WARTIME

WARTIME

Understanding and Behavior
in the Second World War

PAUL FUSSELL

New York   Oxford
OXFORD UNIVERSITY PRESS
1989

Oxford University Press

Oxford   New York   Toronto
Delhi   Bombay   Calcutta   Madras   Karachi
Petaling Jaya   Singapore   Hong Kong   Tokyo
Nairobi   Dar es Salaam   Cape Town
Melbourne   Auckland

and associated companies in
Berlin   Ibadan

Published by Oxford University Press, Inc.,
200 Madison Avenue, New York, New York 10016

Oxford is a registered trademark of Oxford University Press

Library of Congress Cataloging-in-Publication Data
Fussell, Paul, 1924–
Wartime : understanding and behavior in the Second World War /
Paul Fussell.
p.   cm. Bibliography: p.   Includes index.
ISBN 0-19-503797-9
1. World War, 1939–1945—United States—Psychological aspects.
2. World War, 1939–1945—Great Britain—Psychological aspects.
3. World War, 1939–1945—Propaganda. I. Title.
D810.P7U365   1989
940.54'886'73—dc19   89-2875   CIP

1 2 3 4 5 6 7 8 9

Printed in the United States of America
on acid-free paper

Grateful acknowledgment is made to the following for kind permission to quote material in copyright:

Century Hutchinson Ltd.: Excerpts from "Incident, Second World War" by Gavin Ewart, from *The Collected Ewart* by Gavin Ewart. Published by Century Hutchinson Ltd., 1980.

Estate of C. Day Lewis: Excerpts from "Ode to Fear" by C. Day Lewis, from *Collected Poems* by C. Day Lewis. Published by Jonathan Cape Ltd. and The Hogarth Press, 1954.

Estate of Mrs. Norma Millay Ellis: Excerpt from *The Murder of Lidice* by Edna St. Vincent Millay, published by Harper & Row, 1942. Copyright © 1942, 1969 by Edna St. Vincent Millay and Norma Millay Ellis. Reprinted by permission.

Faber & Faber Ltd.: Excerpt from "Peace" by Rupert Brooke, from *The Poetical Works of Rupert Brooke* edited by Geoffrey Keynes (1946); Excerpt from "Dunkirk Pier" by Alan Rook, from *Poets in Wartime* edited by M. J. Tambimuttu (1942).

Farrar, Straus and Giroux, Inc.: Excerpts from "The Omelet of A. MacLeish" from *Wilson's Night Thoughts* by Edmund Wilson. Copyright © 1953, 1962 by Edmund Wilson. Reprinted by permission of Farrar, Straus and Giroux, Inc.; Excerpts from "Eighth Air Force," "Losses," "The Sick Nought," "The Lines," "Solder [T.P.]" from *The Complete Poems* by Randall Jarrell. Copyright © 1943, 1944, 1946, 1947, 1948 by Mrs. Randall Jarrell. Copyright renewed © 1969, 1970, 1971, 1973, 1975 by Mrs. Randall Jarrell. Reprinted by permission of Farrar, Straus and Giroux, Inc. and Faber & Faber Ltd.

Harper & Row, Publishers, Inc.: Excerpts from *Selected Verse* by John Manifold. Copyright 1946 by John Day Co. Reprinted by permission of Harper & Row, Publishers, Inc.

David Higham Associated Limited: Excerpts from "Missing" by John Pudney, from *For Johnny: Poems of World War II* by John Pudney. Published by Shepheard-Walwyn, 1976; Excerpt from "To a Conscript of 1940" by Herbert Read, from *Collected Poems* by Herbert Read. Published by Faber & Faber Ltd., 1966.

London Management: Excerpts from "Steel Cathedrals" by D. van den Bogaerde, from *The Terrible Raid: The War Poets, 1939–1945* edited by Brian Gardner. Published by Methuen London, 1966.

MPL Communications, Inc.: Excerpt from LINDA by Jack Lawrence. © 1944, 1946 John, Linda L., Laura L., and Louise L. Eastman, Jr. © renewed 1972, 1974 MPL Communications, Inc. International Copyright Secured. All Rights Reserved. Used By Permission.

Macmillan Publishing Company: Excerpts from "Chimbly" and "Load" by Lincoln Kirstein, reprinted with permissions of Atheneum Publishers, an imprint of Macmillan Publishing Company, from *The Poems of Lincoln Kirstein*. Copyright © 1964, 1966, 1981, 1987 by Lincoln Kirstein; Excerpt from "The U.S. Sailor with the Japanese Skull" by Winfield Townley Scott. Reprinted with permission of Macmillan Publishing Company from *Collected Poems, 1937–1962* by Winfield Townley Scott. Copyright 1945 by Winfield Townley Scott, renewed 1973 by Eleanor M. Scott.

Methuen London: Excerpts from "What I Never Saw" by Timothy Corsellis, from *The Terrible Raid: The War Poets, 1939–1945* edited by Brian Gardner. Published by Methuen London, 1966.

Oxford University Press: Excerpt from "The Fury of Aerial Bombardment" by Richard Eberhart, from *Collected Poems, 1930–1986* by Richard Eberhart. Copyright © 1960, 1976, 1988 by Richard Eberhart. Reprinted by permission of Oxford University Press, Inc.; Excerpts from "Reading in Wartime" by Edwin Muir, from *Collected Poems* by Edwin Muir. Copyright © 1960 by Willa Muir. Reprinted by permission of Oxford University Press, Inc. and Faber & Faber Ltd.

Paragon House: Excerpt from *Collected Poems* by Louis Simpson. Copyright © 1988 by Paragon House Publishers. Published by Paragon House.

Random House, Inc.: Excerpts from "Under Which Lyre" by W. H. Auden, from *Collected Poems by W. H. Auden* edited by Edward Mendelson. Copyright © 1946 by W. H. Auden; Excerpts from "This Is My Beloved" by Walter Benton. Copyright 1943 by Alfred A. Knopf, Inc. and Walter

*To the memory of
my mother and father,
who sent socks and books*

Preface

This book is about the psychological and emotional culture of Americans and Britons during the Second World War. It is about the rationalizations and euphemisms people needed to deal with an unacceptable actuality from 1939 to 1945. And it is about the abnormally intense frustration of desire in wartime and some of the means by which desire was satisfied. The damage the war visited upon bodies and buildings, planes and tanks and ships, is obvious. Less obvious is the damage it did to intellect, discrimination, honesty, individuality, complexity, ambiguity, and irony, not to mention privacy and wit. For the past fifty years the Allied war has been sanitized and romanticized almost beyond recognition by the sentimental, the loony patriotic, the ignorant, and the bloodthirsty. I have tried to balance the scales.

I am indebted to many people for encouragement, information, and other help, and I must thank Kingsley Amis, William H. Bartsch, Harriette Behringer, James D. Bloom, John Bodley, Alfred Bush, James Cahill, Peter Conrad, Karen Crine, Matthew Evans, Gavin Ewart, Philip French, Betty Fussell, Edwin Sill Fussell, Tucky Fussell, Roland Gant, Paul J. Gartenman, Angeline Goreau, Robert Harper, Doris Hatcher, Elizabeth Jane Howard, Samuel Hynes, William Jovanovich, Arnold Johnston, George Kearns, John Keegan, Donald S. Lamm, H. P. Leinbaugh, Stanley Lewis, Isadore Lichstein, William McGuire, Michele Medinz, Bruce Meyer, Michael Miller, Margaret Mitchell, Reginald Moore, Anthony Powell, John Scanlan, Victor Selwyn, William Skaff, Joseph L. Slater, Humphrey Spender, Roderick Suddaby, Eileen Sullivan, Jeff Walden, Kay Whittle, Michael Willis, Eugene K. Wolf, and Nancy Wilson Ross Young. For permission to quote from manuscript materials in the Imperial War Museum, I must thank these authors and heirs: E. B. C. Aitken, Dorothy Brown, Arthur Deramore, J. Q. Hughes, Robert Rhodes James, R. M. M. King, Peter Royle, Rosemary Meynell, D. A. Simmonds, and H. L. Sykes. And I apologize to memoirists and diarists I have been unable to locate. Judith Pascoe has been an extraordinarily effective research assistant. I am grateful to the Rockefeller Foundation for a Humanities Fellowship in 1983 and to the trustees of the Joseph Warren Beach Lectureship at the University of Minnesota and the Miriam Leranbaum Lectureship at the State University of New York, Binghamton, as well as to Rutgers University and the University of Pennsylvania. I have a debt as well to the people of Company F, 410th Infantry, during 1944 and 1945, especially Spilman B. Gibbs and Robert E. Lawler, memorable colleagues once in absurdity, exhaustion, and fear. And I want to thank two American ex-servicemen, former infantryman Ted Dow and former Marine Eugene B. Sledge, who have generously shared with me their understanding of the war.

Philadelphia   P. F.
August 1, 1988

Contents

WARTIME

From Light to Heavy Duty

Watching a newsreel or flipping through an illustrated magazine at the beginning of the American war, you were likely to encounter a memorable image: the newly invented jeep, an elegant, slim-barrelled 37-mm gun in tow, leaping over a hillock. Going very fast and looking as cute as Bambi, it flies into the air, and behind, the little gun bounces high off the ground on its springy tires. This graceful duo conveyed the firm impression of purposeful, resourceful intelligence going somewhere significant, and going there with speed, agility, and delicacy—almost wit.

That image suggests the general Allied understanding of the war at its outset. Perhaps ("with God's help") quickness, dexterity, and style, a certain skill in feinting and dodging, would suffice to defeat pure force. Perhaps civilized restraint and New World decency could overcome brutality and evil. "Meet the Jeep," said the *Scientific American* in January, 1942. "The United States Army's Answer," it went on without irony, "to Schickelgruber's Panzer Divisions."

At first everyone hoped, and many believed, that the war would be fast-moving, mechanized, remote-controlled, and perhaps even rather easy. In 1940 Colonel William O. Donovan, later head of the American Office of Strategic Services, was persuaded, as he wrote in a pamphlet *Should Men of Fifty Fight Our Wars?*, that "Instead of marching to war, today's soldier rides to war on wheels." For this reason, he conjectured, older men could easily fight the coming war, this time sparing the young. Still hidden in the future were Bataan and Guadalcanal, Saipan and Iwo Jima and Okinawa, Dieppe, Normandy, Cassino, and the virtual trench warfare of the European winter of 1944–45. This optimistic vision of Donovan's is especially curious in light of his having won the Congressional

Medal of Honor while commanding the 69th Infantry in the Great War and earning there the sobriquet Wild Bill. Had time softened his memory of the way ground combat works, the way men will attack only if young, athletic, credulous, and sustained by some equivalent of the buddy system—that is, fear of shame? But by 1940 the Great War had receded into soft focus, and no one wanted to face the terrible fact that military successes are achieved only at the cost of insensate violence and fear and agony, with no bargains allowed. An American woman married in the 1940s to a B-26 tail-gunner for 18 months, after which he was summarily killed, speaks for virtually everybody when she recalls in 1984, "I was naive about pain and suffering."[1] Even the official history of the U.S. Army's Quartermaster Corps admits how innocently far off the mark were early estimates of the number of graves registration units ultimately needed.[2] It would take a skilled pessimist and satirist like Evelyn Waugh to estimate more properly what the war would mean. He notes in his diary in October, 1939: "They are saying, 'The generals learned their lesson in the last war. There are going to be no wholesale slaughters.' I ask, how is victory possible except by wholesale slaughters?"[3]

At the beginning of the war the little light tank, all bolted plane surfaces of one-inch armor plate with smiling men in football helmets looking out, was the standard equipment in the American army's four "mechanized cavalry" divisions. One model carried only machine guns, and the ordnance of the most heavily armed was the 37-mm gun. This light tank, the ten-ton "Stuart" or "Honey," was the one with which George Patton established his reputation as a genius with armor. Assistant Secretary of War John J. McCloy, speaking at the Amherst College commencement on June 14, 1941, recognized that many more such mechanized divisions were called for, but saw no need for heavier equipment. "More like Baby Austins than bloody tanks," commented an experienced British tanker as he watched a shipment of Honeys unloaded at a North African port.[4]

Cavalry mounts were an idea inseparable from the tanks in the first place, as can be inferred from the early American tankers' high laced boots. But at the beginning the cavalry itself still seemed a not implausible arm of the service. In 1941 the United States War Department announced with satisfaction that the army had just supplied itself with 20,000 horses, the most since the Civil War,[5] and in April, 1941, *Life* magazine devoted its cover to a photograph of an earnest "U.S. Cavalryman," Pvt. Buster Hobbs, standing at attention steel-helmeted beside his horse Gip.

Inside, an eight-page "photo essay" celebrated the United States First Cavalry Division, then training at Fort Bliss, Texas. Over half its 11,600 men were mounted, the rest driving armored cars, jeeps, and motorcycles. Their anti-tank defense was the 37-mm gun. At the moment the *Life* reporter visited the division, the troops were hoping for the ultimate delivery of heavier equipment—13 light tanks.

In England the situation was even more touchingly archaic. There, John Verney's Yeomanry (i.e., cavalry) regiment was not mechanized until the summer of 1941. Before then it had been quite prepared to fight with lances and sabers.[6] (And as late as 1949 you could buy a military saber in the cutlery department at Harrod's.[7]) At the outset British armor was as dainty as American, depending on little light tanks dating in design from the 1920s and on such vehicles as a rubber-tired, light-machine-gun-equipped armored car called "Ironsides." Many of the tanks were armed with machine guns only.

Paul Edwards, during the war a Red Cross representative at a number of American cavalry posts, recalls that at the beginning "The romanticism of the cavalry was still very strong. Officers hated giving it up." During the rout of the British on the Malay Peninsula early in 1942, one colonel, says Edwards, "pounded the table" and asserted, "Goddamn it, they'll never [re]take a square foot of it until they get our men down there on horses and donkeys."[8] In this respect the Americans were little more unimaginative than most other victims of the Axis. Witness the behavior of the Polish cavalry in September, 1939, setting out with impressive élan to repel the invading panzers. "In a few minutes," one commentator has observed, "the cavalry lay in a smoking, screaming mass of dismembered and disembowelled men and horses."[9] When in spring, 1940, the Germans swept through Holland, Belgium, and northern France, the Allies, one Briton recalls, simply "gaped, and said, 'What big tanks they've got.' "[10] To help the British deal with the expected German invasion, the United States sent a million rifles. They would have been as effective as the Home Guard's former arms, wooden imitation rifles, against tanks, artillery, bombs, and flamethrowers.

At the beginning military usages in many respects resembled civilian, as if the distinctions between those two worlds could be comfortably reconciled. At first American soldiers were issued white underwear and white towels, as if they were expected to be like other people—civilized and decent. Thus on Guadalcanal an isolated Marine unit was able to signal

HELP by laying out its T-shirts on a hillside to catch the eye of a dive-bomber pilot.[11] This would be impossible very soon, when the new experience in camouflage dictated that everything be olive drab, not just underwear and towels but handkerchiefs, pipe cleaners, and even toilet paper. The U. S. Army's initial innocence of the actualities soon to face the troops is registered in Field Manual 21-100, *The Soldier's Handbook*, issued in July, 1941. By this time France had been conquered and London, Plymouth, Portsmouth, and Liverpool devastated by bombing, and the Germans had captured Crete with paratroops and invaded Russia with thousands of 20-ton panzers. But Field Manual 21-100 was addressing the problem of shelter for the individual infantryman this way:

> At the command FORM FOR SHELTER TENTS TO THE LEFT (RIGHT), the second in command moves to a position on the right of the guide, who is on the right of the right man of the front rank . . . . On direction of the platoon leader, the odd numbers draw their bayonets and thrust them into the ground alongside the outside of the left heel near the instep. The bayonet indicates the position of the front tent pole. . . . At the command PITCH TENTS, each man . . . steps off obliquely with his right foot a full pace to the right front. . . . Each odd-numbered man places a pin in the ground on the spot which he previously marked with his left heel . . . , the odd-numbered man driving the rear guy pin two-and-a-half tent pin lengths from the rear triangle pin.
>
> You will normally pitch your tent where you will be concealed from enemy observation. . . . [In combat situations] the principles of tent-pitching will apply, but there may be no attempt to align the tents.

In the face of such Boy Scoutism, who could imagine the troops in the forests of Europe crouching in freezing holes roofed with logs or railway ties and mounds of dirt to protect against artillery tree-bursts?

As the war advanced the armies reluctantly sloughed off such amenities as two-man tents. Early to disappear was the Sam Browne belt, and as *The Officer's Guide* reported, "The War Department announced on November 8, 1940, that until further instructions the use of the saber by officers on duty with troops . . . will be discontinued."[12] Indeed, before the war is over, officers will have become accustomed to accepting unpleasant facts and dressing like their men, both to raise enlisted morale by lessening the apparent distance between leaders and led and to avoid instant identification by snipers. In the United States Army shiny metal insignia will retire from shoulders to shirt collars, where, in combat, they

can be concealed with a scarf. Officers will abjure tell-tale pistols for
rifles. In the British forces, battledress will become the uniform of all
classes, although not without objection from snobs. At the time of Dunkirk, some officers refused to wear battledress, arguing that they "will
not stand out enough."[13] From an official photograph taken on a balus-
trated patio in Vincennes in October, 1939, you could almost predict that
the British are going to be thrown out of France and the French totally
defeated. Every one of the six high officers depicted there is wearing a
spiffy uniform with ribbons. Four are wearing Sam Browne belts, three,
light-colored cavalry breeches with boots. No one has a weapon. The
Duke of Windsor is there, together with such other losers as General
Howard-Vyse and General Gamelin.[14] All look entirely inadequate to the
cynicism, efficiency, brutality, and bloody-mindedness that will be required to win the war. As Eisenhower recognized in May, 1942, thinking specifically of the U. S. War and Navy Departments, "The actual
fact is that not one man in twenty in the Govt . . . realizes what a grisly,
dirty, tough business we are in."[15] Hence, as late as April, 1943, when
the American plan to shoot down Admiral Yamamoto's plane was being
considered, some scruples were felt, and the Secretary of the Navy was
reluctant to proceed with this assassination until, as John Costello says, he
had "taken the advice of leading churchmen on the morality of killing
enemy leaders."[16]

The inexorable progress from light to heavy duty can be read in the
history of the posters issued on behalf of the American war effort. One
poster of 1942 depicts Joe Louis charging with a slim, long bayonet (soon
to be replaced by the less graceful but more effective short and stocky
version) attached to a long, slender Springfield rifle. He wears a clean
field jacket, properly buttoned. We half expect a necktie. The caption
reads: "Pvt. Joe Louis says—'we're going to do our part . . . and we'll
win because we're on God's side.' " But a year later who is on God's side
seems no longer to matter much, for now open depictions of corpses
begin to displace considerations of moral right. A poster of 1943 shows
the body of a drowned sailor cast up on a beach: "A careless word . . .
A NEEDLESS LOSS." A poster a year later delivers the same message
("CARELESS TALK GOT THERE FIRST") but now with more shocking imagery, a dead paratrooper's body just settling to earth, his head hanging
with closed eyes, his toes just beginning to drag across the dirt. Blood is
conspicuous on his jacket and his hand. And finally, posters will venture

the ultimate revelation—that the war is so brutal, bloody, and terrible to endure that it must be ended (that is, won) without the waste of a single minute more and won by any means, moral or immoral. Thus a poster of 1945 depicts with a harsh photograph, not a painting, the awkward, ugly cadaver of a tank crewman sprawled amidst realistically messy battle detritus—discarded web equipment, unused clips of rifle ammunition, this man's sub-machine gun. His helmet is violently tipped forward, revealing the vulnerable back of his head. Unlike Joe Louis's field jacket, this man's is rumpled and torn, covered with spots of dirt—or blood. The point? "This happens every three minutes. STAY ON THE JOB AND get it over."[17]

By the end, early ideas of finesse, accuracy, and subtlety had yielded to the demands of getting the job over at any cost. If early on the soldiers had spent many tedious hours practicing "marksmanship," by the end it was clear that precision would never win the war—only intensification would. Thus the troops abandoned aiming at precise targets and instead simply poured "assault fire" in the general direction of the enemy while moving towards him. Because the shapely Thompson sub-machine gun took too much time to manufacture, it was replaced by the crude, pressed-metal M-3 "Grease Gun"—which it looked like—since what was wanted, it was finally realized, was a weapon to spew out 45-caliber slugs with more regard for quantity than accuracy. At the beginning company officers in the ground forces were equipped with the little lightweight carbine. It was handy and cute, resembling, one authority has observed, "a sporting arm" more than a military rifle.[18] But before the war had run its course many officers found themselves abandoning it in favor of the heavyweight M-1 rifle. It was less chic but its bullet could penetrate many more feet of wood at once, and many more enemy bodies.

The proximity fuse, devised initially for anti-aircraft use, betokens a similar coarsening of technique. Where formerly you had to aim accurately to hit a plane, now you could achieve the same end by hitting roughly near it. Similarly, "tactics" became a casualty as the war went on, to be replaced by mass wipings-out, bombings, artillery stonks, and frontal flamethrower assaults. The Japanese "defense" of islands like Tarawa, Saipan, or Iwo Jima could hardly be called "combat" at all in the traditional sense. It was suicide stubbornly protracted, and for the Americans the experience argued the uselessness of agility and cunning when sheer overwhelming force was available. More than the Japanese and the Americans died on those islands. Cleverness died too, and fine distinctions. Outmoded now, hopelessly irrelevant, were such former military values and procedures as the alertness of the scout; the skill at topographical notice of the observer in the tethered balloon; the accurately worded message correctly written out (with carbon copy) in the nifty little book of Field Message Forms. Instead, what counted was heavy power, and it is the bulldozers, steam-rollers, and earth graders of the Seabees that constitute the appropriate emblems of the Second World War. "Perhaps there was a time," says Geoffrey Perrett, "when courage, daring, imagination, and intelligence were the hinges on which wars turned. No longer. The total wars of modern history give the decision to the side with the biggest factories."[19] And in Europe as well as the Pacific, the industrial basis of "victory" was even more clear. As Louis Simpson puts it in his poem "A Bower of Roses," in one battle near Dusseldorf

> For every shell Krupp fired,
> General Motors sent back four.[20]

Archibald MacLeish was more precise than perhaps he intended when in *The Atlantic Monthly* in 1949 he declared that the United States had "engineered" a "brilliant victory."[21] One Canadian has remembered: "I knew we were going to win the war when I saw the big Willow Run aircraft factory outside Detroit. My God, but it was a big one."[22] In 1940 Roosevelt called for the building of 50,000 planes. "Asked for a time limit," says Len Deighton, "[he] blandly said that it was the number he wanted each year."[23] Before the war was over the United States had produced almost 300,000 planes, 11,000 of which were in the air over France on D-Day alone.

Thus, abetted by engineering and applied science, the war by its end bore little resemblance to the war at its beginning. It had begun with concern about the bombing of civilians ("BOTH SIDES AGREE NOT TO BOMB CIVILIANS"—*Washington Post*, Sept. 3, 1939) and it ended with not just Hamburg and Dresden but Hiroshima and Nagasaki. If the rubber truncheons issued to British units to repel German invasion of the British Isles were weapons of the beginning, the Tiger tank, the Superfortress, the V-2 rocket, and finally the atom bomb were weapons of the end, after intensification, the "theme" of the war if it has one, had done its work.

"A singular fact about modern war," we are reminded, "is that it takes charge. Once begun it has to be carried to its conclusion, and carrying it there sets in motion events that may be beyond men's control.

British mechanized cavalry on maneuvers, 1938 (Imperial War Museum)

Doing what has to be done to win, men perform acts that alter the very soil in which society's roots are nourished." That's Bruce Catton, and he's referring not to the Second World War but to the American Civil War.[24] At its beginning, say, the Battle of Bull Run (July 21, 1861), light duty was the expectation. A day or two before the battle, congressmen, society ladies, and various picnickers and pleasure-seekers came out from Washington in coaches to watch from the nearby hills what they assumed would be a gratifying rout of the impudent Southern forces. Some women even brought along their evening dresses, expecting a victory ball at Fairfax Court House after the day's successes. But the battle proved a stinging defeat for the North, and now facts had to be faced: the war would be long, bloody, brutal, total, and stupid.

The women who brought along their nice formal dresses were not especially unimaginative. Wars are all alike in beginning complacently. The reason is psychological and compensatory: no one wants to foresee or contemplate the horror, the inevitable ruin of civilized usages, which war will entail. Hence the defensive exercise of the optimistic imagination.

German "King Tiger" Tank in France, June, 1944 (Bundesarchiv)

When in April, 1940, a Heinkel bomber crashed in Clacton-on-Sea, East Anglia, causing great damage on the ground and killing, among others, its crew of four Germans, the war was so new that as the German dead were borne to the local cemetery with full military honors suppled by the RAF, women sobbed for them, and "the gallant foe were laid to rest amidst numerous floral tributes, their coffins being covered with wreaths of lilies, irises, and other spring flowers." Some of these wreaths bore the words "From All Ranks of the Royal Air Force" and "With Heartfelt Sympathy From a Mother."[25] But it wasn't long before soldiers and civilians would be killed in quantity and without scruple, their bodies cremated en masse or tipped into lime pits, and only a couple of years more before A-bombs and the remorseless hanging of German officers convicted of terrible crimes would exemplify the heavy duty the war had necessitated.

Severe trauma was often the result of the initial optimistic imagination encountering actuality. For all her tough-mindedness, the twenty-four-year-old American journalist Marguerite Higgins was appalled when, after years of pleading, she was finally designated a war correspondent and allowed in March, 1945, to inspect the European combat zone. She was delighted that the Allies were winning and anxious to examine the process up close, but as her biographer notes, nothing in her previous experience or knowledge had prepared her for the "mosaic of misery" she was horrified to encounter. Cities ruined and stinking. Dead bodies everywhere, some mangled or torn apart, the American and German equally awful. "More shocking were the wounded, many her own age or younger. Some were blinded, others cruelly disfigured. . . . Many people had lost hands or feet to frostbite." The faces of the Allied soldiers which she had expected to register a degree, at least, of satisfaction over their victories were only "weary" and "bitter."[26]

Marguerite Higgins cannot be blamed for not knowing the truth in advance of experience. The pamphlet *War-Time Prayers for Those at Home*, prepared by U.S. Army and Navy chaplains and published in February, 1943, does a remarkable job of glossing over the distinct possibility of soldiers' deaths and mutilations. The featured prayer, displayed on the back cover, is "A Parent's Prayer for a Son in Service." After asking that all anxiety for the soldier be banished from the heart of the petitioner, it solicits God's help in keeping the boy faithful and victorious in struggles with temptation and sin (sex and liquor are meant), as well as "strong, manly, and cheerful." And the prayer goes on to speak of a just peace and to envisage the troops' happy homecomings. Notably absent is a clause which could be expected by the time of the heavy-duty spring of 1945 and which might go like this: "If it be Thy will that he shall lose his life, receive his soul into Thy safekeeping; if it be Thy will that he shall be maimed, provide him and us with comfort and with hopeful hearts."

Journalists more experienced than Marguerite Higgins tried to perform a public service by exploding the hope that some sort of light duty would suffice to win the war. In late November, 1943, the United States marines secured Tarawa Atoll—less than three square miles—by expending in a three-day assault more than 1000 dead and 2000 wounded. Instructed by the photographs of Marine corpses drifting in long rows along the shore and of cruelly smashed pillboxes and twisted landing craft, those at home began to perceive what sort of heavy duty the war would ultimately demand. Most were horrified, like the mother who wrote Admiral Nimitz, "You killed my son on Tarawa."[27] "This must not happen again," said one editorial, quoted by the *Time* magazine correspondent Robert Sherrod, whose book *Tarawa: The Story of a Battle* (1944) was one of the first to deliver news about the war that was notably less than cheerful. His account does full justice to the inescapable horrors, and in a final chapter he deals with the problem of the American innocence that has kept such truths about the war pleasantly obscure for so long. Deep deficiency of imagination—that has been the cause of the home-front shock. Like the boys they educated, says Sherrod, "the people had not thought of war in terms of men being killed. . . ." Tarawa has finally made clear one terrible truth: "There is no easy way to win a war; there is no panacea which will prevent men from being killed."[28]

2

"Precision Bombing Will Win the War"

A panacea was the natural thing for the audience at home to believe in, since for years it had been lulled into comfort by the conviction that the war could be won by shrewd Yankee technological expedients, like, for example, bombing from costly airplanes flying at safe altitudes. This misapprehension had been in large part promoted by the American government itself. Witness a popular official pamphlet designating the bomber as *The Weapon of Ultimate Victory*. It bears no date, but its insisting that "America cannot lose this war!" suggests the end of 1942, when the issue seemed rather in doubt. The weapon of ultimate victory is specifically the B-17 Flying Fortress, "the mightiest bomber ever built." It is a precision instrument, "equipped with the incredibly accurate Norden bomb sight, which hits a 25-foot circle from 20,000 feet." And the safety of the crew is strongly stressed. One picture caption reads: "Safe within the strong fuselage of his bomber, this master-gunner aims his heavy [50-caliber] weapon." It is as if no such thing as flak had been invented. (During

1942 the U.S. Army Air Corps had called on the War Writers Board to produce materials which might "remove the false impression that the tail gunner's job, which is a hazardous one, is necessarily a shortcut to suicide."[1]) The great height ("seven miles") from which it operates enables the Flying Fortress to "make daylight raids with a greater margin of safety than any other bombing plane." The altitudes at which it will fly guarantee that this bomber will constitute "the poorest target yet developed." Confronted with this advertising, only a deep cynic or sadist could have predicted in 1942 that before the war ended the burnt and twisted bits of almost 22,000 of these Allied bombers would strew the fields of Europe and Asia, attended by the pieces of almost 110,000 airmen. In 1942 it was impossible to imagine the future multitudes empowered to say with the bomber crewmen in Randall Jarrell's "Losses,"

our bodies lay among
The people we had killed and never seen.[2]

The fact was that bombing proved so grossly inaccurate that the planes had to fly well within anti-aircraft range to hit anywhere near the target, and even then they very often missed it entirely. As the war went on, "precision bombing" became a comical oxymoron relished by bomber crews with a sense of black humor. It became obvious to everyone except the home folks reading *Life* and *The Saturday Evening Post* that although you could destroy lots of things with bombs, they weren't necessarily the things you had in mind. Navigation through winds and clouds and turbulence presented such problems that as early as August, 1941, it was clear to even the most naïve in RAF Bomber Command that on a typical mission "only one in ten of the bombers found its way to within five miles of the assigned target."[3] In the first German raids on London, when 500 tons of bombs were dropped, only half fell on the land at all, and only 30 tons hit London.[4] The popular broadcaster J. B. Priestley imagined egotistically that one of the main German targets in this raid was Broadcasting House, where he performed, when actually the Germans were lucky to hit anything in London at all.[5]

One memorable ironic action occurred on May 10, 1940, when a Luftwaffe squadron, setting out to bomb Dijon, by some error dropped its load on its own civilians in Freiburg-im-Breisgau, killing fifty-seven of them. In instantly imputing this atrocity (as it seemed then) to the French, and later to the British, the German propagandists were exploit-

Being carried, the Norden Bombsight, said to be indispensable for precision bombing and so secret that it traveled under guard (Acme)

ing the wide public belief that bombers could hit what they aimed at. Even in the air forces some people were very slow to catch on. They were those who had read, and credited, optimistic books like *The Command of the Air* (1921), by the Italian general Giulio Douhet, which asserted that bombing alone would win future wars. The assumption behind this book was that human beings could do without gross error anything they rationally proposed to do, regardless of natural forces like wind and weather and psychological disruptions of purpose like boredom, terror, and self-destructiveness. At the beginning of the war it was widely believed that poison gas would be used against civilians and that it would be dropped in bombs from aircraft. That it never was indicates less that humane considerations prevailed than that aerial bombing gradually revealed its limitations, reminding the rationalists that man did not control wind direction and force. Diehards like Sir Arthur Harris, head of RAF Bomber

Command, never retreated from their stubborn position that bombing alone could force the surrender of Germany. A virtual sacred text supporting this belief was Alexander Seversky's *Victory through Air Power* (1942). When the Allies bombed the Italians on the island of Pantelleria in June, 1943, General Spaatz, of the United States Air Corps, concluded that bombing "can reduce to the point of surrender any first-class nation now in existence, within six months. . . ."[6]

Thus one staff officer at an RAF Group Headquarters, presented with evidence that an attack had entirely missed its mark, "scrawled across it in red, 'I do not accept this report.' "[7] It was the grave inaccuracy of the bombers that led finally to the practice of "area bombing," whose effect was, in Churchill's memorable euphemism, to "dehouse" the enemy population. And area bombing led inevitably, as intensification overrode scruples, to Hiroshima and Nagasaki. And yet it was not until the war was half over that the presumed accuracy of the bomber was abandoned as a propaganda ploy. The RAF flyer Robert Kee records in his diary in 1941: "I've now been on many raids where owing to total cloud it's been impossible to do anything but fling the bombs out somewhere near the flak and the searchlights, and yet I have invariably read the next morning of 'attacks on rail communications or industrial premises.' "[8]

An unforgettable image of the inaccuracy of bombing is one photograph in Jules Roy's *Return from Hell* showing an RAF Halifax aircraft flying over an enemy agricultural countryside absolutely pitted with harmless bomb craters.[9] "We made a major assault on German agriculture" is a bomber crew's witticism recalled by John Kenneth Galbraith, a member of the postwar U. S. Strategic Bombing Survey, which ascertained, among other findings, that German military and industrial production seemed to increase—just like civilian determination not to surrender—the more bombs were dropped.[10] The Survey found also that 14 per cent of the bombs dropped never went off (ironically balancing out the large number of U.S. anti-tank mines that went off when they weren't supposed to). Was sabotage behind these failures? No, simply error.

It is hard to embrace ironies like this because the human mind, avid for clear meaning, experiences frustration and pain when confronted by events which seem purposeless or meaningless. Hence the all-but-universal impulse during the war to impute specific malign intent to every dropped bomb. When in September, 1940, bombs struck Buckingham Palace, it was assumed on all sides that they had been aimed there and that, as one loyal civilian concluded, the Germans "are trying to drive the King out of London."[11] ("Murderous attack"—*Daily Mirror.*) Scrutinizing the damage to the palace, a policeman observed to the Queen, "A magnificent piece of bombing, Ma'am, if you'll pardon my saying so."[12] Actually, the bombs were more likely jettisoned in a cold panic by a Luftwaffe flyer caught in a searchlight. But simple cause-finders like Vere Hodgson cannot abandon their conviction, so necessary to self-respect as reasoning creatures, that bombs are precisely "aimed" and that thus their damage makes interpretable sense. In September, 1940, she notes in her diary: "Saw the room in the Convent where the incendiaries fell on Tuesday night. Fortunately St. Charles's Hospital has escaped. Were they aiming at the Hospital, or at the Gasometer a few yards away . . . ?" Again, looking at the damage done to Madame Tussaud's one night, she concludes that those bombs were "obviously aimed at Baker St. Station."[13] Vera Brittain combines that sort of rationalist, complacent folk-teleology with a special self-righteousness in interpreting a bombing "incident" which destroyed a large estate house near her country cottage. This was, she is convinced, "no chance hit, but a feat of precision bombing," and the "cause" was specifically the poor discipline and moral laxity of the British troops billetted in the great house. "By day they sat on the green carelessly dismembering their Bren guns; by night their lighted cigarettes defeated the black-out. One evening a German plane came over and planted a bomb neatly on the house, killing seventeen soldiers."[14]

Perhaps the best gloss on Hodgson's *obviously* and Brittain's *neatly* is the scandal of COBRA, the code-name for the immense bombing operation of July 24 and 25, 1944, designed to assist the break-out of the ground forces from the Normandy beachhead near Saint-Lô. The plan was for some 1800 bombers to pulverize the German defenders, after which the Americans were to press forward with, it was hoped, considerable ease. The bombing attack was to occur on July 25, but through a communications blunder many planes dropped their bombs the day before, and so inaccurately that 25 American soldiers were killed and 131 wounded. "Some enraged American units," says Max Hastings, "opened fire on their own aircraft, a not uncommon practice among all the armies in Normandy when suffering at the hands of their own pilots."[15] But worse was to come next day, when the operation was re-mounted. This time the American line was secretly withdrawn thousands of yards to avoid its being bombed a second time, and this time the bombing was even more incontinent, the bombs now falling on the American line to the tune of 111 killed, including Lt. General Lesley McNair, observing

*Digging out the dead and wounded immediately after the COBRA blunder.
(The wartime caption, issued by the U.S. Army in July, 1944: "After
German shelling, Yanks dig out men buried in their foxholes . . .".)
(AP/Wide World Photos)*

from a forward position, and almost five hundred wounded. Men were
torn apart, tanks were tossed around like toys, and troops were driven
insane. After this debacle Eisenhower ("completely dejected," General
Bradley remembers) determined never again to risk heavy bombing to
assist ground attacks.[16] A critical observer might note that the lesson took
a long time to impinge. Weeks before, on D-Day. 480 B-24s had dropped
1,285 tons of bombs before the landings on Omaha Beach. This performance had been, as Bradley notes, "completely ineffective," the 13,000
bombs falling well inland to kill only French civilians and their livestock.[17] The British were slower to catch on than the Americans. Almost
a month after the disaster at Saint-Lô, several hundred Canadian troops
were killed near Falaise when RAF Bomber Command attempted to rein-

force the ground attack. The only comfort available was voiced by Ernie
Pyle, who observed of the Saint-Lô incident, "Anybody makes mistakes.
The enemy made them just the same as we did."[18] Quite so. As Hitler
once declared, "The loser of this war will be the side that makes the
greatest blunders."[19]

Someone Had Blundered

But sanguine misapprehension about the possibilities of aerial bombardment was not the only misconstruction useful to the rationalizing
intellect unable to confront the messy data of actuality. And here the
troops were no more exempt than non-combatants from the tendency to
look on the bright, or orderly, side. Such a habit, indeed, was indispensable if soldiers were to keep their psychic stability and perform their
duties at all. An imaginative infantryman might have inferred what the
battle was going to be like from the presence in each 36-man platoon of
a medic carrying a full load of morphine and bandages, but before experience had enforced understanding, hope rationalized the medic's presence as a precaution against sprains, cuts, insect bites, and heat-stroke. If
confronted openly with the things the medic was going to be faced with,
few could have gone on.

A typical soldier ill-prepared to encounter the facts was the American
Louis Simpson, that is, if we can identify the soldier of the virgin 101st
Airborne Division who fought near Carentan in Normandy with the speaker
in Simpson's poem "Carentan O Carentan." A profound surprise is what
the speaker in this poem registers—surprise at the almost fairy-tale meta-
morphosis a few minutes have wrought in the former strength and discipline of his infantry company. As it advanced cautiously but yet undamaged, it blundered into an ambush:

> The watchers in their leopard suits
> Waited till it was time,
> And aimed between the belt and boot
> And let the barrel climb.

Machine-pistol fire at once catches the speaker in the knee, and as he falls he is aware that others are falling too, and he turns for guidance, if not succour, to the customary authorities:

> Tell me, Master-Sergeant,
> The way to turn and shoot.
> But the Master-Sergeant's silent
> That taught me how to do it.
>
> O Captain, show us quickly
> Our place upon the map.
> But the Captain's sickly
> And taking a long nap.
>
> Lieutenant, what's my duty,
> My place in the platoon?
> He too's a sleeping beauty
> Charmed by that strange tune.

The final words of the poem notate the astonishing fact of the astonishment:

> Carentan O Carentan
> Before we met with you
> We never yet had lost a man
> Or known what death could do.[1]

A disaster like that is rather nearer the norm than not, but people must not be told so, lest the illusion of planning and order be shaken. Why are blunders into ambushes not more rare? Because, for one thing, very few soldiers and officers are masters of their trade. For most, this is the first war they've fought in. They are neophytes and amateurs, plucked from civilian life to engage in deadly on-the-job training in an unfamiliar atmosphere of rigid hierarchical "authority," where orders (sometimes euphemized to "directives" to spare civilian sensibilities) are not to be questioned and are seldom discussed, no matter how absurd, unreasonable, or based on patently erroneous assumptions. A further cause of constant blunders is the frequency of "transfers" into and out of units—no one stays very long. Result: everyone is a newcomer, largely ignorant of the local jargon and way of doing things, and continually starting over in milieus where the pretense is that everyone knows what he's doing. And very often the newcomers have been extruded from their old units for ineptitude or even minor criminality. Coming somewhat dazed into the armed services from individualistic and sometimes anarchic personal backgrounds, the Americans and British committed many more blunders than the Germans or the Japanese. Blunders were almost the hallmark of Allied operations. As the attorney Jim Rowe noted during the Nuremberg trials, "The incredibly large number of cases on the Allied side of mistaken identification were throughout the war the curse of the American and British navies, causing the loss of thousands of Allied lives by their own guns."[2]

The main cause of such fatal errors is simple fear. The planes must not be allowed to get too close, and hence you fire at distances too great for positive identification. The planes *might* be enemy; in fact, they're quite likely to be. Thus it took some time for Allied bombers on their way to the Continent to learn that London was on no account to be flown over. Its amateur anti-aircraft gunners were much too scared. One Canadian bomber pilot testifies that "the jittery army gunners always cut loose at you, despite the fact that we were flying north to south and there were 800 of us. We could hardly be Germans to the most unimaginative mind and yet they always pounded up the flak."[3] (*Always*, notice, used twice.) But the classic recognition error prompted by fear is the one occurring at the invasion of Sicily in July 1943. American navy and ground gunners had been told that transports and gliders carrying the airborne troops would be flying over them, but at the crucial moment they seemed to forget and blasted away, some of them shouting "German attack! Fire!" Before the shooting could be stopped, some 23 planes had been shot down, carrying 229 men of the 82nd Airborne Division to disaster. Three months later a pamphlet issued by the British War Office noted that "Reports from theatres of war contain criticisms of the standard of aircraft recognition amongst the troops taking part in the Tunisian and Sicilian campaigns"—a genteel way of observing that the troops were new and badly scared.[4] Ernie Pyle witnessed the Sicilian debacle but either chose not to mention it in his dispatches or, more likely, was forbidden to. It is still insufficiently known. For example, the volume *The Italian Campaign* (1978) of the *Time-Life* series devoted to World War II doesn't mention it at all.

That is typical behavior for this series, which has done more than perhaps any other popular account of the war to ascribe clear, and usually noble, cause and purpose to accidental or demeaning events. It has thus conveyed to the credulous a satisfying, orderly, and even optimistic and wholesome view of catastrophic occurrences—a fine way to encourage a moralistic, nationalistic, and bellicose politics. It is doubtful that many former World War Two servicemen were particularly astonished to learn, in early summer, 1988, that the American navy had shot down an Iranian airliner, mistaking it for a hostile fighter plane, and killed 290 innocent noncombatants. As usual, fear, or something close to it, was the cause.

So flagrant were these recognition lapses that at the Normandy invasion the gun crews, at least on the merchant ships, were attended, as Max Hastings points out, by "specially trained civilian aircraft recognition teams from the Royal Observer Corps,"[5] not, one might think, a terribly impressive form of safeguard. The same may be said of the safeguard mentioned by Arthur T. Hadley, who "fought with one . . . infantry unit that had shot down so many of our own planes that its antiaircraft machine guns all had little tags on their triggers saying, 'This gun will only be fired under command of an officer.' "[6] At any rate, so many blunders occurred that the most popular Penguin book during the war contained not words but silhouettes. *Aircraft Recognition*, which cost sixpence, ultimately sold three million copies.

Important as fear was in occasioning blunders, especially in the early light-duty stages of the war, it was not the only cause. There were scores of dreadful mistakes without any particular moral or psychological meaning at all. The war began with one. On September 3, 1939, the British passenger liner *Athenia* was sunk by a U-boat, and this attack on civilians—of the 1400 passengers, 112, including 28 Americans, were killed—did much to fuel Allied outrage and to raise the level of violence in return. But as it turned out, the ship was sunk not out of Teutonic viciousness toward women and children but because the submarine commander quite innocently mistook the vessel for an auxiliary cruiser. Indeed, the Germans, anxious that the Americans not be given a new reason for entering the war, were so embarrassed by this blunder that they altered the submarine's log and denied all knowledge of the sinking.[7] The erroneous sinking of ships continued until the end of the war, and even after. In 1943 it was not a Japanese submarine that sank the U. S. Marine Corps transport *McCawley* but a United States PT boat, whose young captain had been assured that any ships operating in his area were enemy.

In October, 1944, the Japanese merchant vessel *Arisan Maru* was neatly torpedoed by the U. S. submarine *Snook*. It sank satisfyingly, together with its cargo, of which its appearance offered no indication. It was carrying thousands of American prisoners being conveyed from the Philippines to safety in Japan. All were drowned. And finally, on August 22, 1945, over a week after the Japanese surrender, a Japanese ship repatriating people from Sakhalin was sunk by an unknown submarine. Over 1700 were lost.

Other kinds of recognition blunders are more personal. A Canadian who fought in Normandy recalls: "I killed a Yank once." The American had mistaken him for a German and wouldn't stop firing at him. There was only one remedy. "I know he's going to get me," says the Canadian. "My intuition tells me I'm for it, so I give it to him. Poor bugger. A corporal from some Texas outfit. . . . He was shooting at me as if I was a German. It's him or me. So I shoot that boy even though I know he's a Yank."[8] And recognition error grows more ironic and insupportable if one is close to the victim. On one occasion RAF airman J. E. Johnson's unit moved up to a new advanced field in France. As he tells it,

> One or two enemy snipers were still at large and they could make life unpleasant. [One morning] an airman had walked into an abandoned enemy strongpoint and had found some discarded German uniforms. To impress his colleagues, he donned one of these garments and shouted to them as he stepped out of the pillbox. His gestures were unfortunately misinterpreted and he was shot stone dead.[9]

Similarly, military Bright Ideas have a way of ending disastrously, and have been doing so at least since the Great War. What reader of Robert Graves's *Good-bye to All That* (1929) can forget the ironic behavior of "the accessory," as the new poison-gas cylinders tried out at the Battle of Loos were euphemized? Manned by inept professors of chemistry from the University of London, the cylinders sent their gas across No Man's Land all right, but the wind changed and blew it back into the British trenches, occasioning a bizarre panic. That bright ideas, far from guaranteeing against blunders, are often their cause is illustrated by the fate of the "D. D." (i.e., dual drive) tanks launched offshore on D-Day. Equipped to float with impermeable canvas skirts, these were to propel themselves to the beach with an ad hoc propeller and then resume normal operation. Thirty-two were launched, their skirts deployed, but in high seas and (doubtless because of fear) too far from land. Twenty-seven sank with their complete crews, a tribute to stubborn hope, for tank after tank was launched *seriatim,* each sinking like a stone, observed by everyone on the launching ship.[10] The *Time-Life* World War II volume dealing with the invasion devotes a full-color page to the D. D. tank without in any way suggesting that something went fatally wrong. "A TANK THAT COULD SWIM" is the caption.[11]

Certainly one of the brightest ideas of the war was the pipeline under the ocean designed to supply the armies in Normandy with fuel after the invasion. It took 41 days to get it into position, but after a few weeks its couplings, hopelessly irreparable from the surface, gave way. A whole new pipeline had to be manufactured and laid down, and fuel flowed through it only in January, 1945, seven months after the invasion.[12] Another bright idea was to equip the troops with one-piece fatigue coveralls: no loose parts to get lost in the wash, no matching of different sizes for jacket and trousers. It wasn't until a number of men had tried going to the toilet while wearing this garment that the designers realized that such an operation required the awkward removal of both arms from the sleeves in order to deal with a problem normally requiring only the dropping of the trousers.

Likewise, much faith was invested in the snappy little Handy-Talkie radio (formally, SCR 536), a hand-held object about as big as two cigarette cartons. Carried by small-unit officers, this was supposed to ease communication between platoon leaders and company commanders, a job accomplished formerly by runners. But while working satisfactorily in training, where company officers were exhaustively schooled in the obligatory jargon ("Fox 6, this is Fox 2. Over."), in combat these little radios failed entirely in woods or whenever a hill got between the two communicators or under any other of a score of "abnormal conditions." One could estimate the maturity and good sense of any infantry unit in the European Theater by the number of these little radios still in use amongst its platoon leaders. One could estimate the educational experience that had taken place on a given road by noticing the number of these pretentious, costly little bright ideas discarded in the ditches. In the same way, it is certainly a bright idea to observe and adjust artillery fire from a light plane rather than, as formerly, from a hilltop overlooking the battlefield. It works fine until the plane strays into the trajectory of the artillery shell, a trajectory it has no way of ascertaining.

If such blunders are occasioned by aspirations to technological cunning, others are the result of zeal and excessive self-righteousness. A British boy witnessed an example when the air warfare was going on daily. "In Wapping," he reports, "a parachutist came down and apparently he was partially blinded. He'd obviously baled out of a plane. He jabbered away to the people that gathered around him in some foreign language. They assumed he was German and they smashed him to death." But actually he was Polish, "which was tragic," the boy goes on, "because he was like a British fighter pilot." The incident is still remembered in Wapping, where "none are prepared to say they took part in it. . . ."[13]

Similar silence has attended one of the most melodramatic blunders of the war, the Great Slapton Sands Disaster, which has been virtually a secret for forty years except among participants and observers. On April 28, 1944, the 4th American Infantry Division and other units were holding an immense rehearsal (Operation TIGER) of the forthcoming invasion. The beaches selected were at Slapton Sands, Devon, near the British naval base at Dartmouth. Two hundred ships took part and 30,000 acres of coastal land were cleared of their residents. The exercise was to be realistic in all ways—air attacks on the beaches, mine fields, live ammunition everywhere. But as the ships were approaching the "landing beaches," actuality intruded. Nine fast 100-foot German E-boats carrying torpedoes set out from Cherbourg and in the dark they got among the American ships. In the immense confusion, not just between friends and enemies but between training and the real thing, the E-boats sank two LSTs and damaged others. The dead amounted to 749 American soldiers and sailors, mostly engineers and quartermaster troops. Their bodies were secretly bulldozed into a mass grave on the Devon farm of Mr. Nolan Tope while the wounded were quarantined at the hospitals and threatened with court-martial if they talked. At the critiques following the exercise, "the British," says Edwin P. Hoyt, "some of whom believed the American troops to be quite hopeless, tactfully kept silent."[14] This blunder was kept secret not just from shame but to avoid compromising the method and date of the actual invasion. There also seemed to be a deep-seated feeling that "training" is one thing and "combat" quite another and that ever to mingle them in this way is so wrong as to be unmentionable. The relatives of the dead were informed that their men had died "in action"— true in a curious way—and it is said that for the record the casualty figures were simply added to the Normandy totals run up some five weeks later. When the real invasion took place, the casualties suffered by the whole corps of which the 4th Infantry Division was a part proved fewer than the number killed at Slapton Sands. But if one believed the *Time-Life* volume devoted to the invasion, the preparatory maneuvers at Slapton Sands were marred only by "traffic jams and confusion."[15]

And one of the last events of the war was one of the costliest blunders. On July 30, 1945, the United States heavy cruiser *Indianapolis* was sunk by a Japanese submarine. Through a whole train of oversights, misunderstandings, and complacencies ("I thought *you* were supposed to check her time of arrival," etc.), it took four days for awareness to sink in at various naval bases that the vessel was overdue—indeed, had quite disappeared. By that time, about 500 men, originally hopeful of a quick rescue, had died on rafts or in life jackets, of thirst, hunger, madness, and shark bites. The event was the greatest loss of life at sea ever suffered by the United States Navy.

Bringing to bear their instinct for civilized irony, the most intelligent contemporary writers have perceived in blunders, errors, and accidents something very close to the essence of the Second World War. To disclose the way someone blundered then is to hint at the crucial imperfections built into the normal or Cold War modern world, a world dependent on predictability, technology, and bureaucracy. The world survives only by assuming that error is not going to launch the rockets or detonate the hydrogen bombs. This is to say that wartime blunders, awful as the worst of them are, constitute a thematic gift to the satirist and moralist intent on exhibiting instructively the uncertainty of the human situation.

Error, for example, is virtually the central character in Evelyn Waugh's wartime diaries, running from December, 1939, to March, 1945. Waugh knew all about error, being himself a vigorously incompetent over-age-in-grade officer in the Royal Marines and for a time a much disliked member of No. 8 Commando. Even before he entered the service he registered in his diary his sense of what the war, conducted by amateurs and bureaucrats, was going to be like:

> Monday, 18 September, 1939
>
> This morning, depressed at the war news . . . , I came down to breakfast and found the registration book for my car, for which I had applied, arrived by return of post. I reflected that there was really a great deal which went through smoothly in England, that we made a great fuss when anything went wrong and disregarded the vast machinery that was working successfully all the time, etc., etc. I then looked at the book and found that it referred to a totally different car. (442)[16]

Soon he is in uniform, in a position both to observe and to participate in the pitfalls attending normal military life. In March, 1940, he reports on a "route march and practical exercise which was disastrous from first to last, and" he adds, "at every stage of the disaster I occupied a conspicuous place" (465). In May, 1940, serving briefly as acting company commander, he notes: "In the afternoon drove to look at training areas for twenty-four-hour field exercise. Thought I had made myself clear but found all I had said was interpreted in an entirely contrary sense" (468). The errors never cease but sometimes they are further removed:

> In the evening [May 22, 1940] a lecture from Fitzgerald who has just come off the *Curaçoa* which was badly bombed in Norway. He described embarking a company and a half of the Leicesters who had the wrong baggage. When that was adjusted they sailed, examined their stores at sea and found the anti-tank magazines empty. This battalion when fully assembled numbered 600 and returned 150 strong. Fitzgerald then described lying in the fjords around Andenes being bombed hourly day by day. The RAF constantly flew without their distinguishing signs and neglected to give answering signals; were constantly fired on and sometimes brought down. (470)

On June 1, 1940, Waugh has two events to record: "A night exercise filled us all with shame" and "One of the men in my company . . . shot himself. . . . Two stretcher bearers confronted with blood for the first time resigned their posts" (471).

Soon Waugh's unit begins preparations for what will become known as The Great Dakar Fuck-Up—the attempt to persuade the French in West Africa to abjure Vichy and cleave to De Gaulle by threatening the port with a naval and landing force. On August 18, 1940, the troops assigned to this mission are moved by train toward Birkenhead, the port of embarkation:

> We left one and a half hours late, at 7:30, with the promise of breakfast at Exeter. . . . There was no breakfast at Exeter, but Bristol at noon provided a cup of contemptible tea and a few biscuits. From then on each station promised us dinner at our next stop. We arrived at Birkenhead at 7 pm having had nothing to eat except what the men could afford to buy for themselves at Crewe in a scurry and scramble. All this time we were carrying emergency rations . . . which Teak, in command of the train, refused to break. . . . The men were not allowed aboard [the ship] until

the nominal-roll had been checked, the equipment strapped down and all
their luggage and weapons brought aboard. It was 10 before they got
food. . . . (475)

Next day it is discovered that two battalions have been embarked in a
ship supposed to carry only one, and one has to get off. "Heavy drinking
in the evening" (475). The day after, "held up by reloading, everything
having been stowed incorrectly. Discoveries at last minute. e.g. that the
ship's boats are run on Dieselite not on petrol." Three days later the ship
actually sails. On the way "The cruiser *Fiji* next to us in convoy put up
a signal which was variously interpreted to mean 'I am dropping depth
charges at 800 feet' and 'I have been torpedoed and am proceeding to
UK.' The latter proved correct" (479). On September 26 the farcical
Battle of Dakar took place. De Gaulle called on the French not to fire,
but they told him to go away and take his naval force with him. The
expedition retreated and after much confusion and delay returned to England. Waugh tries to put together the "general causes of defeat" as follows: "*(a)* initial misconception *(b)* faulty intelligence *(c)* superiority of
French gunnery *(d)* air inadequacy *(e)* signal inadequacy" (482–83). On
the way home, "Three cases of homosexuality in two days" (483).

It was No. 8 Commando that was involved in the disastrous Battle of
Crete in May, 1941, and it is said that Waugh's witnessing numerous
blunders and acts of overt cowardice there soured him permanently on
the army, the war, and the pretense of high purpose claimed by both.
During training for Crete in Scotland the navy repeatedly ran ships around,
there were preposterous orders and more preposterous counter-orders,
sergeants were "paralytically drunk all the time" (493), and a series of
"plans" was laboriously projected and then unceremoniously dumped. The
confusions and delays prompted this graffito scrawled in the troop space
of one of the transports: "Never in the history of human endeavour have
so few been buggered about by so many" (495). On Crete the battle
resulted in an ignominious rout and an ill-managed evacuation, memor-
ably registered later by Waugh in his *Sword of Honor*—the title is outrageously ironic. Pronounced "unemployable" soon after Crete, Waugh
was granted a prolonged leave to write *Brideshead Revisited,* an absurd
anomaly, to be sure, but under the circumstances the handiest way of
removing him, with his satirist's sharp tongue, from contact with troops.
Finally, he accompanied Randolph Churchill on an error-studded mission

to Yugoslavia, which began with an airplane crash, from which Waugh miraculously escaped little damaged, and ended with comic misapprehensions on both sides as Waugh tried earnestly to explain to the Pope the dangers to the Church posed by Yugoslavian communists but got in return His Holiness's "English parrot-talk of how many children had I" and the usual handful of blessed rosaries to take home (618).

Another British connoisseur of service error is the estimable Julian Maclaren-Ross (1912–1964), dandy, eccentric, wit, memoirist, and short-story writer whose works are barely known in the United States and too little valued even in Britain. He is one of those brilliant writers of the second rank to whom the term *stylist*—which does not mean fancy writer—applies, although a reader is likely to be unaware of the appropriateness of that designation while engaged with his prose, only afterward. He catches the whole service atmosphere of error committed, redoubled, compounded, and committed again in a short story like "I Had To Go Sick," first published in Cyril Connolly's *Horizon* in August, 1942. The narrative is spoken by a British soldier who's been in the army no more than a week. On the parade ground he can't keep in step. A sergeant examines his leg and finds a scar on his knee, the result of an old accident with a bicycle. He orders him to "go sick"—i.e., appear next morning at sick-call—and get the medical officer's opinion. Later that same day, an old sweat warns him about MOs: he has gone to one complaining of a stomach ache and the MO has sent him to the dental center where all his teeth have been pulled. In the morning, when the new soldier shows up at sick-call, together with others exhibiting numerous physical defects, he observes: "It's funny how they pass you A-1 into the army and then find out you're nothing of the sort. One of these fellows had flat feet, another weak lungs, a third reckoned he was ruptured" (258).[17]

Examined finally by the medical officer, after the statutory number of insults and delays the soldier is passed on to a specialist, who prescribes "electrical massage" of the leg twice a week. After these treatments, he grows much worse and now limps conspicuously while marching. Some weeks later the MO, puzzled by the worsening of the condition, sends him before a Medical Board for re-classification. While waiting, he returns to his company where, now excused from marching, he clerks for a while until the company commander finds him surplus to the unit's needs for clerks. Back to the MO again, only this time there's a new one, who tells him, "You'd better have a medical board."

"I'm down for one already, sir."

"What? Well why the devil didn't you say so then? Wasting my time. All right. You can go now." (262)

Arriving at the hospital for his Medical Board, he encounters a medical colonel who examines him anew and then tells the reception desk, "Take this man along to Ward 9" (263).

Ward 9 proves to be a gastric ward. There he is bathed, pajama'ed, put to bed, and fed junket. A passing doctor finally confirms that a mistake has been made and that he will have his Board, but "meantime you stay here." He is now given massage daily, and in addition is required to swing a weight back and forth at the end of his "bad leg."

> I used to have to lie down for two hours a day to recover from the treatment. I was limping quite heavily by the time the MO put his head in one morning and said, "You're for a Board today." (264)

As a result he is re-classified B-2, fit for "Garrison duties at home and abroad." But before long the MO sends for him and confesses error: "You should have seen the surgical specialist before having the Board. . . . You'll have to have another Board now." But when the surgical specialist examines him, he arrives at new conclusions: "If you were to jump down into a trench your leg'd snap like a twig. Can't understand how they ever passed you. . . . Oughtn't to be in the infantry with a leg like that at all" (265).

Back to bed in the gastric ward. The next day an entirely new MO shows up, the old one having gone off on a week's leave. This one orders him back to his unit.

> "But he's awaiting a medical board, Doctor," the matron said.
> "Well he can wait for it at his unit. We're not running a home for soldiers awaiting medical boards. I never heard of such a thing."
> "Lieutenant Jackson said . . ."
> "Never mind what he said. I'm in charge here now, and I've just given an order . . . ." (266)

(Those last words suggest the dynamics of a multitude of military errors, namely, the forceful assertion of authority and decision which are actually very insecurely held. The standard response to having one's dubious orders questioned is to insist, and then even add further clauses compounding the original error.)

Back at his unit, the soldier confronts a corporal he's never seen before, to be told that his outfit has left the camp. His possessions have disappeared, and his very bed has been removed. The forty odds and sods left behind march to the train station next day, but our soldier, limping too much to keep in step, is finally trucked there, to the fury of an unfamiliar officer who can't believe he's just been in the hospital. The train proves to be already entirely filled with recruits proceeding to a new camp. No matter: the forty additional soldiers crowd in, no one knowing anything about their destination. Food is brought around, but there's not half enough. "Mistake somewhere," says a captain. Arriving at the new camp, the soldier tries again to have his problem understood:

> In the morning I was down for sick, but the MO at this camp proved to be a much tougher proposition than any I'd yet encountered.
> He said, "What d'you mean, you've had a medical board? How can you have had a medical board? Where's your papers?"
> "I gave them to the officer in charge of the draft, sir," I said.
> "Well, *I* haven't got them. What was the officer's name?"
> "I don't know, sir."
> "You don't know. My God, you give your papers to an officer and you don't even know his name." The MO held his head in his hands. "God deliver me," he said, "from such idiocy." (270)

Examined, the soldier's pay book asserts that he is still classified A-1. The MO accuses him of lying and sends him back to his unit in disgrace. Two days later training resumes, and a new sergeant, finding the man's knee won't allow him to march properly, sends him on sick-call again.

> It was another MO this time and he had my papers, they'd turned up again, and he said I've got to have another medical board. . . . That was a month ago and I'm still waiting. . . . I don't care if they grade me Z-2 or keep me A-1, so long as I don't have to go sick. I've had enough of it. (271)

As that example suggests, Second World War fiction depends heavily on the theme of blunders. They become virtually the fabric of Joseph Heller's *Catch-22*, and perhaps more plausibly of Kurt Vonnegut's *Slaughterhouse-Five*. There, some blunders, ironically, are fortunate, like the clerical error which causes the Red Cross to ship a batch of British POWs 500 instead of 50 food parcels per month. The tons of food resulting enable them to give a lavish banquet to Billy Pilgrim and his fellow GIs when they arrive at the prison camp. But most blunders result in horror. In hospital, Pilgrim's ward neighbor is Eliot Rosewater, Capt., Inf:

> Rosewater was twice as smart as Billy, but he and Billy were dealing with similar crises in similar ways. They had both found life meaningless, partly because of what they had seen in war. Rosewater, for instance, had shot a fourteen-year-old fireman, mistaking him for a German soldier. So it goes. And Billy had seen the greatest massacre in European history, which was the fire-bombing of Dresden. . . . So they were trying to re-invent themselves and their universe.[18]

The tradition that the Second World War can be usefully conceived as a vast theater of errors is resumed in William Wharton's novel *A Midnight Clear* (1981), where the disastrous denouement is occasioned by a slip-up in communication within a single rifle squad. And Derek Robinson's *Piece of Cake* (1984), a novel about the RAF during the Battle of Britain, becomes practically a catalogue of blunders and messes: the RAF shoot down their own planes, constantly mistaking the Messerschmitt 109 for their own Hurricane, while they themselves are fired at regularly by British anti-aircraft. In the early stages of the battle, an RAF fighter squadron proudly shoots down a German bomber. But not quite: it proves to be a British Blenheim.

An author dwelling on such errors is likely to augment his skepticism, and that is likely to have stylistic consequences. Examples are the demotic-ironic idioms devised by Lincoln Kirstein in the United States and Gavin Ewart in Britain for registering their understanding of the war as virtually co-terminous with error. In poems like "Foresight," "Chimbly," "Rank," and "Big Deal," from *Rhymes and More Rhymes of a PFC* (1966), Kirstein forswears standard modern English—appropriate, perhaps, in a world where things go as they're supposed to—and invokes instead an idiom resembling John Berryman's in his last ironic "Henry" poems, wry and twisted, crazily colloquial, as if the speaker is too deeply experienced in the ways of the modern world to honor any longer ideals of "correctness," "good manners," or even "decency." Thus in Kirstein's poems dramatizing blunders we hear of a "dumb officer," "this ass" who "starts to get sore." Another dumb officer, one Major Dabeney, insists that his men build a fireplace and chimney for his tent. They procrastinate but finally find a store of bricks.

> Dabeney due to several delays he become ornery and mean
> We hope his temper improve wunst this excellent brick he seen.[19]

(The bricks prove to be blocks of explosive abandoned by the Germans, and when Dabeney lights his fireplace, the whole thing goes up.) Yet another deplorable officer, "crocked," decorates his drunken remarks with flowers like *shit* and *piss,* earning from a soldier the designation, "this prick."[20]

Similarly informal are the colloquial couplets Ewart uses in 1976 to narrate a bizarre blunder that occurred in England in the early 1940s. It has been officially hushed up ever since.

> Somebody in an office had the very bright idea,

he says in his poem "Incident, Second World War," to conduct a mock air attack on dummies representing troops in vehicles, with the object of developing useful statistics about probable casualties. The question to be answered was

> When the fighters came in to strafe with hedge-hopping low attacks
> how many bits and pieces would be picked up to fill the sacks?
> . . . nobody knew for certain the percentage who wouldn't get up,
> how many would be donating their arms and legs to Krupp.

To find out, the army set up a dummy truck convoy out in the deserted countryside and established a roped-off observation enclosure on a nearby hill. There a number of high-ranking officers assembled to watch the proceedings. As Ewart puts it.

> A grandstand seat
> was reserved for top brass and others, a healthy open-air treat;
> enclosed, beyond the dummies, they stood (or sat?) and smoked
> or otherwise passed the time of day, relaxed as they talked and joked.

Six Spitfire fighters equipped with a new sort of repeating cannon were to appear, strafe the target, and return to their field. But one pilot, either confused about his mission, or embittered, or insane, or God knows what, instead of shooting up the target shot up the observers. Five, it is said, were killed outright: two were generals, three, colonels and majors. Around twenty officers were wounded. And all in dress uniform, "with as much polished leather, brass, scrambled egg bemedalling as possible," recalls Humphrey Spender, then a lieutenant, on duty at the scene as a War Office Official Photographer. "I was told that dummy ammunition would be used," he says.

> I decided that I should lie in front of the leading vehicle so that a part of the vehicle was in the foreground. I was partly protected by the vehicle, but to my alarm I soon discovered that the ammunition used by the planes as they roared over was by no means dummy. Earth spouted up all round me, and I decided, having not been hit on the first run, that I would get away before they came in for the second attack. I ran up a steep bank to the enclosure, and there to my amazement I found officers of all ranks lying around on the ground in great confusion, some obviously wounded; there was blood and groaning.

The errant pilot was rumored, says Spender, (1) to have been Polish, and thus unpredictable; (2) to have been in the employ of German intelligence; or (3) simply to have been driven mad by too much recent combat flying.

Strict secrecy was enjoined on all witnesses of this blunder. Spender's films—he took some fast pictures in the enclosure before a superior stopped him—were confiscated. To his account of this episode he adds: "I saw many such accidents in home-based exercises. The deaths and casualties were always reported to relatives as 'on active service.' All photographs were confiscated and censored." And of the blunder recorded in Ewart's poem, he says, "There can be few people who know anything about this incident."[21] Ewart somehow found out the details, and he learned that his cousin from New Zealand, Penny Matson, was one of those killed. Ewart has dedicated the poem to his memory. It ends sardonically:

> Nevertheless, there *were* results: percentages were worked out,
> how 10 per cent could be written off, the wounded would be about
> 50 per cent or so. Oh yes, they got their figures all right.

Circulated to units. So at least that ill-omened flight
was part of the Allied war effort, and on the credit side—
except for those poor buggers who just stood there and died.[22]

—4—

Rumors of War

A world in which such blunders are more common than usual will
require large amounts of artful narrative to confer purpose, meaning, and
dignity on events actually discrete and contingent. During moments when
clear explanations of purpose and significance seem especially unavailable—as in "What did the pilot think he was doing?" or "What are we
doing here?"—demotic social narrative and prophecy flourish as compensations. During wartime there seems less need for high narrative, like
sophisticated romance or novel, than low. Folk-narrative (or officially
generated pseudo-folk-narrative) blossoms on all sides. The most common
form of folk-narrative is the dirty joke. It survives abundantly in wartime, but it is joined by such psychologically useful forms as the myth of
military heroism and the compensatory rumor.

Widely believed in the dark days of 1942, when America required
relief after all the narratives about surrenders and sinkings and retreats,
was the story of Air Corps Captain Colin P. Kelly. He is said to have
immolated himself in the early days of the war by dropping a bomb, with
the customary early-in-the-war precision, down the main stack of the Japanese battleship *Haruna*, and then, after ordering his crew to bail out,
crashing his bomber into the foundering warship. (By the time of the
kamikazes, this myth had to be forgotten, lest the *kamikaze* pilots be considered heroes rather than madmen.) Actually, what Kelly damaged was
not a battleship but a barely armed troop transport which did not sink,
and he was killed not then but later, when a Japanese fighter jumped his

plane. There is evidence that he tried to bail out before anyone else but was carried down with the plane when his parachute caught on the escape door.[1]

Clearly narratives like the Colin Kelly myth are sophisticated works officially concocted behind the scenes to aid morale. More down-to-earth are wartime rumors. In the prevailing atmosphere of uncertainty for all and mortal danger for some, rumor sustains hopes and suggests magical outcomes. Like any kind of narrative, it compensates for the insignificance of actuality. It is easy to understand why soldiers require constant good news. It is harder to understand why they require false bad news as well. The answer is that even that is better than the absence of narrative. Even a pessimistic, terrifying story is preferable to unmediated actuality.

When Allied troops landed on the beach at Salerno in September, 1943, they expected something close to a walk-in. After all, Italy had just surrendered. But what they found instead was a deadly German defense, so ably conducted that precise reasoners about cause and effect could not by any means regard it as routine. The Germans, it was reasoned, must have known from spies and leaks where and when the landing was to take place. It was said that as the first troops were heading in, they heard from loudspeakers on shore the entirely demoralizing message, "Come on in. We've got you covered." Or in some versions, "Come on in and give up. You're covered."[2] A question no conveyer of this interesting rumor thought to consider is why the Germans would labor thus to taunt their attackers sarcastically—setting up amplifiers and supplying them with power, deciding what to call out, learning the lines in English, getting the whole act approved by higher authority—instead of simply repelling them and thus eliminating the threat to their own safety. Even the commanding general, Mark Clark, believed that the Germans had baited the Americans by loudspeaker as they approached. Some years later, in calmer circumstances, an explanation surfaced. The words the troops heard, or something like them, were what the Allied beachmasters, the earliest arrivals, shouted over their bullhorns to encourage the coxswains of the gingerly approaching landing craft.[3] The shouts from the shore were supposed to be consoling, but to the scared troops they were unexpected and thus could be only menacing. That is, the ferocious, professional German response to the invasion—when the troops had been expecting at worst a feeble Italian gesture—had to have a reasonable cause, and this rumor provided it. In the same way, after the raid on Dieppe had failed so signally in the fall of 1942, folklore assigned shrewd espionage as the cause. Vere Hodgson recalls the contemporary belief that an ad for Sylvan Soap Flakes showing a "Dieppe Beach Coat" that appeared several days before the raid was really "a cryptogram advising the Germans." The ghastly denouement on the French beach confirmed that sinister suspicion: "No wonder we lost half our forces."[4] Thus with the disasters of Salerno and Dieppe even severe breaches of security were more pleasant to imagine than events without psychologically acceptable determinants. And there was this thought too: if the enemy routinely defends his coastlines this way, with what savagery will he defend them when the chips are down, when, say, we ultimately try to land in France? To believe that disaster is the result of hanky-panky rather than ineptitude on our side and superior skill and force on the enemy's is a way of evading a very frightening fact.

Such rumors also illustrate the principle that a complex human motive is more interesting to contemplate than a simple cause. A motive is especially interesting if some inkling of the secret or conspiratorial can be thought to attend it. Hence the perennial rumor in military training camps—popular also in prisons, boarding schools, and colleges—that the authorities are clandestinely adding saltpetre to the victuals to dampen lust and render the men docile and easier to control. Despite one's never meeting anyone whose job it has been to add the saltpetre, this rumor has been a favorite among troops at least since the American Civil War, and the pun lurking in *saltpetre* has doubtless helped contribute to its popularity. To impute an initial lessening of libido in a new, strange, and often hostile environment to disorientation, unaccustomed physical exhaustion, and anxiety would be sensible but uninteresting. Better the melodramatic narrative, with its fascinating hints of conspiracy and cabal, its implicit imagery of crafty orderlies "sworn to secrecy" ladling great doses of white powder into the men's food and drink while they sleep unaware. The sense of mystery generated by the saltpetre rumor has been registered in folk song, and probably not for the last time:

> My cock is limp, I cannot fuck,
> The nitrate it has changed my luck.
> The nitrate it has changed my luck.[5]

Different in function from such "explanatory" rumors are comic or sardonic ones, which operate like midget satires. They represent the spontaneous overflow of powerful feelings—toward civilians, especially 4-Fs;

officers; optimists and euphemizers; and the Great in general. They are the sole weapon of the troops against the Others—all who have victimized them. Rumors of widespread official cynicism, greed, and incompetence are always popular, and the more credible ones often sound as if planted by the enemy. Like the rumor circulating among British troops in the Great War that their government paid the French rent for the use of the trenches, or a counterpart from the Second World War, that Winston Churchill received a royalty of fifty pounds each time one of the tanks named for him issued from the assembly line. In the South Pacific, some believed that the American government paid the Palmolive Company seventy cents for each palm tree destroyed. That military authorities are inevitably mean and unimaginative was the point of the rumor after Dunkirk that U.K. troops who had lost bits of their equipment in the battle would have their pay docked. If the authorities are greedy and unfeeling, they are also morally stupid: witness the rumor that Mrs. Roosevelt insisted that all venereal cases be quarantined on some offshore island before being allowed home. This seemed so credible to many soldiers that she felt obliged to issue a denial.[6]

Many rumors of this type recognize the ludicrous blunders committed by one's own side: no wonder the war goes on so long and is so hard to win. One rumor emanating from British forces in North Africa held that, the army having requested a shipment of one million sandbags, the army received one million bags filled with sand. Another maintained that the London park railings, ostentatiously sawed off early in the war for scrap metal, proved so unusable that they finally had to be secretly dumped into the sea "off Portsmouth." (That last detail illustrates a characteristic of narrative rumors noted as long ago as 1722 by Daniel Defoe in *A Journal of the Plague Year:* the events narrated in a rumor almost always occur at some distance, making verification difficult.) In the United States food rationing was said to be so madly out of control and bungling so extensive that people had witnessed the navy dumping surplus rationed coffee into New York harbor, while tons of it rotted in warehouses as well. There was a shortage of butter, yet vast shipments were sent to the Soviet Union, where it was used as a lubricant for weapons and vehicles. Although beef was rationed, there was so much of it that the army secretly threw away great amounts. While motorists were allowed virtually no fuel, in Texas there was a stream which ran pure gasoline, the guilty excess from the refineries. Faced with canards like these, it is not hard to understand the official attempt to repress rumors (those, that is, not planted by the government itself). "Challenge all rumors and harmful stories about our allies," counsels *The Bluejacket's Manual*, "our inefficiencies or mistakes, the enemy's strength, race dissension or breaches of discipline. Keep scuttlebutt to yourself and tell your shipmates to do the same."[7] But there was as little hope of repressing interesting narrative as of preventing gambling and swearing by prohibiting them.

Undoubtedly planted by the enemy but much circulated, and sardonically enjoyed, by U.K. troops overseas were the rumors that their wives and women were being consoled, usually for money, by the Yanks preparing for the invasion. Some rumors held that the women had opened brothels for the Yanks because of poverty, their husbands' allotments being so tiny by comparison. As Martin Page puts it, "Almost every soldier in North Africa had 'heard' of another who came home unexpectedly, to find that his wife had become a madame, and that his five children had been forced to live in the kitchen, to make room for the GI clients."[8] This obsession found an outlet in a song popular among British troops. A soldier returns home to his Nellie without warning:

> I let myself in quietly and tiptoed up the stairs.
> The thought of being home again had banished all my cares.
> In the bedroom then I murmured, "Nell, your soldier boy has come,"
> When a voice replied in sharp surprise, "Say, Nell, who is this bum?"[9]

Rumors of espionage, sabotage, and treason are universally popular, both because they make the war interesting and because they help explain why one's own side is not winning it faster. On the American home front, ground glass was said to be found in supplies of bandages. The tallest of the Watts towers, in Los Angeles, was really a Japanese radio transmitter broadcasting the taunting of the turncoat Tokyo Rose, a onetime resident, the rumor said, of the Watts area. On the other hand, some said that Tokyo Rose was really Amelia Earhart, who had not been lost in the Pacific but captured by the Japanese, brain-washed, suborned, and wrested from her allegiance to the United States. A German submarine, captured in Florida waters, proved to have in its galley milk from a Miami diary, as well as bread in the wrapper of a local bakery of hitherto good repute.

That one's defeats and disasters are caused by treasonous traffic with the enemy rather than by one's own blundering amateurism is always a popular idea. Thus in the Great War disloyal French and Belgian farmers were believed to indicate the position of British artillery batteries by arranging their livestock in certain patterns visible to the Germans. Likewise, at Pearl Harbor it was believed that Japanese working on Oahu had cut big arrows in the fields to guide Japanese planes toward their targets. In this line there seems no limit to what can be believed, so long as intriguing narrative emerges. Just after the attack on Pearl Harbor, a dog barking on the beach at Oahu was said to be barking in Morse, conveying treasonous messages to a Japanese submarine listening offshore. One reason German bombers seemed to be in the habit of circling British cities for hours is that they were waiting for their agents below to indicate targets. At one point a popular American piano entertainer playing for the BBC was thought to be sending coded information to the Germans by musical means. In North Africa, American troops noticed, one of them says, Arabs plowing "what we fancy is the design of an airplane propeller and guiding arrow, but S-2 does not seem to agree that this may mean an emergency landing field for the Germans."[10] In 1940 the fall of France was widely believed to have been assisted by an internal Fifth Column generating confusion. But as German records reveal, no such thing existed, for it was not needed. As Michael Balfour says, "In not a single concrete case has any evidence been found that the flight of the population was furthered by false orders circulated by enemy agents—they were mostly given by French officials."[11] Signaling from ships, especially troop transports, to enemy submarines is a popular narrative motif, and anyone showing a light or igniting a cigarette on deck is likely to be suspected of disloyalty rather than stupidity.

May, 1940, was an especially nervous time for the British, with invasion fears beginning to shape up. Captain J. R. Strick was occupying a position in Kent, where he wrote: "One gets the impression that we are undermined and that spies are everywhere. We are constantly getting warnings of bogus officers and inspectors going round," and indeed, "various odd things like flashing mirrors have been observed."[12] Since at this time it was easily believed that the Germans were dropping agents or even commandos into England by parachute, and most often disguised as nuns (a classic), it is not particularly surprising that so bright an observer as Virginia Woolf once insisted to Leonard "in a stage whisper" that a nun who had entered their railway carriage was really "a Nazi paratrooper in disguise."[13] You could always secure someone's attention by telling how you'd heard that a nun on a bus had paid her fare with a hairy hand.

Sometimes rumors were originated and transmitted less to assign purpose to the accidental than simply to alleviate the boredom. The British soldier Vernon Scannell recalls the atmosphere in camp just before his battalion took part in the invasion: it comprised "boredom, cold, exhaustion, squalor, lack of privacy, monotony, ugliness and a constant teasing anxiety about the future." Consequently

> fresh rumors were floated almost daily: The battalion was going to be converted to airborne; it was going to move up to Scotland; there had been a rape in the village; General Eisenhower was coming to inspect them; the . . . Division was going to be used as a diversionary assault force on D-Day and it has been written off as totally expendable; the Germans had a secret weapon that would destroy the entire invasion force; Hitler has been assassinated; Vera Lynn was coming to sing . . . ; Churchill was coming to inspect the battalion; the Germans were about to surrender; the battalion was moving to Kent. This last one proved to be true.[14]

Aboard a troop transport off West Africa the young officer Neil McCallum was motivated to fictional narrative by the intense boredom. "Long ago," he notes, "we stopped being gullible but rumors are started deliberately just for the fun of it." He himself experimented with speed of circulation: "I told someone we were to be sent ashore for a route march and the story went round the ship and came back to me in twenty minutes."[15] When the plane carrying Glenn Miller was shot down in December, 1944, the event could be said to be, by that time, almost routine. Narrative imagination therefore set to work: Miller had really been shot in Paris by an American colonel who caught him in an egregious black-market transaction. Or he was killed not in a plane crash but in a fight in a French brothel. Et cetera.

One might think that wartime events themselves would be exciting enough, but no. They must be made even more interesting by having scandal or secrets attached. The American Women's Army Corps was a natural breeding-ground for interesting narrative. Female recruits were said to be required to exhibit themselves naked before male officers in order to enter the WAC. At some installations, it was held, the custom was for the WACs more or less systematically to rape the men. From overseas hordes of WACs had to be returned pregnant, hardly surprising since they were really official whores provided for the comfort of the troops—especially the officers.

Some rumors developed out of jokes or puzzles but became no less gripping for that. For example, the one holding that if you sent the Ford Motor Company a 1943 copper penny, the company would send you a brand new Ford. The catch was that pennies dated 1943 were made not of copper but of steel with a zinc surface. The rumor of the free Ford, which began with this joke, soon spread widely in a serious form. Many members of the Marine Corps believed that free Ford cars would be given the first one hundred marines to set foot on the Japanese main islands;[16] and in the Japanese prison camp at Davao, in the Philippines, Corporal Kenneth Day reports, there were two recurrent rumors collected by a man who wrote down all the rumors he heard and finally amassed a collection of some 2000. The two persistent ones were that Deanna Durbin was dead (why? why on earth?) and that Henry Ford was going to give each prisoner of war a free car when the war was over.[17] Some rumors of this general type avoided the consolatory entirely and focused only on being startling, like the "wild report" about the German plan to empty the Mediterranean by evaporation,[18] or the rumor dear to Scottish troops that the final transport vessel returning them home would be identifiable by its tartan funnel. Every induction center or training camp had its scare rumors, which had to be delivered with a straight face. One was about the square hypodermic needle used for an obligatory injection into the testicles. Another was about the "Umbrella Therapy" for gonorrhea. This involved a device inserted all the way into the urethra, opened like an umbrella when fully inserted, and then pulled slowly out again.

Some rumors (and that one almost qualifies) betray signs of gifted individual authorship. One narrative popular in Germany just after the war when food was extremely scarce could have been written by Poe himself. It was said that a blind Wehrmacht veteran, tapping along the street with his white cane, encountered a healthy and amiable girl and asked her to help him by delivering a letter to a certain address. As she set off she looked back and saw the blind man stepping out briskly, his cane now abandoned. She was so suspicious that she took the letter not to the address indicated but to the nearest police station. The police went to the address and found a shoe shop run by a couple. All seemed perfectly ordinary until the police stumbled upon a concealed cellar full of fresh meat, suggesting a black-market butcher shop. But closely inspected, says Douglas Botting,

> the meat turned out to be human flesh. Until now the police had over-looked the letter which the blind man had given the girl. When they opened it they found a piece of paper on which was written a single, chilling sentence: "This is the last one I shall be sending you today."[19]

As that sort of thing suggests, perhaps rumors should be taken more seriously by students of narrative. Certainly they seem to exhibit an analyzable taxonomy. If some are satires exposing the stupidity of one's own side or demeaning the enemy, others are virtual romances, rendering an optimistic and ideal vision of the future. One large class consists of horror stories emphasizing the enemy's strength, viciousness, and cunning.

General Patton was expert at exploding horror stories. Like the Earl of Warwick in Shakespeare, he knew that

> Rumor doth double, like the voice and echo,
> The numbers of the feared.[20]

One night in April, 1945, it was reported to Patton's headquarters that the Germans had set upon an American hospital column, murdered all male members of the hospital, including the wounded, and raped all the nurses. Daylight revealed that the Germans had killed one officer and two enlisted men, leading Patton to conclude that "the report of no incident which happens after dark should be treated too seriously. They are always overstated."[21] In the same way, his experience taught him that "reports by wounded men are always exaggerated and favor the enemy" and that "a casualty report of more than ten per cent is seldom true, unless people have run away or surrendered."[22]

"Romance" or consolatory rumors, on the other hand, resemble horror rumors turned inside out. Instead of stimulating fear without facts, they propose hope without facts. The simplest type is the most brief: Germany is in revolt; the war will be over by Christmas; you are going to get a free Ford. One such rumor treasured by American infantry troops in Europe was that their division would very soon be withdrawn from combat and return to the States to train new troops. That is, no one could believe the unbelievable—that the destiny of an infantrymen was to stay on the line until wounded, captured, or dead. Or until the end of the war. The division would return, it was said, on the *Queen Mary*. Always the *Queen Mary*. After the campaign in Tunisia, according to General Bradley "an inexplicable rumor spread like wildfire that those divisions that had fought in Tunisia had 'done their share' and would be returned to the States. . . . New Divisions would come over to take their place for future operations." (Hardly *inexplicable*, those familiar with romance rumor's consolatory functions will perceive.) Bradley continues: "When the men were told emphatically that this was not true, there was widespread rebellion" and "many cases of self-maiming were reported."[23]

A standard romance rumor in prisoner-of-war camps is that an exchange of prisoners is imminent. Of course it never takes place. In a German extermination camp like Auschwitz-Birkinau, almost all rumors were consolatory. A persistent one was that on a given day in the near future, "selections"—i.e., gassings—would cease. One had to live only until this target day to survive. Many rumors of this type illogically ascribe secret sympathy and admirable human feelings to the enemy, like the story cherished by British troops in North Africa that if you were seen by the Germans kicking a soccer ball around, they would not fire at you. Indeed, says Olivia Manning, "There was a belief that the enemy never attacked men at play."[24] It was also a consolation to believe that despite the German show of military efficiency and hardihood, individual German soldiers were really quite feeble. In the American infantry it was sometimes believed that German corpses turned green sooner than others—a result of diet deficiency.[25] Just as comforting was the belief that the Germans were not sending off their V-1s with total impunity. Each time they fired one, some said, they lost six men, "killed by the blast."[26] Likewise, it was consoling to believe that the official presence of the London stage magician Jasper Maskelyne among British officers in North Africa was a circumstance of very high military promise. At the moment when he was being spotted, hush-hush, at parties in Cairo, the Germans were advancing steadily and now were only fifty miles from Alexandria. Maskelyne was surely the savior. "He creates illusions," says one true believer in Manning's *The Battle Lost and Won* (1978).[27] Maskelyne was there, but his job was un-mystical and down-to-earth, related to his experience with stage deception: by imposing canvas and wood frames he could make cars look like trucks or tanks. His presence, thus, was scarcely a cause for hope. It argued, on the other hand, a dangerous British deficiency in matériel.

Among the saddest of rumors were those circulating, desperately, around the Philippines early in 1942. General MacArthur had departed for Australia, promising to return. He strongly implied that help for the beleaguered islands was on the way in the form of an immense support convoy from the States. Hattie Brantley, who was a nurse there, remembers that "the main theme . . . was 'Help is on the way!' We evidenced faith, hope, and trust—in God, in General MacArthur, in FDR, in the USA. In fact, anytime anyone looked in the direction of [Manila] Bay and did not see a convoy steaming in it was with disbelief." At night she and her colleagues used to leave a skeleton staff to take care of the wards: they would "go sit on the beach and watch for the convoy that was coming." Private Leon Beck of the army was there too, and he testifies that "people lived on rumors. That was the only hope we had. . . ." Even though everyone knew deep down that the rumors couldn't possibly be true, they had to believe that reinforcements had been sent from San Francisco and that ships carrying lots of food were accompanying the fresh troops. "It was part of the psychology of survival," says Nurse Brantley. "If you had known that you were going to be a captive of the Japs for three and a half years, you wouldn't have existed. You would have given up right then."[28]

Those rumors were created by the believers out of their dire need. Another category includes rumors crafted and carefully planted by the enemy as skirmishes in the psychological warfare battle. The assumption was that the morale of soldiers, obviously a timid, credulous lot, could be undermined if they heard authoritatively that their wives were misbehaving at home; that no one there cared a whit about the misery they suffered; that the pay corps of their army was corrupt and stealing their pay; that their parcels were being stopped and enjoyed by official thieves in the rear areas; or that their civilian jobs, filled now by effeminates or 4-Fs, would never be returned to them after the war. Assigned the task of devising and circulating such rumors among the Germans was the British Political Warfare Executive. "A group of PWE staff," says Michael Balfour, "used to sit around a table weekly at Woburn and scratch their heads to devise stories calculated to inconvenience the enemy." The rumors thus generated were passed on to agents in the field, who would drop them casually in bars and on the streets, and "now and then one of them would crop up in a Swiss newspaper or as something a traveller had heard in Germany."[29]

For the Americans the job was handled by the Morale Operations

Section of the OSS. It enrolled thousands of people. One of its operatives, Elizabeth P. MacDonald, has revealed the way it worked. In Europe it specialized in planting rumors about the mental instability of Hitler, Goering, Goebbels, and the like; suggesting to the soldiers that the home front was letting them down; and stimulating "false hopes . . . which would lead to general disillusionment."[30] The canard that Hitler was an epileptic was the work of the Morale Operations Section. It also devised the rumor, for circulation among German troops in Italy, that Italian units were printing up their own surrender passes instead of limiting themselves to the ones dropped by Allied aircraft. To add to the misery in bomb-torn Berlin, Morale Operations spread the rumor there that exposure to Allied bombing produced both impotence and sterility. In Asia, Elizabeth MacDonald's unit sought to persuade the Japanese troops that their diarrhea was not diarrhea but the effect of poison "love curry" fed them by their inimical Southeast Asian girlfriends. They laced the curry, it was said, with tiny but rigid bamboo hairs which, penetrating the walls of the colon, occasioned internal bleeding which was fatal.[31] In Asia, Morale Operations also managed to inform Japanese soldiers that their government, anxious to increase the population, was encouraging women at home to bear as many children as possible, "with or without the benefit of marriage."[32] In Burma, MacDonald's field unit of Morale Operations employed numerous Burmese agents to plant rumors, and it gave them these tips about spreading rumors successfully:

1. Tell the story casually, and don't give yourself away by being overanxious to launch your rumor.

2. If the low-down is especially hot, tell it confidentially.

3. Never speak your rumor more than once in the same place. If it is good, others will repeat it.

4. Tell it innocently, and don't disclose any source that can readily be discredited.[33]

Both Axis and Allied agents did their work by observing these techniques, spreading in the United Kingdom, for example, the news that numerous rural hosts had been infected with VD by their young evacuees from the cities, and in Germany persuading the troops defending the line in the West that the news that the Russians had already entered Berlin was not true. One morale-deflating item among Americans doubtless kept in motion by Axis operatives was the news that soldiers' V-Mail, handily available on film strips, was being projected on movie screens in state-side army camps to amuse the troops.[34]

Sometimes planted rumors were designed to be believed by one's own side. Thus the British rumor that Lord Woolton's "National Loaf," widely scorned for tasting like sawdust, really possessed remarkable aphrodisiac properties. Or the American one circulated among the troops in Europe that girls had been infected with VD by the enemy specifically to wreak damage on the invaders. It was the task of the Counter Intelligence units operating with American infantry divisions to plant rumors among their own troops naming false destinations and hinting at false plans to mislead enemy agents within whose hearing the Americans were sure to blab. Even more than today, in wartime everything you might hear and read during a day might be false, planted to be passed on to deceive either you or the enemy. Living in wartime thus resembled living in a play, with nothing real or certain. You literally did not know for sure what was going on, and you had to take on faith the public appearance of things, costly as this might prove for perceptual or intellectual life.

One of the most interesting and effective planted rumors, designed to deceive enemy and friend alike, was the British one about the defeat by fire of an attempted German invasion in fall, 1940. Flaming oil set alight in the Channel was the means. The Germans, it was reported, had mounted a full-scale invasion of the east coast, but it was frustrated by a clever British secret weapon—a system of underwater pipes that spread oil over the surface of the sea. The oil slicks resulting were ignited by the RAF, and thus "only blackened bodies ever reached the beaches," as an officer of the American 1st Division, a total believer in the story, asserted.[35] The rumor had great success in London, where it was heard by the young civilian Colin Perry. He recorded in his diary: "I hear . . . that on Saturday night and again on Tuesday invasion was attempted. Not one Nazi returned. Their bodies are still being washed up along our shores."[36] During September, 1940, hundreds of detailed rumors circulated in Britain about the hideously burned bodies of Germans clogging the Channel and washing ashore. Terrible burn cases were overtaxing the German military hospitals in Paris, etc. But the whole thing was, as Michael Balfour has found, "a deliberate British invention."[37]

Some rumors imputing perverseness or oddity to the enemy had a curious way of coming true before the war was over. Early on, Japanese fighter pilots were said to be padlocked into their cockpits to prevent their escaping by parachute, an interesting anticipation of the actual *kamikazes* later in the war. "The enemy is using a new weapon"—that was always popular as an explanation for surprises and setbacks, as Martin Middlebrook perceives.[38] At first the Germans were rumored to have perfected a Death Ray, and then an Engine-Stopping Ray to beam upward at hostile aircraft. Busy with these fantasies, the Allied mind did not notice until quite late that the Germans were actually inventing the V-1 and the V-2 and that not all Hitler's talk about "secret weapons" was bluff. After the attack on Pearl Harbor, United States marines stationed on the East Coast, as if distressed to have been omitted from the action, and the publicity, started the rumor that the Germans were sending dirigibles across the Atlantic packed with paratroops to be dropped in their part of the world. Hitler himself seemed so odd that hundreds of rumors easily attached themselves to him. He was dead. He was insane. He foamed at the mouth and chewed the carpet when angry, which was almost all the time. In 1940 a refugee German industrialist told Chips Channon that Hitler "was certainly a homosexual" and that his failure to ascend to a rank higher than corporal in the Great War "was due to his very pronounced perversion. In later years he reformed. . . ."[39]

But the war was itself so unbelievable that the rumors it generated sometimes behaved anomalously and proved to be true. Like one of the most shocking, the one circulating among European Jews in the early 1940s that they were being sent to the East not for "resettlement" but to be systematically mass-murdered. And in July, 1945, Elizabeth MacDonald's group carefully spread the rumor in Asia, contriving absurd numerological evidence to support it, that some terrible catastrophe would befall Japan during the first week of August. These light-hearted rumormongers knew nothing about the new kind of bomb that would go off above Hirsohima on August 6th, when what they designed to be false turned out to be all too true.

Unlike such scare rumors, the most popular military rumors are the ones fostering irrational hopes and proposing magical outcomes. Closely related by the motive to influence the future mystically are wartime military superstitions. Their mode is a form of instant protective prophecy, and each implies a consoling projected narrative—the New Testament in the breast pocket *will* charm away bursts of machine-gun fire, the tiny bone elephant carried in the pocket on every bombing mission *will* deflect the flak. Rigorous attention to such usages will guarantee for the believer a lucky, seamless personal narrative, enabling him to come out of the war as undamaged as he went in.

The talismans treasured by the troops resemble those popular in the Great War: special coins (Eisenhower had a lucky set of seven, which he rubbed before crucial operations); St. Christopher medals; key and watch-chain fobs and medallions. But one thing distinguishing the Second War talismans from the earlier ones is their open connection with sex. Bras-sieres and silk or nylon stockings and panties were especially lucky items, not to be parted from, especially among bomber crews, who also insisted on wearing special pieces of clothing which had saved them in the past. Scarves and the like would sometimes "remain unwashed for months for fear that [their] owner might be called upon to fly without [them]."[40] As in many other things, the RAF went in for special eccentricity in talismans, as if sometimes to suggest pampered aristocratic boyhoods, like Sebastian's in *Brideshead Revisited*. His teddy bear Aloysius would have made a perfect talisman to accompany a crew on a bombing mission. An RAF staff officer once observed a bomber crew waiting for interrogation attended by their black rag-doll buddy. "In one chair sat a golliwog, their mascot. Someone happened to knock this chap off the chair and one of these tired men just picked him up, dusted him and sat this grotesque creature in his place. Golly had been on every trip and had never missed an interrogration. . . ."[41] (This use of the golliwog may reflect the Brit-ish folk belief that blacks are carriers of luck. One African air-raid war-den reported that the people in his district so fervently believed him to be a lucky omen that in a shelter on the verge of panic he once calmed the crowd by simply shining a flashlight on his own face.[42])

Another lucky thing to carry was a bullet that had missed one earlier, a usage apparently related to the belief that no two shells or bombs land in the same place and thus that a shell crater or a bombed site is a good place to hide. Julian Maclaren-Ross was working in the butts on a firing range when a wayward bullet glanced off his helmet. "For years," he says, "I carried this bullet about as the One with My Name On It, possession of which, according to army superstition, guaranteed immor-tality, at least for the duration."[43] He was seriously upset when he finally lost it down a London street drain.

As in the Great War, numbers assumed powerful mystical and pro-phetic significance. Fliers found it easy to believe that accidents in train-ing came in threes, and one soldier landing at Anzio warned another (with some irony, to be sure) to be especially careful on his third, seventh, and thirteenth invasions. Constantly counting their missions and determining how many they had to go before reprieve, bomber crews were especially number-obsessed. Disaster could be avoided by designating the thirteenth mission number 12-B. There was a belief among American crews that if you returned safely from five missions, of your required twenty-five, thirty, or fifty, you would come through them all. Sixteen, on the other hand, was the magic number for the more sardonic American prisoners of the Japanese accidentally bombed by their comrades: if during an air raid you could count to sixteen, you were OK. "If you didn't get to sixteen it was all over."[44] And some words, if said at the right moment, possessed magical properties. Among British troops saying *rabbits* first thing upon waking on the first day of each month was held to be efficacious, and some thought *white rabbits* worked even better. Omitting this ritual could be disturbing. Thus Captain M. J. Brown, in North Africa, notes in his diary on the first of March, 1943, "I forgot to say 'rabbits' this morning—I always do in the first of the month, with unfailing regularity."[45]

Among the British, Bomber Command was the branch of service most in need of the consolations of superstition, for there the odds of surviving were the worst: out of 100 men, only twenty-four, on an average, could expect to live. When thirty missions constituted a tour, releasing an airman from further obligation, the average number of missions completed was fourteen. No wonder golliwogs were required. No wonder bomber crews chose to believe that empty beer bottles dropped from their planes had the power to blank out German searchlights. "It was unwise to laugh at this practice," reports Hector Bolitho, "so widely and deeply was it believed."[46] Another way for bomber crews to secure their survival was to urinate communally on their plane's tail wheel before taking off on a mission, or sometimes to do the same—as a ritual of thanksgiving—upon returning.

In the RAF, horoscopes were also popular, but probably no more so than everywhere else. So carefully attended to were the predictions of "Lyndoe" in the *Daily Express*, "Archidamus" in the *Daily Mail*, and "Mme. Tabouis" in the *Dispatch* that Professor C. E. M. Joad came on the radio to debunk the whole thing. Both the Allies and the Axis used astrological prediction as a propaganda weapon. The British dropped leaflets predicting a ghastly future for the Germans, and Goebbels retaliated by scattering ominous prophecies—many said to be derived from Nostra-

damus—among Allied personnel, as well as issuing encouraging horoscopes for home consumption, which noted that as soon as the dark places
had been passed, a bright future was inevitable.

The Second World War was a notably secular affair. When superstitions that could be considered "religious" do surface, they are likely to
carry with them a taint of skepticism, or at least wariness. Marching
nearer and nearer the Japanese border, British lieutenant Robert Rhodes
James reacts thus to the suggestion that his endangered unit might profitably listen to nightly readings from the New Testament: "The idea that
one should use God as a form of artificial respiration or blood transfusion
to be used only in extremity has always appeared to me to be . . . particularly crude. . . ."[47] And some invocations of religious comfort suggest not piety but simple insanity. With total conviction Sir James Stephen writes in his diary: "They can't kill me—God won't let them."[48]

John Steinbeck once sent back this dispatch to the *New York Herald
Tribune:*

BOMBER STATION IN ENGLAND,
June 30, 1943

It is a bad night in the barracks, such a night as does not happen very
often. . . . Nerves are a little thin and no one is sleepy. The tail gunner
. . . gets down from his bunk and begins rooting around on the floor.
  "What's the matter?" the man on the lower bunk asks.
  "I lost my medallion," the tail gunner says.
  No one asks what it was, a St. Christopher or a good-luck piece. The
fact of the matter is that it is his medallion and he has lost it. Everyone
gets up and looks. They move the double-decker bunk out from the wall.
They empty all the shoes. They look behind the steel lockers. They insist
that the gunner go through all his pockets. It isn't a good thing for a
man to lose his medallion.

In a world whose behavior seems to define it as nothing but mad, "You
cannot call the things that happen to bomber crews superstition."[49] In the
midst of calmly committed mass murder, reliance on amulets will seem
about the most reasonable thing around.

School of the Soldier

ll wars are boyish, and are fought by boys." Thus Melville in his poem "The March into Virginia." War must rely on the young, for only they have the two things fighting requires: physical stamina and innocence about their own mortality. The young are proud of their athleticism, and because their sense of honor has not yet suffered compromise, they make the most useful material for manning the sharp end of war. Knowledge will come after a few months, and then they'll be used up and as soldiers virtually useless—scared, cynical, debilitated, unwilling.

A notable feature of the Second World War is the youth of most who fought it. The soldiers played not just at being killers but at being grown-ups. Enacting a child's parody of a murderous adult society, boys who had never shaved machine-gunned other boys creeping up with *Panzer-fausts* in their adolescent hands. Among the horribly wounded the most common cry was "Mother!" It was his mother who affectionately cut a young soldier down to size when, training at Fort Benning, Georgia, he bragged in his letters about his manly expertise in night combat exercises. "The fact of the business," she reminded him, "is that most of you still need nursing bottles instead of Night Infiltration."[1] Women especially were struck by the anomaly of teen-agers turned soldiers, and not just in America. Observing the Finnish War in December, 1939, Martha Gellhorn visited a squadron of fighter planes and observed, "As always, one is astounded by the age of the pilots; they ought to be going to college dances, you feel, or cheering at football games." And later, in China in March, 1941, she notes of the soldiers of a Chinese army bodyguard provided for her party, "They all looked twelve years old and were probably nineteen."[2] Devising a military hero for her *Levant Trilogy*, dealing with the British desert war, Olivia Manning makes her Lieutenant Simon Boulderstone twenty years old. At one point he says of a major that he is "an old fellow, thirty-five or more."[3] In a world where anyone over twenty-seven or twenty-eight was likely to be called "Dad," thirty was dangerously old and thirty-five close to senile. A Canadian navy veteran recalls being badly led. The reason: "Our senior officers were what we called boffins, old fellows of 35 years or so who wanted to see the war out. . . ."[4] Like Evelyn Waugh himself, Guy Crouchback, the protagonist of *Sword of Honor*, feels distinctly superannuated, being almost thirty-six at the start of the war. Only in an atmosphere where extreme youth is normal could a twelve-year-old fight in the Canadian army in Italy "before his parents got a line on where he was and the army kicked him out. . . ."[5]

But were the soldiers particularly young, or did they just seem so, marked by some special 1940s signs of immaturity? When British conscription began, the minimum age was twenty. It was finally lowered to eighteen. The Americans started at twenty-one, but ultimately dropped the age to eighteen also. By late 1944, boys of the *Hitler Jugend*, aged sixteen or seventeen, and a few as young as fourteen or even twelve, were being thrown into the German line. One defending Berlin at the last, unarmed because there were not enough rifles to go around, asked what he was supposed to do. Cheer, he was told.[6] In the Great War, soldiers were young too—by the end, the British were taking seventeen-year-olds—but the world hadn't yet learned what a good front-line investment the very young were. The ages of some well-known Great War soldiers provide a useful contrast. By 1918, Edmund Blunden was twenty-two, Robert Graves twenty-three, Wilfred Owen twenty-five, Ivor Gurney and Isaac Rosenberg twenty-eight. Siegfried Sassoon and Frank Richards were almost elderly—thirty-two and thirty-five respectively. Sassoon was a company commander, and so was one Lieutenant Wilson who led a rifle company fighting in the Saar in March, 1945. At one point, his company clearing out a village house-to-house, he leaned out of an upstairs window to direct his men in the street below.

> Suddenly he jerked. He staggered back from the window. "My God, I'm hit!" he cried, his voice full of disbelief. Abruptly he thrust out his legs, as if he were trying to brace himself, in a last desperate attempt to fight off death. "Slap my face!" he commanded. "Slap my face!"
> A soldier dropped his rifle and struck him across the cheeks. To no

German boy soldiers surrendering at Cisterna di Latina, Italy
(George Silk, Life Magazine © 1944 Time Inc.)

avail. He dropped to the floor and with his last burst of energy, slammed his boots against a heavy oaken table, kicking it across the room.

A man in the company who examined the body later took from it Lt. Wilson's officer's identification card. It disclosed something his men hadn't thought about much until his destruction:

> He was only twenty-one and as he lay there he didn't look anywhere near that. His hair was cropped close and he had no beard at all. . . . When he died the spirit of the company died with him.[7]

At the outset, with events like that well hidden in the future, what a young person thought might happen to him seemed to depend on his intellectual sophistication. For Irving Howe and his crowd of young New York intellectuals "the thought of surviving to old age," he remembers, "seemed an implausible vulgarity."[8] And Philip Larkin, entering Oxford at the beginning of the war, found in himself and his friends (including Kingsley Amis) an "almost-complete suspension of concern for the future. . . . National affairs were going so badly, and a victorious peace was clearly so far off, that effort expended on one's post-war prospects could hardly seem anything but a ludicrous waste of time."[9] More innocent and optimistic were the largely rural American high-school youths preparing for the portentous unknown in the army and Marine Corps. "Maybe it was the naive optimism of youth," says E. B. Sledge, an eloquent memoirist of Marine horrors,

> but the awesome reality that we were training to be cannon fodder in a global war that had already snuffed out millions of lives never seemed to occur to us. The fact that our lives might end violently or that we might be crippled while we were still boys didn't seem to register.[10]

To young men whose main news about life has come from an acquaintance with "school," military training cannot fail to arouse ironic echoes. What had been liberal learning is now vocational training, and with a vengeance. And the more murderously vocational, the more irony, the more curious the parallels. "I walked through the gates alone," says Rupert Croft-Cooke of his arrival at his first training camp in 1940, "feeling some of the shyness of a new boy entering a school, half expecting to be asked by one of the old hands in khaki what my father did for a

(National Archives)

living."[11] A continuation of boarding school by other means—the army could seem that, especially in Britain. Croft-Cooke continues: "Life . . . became a sort of parody of life in a preparatory school, with new boys arriving, 'frightful rows' going on, football matches against rival establishments, favoritism, whispered confidences, and if not tuck-boxes at least pocket-money to spend in the canteen."[12] Everyone noticed how closely military instructors and superiors resembled the eccentric schoolmasters of one's boyhood. General Bernard Montgomery often impressed his audiences this way, with his pedantic lectures, his self-congratulatory attention to the "lessons" learned after every battle, his vicious, finely honed temper. One major testifies: "Only two people have ever made me shake in my shoes—Monty, and a very great headmaster at Rugby where I was at school."[13] In the service one was graded and "marked" constantly, just as at school, and the "Remarks" in RAF log books, entered periodically by the commanding officer, had a familiar ring: *Exceptional; Above average; Average; Below average.* Likewise the "Report Card" comments on officers' efficiency reports: "Tries hard"; "Good reliable performer"; "Can do better"; "Shows some improvement since last report." Quasi-academic "lecturing" was a skill every officer and NCO was supposed to acquire. At one British air-crew school, a veteran remembers, the students were "given a lecture on how to give a lecture. The lecturer told us that 'Marks will be given for the way the subject is treated and delivered. They will, on the other hand, be deducted for any showing of distracting idiosyncrasies such as . . . swinging keys round the fingers, juggling with a piece of chalk, etc.' "[14]

After a couple of years of this sort of thing, it became natural to import academic expectations and idiom into combat. If training required a number of literal tests, the "finals" were what you were anxious about "passing": combat, killing, the fear of death. Having survived the Battle of Alamein, Keith Douglas spoke of it as "an important test, which I was interested in passing."[15] If you failed on a mission or revealed undue anxiety, you blotted your copy-book, or fell, like George Orwell at St. Cyprian's, into "bad favor."[16] But if, like one troop of the Royal Artillery in North Africa, you remained "calm and steady" when menaced by 36 German tanks, you received "full marks."[17] No one knew until the war was over whether he would really "pass" and "graduate." It was finally an inexpressible relief to know, as the naval officer Louis Auchincloss said when Japan surrendered, that "I had 'made the grade'—however much by the skin of my teeth—and America had made the grade."[18] After the war, Evelyn Waugh observed the trials at Nuremberg, and it was as a pack of inept, contemptible schoolteachers—as scrutinized by the brightest students—that he saw the defendants, Ribbentrop especially, who seemed like

> a seedy schoolmaster being ragged, who knows he doesn't know the lesson, knows that the boys know, knows he has done the sum wrong on the blackboard, knows he has nothing to hope for at the school, but still hopes if he can hold out to the end of the term to get a "character" for another post. He lied instinctively and without apparent motive.[19]

The loss of freedom and the fear occasioned by the war, even if one escaped being in the armed services, was for the British aesthetic sensibility comparable to the dread punishment of "being sent off to boarding school." Whenever as a boy he was especially naughty, says Jocelyn Brooke, he was threatened with this terrible destiny. And finally the dire threat materialized. One day his mother made the irrevocable announcement, "more in sorrow than in anger as it were—rather as Chamberlain announced the outbreak of war in 1939." As the war ground on, it began to seem like an interminable series of terms at school, only now and then there was a bright moment. "After Alamein, the chase across the desert, the landings in Algeria, it began to seem that the War might one day be over: the 'end of term' was in sight, one would be going home for the holidays."[20] Those in the service noticed more specific ironic allusions to school. Vernon Scannell, taking part in an attack in North Africa in 1943, was struck by the "sheer absurdity" of "the white tape at the starting point, parodying a school sports day. . . ."[21] In one RAF unit the problem arose of keeping or transferring out those sergeants awarded commissions, lest social and command embarrassments ensue. The adjutant, after some thought about analogous school usages, decided against transfer: "It's rather as though a man had been made a prefect," he said. "Nobody is jealous."[22] And anyone witnessing the horseplay in the mess of that, or any other, RAF unit, watching, for example, the brigadier and another officer firing soda-water at each other from siphons, might imagine himself in "the sixth form on the last night of term."[23]

The airmen in Bomber Command were so close to their schooldays that after parties off the base, it was the convention to bring back such schoolboy trophies as toilet seats and street signs. And during the Battle of Britain the newshawkers' posters resembled adolescent cricket or football scoreboards: "Theirs, 78; Ours 17."[24] The overlap between school and the military struck Anthony Powell when he was attending an intelligence officers course at Cambridge. Because of frequent errors in the honorific initials following students' names on the roster, some Masters of Arts were conflated with holders of the Military Cross, and vice versa, as if ultimately MA and MC betokened roughly the same thing, that one had "passed."[25] And the snobberies associated with the British Public Schools of the Headmasters Conference survived remarkably well. One British officer taken prisoner in Italy was awed to arrive at his POW camp and to find there comfortably installed an exclusive club of men who had gone to Radley. "It's quite unbelievable," he said, "but they've formed an Old Radleian Society and they all sit around talking about when they were at school together."[26]

The school feeling was a property of not just the men in the services. Civilians experienced it too, and "suddenly," as Martin Green notes, "the whole nation was a school again." One lived in "an atmosphere of dos and don'ts, of punishments and reports, of lights out and school meals and pedagogical praise and blame," as well as of "solicited sacrifices and exhortations to show the right spirit."[27] All this made civilians feel, as many have observed, young again. The effect of the war was apparently to take years off everyone, and Jan Struther's Mrs. Miniver senses the reason: everyone, for a change, was learning something—first aid, knitting, fire-extinguishing, food-saving, vegetable gardening, tire and clothing preservation. "Almost everybody you meet is busy learning something," cheerful Mrs. Miniver finds, "whereas in ordinary times the majority of grown-up people never try to acquire any new skill at all, either mental or physical: which is why they are apt to seem, and feel, so old."[28]

Americans also sensed that the military was, oddly, still "school," although the greater variety of such institutions in the United States— public, private, parochial, state, Ivy, Liberal Arts, vocational, even military—made the analogies seem more complicated. The anxious competitiveness and status-consciousness in American education attached likewise to the numerous military and naval training programs, and getting admitted to, and risking "washing-out of," the various officer-training schemes was very like doing the same with the literal schools they aped. There were subtle social distinctions: the Navy V-12 program seemed the equivalent of Ivy, while going to Fort Sill, Fort Benning, or Fort Belvoir for ground-force officer training was like attending a state university. The textbooks familiar in American high schools and colleges had their counterparts in the military and naval training manuals, especially such elementary "introductory texts" as *The Soldier's Handbook* and *The Bluejacket's Manual,* issued to newcomers. The sailor's textbook could shock, delivering as it did useful hints for those cast away on desert islands. "All animals are safe to eat, but be careful about poisonous snakes. . . . Grubs and grasshoppers make good food. Pick off legs and wings before cooking. Do not eat caterpillars."[29] "School of the Soldier" is the title of one chapter of *The Soldier's Handbook*. There the recruit would learn, not about West Point, as some might expect, but about the rudiments of close-order drill. Ross Parmenter, author of a memoir about his experience in the army, explains that he has titled his book *School of the Soldier* because "to a civilian the army as a whole is a vast school. . . ."[30] Quite naturally, then, the troops called the little guidebooks about local manners and sensibilities issued before landing on strange shores (like the *Soldier's Guide to Sicily*) "invasion textbooks."

For those recently hazed in college fraternities, the sadisms and humiliations visited on newcomers in the services seemed merely an intensification of the familiar, and satire of the army and navy's refraction of "school" often surfaced in song. This one was sung mock-reverently to the melody of "Far Above Cayuga's Waters":

> High above the Chattahoochee,
> And the Upatoi,
> Stands our noble Alma Mater,
> Benning School for Boys.
>
> Salt in Tablets, scorching sun,
> Touch your toes on count of one,
> Expert, bolo, school solutions,
> Phenix City institutions.
>
> Hail to Benning, Hail to Benning,
> Follow Me's the cry.
> You must use the school solution.
> Follow me, or die.[31]

Training at an Air Corps field in Illinois in 1943, Randall Jarrell wrote his wife:

> I marched to KP with a wonderful barracks, 407; they are wonderful because they all sing, like angry cattle, the best song I've heard in the army. They begin to bawl without warning . . . to the tune of "The Stars and Stripes Forever" . . .
>
> > Three *cheers* for the *Jones* Junior *High*,
> > The *best* junior *high* in *Toledo*,
> > The *boys* and the *girls* they are *fine*,
> > You will *never* meet a *better* groo oo oo oop . . .
>
> (In measured cadence:)

Rah . . . Rah . . . Rah . . . Rah . . .
Jones . . . Junior . . . High . . . School . . then
    . . . 'Our class won the Bible.'
Then as an afterthought: 'TWICE!'[32]

To sing that straight-faced while marching was to say many things:
(1) Toledo is ipso facto funny; (2) the army is childish; (3) we secretly
miss our former life at public schools and resent the military's aping such
wholesome, innocent institutions; (4) youths claustrated in junior high
schools are silly and sweet, and their enthusiasms are to be admired, at
the same time they're patronized and pitied; and (5) being in the army
has taught us a style for ridiculing mass movements, group-sing and group-
think of all sorts. The innocence half-mockingly celebrated in "Jones Junior High" is reflected in the diary kept by a young American sailor on
terribly dangerous duty in the Pacific. In November, 1943, just after
shooting some Japanese to ribbons with his 20-mm installation, he pauses
to record news from his hometown paper: "Waltham [Massachusetts]
High is still undefeated [in football]. It looks like they will be state
champs this year." One page later he enters dispassionately details of the
casualties suffered aboard the nearby USS *Denver:* "Men with broken
backs, eyes blown out, bodies crushed, etc."[33] And what American boy
could watch the detonation of white phosphorus shells without recalling
the high-school or college chemistry lab, with the white phosphorus safe
in its jar of liquid, ready to flame out upon contact with the atmosphere?

Just as "school" colors the war, the war colors school. John Knowles,
in *A Separate Peace* (1960), perceptively senses the "invasion"—his word—
of an American private school by the contours and textures of the war.
The year is 1942, rock-bottom for the Allies, what with the loss of Singapore, Hong Kong, and the Philippines, the sinking of the *Prince of
Wales* and *Repulse,* the Japanese invasion of the Aleutian Islands, the British retreat at Tobruk, and the disastrous Dieppe raid. The metaphors
with which school life is rendered overlap inevitably with those appropriate to military and political situations well outside: situations are *hopeless,* areas are *overrun, countrysides* are *ruined,* there is *desolation* everywhere—and yet only life at a boys' school in remote, peaceful New
Hampshire is being depicted.[34]

Comparing the writing from the Great War with writing from the
Second, one perceives a curious difference. Wilfred Owen elegizes doomed

youth without imagining it in the classroom, and what Siegfried Sassoon's soldiers miss is not the life of school or campus but

> Bank-holidays, and picture shows, and spats,
> And going to the office in the train.[35]

But the writers of some of the most memorable Second War poems were university teachers, either actual or aspirant. And even those who weren't were intimate with the idea of the uses of the intellect and of art and curiosity as defined by the university. And even its social terms have become widely familiar. Thus Lincoln Kirstein specifies the troopship carrying 10,000 American soldiers to England as the former liner that

> Once shipped sophomore and cardsharp to Le Havre and
> Southampton.[36]

Meditating on innocence and its liability to damage, by the world and specifically by the war, Jarrell sets a poem on a campus, where "The Soldier Walks Under the Trees of the University." There, the students

> are, almost, sublime,
> In their read ignorance of everything.[37]

And in his poem "Losses" the airmen are depicted specifically as high-school students wholly unprepared for the tasks now laid upon them. "When we left high school," they say,

> nothing else had died
> For us to figure we had died like.

Regardless,

> In bombers named for girls, we burned
> The cities we had learned about in school. . . .[38]

Jarrell's ball-turret gunner is pointedly not a grown-up: his life explodes in a flak-burst before it's really begun. And the bomber crews of "Eighth Air Force" are like school kids. They

> play, before they die,
>   Like puppies with their puppy. . . .[39]

But such children have been through such "schooling" as the army has vouchsafed them. "What have you learned here?" the questioner asks the soldier in 'Soldier [T.P.]"—i.e., "Title Pending," not yet classified for a specific job. What has the soldier learned in this parody of school?

>   To bear, and be silent.
>   To do what I must, as I must: that is, to die
>   What are the soldier's answers? Yes, sir;
>   No, sir; no excuse, sir. . . . *But (sir) there is no room there,*
>   *to die—*
>   *To die or to live.* . . . Hush, no-one is listening.
>   Ask as you please, there is no one here to reply.
>   Here what they teach is other people's deaths;
>   Who needs to learn why another man should die?
>   Who has taught you, soldier, why you yourself are dying?
>   And there is no time, each war, to learn.
>   You must live or die as the dice are thrown on a blanket;
>   As the leaf chars or is kindled; as the bough burns.[40]

Not as sentimental as that is Henry Reed's very British three-part poem "Lessons of the War." It is, rather, witty, parodic, and satiric. But it is as obsessed with "lessons" as Jarrell's poems about his schoolchildren-soldiers, and Reed's NCO "teachers"—of rifle nomenclature, distance-judging, and unarmed combat—are just as ludicrous and innocent of their double-entendres as the fatuous masters in some remembered school.

   Jarrell's wartime identity as a teacher of celestial navigation in the Air Corps was superimposed on his identity as a teacher of English. Similarly Richard Eberhart: in the navy, a teacher of aerial gunnery; otherwise, a teacher of English. His well-known poem "The Fury of Aerial Bombardment" devotes three-quarters of its substance to a search for a language adequate to the inexpressible power and horror of bombing. After posing a series of questions unanswerable because of their magnitude and abstraction, the speaker tries to suggest what he's getting at by descending to particulars, his schoolboy students of the 50-caliber machine gun. To do this he imagines a military roster and feels his eye running up the names from bottom to top:

> Of Van Wettering I speak, and Averill,
> Names on a list, whose faces I do not recall . . .

And then a final elegiac gesture restrained from excessively destructive emotion by a sardonic comparison between this mortal "school" and the real schools his pupils so recently left:

> But they are gone to early death, who late in school
> Distinguished the belt feed lever from the belt holding pawl.[41]

During the war W. H. Auden taught English at Swarthmore and Bryn Mawr, and just afterwards he scrutinized the destruction wrought by the bombing of Germany as an anomalous member of the Morale Division of the American Strategic Bombing Survey. ("The work is very interesting but I'm near crying sometimes."[42]) Returning to the United States, he wrote "Under Which Lyre," the Harvard Phi Beta Kappa poem for 1946. "As far as I know," says Lincoln Kirstein, "[Auden] never wrote about the Second World War. . . ."[43] But he came close to doing so in this poem. Comically opposing the academic humanities (good) to the academic social sciences (bad), Auden by means of jokey imagery conflates university and military life. The time is the first year of the G. I. Bill. The colleges are bulging with just-released veterans awed by the mystique and prestige of liberal study after their years of vocational learning, and learning in the service of murder and devastation. Now their schooling is equally demanding, but different:

> . . . nerves that steeled themselves to slaughter
> Are shot to pieces by the shorter
> Poems of Donne.

And the "war" continues, but now between two "sides" within the university:

> Let Ares doze, that other war
> Is instantly declared once more
> 'Twixt those who follow
> Precocious Hermes all the way
> And those who without qualms obey
> Pompous Apollo.

That is, the playful and the useful, who now fight it out in school in a parody Second World War:

> Lone scholars, sniping from the walls
> Of learned periodicals,
>   Our facts defend,
> Our intellectual marines,
> Landing in little magazines,
>   Capture a trend.

Images of the *underground* and of *ambushes* and of *morale* and *routs* and *battalions* conduct the reader to the closing mock-Decalogue, which includes such injunctions to the student as

> Thou shalt not answer questionnaires
> Or quizzes upon World-Affairs,
>   Nor with compliance
> Take any test. Thou shalt not sit
> With statisticians nor commit
>   A social science.[44]

Lightweight, to be sure, but yet a telling registration and reminder of the Second World War's "school" dimension.

In 1947 Don M. Wolfe, normally a professor of English, published *The Purple Testament*, a collection of brief narratives by fifty-three severely disabled veterans of the war. Their depositions, collected while they were re-learning life at American University in Washington, abundantly testify to their youthful physical stamina and their young innocence. Miraculously, they have survived physically, and their lack of cynicism has enabled them to survive psychologically. "Among friends," Wolfe writes,

the veteran is not self-conscious about his wounds; he is willing often to talk or write about his last battle and his hospital ordeals. To cope with life, whatever comes, he had a preparation deep in his youth. Did we not choose him for his health, both mental and physical?[45]

Unread Books on a Shelf

I t was common . . . throughout the [Okinawa] campaign," says the U. S. marine Eugene Sledge,

> for replacements to get hit before we even knew their names. They came up confused, frightened, and hopeful, got wounded or killed, and went right back to the rear on the route by which they had come, shocked, bleeding, or stiff. They were forlorn figures coming up to the meat grinder and going right back out of it like homeless waifs, unknown and faceless to us, like unread books on a shelf.[1]

"Their faces I do not recall," says Eberhart's gunnery instructor, only that

> they are gone to early death.

Uniform and anonymous, undifferentiated in essentials whether Marine replacements or aerial gunners, these boys turned by training into quasi-mechanical interchangeable parts reflect the success of human mass-production between the two world wars, a process fueled by dramatic increases in population and assisted by the rapid rise of "media culture," with its power to impose national uniformities. A result was that servicemen in the Second World War seemed even more anonymous and bereft of significant individual personality than their counterparts in the Great War. Mistaken as she may have been about the accuracy of aerial bombing, Vera Brittain was right to sense that the Second World War owes much of its uniqueness to between-the-wars developments in mass production and propaganda. The Second War, she notes, "soon revealed it-

66

self as less a struggle of men with men than a contest in methods of mass production which were to debase the intrinsic value of martial daring." Moreover, the war from the beginning constituted "a bewildering duet, and later a whole orchestra, of propaganda carried out by all the new instruments of communication developed between the wars."[2] (Radio especially, of course, but also such an invention as the weekly newsmagazine.)

In contrast to the faceless young automatons of the Second World War, the characters of John Dos Passos's Great War novel *Three Soldiers* (1921) spend much of their time asserting their persisting individuality as they buck against the forces opposed to their uniqueness. And significantly, those characters have names. Not so the memorable servicemen of the Second World War, who are as devoid of personal identity as the soldiers in Jarrell's poems of the war. James Dickey has noticed that there aren't really any people in them, just "The Ball Turret Gunner," "A Pilot from the Carrier," "The Wingman," and, as Dickey says, "assorted faceless types in uniform." (Even the unfortunates detailed to clean up the mess of the ball-turret gunner with their steam hose consist merely of "they.") Because Jarrell's servicemen are "just collective Objects, or Attitudes, or Killable Puppets," the reader observes their frustration or destruction with an apparently inappropriate detachment. "You care very little what happens to them," says Dickey, "and that is terrible."[3] But terrible or not, that is precisely the effect of the wartime anonymity Jarrell is pointing to. The detachment may be heartless, but it makes it possible for sensitive people to survive the war relatively undamaged. Jarrell's poems constitute both an appreciation and a critique, none the less strenuous for being so apparently bland, of that necessary heartlessness. In "The Sick Nought," a poem addressed to a convalescent soldier, Jarrell says with a complex tone,

> You are something there are millions of

and confesses that, try as he will to overcome the implications of the multitudinousness and the uniformity and to consider this soldier as a unique person, he can't make it:

> How can I care about you much, or pick you out
> From all the others other people loved
> And sent away to die for them?[4]

Morning physical training at Camp Roberts, California
(National Archives)

Thirty years earlier things were different. A poem from the Great War like Edmund Blunden's "Pillbox" names the people in it—Worley, Sergeant Hoad—and even nicknames them: "Bluffer." Even if unnamed, the sergeant in Ivor Gurney's "The Silent One,"

> Who died on the wires, and hung there. . .
> Who for his hours of life had chattered through
> Infinitely lovely chatter of Bucks accent,[5]

cannot easily be mistaken for anyone else. Nor can Yeats's Major Robert Gregory, Robert Graves's "Sergeant-Major Money," or E. E. Cummings's Olaf,

> glad and big
> whose warmest heart recoiled at war.[6]

But in the Second War such individual designations seem out of style, somehow not consistent with "the war effort," evidence that the war has powerfully augmented what Jean Cocteau has called "the conspiracy of the plural against the singular."[7] This formulation is enacted in the unforgettable images of Russian infantry attacking, rushing forward by the thousands with their long overcoats and sub-machine guns. There, individual distinctions are unthinkable, not just because these men are Soviets but because this is the Second World War.

To recall the sights and sounds and smells of the war is to invoke the memory of crowds everywhere—in trains and restaurants, bars and pubs, theaters and bus stations. Especially bus stations. The bus, indeed, can be thought of as the Second War's emblematic vehicle. At least on the American scene. Jarrell uses it as a handy totem of his "noughts' " loneliness and distress, and so do others, like Louis Simpson. In Simpson's poem "Basic Blues" three servicemen, nameless, go into town in search of women. Not finding them, they walk aimlessly away from the center of town. They sit on park benches. After a while

> A vagrant breeze rustles the leaves
> and they become aware that time is passing.
> They take the bus back to town.

Then they go to "the" movie. Finally it's time to return to camp, on the bus,

> looking at fields,
> small trees,
> houses like wooden boxes,
> a church that says 'Praise the Lord.'

The bus ride back to camp takes hours, and

> When the bus brakes for a stop
> the sleepers stir
> and someone asks, "What time is it?"

The bus has conveyed them through nothing but "dark and desolate" streets past objects which in their lack of distinction serve as unshakeable images of a uniform desolation:

O, all the wars in Germany
and Russia will not make them grieve
like a Shell station, and Lone Star Bar,
and the Hotel Davy Crockett.[8]

If in the First World War you're one of over four million uniformed Americans, you're actually pretty anonymous. But if in the Second World War you're one of sixteen million, you're really nothing. You might as well be an inert item of Government Issue, like a mess kit or a tool, entrenching. You are in an army where an editorial writer in the *Infantry Journal* conceives your anonymity specifically as a virtue. In a piece titled "Who Created G.I. Joe?" this writer quotes with satisfaction a civilian friend who has asserted that *G.I. Joe* is a "wonderful phrase that completely expresses the utter anonymity of the private soldier. . . . The proud anonymity of the uniform demanded a name as proud and as anonymous as itself and got it in 'G.I. Joe.' " And this editorialist asks, "Who in uniform would want it otherwise?"[9] Those sentiments were uttered in January, 1945, by which time anonymity and uniformity had become so insistently the style of the period that few would have smiled at the oxymoron *proud anonymity*.

The ex-soldier never forgets his serial number. Nor, if he had no middle name, the way one was supplied, in the army NMI (No Middle Initial), in the Marine Corps NONE, so that he ended as John NMI Jones or Frederick NONE Smith, in name as little different as possible from other people. The British army honored this principle by officially not noting, for the duration, titles of nobility held by officers. The year 1943 was the moment not merely of the gathering of the great faceless armies required for the invasion of Europe. It was also the moment of Aaron Copland's *Fanfare for the Common Man*. Returning to the United Kingdom in 1944 after a tour of duty in the Mediterranean, a young British flier makes a semi-sardonic note in his diary about the prevailing maritime procedures. "A man falls off the *Capetown Castle* and is drowned. The convoy does not stop. All flags are lowered to half-mast."[10]

In wartime, fiction, memoirs, and plays swarm with bizarre male individualists. They are doubly welcome as lost ideals in this drab culture of anonymity and uniformity. There is "Ginger," Osbert Sitwell's all-but insane father. There is the eccentric parent of *Life with Father*; the outrageously witty bully of *The Man Who Came to Dinner*; the crazed elderly relative of *Arsenic and Old Lace*, given to rushing up the stairs flourishing

Admiral Mountbatten addresses officers and men of the USS Saratoga
(National Archives)

an archaic sword and shouting "Charge!" In addition there's the colorful Gully Jimson of Joyce Cary's *The Horse's Mouth* and the gentle dipsomaniac of *Harvey*. Not to mention such popular films featuring notable individual male characters as *Goodbye, Mr. Chips, Citizen Kane, Wilson, Casablanca,* and *Henry V*. And there are such flagrant egocentrics as George Minafer Amberson in *The Magnificent Ambersons* and Waldo Lydecker in *Laura,* of whose personal style it is sufficient to say that he was played by Clifton Webb. Gary Cooper's *Sergeant York,* eccentric, moody, Bible-obsessed, could be an oddity because his combat occurred in 1918. In the 1940s he would have been beaten into the common mold in no time. All these characters suggest, in various degrees, a resistance, as Roland Blythe says, "to the new facelessness" required by "military expediency." The gestures these characters make assert that "salvation and hope begin with the discovery of one's own identity and its maintenance against all the pressures of the emergency."[11] It was in the midst of the war, in 1943, that George Orwell conceived the work which would become *Nineteen Eighty-Four,* depicting Big Brother's hatred of individuality and eccentricity, the common attendants of what is known in Newspeak as *ownlife.*

The troops had their own poignant ways of countering the pressures of anonymity. Forbidden to embellish their uniforms with individual touches, they could assert a small degree of selfhood by wearing rings. When he joined the British army, Rupert Croft-Cooke hastened to buy a ring, and a rather vivid one, a garnet in a Victorian setting, although he'd never worn a ring before and rather disapproved of the wearing of jewelry by men. But now he sensed that he needed a ring. "I think I had an idea," he explains, "that in uniform I should want some personal touch, a link with less regimented times of freedom in dress."[12] Kiedrich Rhys, in his poem "Letter to My Wife," comments on a locket containing her picture which he wears out of sight under his shirt with his dog-tags. This collocation of objects triggers various quiet ironies on the topic of one's "identity" in the service:

> I will wear the old-fashioned locket (cum-identity disc) always!
> Although this must seem a little sentimental for nowadays.
>
> But after all I'll simply have to hang onto my identity,
> Otherwise how carry the sayings and small things for posterity.[13]

Even the infamous Zoot-Suit Riots in Los Angeles and San Diego in June, 1943, doubtless reflect the resentment of soldiers and sailors at the flamboyant finery the Mexican-American youths' civilian status gave them a chance to exhibit. The motive in beating up a "Pachuco" was partly racial fury and partly anger at his not being in the service, but it was also simply envy of his freedom to dress in any bizarre way that took his fancy.[14]

Wartime journalism about the troops, conscious that one thing they missed most was their prewar individualities, was conscientious in attempting to reimpose some identity upon them. Ernie Pyle was always careful not just to name the soldiers he described, but to locate them in individual peacetime residences. "My two 'roommates' were Corporal Martin Clayton, Jr., of 3400 Princeton St., Dallas, Texas, and Pfc. William Gross of 322 North Foster Street, Lansing, Michigan."[15] If zip codes had been invented, Pyle would have been happy to include them. Sensing that to locate a man in a pre-army place is to provide some stay against non-identity, Pyle even has in his last, posthumous book (*Last Chapter*, 1946) an index arranged by towns and cities, thus:

> ALBUQUERQUE, New Mexico
> Robinson, Maj. Gerald . . .
> Trauth, Pfc. Dick . . . , etc.

Evelyn Waugh's *Put Out More Flags* (1942) explores among other things the theme of the Uniform Many and the Personal One which the war was forcing on everyone's attention. At the outset, for example, Lady Cynthia Seal senses how useful the military's influence is going to be in taming her son Basil's troublesome, indeed caddish, individuality. As she explains to a friend,

> "Sometimes, lately, I've begun to doubt whether we shall ever find the proper place for Basil. He's been a square peg in so many round holes. But this war seems to take the responsibility off our hands. There's room for everyone in war-time, every *man*. It's always been Basil's *individuality* that's been wrong. . . . In war-time individuality doesn't matter any more. There are just *men*, aren't there?"[16]

On the other hand, the socially naive, dutiful Cedric Lane, "a very conscientious officer," as he is called, and thus Basil Seal's apparent antithesis, is serving in France just before Dunkirk as a regimental intelligence officer. He is happy to confront the opposition between individual and mass from the other side than Lady Cynthia. Ordered to make contact with a unit on his regiment's left, he consciously sets out by himself, seeking relief from the mass and leaving even his orderly behind:

> It was against the rules, but he was weary of the weight of dependent soldiery which . . . encumbered him and depressed his spirits. As he walked alone he was exhilarated with the sense of being one man, one pair of legs, one pair of eyes, one brain, sent on a single, intelligible task; one man alone could go freely anywhere on the earth's surface; multiply him, put him in a drove and by each addition of his fellows you subtract something that is of value, make him so much less a man; this was the crazy mathematics of war . . . there's danger in numbers; divided we stand, united we fall, thought Cedric, striding happily towards the enemy, shaking from his boots all the frustration of corporate life.[17]

But the war won't allow it. He is shot and killed instantly while still a quarter of a mile from the neighboring regiment. The war's intolerance of such individualistic performances is the theme of a whole wartime and postwar literature and the substance of numerous remembered real-life "plots." An exemplary one involves "Thomas," a Cree Indian in the Canadian army who "just loved to fight." In Italy, he often volunteered to go on patrol alone, and "just before dawn," a fellow soldier remembers,

> you'd be on sentry go, and he'd scare the shit out of you because there's nobody there and suddenly there he is. If the officer wanted a prisoner, he'd usually have one all trussed up, or a *paisano*, or he'd have the gen written down in a little note pad, so many guns, artillery, where the Germans were.

But once, stepping carefully through a minefield, fifteen of Thomas's fellow soldiers get through by treading only in each other's tracks. Thomas picks his own route—

> and then *boom* and there's this smoke and dust and I remember the sergeant saying, "Goddamn it all to hell, they got our Injun."
>
> It sort of took the stuffing out of us for that day. That night we're hanging around the basement of this house and somebody says that 15 guys go through and then Thomas is next and he's blown to ratshit and how come? The sergeant says he used to watch Thomas, and he never did

go where the rest of the patrol went. He walked his own way, and once too often.[18]

But a violent denouement like that comes only at the end of a great deal of nothing. Most of the time, the mass of unread books stands in rows, waiting. Waiting itself and nothing else becomes a large element in the atmosphere of wartime, for both soldiers and civilians. You are waiting for induction into the services, waiting for D-Day, for someone to come home on furlough, for a letter, for a promotion, for news, for a set of tires, for the train, for things to get better, for your release from POW camp, for the end of the war, for your discharge. Attention—as always, but with a special wartime intensification—focuses not on the present but on some moment in the future. "Waiting gets to be a thing you can touch," says Martha Gellhorn, exhausted waiting for bombers to return from a mission over France. "First you wait for them to go and then you wait for them to get back."[19] Jarrell is skilled at contemplating his anonymous "replacements" and non-entities waiting in line, the ultimate posture of proletarianization. Thus a poem like "The Lines," a virtual census of all the lines a soldier must stand in, from the naked line of the draftees' medical examination through

> the basic line
> Standing outside a building in the cold
> Of the late or early darkness, waiting
> For meals or mail or salvage . . . .

to, finally, the ultimate discharge line, waiting "for papers, pensions," after which the men will finally be "free."[20] They all share the feeling registered by the British soldier D. van den Bogaerde (after the war the actor Dirk Bogarde) in his poem "Steel Cathedrals":

> It seems to me I spend my life in stations.
> Going, coming, standing, waiting,

surrounded by service anonymities like

> Sailors going to Chatham, soldiers going to Crewe.

And withal, nothing to do:

*U.S. ground troops in the Ardennes, Fall, 1944, lining up
for assignment to rest billets (National Archives)*

The station clock with staggering hands and callous face
   says twenty-five-to-nine.
A cigarette, a cup of tea, a bun,
   and my train goes at ten.[21]

"Endlessly waiting in a dirty, grey railway station waiting-room"—that's an image Leonard Woolf proposes to convey the feeling of "negative emptiness and desolation of personal and cosmic boredom" of war. People his age, he says, already know the feeling from their experience of the Great War, and that is one thing that makes living through the Second one so appalling. The expectation of the boredom, the knowledge that there is no escaping it—that's all but insufferable.[22]

If you were a civilian, daily life was boring. If you were a soldier, daily life was very boring. But it was most boring to be a prisoner of war. By establishing the principle that captured officers were to do no work and that NCOs could work only as supervisors of the work of privates, the Geneva Convention guaranteed that life in POW camps would be for many an experience of unprecedented ennui, against which some often fantastic defenses were required. In one German *Stalag*, an American lieutenant with nothing to do "counted the barbs in one section of the barbed wire fence and then estimated the total number of barbs around the encampment. When he announced this number, his fellow kriegies not only didn't consider him mad, they formed teams to check him out with a barb-by-barb count."[23] There certainly was little escape from boredom to be had by moving upwards, toward high ranks and the centers of power. One of the most tedious places during the whole war was Hitler's own dinner table, which he dominated with interminable nightly monologues on strategy, history, eugenics, and what have you. Even his toads found the boredom of this unvarying *Tischgespräche* almost unendurable. Generals and field marshals nodded, and Albert Speer recalls "the sense of stifling boredom."[24]

There was no escape either in opting out of the whole thing and becoming a conscientious objector, as the British CO Edward Blishen discovered. Farm work, he found, was so boring that he came to relish irrationally the tiniest variation from the daily routine. His brother, in the navy, kept in touch by letter, and asserted often that life in the navy was similar in "idiotic" boredom to life on the CO farm. "A long apprenticeship to bugger-all," he called it.[25] Another sailor, who makes an appearance in Humphrey Knight's short story "The Sea and the Sky," testifies that the sea air wears on you because "it never smells of anything." The result, he says, is that "my nostrils are *bored*." Is training to become an officer less boring than learning to be a soldier? No. "The work is very hard," writes a man in British officer training school, "and madly boring—so boring in fact that boredom down here becomes a mystical experience."[26] And if training is boring, no training is equally boring, and even passes and leaves and furloughs provide little relief. John Steinbeck writes his wife from London in the fall of 1943 about the lonely soldiers walking the streets with their "apathetic shuffle." They seem to be searching for something. "They'll say it's a girl—any girl, but it isn't that at all."[27] And one should not get the idea that the officers managing these men imagine that life in the services is something other than boring. They know better. One British brigadier is recorded as uttering deep service wisdom on this point. "The more you can train soldiers to stand boredom and then come to life when required," he said, "the better."[28]

Some antidotes to boredom took literary form. In relatively inactive theaters like India, bright British soldiers kept copious literary diaries, which they composed carefully, even artfully, writing sometimes 2500 or more words a day. That such diaries were strictly forbidden added to the pleasure. One man stuck in Syria wrote a diary "to prove," he said, "that I am alive."[29] Captured at Hong Kong and kept in a Japanese POW camp for four years, Lieutenant R. M. M. King copied things out into his diary, either from memory—the words of "These Foolish Things Remind Me of You"—or from books, like a passage from H. V. Morton's *In Search of England* describing the charms of rural churchgoing.[30] As always, chess was a consolation, and by the device of correspondence chess, you could stretch out a game sometimes as long as four months. One would imagine that a captain in the Royal Army Medical Corps would be presented with plenty to do in Normandy in the summer of 1944. But Captain Douglas G. Aitken found himself so bored and lonely that he developed a new appreciation of correspondence, saying, "I never realized before what a lot the post could mean and must write to *everyone I ever knew* [my emphasis] in the hope that they will write back."[31]

But the ultimate antidote to tedium was sleep. Olivia Manning's understanding of the soldier's psyche is remarkable, as appears when she is imagining what it would be like to be young Simon Boulderstone, her subaltern hero in *The Levant Trilogy*. Before being shipped to North Africa, he had "regarded sleep as a time-wasting necessity," but he now "discovered it could be bliss. Whenever he had nothing better to do, he would get into his sleeping-bag . . . and hiding his face from the light, would sink into sleep." By long and repeated experience, he learned what all soldiers learn, that "sleep devoured boredom."[32]

7

Chickenshit, An Anatomy

At the beginning of the war nineteen-year-old Timothy Corsellis, brimming with high purpose and the spirit of self-sacrifice for a noble end, joined the RAF. As he reports in his poem, "What I Never Saw,"

> I was ready for death,
> Ready to give my all in one expansive gesture
> For a cause that was worthy of death.

Thus he enlisted,

> ready to fight and to die.

But he soon saw that his early visions had not been complete:

> What I never saw
> Were the weary hours of waiting while the sun rose and set . . .

He found further that none of his fellow fliers seemed at all interested in even considering what the war could be said to be about. Instead,

> We sat together as we sat at peace
> Bound by no ideal of service
> But by a common interest in pornography and a desire
>   to outdrink one another.

The dreary, demeaning lining-up was something he'd not anticipated,

the queueing, the recurrent line of pungent men
Dressed in dirt with mud eating their trouser legs. . . .

But even worse than "the boredom and the inefficiency" were what really
distressed him,

The petty injustice and the everlasting grudges.

It is these more than anything that persuade him that the sacrifice he is
making is

greater than I ever expected.[1]

In 1941, when he was twenty-one, Corsellis was killed. If he could testify
now, he might say that he minded even dying less than "the petty injustice and the everlasting grudges." That is, the chickenshit.

What does that rude term signify? It does not imply complaint about
the inevitable inconveniences of military life: overcrowding and lack of
privacy, tedious institutional cookery, deprivation of personality, general
boredom. Nothing much can be done about those things. Chickenshit
refers rather to behavior that makes military life worse than it need be:
petty harassment of the weak by the strong; open scrimmage for power
and authority and prestige; sadism thinly disguised as necessary discipline;
a constant "paying off of old scores"; and insistence on the letter rather
than the spirit of ordinances. Chickenshit is so called—instead of horse-
or bull- or elephant shit—because it is small-minded and ignoble and
takes the trivial seriously. Chickenshit can be recognized instantly because
it never has anything to do with winning the war.

If you are an enlisted man, you'll know you've been the victim of
chickenshit if your sergeant assigns you to K.P. not because it's your turn
but because you disagreed with him on a question of taste a few evenings
ago. Or you might find your pass to town cancelled at the last moment
because, you finally remember, a few days ago you asked a question during the sergeant's lecture on map-reading that he couldn't answer. If you're
an officer, you may find yourself performing very often as company duty
officer or officer of the day or carrying out kitchen and garbage inspection
because, you now realize, a while ago in the officers' mess you briefly
interposed a mildly "liberal" observation after the major had descanted

for fifteen minutes on the unsuitability of "nigras" for combat. If your comment had gone a bit further, you'd be likely to find yourself transferred soon to a distant and much worse unit. Or if you'd uttered your mild remonstrance while in combat instead of in camp, you might find yourself repeatedly selected to take out the more hazardous night patrols to secure information, the kind, a former junior officer recalls, "we already knew from daytime observations, and had reported."[2]

All such treatment falls into the general category of chickenshit. So does the military obsession with haircuts. So does all pleasure taken in rank for rank's sake. So does the practice of public verbal humiliation ("chewing ass," in the parlance). Snap inspections are a useful chickenshit device, especially when the inspecting officer knows already that something crucial is missing or ill-maintained. Chickenshit has a way of locating its victims according to time-honored middle-class canons of contempt: for the Jew, the "long hair," the artist, the "so-called intellectual," the sneerer at athletics, the "smart ass," the "stuck-up," the foreigner—anyone conceived to be "not our crowd." Chickenshit's favored term of reprobation is, in the USA, *sloppy*. In the UK, *slack*. Because chickenshit shifts the emphasis from reality to appearance, its favored terms of approbation are, respectively, *smartness* and *swank*. It is chickenshit that requires that brass and leather care occupy so important a part of the service day, that saddle soap and leather polish, Brasso and the Glad Rag become such indispensable elements of bellicose equipment.

Frequent unnecessary inspections—of personal appearance, barracks, weapons, vehicles, kit—remain the commonest ways of indulging in chickenshit. As a way of "keeping the men on their toes," the barracks inspection on Saturday morning, when passes can be withheld at the last moment and plans for good times frustrated, is effective. For its victims it has its own serial psychological structure generating maximum anxiety over matters of minimum significance. Its stages are "the nervous waiting, the last-minute flurry, the final resignation, the sagging aftermath."[3] An experienced ex-soldier has conjectured that military inspections have a purpose that goes beyond mere temporary shows of authority and the official power to inconvenience. As Louis Simpson observes, "The aim of military training is not just to prepare men for battle, but to make them long for it. Inspections are one way to achieve this."[4] In the American army at the beginning, when it still contained a large proportion of regulars, and in the British army throughout, clever soldiers, obliged to lay out their kits on their beds every Saturday morning, kept a secret dummy kit duplicating all the articles—shaving brushes, unopened packets of razor blades, rolled-up extra socks—of the real kit and kept pristine and useless except for purposes of weekly display. Soldiers really sensitive to chickenshit would make their beds tautly and lay out their kit on them with unimpeachable precision the night before, then sleep on the floor. Ultimately the only way to escape most of the chickenshit was to be in combat and so far forward as to be virtually unreachable and surely uninspectable. "The needle is only so long," a Vietnam veteran notes. "You can escape it by going forward into combat."[5] And maybe, as Louis Simpson wonders, that is the perverse point of it all. During the war the only solace one could find for Allied chickenshit was knowing that Germans, Italians, and Japanese were saddled with it too, their efficiency and morale similarly drained off into annoyance, bitterness, and cynicism.

Some of the Second World War masters of chickenshit became famous for it, like General Patton. He insisted that members of his Third Army dress genteelly in the combat zone, and many men died with their neckties tucked in between the second and third shirt buttons. The war's champion practitioner was probably Hitler, with his insistence on appearing to win the war instead of winning it, and his devotion to the heroic façade regardless. General Paulus at Stalingrad begged to relieve the suffering by surrendering while some troops were left alive. He addressed the Führer in these terms:

ARMY REQUESTS IMMEDIATE PERMISSION TO SURRENDER
IN ORDER TO SAVE LIVES OF REMAINING TROOPS

and added a heartrending recital of disaster, including the destruction of five whole divisions, with 18,000 of the wounded unattended in their agony. Paulus concluded: "COLLAPSE INEVITABLE." To this Hitler sent this monumentally chickenshit reply:

SURRENDER IS FORBIDDEN. SIXTH ARMY WILL HOLD THEIR POSI
TIONS TO THE LAST MAN AND THE LAST ROUND AND BY THEIR
HEROIC ENDURANCE WILL MAKE AN UNFORGETTABLE CONTRI
BUTION TOWARDS THE ESTABLISHMENT OF A DEFENSIVE FRONT
AND THE SALVATION OF THE WESTERN WORLD.[6]

Indeed, it was doubtless in Germany that chickenshit reached its wartime apogee. Consider the activities devised for inmates of camps like Bergen-Belsen and Auschwitz—digging holes to fill in again, endless "roll calls" in freezing weather with the dead falling in place: these are merely chickenshit raised to the highest power. And one must not overlook the infamous 148 steps in the rock quarry at Mauthausen, which prisoners were required to ascend repeatedly carrying large rocks in wooden platforms on their backs, until they died.

The literature of chickenshit is extensive, and not surprisingly, since so many authors-to-be were, in the services, precisely the types that are chickenshit's eternal targets, bright Jewish boys like Norman Mailer and Joseph Heller, or intelligent sarcastic kids from good colleges, like Kingsley Amis. Because it would be hard not to notice the proximity of Allied chickenshit to certain stigmata of Fascism, all sorts of opportunities for irony present themselves. It is notable how much of the writing from the Second World War tends not so much to convey news from the battlefield as to expose the chickenshit lurking behind it. (The exception is popular fiction like that of Leon Uris and Herman Wouk. Their audience being untrained in irony, in their novels, especially Wouk's over-produced ones, there are few blunders and errors and everyone does what he's supposed to do, with minimal chickenshit. Result: Victory.)

One of the first American novels about the war, Robert Lowry's *Casualty* (1946), is about little but chickenshit, and its appearance the moment the war was over suggests the propellant of deep anger. Clearly the characteristic of the army that has most impressed Lowry during his 23 months with the Air Corps in Africa and Italy is the constant chickenshit. As his hero Pfc. Joe Hammond observes, "The army brings out the worst in everybody."[7] Hammond, who is finally run over and killed by a truck in an Italian town after being punished for taking over a friend's guard duty, is projected as a casualty of pure chickenshit. Like Mailer in *The Naked and the Dead,* Lowry depicts the army as a quasi-fascistic institution, perhaps illustrating what John Keegan has termed the "culture shock" experienced by Americans who found themselves in the military. Although the war killed few Americans (in contrast, say, to Russians), it "exposed over 12 million of them," says Keegan, "to a system of subordination and autocracy entirely alien to American values."[8] One small and gentle measure of the shock is the way men in the American army responded to a questionnaire in 1942. One soldier said: "We are entitled to the respect we have worked for and earned in civilian life." Another: "I thought the caste system was restricted to India."[9]

Forty years after the war, when one might imagine the harsher memories of chickenshit had mellowed, a former Boy Seaman in the Royal

Navy vividly recalls that the war seemed almost as much an effort to humiliate Allied enlisted personnel as to destroy the proclaimed enemy. As Tristan Jones says in his memoir *Heart of Oak* (1984), "It was quite obvious, from the moment I stepped on board [the destroyer] *Eclectic*, that the crew considered the Jinny [executive officer] to be a far greater enemy than any German." That particular Jinny was "a martinet who should by rights have been . . . in a mental hospital" (131).[10] But he was standard. Jones had been encountering his type ever since enlisting in 1940. At *HMS Ganges*—actually a mere training camp, cutely named— he suffered all the sadistic torments normally visited on newcomers. There, one emblem of bullshit—the term for chickenshit in the Royal Navy— was the Polished Floor. Almost half the length of the barracks, it was never to be walked on. Like the dummy kit for inspections, it was reserved solely for purposes of impressing an inspecting officer. So persistently irrational was the "mindless bullying" that "each week the regular ambulance left *Ganges* taking three or four trainees . . . , off their heads, to the mental hospital in Chatham"(36).

A constant wonder to Jones is the assiduity with which bullshit is made to attend the most grave contingencies. It is never laid aside. Passing through the railway station at Birmingham just as it is being bombed, Jones takes shelter together with a crowd of other servicemen, and after the All Clear they lend a hand cleaning up the carnage, disordering their leave uniforms in the process.

> When the last of the salvage-rescue teams roared away in their trucks to dig someone else out from under the blasted rubble, the red-caps—now joined by naval policemen—all ramrod straight and regimental still, strode around . . . . "Get your hat on straight, lad. Where do you think you are, Bertram Mills' Circus?" (54)

One scene nicely conveying Jones's perception of the absurdity of combat bullshit takes place aboard the armed merchant cruiser *Cameroon*. On this vessel Jones has been made to polish much external brass during rainstorms and has come to perceive that even in the midst of death and calamity, the bullshit, as specified in posted King's Regulations and Admiralty instructions, must go on. Torpedoed and afire, the ship is abandoned as burnt men stagger around and bodies block the passageways.

> The port main passage was a wreck, with most of the paintwork burned and blistered—all except the ship's notice board. It was still, by

some miracle, pristine, and I clearly remember reading, as if in a daze, the heavily printed ". . . *shall suffer death by hanging or any other punishment hereafter mentioned , . . .*" It is strange how in times of stress certain images impress themselves upon the mind and memory. I suppose I ought to have remembered more the appearance of the dead men . . . all black and blistered with their eyes staring out of their heads, and their hair, in many cases, completely burned off. I ought to remember more the shouts and screams of the men too injured to be moved. But no, I see it clearly now, that appalling sentence on the brown varnished poster . . . and I clearly recall wondering if one of the punishments hereafter mentioned was burning to death. (91–92)

Reassigned to another ship, as he approaches the gangway to go aboard in the dark and the rain, lugging his hammock and sea bag, he hears a shout "from inside the dark and gloomy, but warm and dry gatehouse . . . loud and fierce, 'That man *there!* Get your hat on STRAIGHT' " (123). Amid the gunfire and mines and depth-charges and torpedoes of the North Atlantic the bullshit is unremitting. The *Hood* is sunk (1400 killed), and so is the *Bismarck* (1900 killed), and so is the *Scharnhorst* (another 1900), and so are the countless merchant ships, convoyed by the destroyers Jones serves on. He notes that "at odd times we would have a matelot clomping around the upper deck with a Lee-Enfield held at arm's length over his head. 'Get those bloody knees UP!' to a background of heavily loaded merchant ships plodding on and on" (204). At moments of deep anxiety, the navy's "punishment verse and chapter" exhibited on the notice board "seemed the most ridiculous, the most insane."

> How can a man already probably under sentence of death, already suffering cold and malnutrition from unheated meals, already worried to death over lack of mail from his missus in Yankee-crowded Britain, be further punished? But punished we were, and sometimes for the most trite offenses—being late on muster, being out of the rig of the day at anchorages, fighting (although that was most rare), or being found wanking in the heads and accused of skulking. (204)

From all this Jones carried away a precious lifelong conviction: "The individual is important . . . . Mindless bureaucracy is a grave danger to the individual spirit of Man and is to be questioned and if need be attacked at every turn." [11]

Julian Maclaren-Ross is not just a connoisseur of service blunders.

He is an astute student of chickenshit as well. When he met the poet Alun Lewis, a shy young lieutenant, he noticed that Lewis's hair was cut unbecomingly short and inferred that "his OC had talked about curling pins and violins."[12] Maclaren-Ross's exploration of service blunders in "I Had to Go Sick" finds them nearly allied to the constant chickenshit, their signal and frequent cause. One morning the man with the bad knee, eating bland foods in the gastric ward, is surprised by the entrance of an unfamiliar Medical Officer, a captain.

> "Stand by your beds!" he called out as he came in.
> The ward had filled up in the last week or so, but most of the patients were in bed, so they couldn't obey. The five of us who were up came belatedly to attention.
> "Bad discipline in this ward, Matron," the captain said. "Very slack. Who's the senior NCO here?"
> There was only one NCO among the lot of us: a lance-corporal. He was up, as it happened, so he came in for an awful chewing-off.
> "You've got to keep better order than this, Corporal," said the captain. "See that the men pay proper respect to an officer when he enters the ward. If I've any further cause for complaint I shall hold you responsible. Also the beds aren't properly in line. I'm not satisfied with this ward, not satisfied at *all*. I hope to see some improvement when I come round tomorrow. Otherwise . . . ."[13]

But sensitive as Maclaren-Ross's nose is for chickenshit, as a registrar of it he is surpassed by Kingsley Amis, who gathered his views of it while a lieutenant in the Royal Corps of Signals. Many of the short stories in *My Enemy's Enemy* (1962) concern a signals unit commanded by Amis's particular bête noire, a Major Richard Raleigh. His talent for chickenshit is exhibited first in the story "Court of Inquiry."

Raleigh's company is in Belgium, and the end of the war is very near. He has determined to convene a court of inquiry (only doubtfully legal) to "look into" the disappearance of a battery-charging engine. This has been left behind on a motor march by a section under the admittedly incompetent command of Lieutenant Frank Archer. The narrator, a person of perhaps insufficient administrative courage but impressive perception and sense of moral comedy, is collared to serve as a member of the three-man court. The object of the inquiry is not to recover the lost charging-engine or its value or in any way make amends for its disappearance: it is rather to deluge chickenshit over the head of luckless young

Archer, who strikes the Major as, in general, "slack." Everyone admits the charging-engine was worthless—wouldn't work, never did work, and has already been informally "replaced" by an unauthorized newer model kept hidden from inspectors. But twenty-one-year-old Lt. Archer must be tormented. The narrator, a hater of chickenshit but ranked too low to object to it in this case, tries his best to mitigate Archer's crime by getting Major Raleigh to admit that the lost item was worthless, both obsolete and surplus. Raleigh answers immediately: " 'That's not the point. This one was on young Archer's charge. The Quartermaster has his signature' " (42).[14] The "court" assembles in Raleigh's office—on the way there the Major pauses "to exhort a driver, supine under the differential of a three-tonner, to get his hair cut" (45)—and begins interviewing the witnesses. But when it is Archer's turn to testify, he undercuts the chickenshit by confessing his culpability and cynically affecting contrition. And he goes even further:

> "I'm so sorry to have let you down personally, Major Raleigh. That's what gets me, failing in my duty by you, sir. When you've always been so decent to me about everything, and backed me up and . . . and encouraged me." (48)

These lies succeed in embarrassing Raleigh so badly that the inevitable "finding" of the court, a reprimand for Archer, is made to seem inappropriate and even cruel. As the cunning Archer explains later,

> "If I'd stood up for my rights or anything, he'd just have decided to step up his little war of nerves in other ways. As it was I think I even made him feel he'd gone too far." (51)

Another story of Amis's about chickenshit, "My Enemy's Enemy," deals with the adjutant's harassment of Lieutenant Dalessio, a natural victim for three reasons: his Italian background, his uncut hair, and his visible contempt for military trivialities. The method here is the snap inspection—Dalessio's section is notoriously slack—but as in "Court of Inquiry," here too the chickenshit is deflected: someone warns Dalessio in time for him to perform a rapid superficial clean-up. The adjutant is defeated and a captain who has had the chance to warn Dalessio but who, momentarily siding with the chickenshit practitioners, has not, is humiliated.

But Amis's masterpiece in this line is his long short story, almost a novella, "I Spy Strangers." Here Amis has proposed, in only about 20,000 words, a compressed "war novel" registering the moral meaning of his military experience against a background of European politics and the British social framework. Bernard Bergonzi is one among many to regard "I Spy Strangers" "not only Amis's finest story, but one of the best pieces of fiction to have come out of the Second World War."[15] And it's worth noticing that "one of the best pieces of fiction to have come out of the Second World War" is not about combat at all. The European war is over. The Signals company where the moral action takes place has "completed its role in the European theatre of war without having had to walk a step or fire a shot." (60). The story is not about damage to the body but damage to principles and to personal freedom and integrity. It is about the natural alliance between chickenshit and totalitarian conceptions of personality.

The two main characters, again, are Major Raleigh, artist of chickenshit, and Lieutenant Archer, its recipient. Throughout the story Major Raleigh's dignity and self-importance suffer repeated assaults and diminishments. Because someone else has been chosen to command the communications unit serving the Potsdam Conference, he has lost prestige, together with opportunities for drinks and dinners with important people who might be useful later. (He is the sort of man who would have fully understood the term *networking* forty years before it was invented.) The Major now commands only a motley collection of strays with no loyalty to him. At the moment he is extremely depressed by the unmilitary freedom and impudence of the debate in the moot parliament established to give the troops something to occupy them until their discharge. One Hargreaves has been a vocal radical presence there, calumniating the Crown and all the conservative decencies, and Archer is his officer. Worse, Raleigh's attempt to deliver as a counterweight a sentimental speech in praise of the class system has been rudely rebuffed—as a mere observer at the parliament, he can speak only on its sufferance, and after Raleigh's reactionary speech, Hargreaves has uttered the phrase "I Spy Strangers," proposing that, unless there's objection, the House withdraw permission for the observer to be present. As Speaker of the House, Lieutenant Archer directs Major Raleigh to leave. Ignominy. Smarting under this humiliation, with its strong suggestion that his political views are noisome to his command, Raleigh also suffers rebuff in attempts to enlarge his authority by taking over neighboring units. He fantasizes a lieutenant-colonelcy, which is not to be his. And all the while it is clear, and not just by the informalities of the moot parliament, that distinctions of rank are beginning to soften sadly.

At one point Raleigh asks Archer what seems to be the matter with Hargreaves, and the following conversation, so acute as an analysis of the dynamics of chickenshit, ensues:

> "What's the matter with Hargreaves? Basically the matter?"
>
> "That's very simple, sir. He doesn't like the Army."
>
> The Major laughed through his nose. "I should imagine very few of us would sooner be here than anywhere else. If a man isn't a cretin he knows it's a question of getting a job done. A very important job. I take it you agree?"
>
> "Oh yes, sir. And Hargreaves is clear on that too. But it isn't being in the Army that gets him down. It's the Army."
>
> "I'm afraid you're being too subtle for me, Frank."
>
> "Well, as far as I can make him out . . . people have been nasty to him in the Army in a way they wouldn't be in civilian life. The Army puts power into the hands of chaps who've never had it before, not that sort of power, and they use it to inflict injustices on other chaps whom they happen to dislike for personal reasons. That's the way the Army works. According to Hargreaves." (89)

Disliking Hargreaves for views like that and for his political impertinence, Major Raleigh imagines an "unwholesome" relation between him and his buddy Hammond, a switchboard operator in Archer's section. Raleigh seizes an opportunity to get rid of Hargreaves by transferring him to Burma—thus perhaps consigning him to death in the Japanese war—and Archer mischievously but sympathetically adds Hammond's name to the transfer roster as well. The denouement occurs at the officers' club. Raleigh is in drink, but less deeply than a visiting colonel. Hargreaves enters to apologize for his rudeness in expelling the Major from the parliament. At this point all Raleigh's fury boils over. Wild-eyed, he accuses Hargreaves and Hammond of buggery and asserts that Archer is "tarred with the same brush" (110). The colonel intervenes in what threatens rapidly to become a fistfight, even drawing his pistol. Inadvertently pressed against a frail bannister, as it gives way the colonel falls to the floor below: *coup de théâtre*. He suffers a concussion and a broken arm. Frustrated and humiliated as he has been, Raleigh still hopes to torment Archer by sending him to Burma too, but he learns that Archer has been accepted for a scheme that will let him escape the army almost immediately and return to Oxford for liberal study. That is a severe blow for the Major, but there's a final one in the 1945 election results from the U.K. His borough has gone Labour for the first time in a decade, and the badly defeated Conservative candidate, a representative of all the old nationalistic chickenshit, might be Raleigh himself. "The major dropped his head into his hands" (115).

In one way this story is a highly compensatory fantasy concocted by an author who has endured a great deal of chickenshit. It suggests the way ordinary soldiers, who are far from being authors, also defend themselves against the grosser kinds of chickenshit by devising compensatory brief narratives—rumor-jokes, they might be called. If good enough, these will fly on their own wings all over the army. For example: General Patton, inspecting a hospital in France, profanely chews out one man for not coming to attention in his presence. The man replies: "Run along, asshole. I'm in the Merchant Marine." Another: it is summer in a stateside army camp. In the recreation hall, a man in filthy suntans is reprimanded for the state of his uniform by a major. Man: "Fuck you, buddy. I just came in from town to fill the Coke machine." Another standard compensatory gesture providing some comfort in the face of chickenshit is dwelling upon the mean social positions presumably occupied in civilian life by officers now putting on airs of importance. To conceive of majors, colonels, and even generals as originally stock-room clerks, garage mechanics, or septic-tank-suction operators is a distinct comfort. And the principle was not limited to just the Allied armies. A captain of a German U-boat recalls his status in wartime: "You were almost a god," he says. How the crew of a U-boat must have trembled once before Kapitänleutnant Emil Klusmeier, for example, and how they would delight to know that, as of 1978, "he is . . . a household appliance dealer in Bochum."[16] Another U-boat commander, Kapitänleutnant Heinrich Müller-Edzards, after the war became—what? An officer of a corporation? the governor of a *Land*? an important publisher? No, a schoolteacher.[17]

The chickenshit that demeans the already low like Maclaren-Ross's soldier with the bad knee and Amis's Hargreaves and Hammond must invoke its own idiom to work properly, an idiom implying that contempt for persons and things is a matter of course, almost of necessity. Everything must be lowered and calumniated, even foodstuffs. Creamed chipped beef becomes *shit on a shingle,* and sometimes *creamed foreskins.* In the U.S. Marine Corps, mustard becomes *babyshit.* The two most common kinds of sandwiches, baloney and cheese, are designated respectively *horse-cock* (sometimes *bull-* or *donkey-dick*) and *choke-ass.* Indeed, without *ass* military discourse would be virtually dumb. The sergeant does not order, "Move over there" but "Move your ass over there." Never "Let's get out of here" but "Let's haul ass." Never "You're right" but "Fuckin' A," meaning "You can bet your fucking ass on it." The variations are endless:

> Get your ass into the orderly room.
> "   "   "   messhall.
> Get your ass moving.
> "   " out of here.
> Who told you to park your ass here?

Inconvenience visited upon the enemy by artillery is accommodated to the chickenshit paradigm by pronouncing *harassing fire* with the stress on the *ass,* rather than, as dictionaries advise and genteel civilian usage suggests, on the first syllable. And the army *ass* habit is not easy to break. As Bill Mauldin, now in his sixties, said recently of the FBI's surveillance when after the war he was asked to address the troops at Fort Bliss, Texas, "I was the army's fair-haired boy and there they were investigating my ass!" [18] *Shit* likewise is indispensable. (As, indeed, in *chickenshit.*) It is not just an all-purpose expletive but a device for registering a general knowing disdain. Thus in the United States Army, pay-day is *the day the eagle shits.* A Marine Corps trainee is a *shitbird.* The cartoon character Sad Sack of course derives his name from the NCO's favorite term for a despised subordinate, *a sad sack of shit,* a bit of nomenclature reducing the addressee to a bag of noisome matter equipped, as if by some accident, with arms and legs. (On the other hand, not so bad as *a sad sack of shit,* even rather likeable in his way, is a *flatpeter*—a man so stupid and awkward as always to be stepping on, or stumbling over, his own penis.)

Contempt for insignia, one's own or others', can be expressed by various excretory compounds. Thus the ignited old-fashioned bomb constituting the insignia of the U.S. Ordnance Corps becomes *the flaming horse turd* (sometimes *flaming piss-pot*). And a way to gauge the singularity of such verbal practices is to try to imagine similarly demeaning terms for other emblems, like the Christian or the Red Cross, or the scales of justice, or the seals of the more distinguished universities. The demeaning impulse, a compound of both hatred and fear, seems appropriate only to the services. The soldier's overseas cap, the one that opens up along the top, is called a *cunt cap:* it's hard to imagine any other piece of conventional headgear, like a policeman's visor cap or a bishop's miter or a motorcyclist's helmet treated automatically with such obscene disrespect. In the same way, in the army if you regularly spend nights off the post with a woman, you're not *sleeping with* her or *living with* her—you're *shacking up,* a metaphor demeaning both the sex and the setting.

The infantry seems the arm of the service most habitually debased by language. An infantryman is a *dogface,* and he sleeps in a *pup-tent* (in the American Civil War, a *dog-tent*). Around his neck he wears *dog-tags* (officially, *identity tags* or [British] *identity discs*). Thus his animalism is brought to his attention, as it is on the line, when he digs and occupies a *foxhole,* or when he momentarily vacates it, shovel in hand, to go off and dig a *cat hole* to excrete in and then fill up. When he resumes his pack to move on, he will be following the command to *"Saddle up!"* And in one respect at least the American infantry considers itself even less worthy of self-respect than the British. The colorful piece of fabric a British infantryman wears at the top of his left sleeve identifying his division is a *flash.* That's a word with some suggestions of swank and even "pride in unit." In American military usage the same item suffers programmatic degradation—to a *patch,* term carrying suggestions of poverty, defect, and the second-rate. *Chambers's Twentieth-Century Dictionary* doesn't even recognize the military meaning of *patch,* but instead devotes itself to such definitions as involve deficiency and the hasty concealment of defect, like *mend, hurt, scrap, fragment, hastily, clumsily,* and *temporarily. Patch* seems especially meaningful when its alternatives are considered, not just *flash* but words like *insigne, sign, emblem,* or even *blazon*—all rejected in favor of *patch.* It would seem a willing degradation, like calling a man "a G. I.," a term suggesting such low items of government issue as smelly, coarse yellow laundry soap and the standard galvanized-iron garbage can. But, on second thought, why not? Soldiers wear dirt-colored clothes, stimulating at least British naval and RAF people to refer to them as "Brown Jobs."

Indispensable to the proficient practice of chickenshit and the fullest exercise of self-contempt is the adjective *fucking.* This modifier had been standard among English speakers in the Great War, where it had often been deployed with considerable art and comedy, as in "I hope my mother's keeping the home fuckin' fires burning." It was left to the more

embittered soldiers of the Second World War, especially those then designated "Colored," to improve this to *motherfuckin'*. By the frequent interjection of *fuckin'* and by certain rhythmic devices one produces the
dialect Tom Wolfe has termed "Army Creole," so intimately the sound
of a life lived within the purlieus of chickenshit:

> "I tol'im iffie tried to fuck me over, I was gonna kick 'is fuckin' ass,
> iddnot right?"
> "Fuckin' A."
> "Soey kep'on fuckin' me over and I kicked 'is fuckin' ass in fo'im,
> iddnot right?"
> "Fuckin' A."
> "An so now they tellin' me they gon' th'ow my fuckin' ass inna fuckin'
> *stoc*-kade! You know what? They some kind fuckin' me over!"
> "Fuckin' A well tol', Bubba."[19]

Although equally forbidden in all American services ("The use of profane
or filthy language is forbidden"—*Bluejacket's Manual*, 1944), obscenity
is equally popular in all and seldom reproved. In the Marine Corps dialogue like this takes place:

> "Hey Bull, you going on liberty?"
> "Fuckin' A doodle de doo."[20]

And one unit of army paratroopers hurled themselves out of their planes
shouting not the officially sanctioned "Geronimo!" or even the genteel-
comic variant "Umbriago!" but the demotic "Fuck it!"

All told, however, it is the British who have the most entertaining
way with *fuckin'*. Sometimes it is reduced to a bare minimum, as if only
a sketch is required:

> "How are things up ahead, mate?"
> " 'kin 'ell."

Sometimes repetition and alliteration produce memorable effects. Assem-
bling German prisoners into groups of five for easy counting, British
guards would be heard to shout, "All right, you fuckers, get in your
fuckin' fünfs," and in one Japanese prison camp a British NCO, super-
vising a work detail of his fellow prisoners and seeing a Japanese guard

approaching, exhorted his detail to look busy by uttering the one word "Guyferkinyaferkinferkers."[21] One RAF sergeant-major was renowned for his vigorous abusive word-hoard. One day he marched a squad of airmen to church for a funeral service. "As he led the squad to the church door, he stepped aside," a witness remembers, "but kept the left, right, left, right cadence as we proceeded inside. A sergeant in front of me tried to enter wearing his cap but the sergeant-major snatched it off his head roaring, 'Take yer fuckin' 'at off in the 'ouse of God, cunt!' "[22] In the British forces especially *fuckin'* could serve as a social-class signal, used less by the officers than the men. One sailor in the Royal Navy reports hearing another declare, "Mother love—that's what spoils everything . . . Damned mother love," and comments: "Roger was the only matelot I can ever remember who used the word 'damned,' " a modifier distinctly for the wardroom, where *fuckin'* might betray an unfortunate social past.[23] Even among conscientious objectors *fuckin'* signaled class division. Edward Blishen was struck by one of his fellow COs, a working-class boy named "Moke," who, says Blishen, was "remarkably versatile in making *[fucking]* serve for all parts of speech whatever."

> On one occasion he was expressing uncertainty as to the entertainment he would seek out on the evening to come. Should it be the cinema? He frowned over the problem, and canvassed opinions . . . .
>   "Sometimes," he declared at last, "I fink I fucking will, and sometimes I fink I fucking won't."
>   "I fucking wouldn't," Phil Perkins had suggested.
>   "You fucker," he'd commented. . . .

Once another CO, engaged with Blishen in farm work, noted with surprise how large a load a certain truck could hold. " 'You'd never fink . . . that this fucking lorry could carry so much fucking corn.' 'Oh quite,' [answered Blishen] 'it's unexpectedly capacious.' The man collapsed in helpless laughter, shouting, 'Oh Gawd! . . . Oh Gawd's truth!' "[24]

The use of *fucking* as the adjective and *fuckers* as the noun of all work was so common among British troops that it was noticed in an official War Office pamphlet of October, 1941, issued not to reprehend the usage but simply to warn against careless identification of strangers. In North Africa a German spy dressed in British uniform had succeeded in deceiving a British unit because he spoke impeccable Other Ranks English. The War Office pamphlet warned: "It should . . . be impressed on all ranks that the use in conversation of 'f------s' and 'b-------s' is *not* necessarily a guarantee of British nationality."[25] Now and then even the troops wearied of *fucking* and tried substituting equivalents like *conjugal* or *matrimonial*, as in "Where's the conjugal NAAFI in this camp?" or "What the matrimonial bloody hell do you think you're doing?" *Fucking* was so common and boring by the time of the Vietnam War that the Americans merely alluded to it and accommodated it to the more modern abbreviation habit. Thus a new arrival was a FNG or Fucking New Guy, and, as an army nurse remembers, a little rubber boat used for frolics while swimming was a LFRB, short for Little Fucking Rubber Boat.[26]

After several years of *fucking*, one did not have to be a puritan to find it tedious. On Guadalcanal, Sherwood F. Moran, a Japanese language expert, said wearily to one marine, "Yes, I know, you saw the fucking Jap coming up the fucking hill and raised your fucking rifle and shot him between the fucking eyes."[27]

Ernie Pyle is also reputed to have had enough, even if his remonstrance took ironic form. "I am sick and tired of that word ----," he once said. "If I ever hear the ------- word again I'm going to throw up."[28] But the use of the term could never be curbed because it was so essential to military meaning:

> Once, on a misty Scottish airfield, an airman was changing the magneto on the engine of a Wellington bomber. Suddenly his wrench slipped and he flung it on the grass and snarled, "Fuck! The fucking fucker's fucked." The bystanders were all quite well aware that he had stripped a bolt and skinned his knuckles.[29]

Indispensable both to those administering chickenshit and to those receiving it, *fucking* helped express the resentment of both sides, the one resenting the constant frustration of its authority, the other resenting its constant victimhood. Among the working class *fucking* had always been a popular intensifier, but in wartime it became precious as a way for millions of conscripts to note, in a licensed way, their bitterness and anger. If you couldn't oppose the chickenshit any other way, you could always say, "Fuck it!"

8

Drinking Far Too Much,
Copulating Too Little

The soldier, especially the conscript, suffers so deeply from contempt and damage to his selfhood, from absurdity and boredom and chicken-shit, that some anodyne is necessary. In Vietnam drugs served the purpose. In the Second World War the recourse was to drunkenness. In its alcoholic culture, this war was very different from its 1914–18 predecessor, at least as that earlier one was experienced by Americans. Although then drink was much sought after, the wartime atmosphere was gathering to the thunderhead that would burst into the Volstead Act. Cantonments and bivouacs, and even places fairly near the front lines in France, were frequented by thousands of do-gooders, Christers, and snoopers—YMCA secretaries, teetotal lecturers, anti-saloon-league zealots, and similar temperance fanatics who kept the troops under close surveillance and who were quick to note and repress signs of excess, or more often even indulgence. No drink, not even 3.2 beer, was available in army camps. These vocal hordes opposed to drink in any form are easily forgotten because few survived the repeal of the Eighteenth Amendment in 1933, and by the time of the Second World War, the notion that everyone has a perfect, even a Constitutional, right to a binge was thoroughly established in the United States.

In Britain that understanding had never gone underground. In one demoralized and unruly British unit in North Africa, we are told, "In a large marquee . . . a wet canteen was opened and Battalion Orders bore the amazing instruction that all ranks might get drunk provided they stayed within camp lines."[1] Although in the States the song "Rum and Coca-Cola" was popular, nothing there went so far in brassy alcoholic

96

frankness as the British "I'm Gonna Get Lit Up When the Lights Go Up in London."

In Canada "drink became a national craving," says one observer. "Perhaps it was a reaction to the depression . . . perhaps it was simply because the stuff was rationed; but in Canada during the war, everyone seemed to go loony about booze . . ."[2] And what you drank didn't matter much, so long as the anodyne worked. One Canadian girl speaks of learning to drink at servicemen's dances in Winnipeg by consuming Southern Comfort "right out of the neck of the bottle."[3] It seems evocative of the alcoholic atmosphere that when W. H. Auden meditates about the outbreak of the war he finds himself doing so while sitting "in one of the dives / On Fifty-second Street" and that Martha Gellhorn opens her section on the Second World War in *The Face of War* by recalling her whereabouts and activity when, in Mexico, she heard the news about Pearl Harbor: "We were drinking daiquiris in a mingy little bar."[4] A measure of the psychological distance of the Second War from the First is the rarity in 1914–18 of drinking and drunkenness poems, and their corollary, hangover poems, like Peter A. Sanders' "Tripoli":

> I've a mouth like a parrot's cage
> And a roaring thirst inside,
> My liver's a swollen, sullen rage—
> Last night I was blind to the wide.
>
> Canned as an owl, last night,
> Drunk as a fiddler's bitch,
> Oiled and stewed and pissed and tight,
> Sewn-up, asleep, in a ditch,

and so on.[5] Foreign to the Great War tradition are works like Gavin Ewarts's "Officers' Mess," Louis MacNeice's "Bar-Room Matins," and Julian Symons's "Pub." There's clearly something about fighting another war against the same enemy fewer than twenty-five years later so depressing and cynical-making as to propel anyone toward the saloon.

And in wartime there's an understanding that, considering the violence and the risk to life and limb and in the absence of a great deal of publicity and tut-tutting about "alcoholism"—that would come after the war—drink is largely natural and harmless, very like cigarettes in the 1940s. Thus Phyllis Moir, in an article "I Was Winston Churchill's

Private Secretary" in *Life* magazine, calmly notes, without raising an eyebrow, that "Mr. Churchill enjoys a drink":

> At home or on travel, at work or on holiday, Churchill drinks a glass of dry sherry at mid-morning and a small bottle of claret or Burgundy at lunch. To Mr. Churchill a meal without wine is not a meal at all. When he is in England he sometimes takes port after lunch, and always after dinner. It is at this time that his conversation is most brilliant. In the late afternoon he calls for his first whisky and soda of the day. . . . He likes a bottle of champagne at dinner. After the ritual of port, he sips the very finest Napoleon brandy. He may have a highball in the course of the evening.[6]

Thus drinking at the top, but lower down the picture was similar, as anyone can verify by turning to a wartime diary like Strome Galloway's *With the Irish Against Rommel* (1984). Galloway was a young Canadian infantry captain serving with the British in North Africa. Through such devices of toleration if not encouragement as "the officers' mess allowance," he was supplied with whisky throughout the campaign, as well as additional supplies of gin and other intoxicants, whose use he records freely. Any assembly of officers at any hour of the day is marked by drink, and most evenings when combat conditions permit are spent drinking and arguing, "on such topics as 'the abdication of Edward VIII,' 'What are we fighting for?', 'Will the British Empire survive this war?', and so on" (120).[7] On one occasion in March, 1943, "during the evening's usual tête-à-tête . . . Dunhill told an amusing story about the *Sitzkrieg* in France" while "a bottle of Gordon's gin disappeared" (123). A few days later, as Galloway is about to leave the unit on transfer, the major "put on a 'farewell party' for me in the Company Office tent, during which we killed two bottles of Scotch" (127). Four days later: "This evening I spent a couple of hours trying to find the Hampshires on my motor-cycle. I finally located their adjutant in a slit-trench and gave him the Brigadier's message. . . . Two slugs of whisky, which he offered me from an almost full bottle, warmed me up nicely, as the night air is very cold. The drinks also steadied my nerves, as the ride through uncharted ways in the pitch black was most nerve-wracking" (136–37). One week later: "We arrived at the . . . reception camp . . . a little the worse for the issue rum we had been indulging in—Teed having had a couple of Jerry waterbottles full of it when we left the Brigade area!" (145). For

Galloway, few events even remotely classifiable as social are unattended by drinks, but from his account there emerges the understanding that an "officer" is in part identifiable as someone who has learned through long, intense experience to hold his liquor. During one German attack, when Galloway was perilously directing the defense from the front and bullets were cracking overhead and enemy grenades were going off nearby, "the [Company Sergeant Major], disregarding my orders and my private property, was [a bit to the rear] getting slightly drunk on my whisky."

> He then saw a couple of Boche sneaking up from what had been our night positions, which they had over-run. Instead of waiting until they got up to the gap in the wall which he was covering, he jumped out through the gap and rushed up to them, apparently intent upon making a capture. As a result he was shot and killed. His body lay in a grotesque attitude throughout the day. One of the men told me he was quite drunk.

Later, checking the contents of his whisky bottle, Galloway finds it half empty and in a fury smashes it against a wall, angered doubtless both at himself and at the Sergeant Major's "need for Dutch Courage" (78–79).

If that's a covert reason for getting drunk, the overt reasons were many. One was that a traditional holiday had to be celebrated, like Christmas and, among the British, Boxing Day. On Boxing Day, 1941, on Malta, says one diarist, "Sgt.-Major Hunt and Sgt. Sandy were quite incapable and more often than not unconscious for two days." In the same unit and on the same holiday, we are assured, "one officer attended a Court Martial in which all the members were drunk, and the proceedings were thus postponed for several days."[8] Three years later, in Egypt, the custom was of course still being honored. "A heavy drinking session . . . started at noon on Christmas Eve," reports one RAF Pilot Officer, "and continued at a good pace most of the night, during which I managed to drink two bottles of brandy." By Boxing Day some few hours later he felt recovered enough to knock back eleven additional brandies.[9]

Drinking to "overcome" fear was a practice openly admitted by all hands. On a transport headed for North Africa in the fall of 1941, "Bill," designated by Robin Maugham as "one of our regular drinking officers," asked his "native" table steward to bring him some port. The steward, Maugham says, "bent over him and whispered confidentially, 'No need for Port now. We no more longer in danger zone.' "[10] An RAF pilot flying from a North African field reminds himself in his diary, "Must

British troops engaged in a drinking contest, Normandy, July, 1944
(Imperial War Museum)

remember not to drink too much [today] in case we are called out to operate. Although a wee drink or two does one good before a night take-off. Am very jumpy nowadays. I wonder if I am feeling the strain of flying." A couple of months later, this pilot notes with satisfaction that he has managed to cut his evening drinks, as he says, "down to a round dozen."[11] Attacking enemy shipping with Blenheim bombers was a hairy business, a gunner in one of them remembers: "One could die suddenly, receive some nasty jagged holes, acquire a galloping twitch, or develop a craving for copious draughts of brandy without soda."[12] The Canadian bomber pilot J. Douglas Harvey testifies that "fear of death . . . was so strong in some of the aircrew that no form of discipline was effective. These were the ones who had convinced themselves they would be killed and everything else was therefore trivial." One such was a colleague named

Joe. "He became the mess drunk."[13] An American soldier living in a hole at Anzio found "a slug of the old *vino*" taken before retiring sufficient to provide "catacomb courage" for the shellings of the night.[14] And as in the earlier war, the British dispensed rum freely to stimulate their infantry before the demoralizing tasks they were obliged to perform. Recalling Tunisia, one soldier says of the rum analgesic: "Eventually it became unthinkable to go into action without it. Rum, and morphia to silence our wounded."[15] (The German equivalent of the British rum was Schnapps, and few attacks were mounted without a good supply. It could be smelled in the air sometimes as the German soldiers formed up. And more Germans than the front-line troops needed an anodyne, to the degree that the end of the Third Reich resembled an alcoholic apocalypse. Somehow eloquent of the whole mad mess was William Joyce's final Lord Haw Haw broadcast from Hamburg on April 30, 1945. His topic was Hitler's suicide, and he was audibly and wildly drunk—perhaps intelligent behavior in view of what he must have suspected, that he was destined soon to be hanged by the conquerors.)

For the ground forces, performing one's duties was undeniably hard without some alcoholic insulation against reality. One man in the Normandy invasion remembers an American colonel who "couldn't take combat." Well before the landing, "he was just stoned out of his mind." Once ashore, "he came walking by, hanging onto his command car because he was so drunk."[16] On Okinawa the American soldier John Garcia consumed a fifth and a half of whisky daily. "It was the only way I could kill," he says. "I'd get up each day and start drinking. How else could I fight the war?" Once the war was over, he stopped drinking entirely, on the night of August 14, 1945, and "I haven't touched a drop since."[17] The canteens of those at the cutting edge contained brandy, whisky, or gin almost as often as water, and even Ernie Pyle finally took to drink so that, as he explained in a letter to his wife, going drunkenly to sleep "you wouldn't hear the guns and planes."[18] At one point, in the fall of 1944, after five whole years of it, the sheer multitudinousness of the war was beginning to get to one RAF pilot. He allowed his imagination to roam over the idea of vast quantities of men and matériel and their insensate wartime multiplication. Then he wrote in his diary, "There must be hundreds of aircraft at the bottom of the Mediterranean." But enough of such grim imagining. He goes on immediately: "I intend to have a few double brandies. . . ."[19]

Far away, in London, a great many double brandies were needed too, from the Prime Minister on down. Much of the drink was required, said the drinkers, to "calm nerves." The front page of the *Evening Standard* for December 30, 1940, offers a pregnant juxtaposition. A headline reads

SEVEN FAMOUS CHURCHES HIT IN FIERCEST LONDON RAID,

while a box in the upper right-hand corner of the same page proclaims

NICHOLSON'S GIN
It's Clear   It's Good

"I am drinking far too much—like most people in Whitehall these days," says the civil servant Robert Bruce Lockhart. "The ministers are no better; [Hugh] Dalton [Minister of Economic Warfare] has a strong head, drinks hard and has a particular liking for brandy. Brendan [Bracken, Minister of Information] is rarely completely sober after 11 pm, and even Eden takes a man's full share in the evening. War's effect on nerves, I suppose." [20] An aspect of British upper-class (or would-be upper-class) style might be inferred from Freddie Birkenhead's reporting, in July, 1944, that Evelyn Waugh was "always drunk," and Randolph Churchill's rages and contumelies when elevated were notorious and much feared. [21]

But even the British were sometimes horrified by American excesses. One Royal Army Service Corps officer in North Africa, just after the American defeat at Kasserine Pass, notes his satisfaction that British and American troops are being kept apart. "Though we are not angels," he says, "an army which is drunk all day is no good to be associated with." [22] And on the other side of the world, "In my outfit," James Jones says, "we got blind asshole drunk every chance we got"—on what the troops termed *swipe*, an ad hoc distillate of sugar, canned fruit, potato peelings, and other such ingredients. [23] In Europe the U.S. Army Medical Corps discovered that the troops were so eager for drink that numbers of them consumed captured buzz-bomb fluid (i.e., methyl alcohol) and died. Most were ground combat troops, and the Official History reports that "During the period October 1944 to June 1945 . . . there were more deaths in the European theater due to a single agent, alcohol poisoning, than to acute communicable disease." The History draws the inevitable conclusion: "In future operations the problem of alcoholic beverages . . . needs serious consideration. The American soldier will find a substitute which may be poisonous, if a supply is not available."[24] During and after the battle for Manila, the bad-alcohol problem grew so grave that billboards were put up to warn the troops: "Deaths from Poison Liquor to Date: 48." A soldier who was there saw what such deaths were like. "A young soldier lay in the gutter," he remembers, "his foam-flecked mouth emitting groans as he stared blankly at the sky. I paused to help him, but I knew it was hopeless. He was one of many who had drunk poison liquor purchased from Filipino moonshiners."[25]

Although not widely publicized in the civilian world, very heavy drinking of hard liquor had been a notable custom in the peacetime American army. It takes some reading between the lines about, say, General Wainwright and his wife to discover that they were close to drunks, and one can infer that they were not terribly anomalous among their colleagues. At high army headquarters in the European theater, the flagrantly intoxicating French 75 was a common drink, and so was an even more vigorous version, the "170," popular at Patton's headquarters and probably named after the German 170-mm gun. Instead of 75 per cent champagne and 25 per cent cognac, like the French 75, this consisted of half and half.[26] Army public relations labored to conceal the facts about military drinking from the public, stressing that the beer served at the training camps contained only 3.2 per cent alcohol and glossing over the ease with which you could get fighting drunk on it if you tried. Public relations omitted also to disclose the officers' two-bottle-a-month hard liquor issue, doled out whether wanted or not. In December, 1942, it was apparently necessary for the Office of War Information to lay to rest suspicions that the troops in training were drinking too much. It issued a soothing pamphlet in co-operation with "The Conference of Alcoholic Beverage Industries" aimed, one gathers, largely at citizens living near army camps and nervous about enormities. Titled *A Survey of Drinking Habits In and Around Army Camps*, it concluded, after an inquiry extending from coast to coast, that there was no problem. Indeed, it found that "no American army in all history has been so orderly." The provision of 3.2 beer on army posts is so little a cause of trouble that it's "a positive factor in Army sobriety." But actually, the pamphlet went on, beer is not very popular, the best-selling drinks in and around the camps being coffee, milk, milk-shakes and malts, and soft drinks. What's caused all the

(Standard Oil, N.J., Collection,
University of Louisville Photographic Archives)

rumors about army drunkenness is simply the uniform, which makes its wearer conspicuous and the object of constant would-be censorious scrutiny. "One unruly delinquent in a G. I. blouse, a half-dozen prankish privates tipsy with a few drinks and furlough freedom, can start stories which, pyramided in telling, give the impression . . . that service carousals are hampering our training for war." The very small number of arrests for drunkenness in towns near the camps tells the story of military temperance, the pamphlet says.

When in 1966 Ronald Blythe published his anthology of stories, poems, and essays of the Second World War titled *Components of the Scene*, he had been mulling over Second War writings for years, imbibing their aromas and inhaling their atmosphere. It is therefore hardly surprising to find him commenting in alcoholic and hedonistic terms about Cyril Connolly's *The Unquiet Grave*. Connolly's book, he finds, is "a profound distillation of melancholy, which, exuded drop by aphoristic drop, gets the reader wonderfully drunk."[27]

If drink was indulged in freely, the other traditional comfort, sex, seemed often in short supply. The reasons were social and legal, and they sound so quaint today that anyone trying to indicate the public view of sex in the 1940s hardly expects to be believed. Now, when the urban newstand flaunts its pornographic wares which, if not heady enough, can be eked out with the bolder materials at the nearest Adult Bookshop, and when your local X-rated film theater routinely and legally depicts scenes formerly viewable only at stag parties, it is almost impossible to realize that things were once quite otherwise. Not just unimagined in the 1940s but unimaginable then was the video cassette recorder, allowing you to enjoy dirty movies right in your bedroom by means of your own television (what's that?). In wartime, before all this, the American Postmaster General was empowered to act as a moral censor of anything sent through the mails, and in the United Kingdom the Lord Chancellor made sure that the minimum of sexually exciting material reached stage or screen. He was the one who stipulated that the very chaste nudes in the pseudo-high-minded tableaux at the Windmill Theatre, Picadilly, stood like statues—any movement seemed too suggestive of bumps and grinds. There was no *Playboy* or *Penthouse* or *Hustler*, and certainly no *Squeeze, Rapture,* or *Adult American Dreambook*. The sexiest magazine generally available was probably *Esquire*, with its drawings by "Petty" and "Varga" of languorous girls with immensely long legs—thought more exciting then than now—and precisely delineated breasts. On June 7, 1945, the London edition of *Stars and Stripes* cheered its readers no end by announcing that the U.S. Court of Appeals had upheld *Esquire*'s mailing privileges and that it was now free to circulate its Petty and Varga imagery without further interference from the postal authorities. Milton Caniff's comic-strip "Terry and the Pirates" also offered some good breasts, usually very pointed, but encased in black satin. Throughout the war the London *Daily Mirror* ran a comic-strip depicting the scantily clad "Jane," much relished by the troops. Only on VE-Day did she go so far as to take off everything. This created a sensation, and many were not sure what they thought about it. Pocket-size magazines like *Pageant* and *Coronet,* and in the U.K., *Lilliput,* occasionally ran an art photo showing a girl's back or even breasts, and a chaste artistic nude now and then appeared in *Popular Photography.* In sophisticated places one might buy a copy of a magazine like *Sunshine and Health,* showing stout nudists enjoying volleyball with air-brushed genital organs. Rare was a burlesque or strip show in which a woman displayed, finally, her actual nipples: local ordinances commonly required a small bra, or at least "pasties." If such a performer omitted a G-string, you were probably not in a theater but a bawdyhouse. It was only a few years before the war that men had begun leaving off their bathing-suit tops, and a two-piece suit for women was thought bold. Dressed for swimming, one did not generally exhibit one's navel.

In the United States, films were regulated morally by the "Hays Office," which went to work in a strictly binary way. There were no classifications like G, PG, R, and X. A film was either acceptable or unshowable. The most daring film was probably *Ecstasy* (1932), in which Hedy Lemarr first ran around in the nude evading a horseman on a white stallion and then simulated orgasmic facial expressions. But a film like that was one of a kind, for you didn't normally expect erotic experience at the movies. It was so rare that in one U. S. Army unit in Italy *Ziegfeld Girl* (1941), starring Lana Turner, was notorious as the film where "you can see her tits when she bends over to pick the flowers. . . ."[28] An experience one sailor found worth recording in his diary was a second viewing of the technicolor film *Arabian Nights* (1942) featuring the actress he called "Maria 'Oh Those Boobies' Montez." "All boys were satisfied," he notes.[29] In wartime films, a very little innuendo or double entendre had the power to shock. An American soldier, on maneuvers in the States, once attended an army film-showing to which some local civilians were invited. The feature was *Topper Takes a Trip* (1938), with Roland Young and Constance Bennett, set on the Riviera. The soldier observed in his diary: "Show started at 7:30. Rancher, wife, and another woman. 2 small girls and a baby also present." And he adds the comment: "G. I. movies a bit spicy—hardly fit for girls."[30]

Sex before marriage was regarded as either entirely taboo or gravely reprehensible. "Most of the girls said it was either marriage or nothing," one woman remembers.[31] There was of course no Pill, and contraception was mechanical and barely trustworthy. The consequent fear of pregnancy added to the general wartime anxiety. A bit of apprehension attended every embrace. One woman recalls: "It was no joke to try to do everything right and still put your heart into the whole thing. There wasn't anything foolproof except abstinence, and who needed that?"[32] Some women insisted on their beaux's wearing two condoms at once and even then required them to withdraw before ejaculation.[33]

In this ambience of public puritanism and sexual anxiety, literature didn't have to go very far to be thought highly provocative. Kathleen Winsor's historical novel about a naughty girl, *Forever Amber* (1944), would doubtless strike today's readers as tediously chaste, but a representative group of deprived United States marines found it intensely sexy. "Jeez, they were horny!" reports one who watched them pore over the book, the dirtiest available on their ship. "If you've ever seen books that were completely worn out by reading, it was the copies of *Forever Amber* on our LST."[34] Considered similarly hot was Erskine Caldwell's *God's Little Acre* (1933), which Ensign Pulver, in Thomas Heggen's *Mister Roberts* (1946), had read twelve times and whose most salacious passages, says Heggen, "he could recite flawlessly."[35] Another literary aphrodisiac was Nicholas Monsarrat's *Leave Cancelled* (1945), packaged in a pink dust-jacket displaying a cupid with holes punched in him. Sparse and genteel as the lubriciousness was, it was sufficient to excite numerous males in the service.

Their loneliness can be inferred from their inordinate fondness for popular songs warm with sexual allusion like "Why Don't We Do This More Often?", "In the Mood," or "That Lovely Weekend." The vivid requirements of the imagination among the sexually needy can be estimated from this little song popular among British troops. It is titled "In the Moonlight":

> I love you in your negligee,
> I love you in your nightie,
> But when moonlight flits across your tits—

and then the heartfelt climax,

> By Christ all-fucking-mighty![36]

It is easy to understand if not, perhaps, to forgive the Norwegian pilots trained in Canada on their way to England on a transport, who lay in their bunks "masturbating for all the world to see, so that you walked the decks whether you wanted to or not."[37] Or to sympathize with the soldiers who, as a Canadian remembers, "get a letter from their girl and go right into the can and masturbate—you could tell by the looks on their faces when they came out."[38] Exemplary among the deprived are the American soldiers in Lincoln Kirstein's poem "Load." Waiting in their cots for shells to arrive from a long-range German railway gun, they masturbate out of sheer anxiety:

> Well aimed from forty miles away
>   Are steel-turned tubes the Jerries use,
> But the most harm their banging does
>   Is stiffen us to self-abuse.
> Waiting the next note from their gun,
>   A hot hand strokes an aching hard.
> Nervousness exceeding fun
>   Jacks a poor peter to its yard.[39]

Interesting as this is, it is notably what front-line troops would stigmatize as a rear-echelon problem. Sexual deprivation and inordinate desire generally did not trouble men on the front line. They were too scared, busy, hungry, tired, and demoralized to think about sex at all. Indeed, the front was the one wartime place that was sexless.

Behind the lines, desire was constantly seeking an outlet it seldom satisfactorily found. The official attitude of the Allied forces seemed to be that copulation among the unmarried did not take place but that when it did a condom—issued free to people going on pass or liberty—had to be used and a prophylactic station visited immediately after. Acquiring a venereal disease was a punishable offense, and the services labored to keep the rate of infection under control, the Americans largely with earnest movies like *Good Girls Have VD Too*, the British, perhaps more comfortable with verbal wit, with slogans like the one used in Egypt, "Remember, flies spread disease. Keep yours shut!" The proximity of women service personnel caused complications, requiring high steel-mesh fences topped with barbed wire, guard dogs, and bothersome chaperonage. On official social visits to ships of the Royal Navy—dances and the like—members of the Women's Royal Naval Service (WRENS), who normally lived claustrated in what sailors called Wrenneries, were obliged to wear for the occasion, and to have verified by inspection, "blackouts," rugged black knickers with stout elastic at waist and knee.

One curious thing is that, compared with passionate writing in the

Great War, the convention in the Second is that love is strenuously het-eroerotic. From the Second War there seem to be none of those poems fantasizing loving "lads" that the lonely imagination threw off in Flan-ders and Picardy. In *Rhymes of a PFC*, to be sure, Kirstein does sketch a couple of episodes of homosexual interest, but that sort of thing, either in actuality or in writing, is so rare as to engender special notice and comment. If we do hear now and then of such "minority" sexual compen-sations, they seem largely limited to the POW camps, with their extreme circumstances of deprivation. In one Japanese camp, for example, ho-mosexual liaisons were so common that an American medical officer con-ducted, we are told, "a weekly marital relations clinic, in an effort to keep the couples happy. . . ."[40] And in a German POW camp a British prisoner once observed an interesting scene: "I attended a theatrical enter-tainment in which the equivalent of the stalls were packed with French officers in elegant uniforms and women in evening dress with elaborate hair-dos, who were not women at all but had rubber tits."[41]

But free to forage where they wanted to, the troops sought out such women as could be found, and as heavy duty began to reveal itself un-mistakably as the style of the war, sex surfaced with an insistence and violence which suggested that the troops had had too little for too long. In the months before the invasion London swarmed with prostitutes of all ages, who would either take you into one of the parks or vouchsafe you a "wall job" or "knee trembler," standing up in a not so dark street around Picadilly. "I never saw so many whores in my life," one Canadian soldier remembers, and another explains:

> We were going to open a Second Front. Everyone knew that and that a lot of men were going to die. . . . I won't describe the scenes or the sounds of Hyde Park or Green Park at dusk and after dark. They just can't be described. You can just imagine, a vast battlefield of sex.[42]

Once the invasion troops had departed for Normandy, there was conster-nation among the prostitutes. The pubs where they used to meet clients were suddenly empty. The George, a pub near the BBC which American officers had made their own, ever after was referred to as The Whore's Lament. But license was not universal. Canadian boys in particular were "naive by any standard," says J. Douglas Harvey, who was with the RAF:

Not only about the war and the world but about much simpler things. Sex for instance. It can never be determined how many aircrew died in a virgin state, but it was undoubtedly a very high percentage.

When these Canadian youths arrived in the U.K., he says, "The English girls must have thought a flock of eunuchs had landed in their midst."[43]

Such surely had frequent recourse to "the old five-fingered widow," as one of the NCOs recalled by Brian Aldiss puts it. This British novelist is probably the most acute and comic registrar of wartime sexual deprivation and its effects. He is better known now as a science-fiction writer than as the author of the Horatio Stubbs trilogy, comprising the novels—their titles nicely imply the subject—*The Hand-Reared Boy* (1970), *A Soldier Erect* (1971), and *A Rude Awakening* (1978). All are now out of print in the United States. During wartime they would have seemed gravely pornographic and certainly unpublishable. Aldiss was born in Norfolk in 1925, went to boarding schools very like those in *The Hand-Reared* Boy, volunteered in 1939, served in the Signals in Burma, India, and briefly, after the war, in Sumatra. During his spare hours in the service he spent his time doing two things primarily: reading *Palgrave's Golden Treasury of Songs and Lyrics* and thinking of ways to relieve his deep sexual frustration. "Fictional autobiography" he has called his trilogy, and there is no reason to infer a very wide distance between Horatio Stubbs and his creator.

From the outset Horatio's sexual instincts have been prodigious. Beginning with fascination with the wee-wees of others in kindergarten, he proceeds to infantine masturbation, instructed by his older brother and observed by his younger sister. These "regular wanking sessions"[44] within the confines of the family yield finally to more ambitious masturbatory exhibitions at boarding school and to precocious intercourse, at age twelve, with the family maid at the family beach house. In 1939, aged seventeen and in his last year at school, Horatio encounters Sister Virginia Traven, and they prosecute a torrid affair in the school infirmary at the moment the BEF is going over to save France. As *The Hand-Reared Boy* comes to an end, Horatio has discovered not just that Virginia is perfidious but that she is insane. He is now ready to go into the army, and his middle period, his age of monumental sexual deprivation, is about to begin. This is the subject of the best novel of the three, *A Soldier Erect*.

Narrated, like all three, in the first person, the novel opens with a bizarre comic farewell-party given Horatio by his puritanical parents.

"Jesus, what a wet dream of a party that was!" (10),[45] Horatio says, recalling the witless guests, largely his father's colleagues from the branch bank where he works, and the odd elderly relative or two. His sister has brought along Sylvia Rudge, and it is to her attempted seduction that Horatio devotes his abundant erotic energy while the rest of the party of sixteen is regaling itself with a little bit of wine and lots of cake. Someone puts on the gramophone Len Camber singing "That Lovely Weekend":

> The ride in the taxi when midnight had flown,
> And breakfast next morning, just we two alone.
> You had to go, time was so short,
> We both had so much to say.
> Your kit to be packed, your train to be caught—
> I'm sorry I cried but I just felt that way . . . (20)

The effect of that is to stimulate in Horatio a wild farewell-occasion kind of lust which Sylvia is about to gratify in the Stubbs family's backyard air-raid shelter when Horatio's mother appears at the entrance and insists they return to the house:

> So we went in past her, Sylvia blushing with shame, me a twenty-year-old infantryman, pride of the Royal Mendips, about to die for Old England, erections every night up to my armpits—sometimes you wonder what the fucking hell you were fighting for! (22)

The party over, Horatio's erection will not subside, and up in his room he fantasizes a knee-trembler with Sylvia while he masturbates. At that moment—like the German shells in Kirstein's "Load"—a flight of Dornier bombers "heading for Birmingham again, third night in succession, throb-throb-throb" passes overhead. "As they come over the chimney-tops, I come over my fists and stand alone panting in the dark . . ." (24). That is the first of many, many onanistic performances with which Horatio will solace his military horniness.

Assigned to the British 2nd Division, Signaller Stubbs arrives in Bombay in October, 1943. He finds the scene one "that England could never envisage, noisy, unregulated, full of colour and stink" (31). While being transported by train and truck to barracks at Kanchapur, Stubbs and his fellow Other Ranks goggle and gape at the odd world they've been set down in, fascinated by "the three-legged dogs, the ruffians spitting and peeing from squatting positions; . . . the women washing and drinking at a water tank; the monkeys sitting or squabbling on shed roofs; the aimless people, probing into their crutches for wild life as they watched everything fade into dust" (34–35). Stubbs's company is finally installed at its station, and it's here that Horatio begins to realize what he's in for, sexually. The Commanding Officer addresses the newcomers, delivering warnings appropriate to the hot and filthy environment: stay away from alcohol, take plenty of salt, " 'also, keep away from local women, all of whom have the pox. You may be offered women down in the bazaar. Refuse them. Don't be misled. They will have the pox, so stay away from them. It's a hot climate, so keep yourselves morally pure,' " to which the troops grumble, " 'Morally fucking pure . . . What does he think we are . . .' " (41–42). An old-service corporal later underlines the CO's warnings, and to the question, "What are we supposed to do?" he replies, " 'Stick to the old five-fingered widow! Stick to the old five-fingered widow and you won't go far wrong' " (43). Horatio confesses that he avidly followed the corporal's advice: "The five-fingered widow was my own constant companion. Never a day went by but a marriage was arranged" (43).

Once, Horatio is enticed into the brothel area of the town but caught and warned by the MPs before he can settle in for a bout with a beautiful young girl he fancies there. He does sneak back later and enjoy her, but frustration sets in again as the company moves to a worse town, Belgaum, for training. Fighting the Japanese in Burma is their rumored destiny, but Horatio's "problem" grows worse and worse. Hearing of a woman plying her trade in a shack near a fetid lake nearby, he shows interest and experiences some hope, but he is warned by a fellow soldier again to stay away from all local women:

> "They're none of them any good. . . . Rotten with syph. Even the bloody ground's rotten with syph here—that's why nothing grows. Take the advice of an old soldier, Stubby-boy, and keep off 'em. Fuck your fist, same as I do, and you're safe. Honeymoon in the hand." (80)

But Horatio seeks out the girl in the lakeside shed. He is about to approach her when he sees one of the slimiest of the cooks leaving her, and he simply can't. Instead, he decides to wade out into the lake, pretending to swim, and masturbate there. But he is seen by a strolling sergeant and reprimanded for swimming without permission in filthy water. Doesn't he know about bilharzia, etc? Horatio has now entirely lost sexual self-respect: "Failed fucker, failed wanker was an inglorious double billing" (86).

Back, finally, to Kanchapur and more sexual frustration, which Horatio manages to relieve now and then with a local prostitute, regardless. The gossip now is about the native *gobble-wallahs*, young men who for a small fee will relieve the troops with their mouths. One of Horatio's platoon mates, eighteen-year-old Jackie Tertis, who confesses that he's a virgin, suffers intensely from frustration and shame: " 'I have to keep on bashing my bishop,' " he tells Horatio. " 'It makes me feel awful. It's twitching in my pants if I just mention its name' " (107). Tertis and others find some satisfaction in the barely literate local pornography, especially *The Night Times of Michael Meatyard*, a work which passes from hand to hand around Horatio's platoon. "Who wrote the immortal *Michael Meatyard?*" Horatio wonders.

> Meatyard's antics must have delighted thousands of British troops. . . . The setting of the book was Venice, which may have meant only that the writer had read his Casanova. No use was made of the Venetian setting, unless one counts the early scene in the book where Michael attends a masked ball. There he dances with a buxom matron, masked as he is; they become excited by each other and go to a nearby bedroom. Only when the lady opens her legs does Michael recognize—his mother! (164)

While the bulk of his unit ships out to fight in Burma, Stubbs remains behind temporarily on a supply detail. Working one day at the railway station, his group is talking about sex as usual, with Jackie Tertis especially lamenting his condition, when a local young man sidles up and addresses him: " 'You like gobble, Johnny? Nice sweet mouth open only five rupee. . . ?' " Anxious to provide for Jackie, the group bargains the price down to two rupess eight anna, and the *gobble-wallah* leads Jackie away behind some crates, whence in a few minutes he emerges "pale and sweating," and thoroughly ashamed (170).

Horatio is soon passing through Calcutta and sampling its brothels. A friend is kind enough to pull various strings to delay his and Horatio's shipment to combat in Burma, but the inevitable cannot be postponed forever, and before Horatio knows what's happening he's in combat, digging slit trenches and marching up and down mountains. He is still wanking twice a day, but sexuality retires as excitement and fear mount, and Horatio learns that nothing curbs desire, drives it completely out of one's mind and meat, like being mortared by the Japanese. Leeches on one's legs and lower body don't help either, nor is the stench of human bodies rotting in the jungle anything like an aphrodisiac. "I never dreamed of home or sex," Horatio says now (251).

If battle extinguishes desire that way in *A Soldier Erect*, peace re-ignites it in the final work of the trilogy, *A Rude Awakening*. It is 1946, and Sergeant Stubbs is now with the occupying forces in Sumatra. The Awakening of the title is Horatio's perception that the Second World War is mutating before his eyes into the Third—the colonialist, anti-insurgent war that will end disastrously for Europeans by conferring Southeast Asia very largely upon indigenous communists and socialists and dissolving former French, British, and Dutch presence there. But this political understanding is not the center of *A Rude Awakening*. Sex is, in the person first of Margey, a Chinese girl who wants to accompany Horatio back to England upon his imminent demobilization, and then in Katie Chae, an accomplished Chinese prostitute, Margey's rival for Stubbs's affection as well as for his gifts from NAAFI stores. But despite the skill of both Margey and Katie in providing relief, Horatio's libido is so pow-erful that he remains an avid wanker on the side. Jackie Tertis reappears here, transformed now from the shy client of the *gobble-wallahs* into a vicious official torturer of captured guerillas. Katie's brother Tiger Balm on one occasion acutely diagnoses Horatio's trouble and in doing so illu-minates the whole emotional predicament of human beings pressed into military service. " 'You are a soldier, Sergeant Stubbs,' he says, 'so you are not a complete person. You are partly a uniform.' "[46] Horatio real-izes now that his hope for himself resides in flight from the army and the obsessions that have accompanied his career in it—political, administra-tive, and sexual power, and he flies off alone toward his freedom. Margey and Katie will have to find new friends and customers.

Aldiss's Horatio Stubbs trilogy is not the best writing to come out of the war but it does offer the most clear-sighted view, necessarily comic, of the pressures engendered by sexual deprivation in a bizarre context of male bonding with a vengeance. If one enemy was the Japanese, others almost as destructive, wartime made clear, were chastity, claustration, puritanism, repression, and hypocrisy.

9

Type-casting

he Chinese are fine fighting men," declares one of Horatio Stubbs's
fellow soldiers. "Your Chink is brought up to fight on a handful of rice
a day. A Chink'll go for days on just a handful of rice."[1] That's an
example, if a rather low one, of the kind of cliché classifications indispensable in wartime. If war is a political, social, and psychological disaster, it is also a perceptual and rhetorical scandal from which total recovery
is unlikely. Looking out upon the wartime world, soldiers and civilians
alike reduce it to a simplified sketch featuring a limited series of classifications into which people, in the process dehumanized and deprived of
individuality or eccentricity, are fitted. In the Second World War many
more things than conscripts underwent classifications from 1-A to 4-F.
The British working girl Louie, in Elizabeth Bowen's *The Heat of the
Day* (1948), receives the classifications determining her vision in 1942
from the newspapers she follows devotedly:

> Was she not a worker, a soldier's lonely wife, a war orphan, a pedestrian,
> a Londoner, a home and animal-lover, a thinking democrat, a movie-
> goer, a woman of Britain, a letter-writer, a fuel-saver and a housewife?[2]

Within the soldier's world, the classifications are clearly indicated by
insignia of rank and branch of service. The result is that with people,
you always know what to expect. A captain of artillery will be a certain
type, and so will a major in the Judge Advocate General's department, a
first lieutenant of Ordnance, and an infantry staff-sergeant. You can count
on it. And gazing outward toward the civilian scene, the soldierly imagination rudely consigns people to four categories:

1. The female, consisting of mother, grandmother, and sister, on the one hand, and, on the other, agents of sexual solace.

2. Elderly men, who are running the draft boards, as well as the rationing, transportation, and propaganda apparatus.

3. The infantine, who will be in the war if it lasts long enough.

4. And the most despised of categories, the 4-F or physically unfit and thus defective, the more despicable the more invisible the defect, like a heart murmur, punctured ear-drum, or flat feet.

One might think the most vigorous soldierly contempt might be directed at conscientious objectors, but no: since most of them were set to hard labor in camps, they were regarded as virtually members, if a bit disgraced, of the armed services, and their circumstances were conceived to be little more degrading than those of the troops in, say, the non-combatant quartermaster corps. That the COs endured lots of chickenshit made them like brothers. Civilians were different, more like "foreigners," indeed rather like the enemy.

For the war to be prosecuted at all, the enemy of course had to be severely dehumanized and demeaned, and in different ways, depending on different presumed national characteristics. One way of classifying the Axis enemy was to arrange it by nationalities along a scale running from courage down to cowardice. The Japanese were at the brave end, the Italians at the pusillanimous, and the Germans were in the middle. This symmetrical arrangement also implied a scale of animalism, with the Japanese accorded the most feral qualities and the Italians the most human, including a love of music, ice-cream, and ostentatious dress.

Americans detested the Japanese the most, for only they had had the effrontery to attack the United States directly, sinking ships, killing sailors, and embarrassing American pretenses to alertness and combat adequacy. They must be animals to behave thus, and cruel ones at that. "Bestial apes"—that is what Admiral William F. Halsey termed them and added the good news that "we are drowning and burning [them] all over the Pacific, and it is just as much pleasure to burn them as to drown them."[3] A marine on Guadalcanal could perceive the Japanese only as beasts of various species. He told John Hersey, "They hide up in the trees like wildcats. Sometimes when they attack, they scream like a bunch of terrified cattle in a slaughter house." Another said, "I wish we were fighting against Germans. They are human beings, like us. . . . But the Japs are like animals. . . . They take to the jungle as if they had been bred there, and like some beasts you never see them until they are dead."[4] What harm, then, in cleaning, polishing, and sending home their animal skulls as souvenirs, so that a standard snapshot depicts a soldier or marine proudly exhibiting a cleansed Japanese skull, while a poem of the period, by Winfield Townley Scott, meditates without moral comment on "The U.S. Sailor with the Japanese Skull":

> our
> Bluejacket, I mean, aged 20, in August strolled
> Among the little bodies on the sand and hunted
> Souvenirs: teeth, tags, diaries, boots; but bolder still
> Hacked off this head and under a Ginkgo tree skinned it.[5]

Then dragged it behind his ship for many days and finally scrubbed it thoroughly with lye and had a perfect souvenir. Dealing that way with the skull of a German or Italian, that is, "a white man," would be clearly inappropriate, perhaps sacrilegious. This treatment of Japanese corpses as if they were animal became so flagrant as early as September, 1942, that the Commander in Chief of the Pacific Fleet ordered that "No part of the enemy's body may be used as a souvenir. Unit Commanders will take stern disciplinary action. . . ."[6]

The civil, unbloodthirsty American sailor James J. Fahey, a Roman Catholic from Waltham, Massachusetts, and a respecter of all the decencies, after a *kamikaze* attack on his ship wrote home that "one of the men on our [gun] mount got a Jap rib and cleaned it up" because "his sister wants part of a Jap body."[7] No censorious reaction whatever from Fahey, for that rib is like one you can buy in a meat market. "Oh, the inhuman brutes!" exclaimed Mrs. John Milburn, as news of Japanese behavior reached the United Kingdom.[8] Among the Allies the Japanese were also known as "jackals" or "monkey-men" or "sub-humans," the term of course used by the Germans for Russians, Poles, and assorted Slavs, amply justifying their vivisection. Personnel of the United States Marine Corps sought to popularize the term *Japes* (*Japs* + *apes*), but the word never caught on, and the Japanese remained *Japs*, or, slightly less contemptuously, *Nips*. Like the *Huns* of the Great War, *Japs*—"the yellow Huns of the East," Australian General Gordon Bennett called them[9]—was a brisk monosyllable handy for slogans like "Rap the Jap" or "Let's Blast the Jap Clean Off the Map," the last a virtual prophecy of Hiroshima. It is a truism of military propaganda that monosyllabic enemies are easier to despise than others. A *kraut* or *wop* is instantly disposable in a way a

Caricature by Arthur Szyk (San Francisco Archive of Comic Art)

German or Italian isn't quite, just as in the Great War a *boche* or a *hun* betrayed by their very names their vileness and worthlessness. Like the later *gook*. In July, 1943, a large sign on the damaged bow of the U.S. Cruiser *Honolulu* quoted Admiral Halsey urging everyone to

> Kill Japs. Kill Japs.
> Kill More Japs.[10]

Because they were animals, Japanese troops had certain advantages over Americans. They could see in the dark, it was believed, and survive on a diet of roots and grubs. The very tiny-ness of the Japanese was another reason for contempt. They were little the way insects and rodents are little—little but nasty. In 1942, in the pamphlet *Individual Battle Doctrine*, the United States Marine Corps assured its members of Japanese combat inferiority by pointing out that "the Jap is much too short to enter the Marine Corps." One result of this puniness is that "he is really a poor bayonet fighter." Americans held in Japanese prison camps noticed the way their captors liked to get up onto something, a box, podium, platform, or stand, when haranguing the prisoners. "They loved to elevate themselves," one prisoner said.[11] Americans of standard height could understand the Japanese problem immediately as the "Runt's Complex," familiar from high school, the need of the short to "get back at" people of normal height and their customary use of guile or fraud to do so. The "sneak attack" on Pearl Harbor thus explains itself.

A rumor popular during the war told of a mother receiving a letter from her soldier son in a Japanese POW camp. He tells her that he is well and surviving OK and not to worry, and he adds that she might like to soak off the stamp on the envelope to give a friend who's a collector. When she does so, she finds written under the stamp, "THEY HAVE CUT OUT MY TONGUE." Given the notorious cruelty of the Japanese, in wartime that story could be received as entirely credible, making everyone forget that letters from captured soldiers bear no postage stamps. Type-casting assured that the Pacific War would be particularly cruel, and the cruelty was on both sides. The Japanese, as former marine E. B. Sledge says, "killed solely for the sake of killing, without hope and without higher purpose," and so did the Americans. The Japanese fired programmatically on stretcher-bearers and tortured to death Americans who fell into their hands. Sledge once encountered a group of dead marines whose bodies had been defiled, one man's penis having been sliced off and inserted in his mouth, another man's head and hands having been chopped off.[12] Similarly, the marines loved to use the few Japs who came forward to surrender as amusing rifle targets, just as they felt intense satisfaction watching them twist and writhe when set afire by the napalm of the flame-thrower. Japanese skulls were not the only desirable trophies: treasured also were Japanese gold teeth, knocked out, sometimes from the mouths of the still-living, by a USMC Ka-bar knife-hilt. During wartime it was impossible to complicate "the Japanese character" in any way, to recognize that the same auspices were behind the Bataan Death March and the Noh drama. It was not to be widely publicized that the same "types" who had bayoneted hospital patients in Hong Kong also flew out over the sea where they had sunk HMS *Repulse* and *Prince of Wales* and dropped a memorial wreath on the water. Once the war was over and the Americans were installed on the home islands as occupiers, the Japanese capacity for subtlety and delicacy could again be recognized. Then, Admiral Nimitz, doubtless with Halsey and such in mind, reminded his subordinates that "the use of insulting epithets in connection with the Japanese as a race or individuals does not now become the officers of the United States Navy."[13]

If the Japanese were type-cast as animals of an especially dwarfish but vicious species, the Germans were recognized to be human beings, but of a perverse type, cold, diagrammatic, pedantic, unimaginative, and thoroughly sinister. We had submarines, but they had U-boats. Their instinct for discipline made them especially dangerous, and their admitted distinction in technology made their cruelty uniquely effective. That it was the same people who were shooting hostages and hanging Poles and gassing Jews, on the one hand, and enjoying Beethoven and Schubert, on the other, was a complication too difficult to be faced during wartime. In March, 1942, John Steinbeck found that he had seriously misjudged the popular necessity of type-casting German troops as simply wicked. In his novella (later a play) *The Moon Is Down*, he depicted the Germans occupying a Norwegian town as human, subject like other people to emotions of love, pride, envy, and jealousy. None was characterized as an anti-Semitic monster. To his astonishment, a cascade of intellectual and moral abuse fell upon him. Artistically he may have deserved it: *The Moon Is Down* is a sort of narrative *Our Town* relocated to a wartime Continent. The story overflows with folksiness and jocosity, and the small-town scene is peopled with sentimental would-be lovable characters. But the badness of the book lies rather in its aesthetic clumsiness than in any ideological defect. As a writer dependent on popular suffrage, Steinbeck had simply not noticed that the days of light duty were past and henceforth Germans, all Germans—Wehrmacht, SS, sailors, housewives, hikers, the lot—had to be cast as confirmed enemies of human decency.

In normal times, the characteristic most often imputed to the Germans, thoroughness, would have constituted a compliment. But in wartime it was a moral defect, implying an inhuman mechanism, monotony, and rigidity. Heartless classification and analysis were considered a German specialty, and German soldiers were said to have a passion for straight lines and rigid postures. In one British theater showing a newsreel scene of German soldiers standing at exaggerated attention, someone was heard to shout, "Take t'coat hanger out then." [14] RAF bomber crews were not often deceived by decoy burning cities located five to ten miles from the actual ones because the fake fires were disposed in lines that were too straight. One photograph in Len Deighton's *Fighter* (1977) carries this legend:

> *Junkers JU 88 Bomber Crews Go to Work.* Most of the photographs . . . of the airmen, German and British . . . are strikingly alike—as the fliers pat their dogs, play chess, or relax near their aircraft—but it would be difficult to imagine RAF crews marching to their aircraft in the long rays of the early-morning sun singing as these men do. [15]

The German aircrewmen depicted there are marching in three precise files, an officer at their head, past a line-up of planes. And of course the group singing of such troops was more objectionably disciplined than that of the British or Americans could ever be. British General Sir John Hackett heard a lot of German army singing during his months as a prisoner of war, and he found himself offended by the communal abrupt "shortening of the final note of any line, as though according to a drill." [16] As a German characteristic, "thoroughness" was recognized even by the Germans. Visiting a Luftwaffe establishment in France in 1940, Josef Goebbels notes with satisfaction that it's operated with "German thoroughness," although it is "a very complex organizational machine." [17] Popular historiography especially preserves the German reputation for being foolishly "methodical." Thus Seymour Reit's *Masquerade: The Amazing Camouflage Deceptions of World War II* (1978) speaks critically of "the very methodical and systematic way" the Germans went about their visual deceptions. "Teutonic thoroughness" is the term for their technique,[18] and there is clearly something reprehensible about it.

While the Japanese were calumniated for being animals, the Germans were simply "sick," the very embodiment of disease. Hearing that the Germans have been manacling British prisoners of war (actually, in retaliation for the British order to handcuff prisoners taken at Dieppe), Mrs. Milburn explodes: "One can't think of anything bad enough for these diseased Germans. Their minds are all wrong."[19] Indeed, "They are like a loathsome disease spreading and spreading over Europe."[20] And a disease is what they were held to resemble in a whimsical "receipt" by which General Troy Middleton took over the town of Bastogne from the 101st Airborne Division in January, 1945. The condition of the town was said to be "Used but Serviceable," and it was held to be "Kraut Disinfected."[21] Sick or not, the Germans were different in every way. Even their planes sounded different. Flying over England, their motors seemed to throb, sounding like "grunt-a-grunt-a-grunt-a-grunt-a." Some heard in the throbbing sound the message, "It's for you, It's for you, It's for you." One report printed in a newspaper ("ROUGED GERMAN AIRMEN") could never have been fastened on the bestial Japanese, namely, that some captured German fliers were found to have rouged cheeks, together with waved, hair, lipstick, and painted finger- and toenails.[22]

Social envy and social snobbery, respectively, seem to lie behind Hitler's view of Churchill as "a superannuated drunkard supported by Jewish gold" and Churchill's view of Hitler as a "bloodthirsty guttersnipe."[23] Down below, where the troops were, the Germans had some respect for British soldiers but none for Americans. The Americans were spoiled, lazy, ignorant, unpolitical loud-mouths, and, as Goebbels put it, they seemed afflicted with "a spiritual emptiness that really makes you shake your head."[24] Few in Germany had any idea why the Americans had invaded Europe. One German officer could conclude only, as he told his interrogator, that they had attacked the Reich "in order to save Churchill and the Yews."[25] It was only their superiority in numbers, ordnance, and equipment that brought any victories to the Americans—and the British as well. High British officers privately admitted as much. Max Hastings observes of the state of Allied sensibility just before the invasion of Normandy:

Four years of war against the Wehrmacht had convinced Britain's commanders that Allied troops should engage and could defeat their principal enemy only on the most absolutely favorable terms. Throughout the Second World War, whenever British or American troops met the Germans in anything like equal strength, the Germans prevailed.[26]

It was only wealth that tipped the scales in favor of the Allies.

A sensitive German woman, Christabel Bielenberg, accidentally came upon an American flier hidden in a room in her small town. She instantly perceived that the war was lost when she observed "the general air of health and well being, of affluence, about him." What struck her was

> the quality of the stuff his overalls were made of, his boots and the silk scarf which he had tied into his belt, and a soft leather wallet he held in one hand. Suddenly I felt shabby, old, dilapidated, and defeated. Everything he had on was so real: real wool, real leather, real silk—so real and he looked so young.[27]

German troops could often tell when the "Amis" were nearby. Their positions seemed to give off a sweet smell, probably because they smoked Virginia, rather than "Turkish" and ersatz, tobacco.

Those fighting on the same side type-cast each other just as enemies did. One reason the Italians were held in such contempt by the Germans is that they seemed to resemble the Americans, with their unmilitary concern with comfort and their lack of the sacrificial impulse. But the Italians were patronized even by the Americans. One American officer in the North African desert was outraged to hear a German prisoner, asked what he thought of the American troops he'd encountered, assert: "The Americans are to us what the Italians are to you."[28] If the Germans were sadists and bullies, the Italians were dandies motivated by both vainglory and cowardice. Popular culture had them surrendering not just en masse but pomaded and scented, accompanied by framed pictures, birdcages, and similar domestic amenities, their elegant spare uniforms neatly folded in extra suitcases and trunks. One British prisoner of the Italians who was often moved from camp to camp was astonished at the Italian understanding of the comforts appropriate to commissioned rank, even when held by an enemy. He was allowed two suitcases, a pack, a blanket roll, and a case of books. "It never seemed to worry the Italians how much kit we took," he says, "since they regarded it as quite normal for officers. Their own took thirty large trunks, mostly full of different uniforms, wherever they moved, even on active service."[29]

Since it was not until late in the war that the Allies entered France, and since by that time there was little food there, Italy, even afflicted as it was by widespread starvation, became a place where the troops' food fantasies could sometimes be realized. In Taranto in June, 1944, one British soldier had an experience he set down in his diary this way: "Wonderful meal in T. Steak—eggs—cherries—white wine—macaroni—and Marsala." He added: "We should never have fought these people."[30] The Italian reputation as the surviving custodians of the cuisine depended in part on their fame in London as waiters and chefs and restaurant owners. Many were interned in the United Kingdom to be shipped to Canada out of harm's way. When a ship carrying them, the *Arandora Star*, was torpedoed and sunk, "a number of London's most famous *restaurateurs*," says Vera Brittain, "perished in the Atlantic."[31] Because the Italians were also associated with ice cream—making it, selling it, and eating it—British soldiers seldom let the idea of "Italians" pass through their understandings without some half-melancholy, half-contemptuous allusion to ice cream, a commodity rare in the British army. In one battalion magazine for February, 1941, a comic story, "Wops in Action," introduces its characters thus: "Alphonse and Toni were two soldiers in a crack Wop infantry regiment. On their right arms they wore three enamel ice cream cones, awarded by their C.O. for the smartest pair of heels."[32]

If the Germans were held to sing with conspicuous group discipline, "shortening . . . the final note of any line, as though according to a drill," the Italians were likely to burst into song out of the sheer "Latin" joy of being alive, a feeling intensified beyond measure by the hazards of wartime. Whan Farley Mowat's unit invaded the Italian mainland near Messina, there were no Germans about, and "since the Italian troops manning the coast defenses already knew that Mussolini had fallen, they were in no mood to die heroically in a lost cause." Thus,

> as the Allied column labored upward like an attenuated khaki-colored snake, another descended parallel to it, this one bluish-green in hue. The Italian soldiers came down from the hills, not like members of a defeated army but in a mood of fiesta, marching raggedly along with their personal possessions slung about them, filling the air with laughter and song.[33]

"A lot of opera singers" was Roosevelt's characterization of resident Italian aliens as he decided not to intern them in 1942.[34] And speaking of the association between wartime and cliché, "*O Sole Mio*" was the song actually being sung when Edward Blishen saw a group of Italian prisoners in England for the first time,[35] while some of the British in North Africa maintained that it was "to the strains of *Aida*" that the Italians planned to march triumphantly into Egypt. Says Tanker H. L. Sykes, "We actually found the music, the instruments, and the ceremonial dress they intended to use."[36]

When in the earlier war Frederic Henry, in Hemingway's *A Farewell to Arms* (1929), feels some guilt about deserting, Catherine Barkley comforts him by reminding him that "It's only the Italian army."[37] This myth of Italian military haplessness served a useful psychological function in the Second World War, helping secretly to define what Allied soldiers wanted the "enemy" universally to be—pacifists, dandies, sensitive and civilized non-ideologues, even clowns. The antithesis of committed, fanatic National Socialists. At the same time the Italians could serve as the definition of incompetence, fraudulence, and cowardice: no one really wanted to be like them to be sure, but how everyone wished it were possible! The world was laughing at Italy, and yet the Italians were sensibly declining to be murdered. The Allied soldier couldn't help wondering that if contempt and ridicule are the price of staying alive, perhaps the price is worth paying. While constituting one of the war's most simple-minded clichés, the Italians thus posed a challenge to cliché, shaking up and complicating the standard uncomplex attitude toward "the enemy." It was their presence in the war that kept a degree of ambiguity and paradox alive in a wartime world of stark and easily dealt-with oppositions. Were the Italians properly sized up by ridicule, as in the popular London dance-step The Tuscana ("based on the Italians' way of fighting, . . . one step forward, two steps back")?[38] Was A. P. Herbert right to refer to Mussolini on the BBC as "the Top Wop"? Or were they a serious enemy, more correctly treated respectfully? One who fought them, Peter Cochrane, in his book *Charlie Company* (1977), praises their courage, flair, and discipline, and goes out of his way to celebrate Italian skill in road engineering and artillery ranging and to note Italian compassion toward wounded prisoners. Is that the correct view? Or did General Montgomery have the right attitude when he told the troops preparing to invade Sicily,

"Someone said to me a few days ago that the Italians are really decent people and that if we treat them properly they will come over to us. I disagree with him. Our job is to kill them. That is what we have to do. Once we have killed them we can see if they are good fellows or not. But they must be killed first."[39]

Whatever the Italians actually were, the myth that they were the sweetest people in the war survives. The cover illustration of the American magazine *Men Today* for July, 1963, depicts a scene from one of the sado-erotic narratives within. Two girls are busy torturing an American soldier of the Second World War. He is tied to a chair. One girl, dressed in tight blouse and short shorts, is playing a blowtorch over his chest. The other looks on, coiled whip at the ready. The first girl is shouting, "Scream for my kisses, Amerikaner Soldat!" She wears a swastika armband. The other girl wears a German officer's jacket and cap.[40] The Italian wartime image becomes doubly clear if one tries to imagine the insignia and trappings of Italian fascism used with significations like these. They would produce not a frisson or even an erection but a laugh.

The force and to a degree the validity of wartime type-casting can be appreciated by trying to imagine German troops crawling on their stomachs through the malarial jungles of the South Pacific. Just as hard to conceive as Japanese soldiers defending the Apennines from behind mountain barricades built up from stones or determined Italian youths resisting to the death the American assault on the Rhine or the Russian assault on Berlin. Each enemy has taken on the characteristics of his primary geography, both literal and otherwise, and it is impossible to imagine them any other way. Similarly it is impossible to believe about one enemy what it is easy to believe about another. For example: according to Captain M. J. Brown, British troops once came upon a highly desirable billet abandoned by the Germans whose front door was invitingly half-open. Entering cautiously through a window to avoid the likely booby-trap, they approached the front door from inside and found attached to it the expected explosive charge set to go off when the door was moved. They left the house carefully and tied a string to the outside knob of the front door, taking cover in a slit-trench across the road. When they were all in the slit-trench, they pulled the string and the slit-trench exploded, killing them all. "The layer of the trap had anticipated their process of reasoning," notes Captain Brown, "step by step."[41] The Japanese would probably not think such a caper funny enough to be worthwhile. The Italians would, but would be too "unmethodical" to set it up efficiently. The Americans and British would like the idea but would be too lazy to waste time on it. But assigned to the Germans, the story, apocryphal as it may be, rings true.

And although a whole book could be devoted to the sort of stereotyping necessary for Americans (and British) to see themselves as attractive, moral, and exemplary, some of the conventions can be noted briefly. A good way to get a feel for the subject would be to go through any number of *Life* magazine, or *Look*, or *Collier's*, or *The Saturday Evening Post* issued from 1942 to 1945. Attending to the display advertisements, mostly in color, one would immediately understand the wartime thrill Americans achieved by imagining themselves good-looking Aryans, blond and tall, beloved by slim blonde women and surrounded by much-desired consumer goods. If the illustrations are to be believed, all young men are in the Air Corps, where they are officers almost by definition (or, in 1942, cadets destined soon to be officers). If by some misfortune they are in any other part of the army, they are almost never privates or NCOs but young officers beaming on their fiancée's assiduity in accumulating flatware of International Sterling. Notable is the absence of any features which might be interpreted as Jewish, or Central European, or in any remote way "Colored." The people on whose behalf the war is being fought are Anglo-Saxons, "nice people"—that is, upper-middle class. Readers of these advertisements could not help inferring that the war was designed primarily to defend and advance the interests of such tall, clean blonds, as well as the suppliers of the cars, tires, and refrigerators the blonds will own and exhibit once the war is won. If the Jews, like those in New York, liked to think the war was in some way about them, it's clear that most people didn't want to be like them in any way or even reminded of them. You could spend your life studying the magazine ads of wartime without once coming upon a yarmulkah or prayer shawl, or even features suggestive of Jewishness. Philip Roth's Alexander Portnoy, too young for the war but not too young to associate himself with the thrill of being on the winning and the righteous side, conceives of it as entirely an upper-middle-class Anglophile-American victory, less about the right to wear phylacteries than argyle socks and loafers.

The advertising artists sometimes had to face facts and recognize that many of those fighting the Axis were, regrettably, quite unromantic enlisted men, but such are generally depicted without women and usually alone, unwrapping a gift watch sent by the folks, celebrating the possession of a candy bar ("Boy! I'm strong for Milky Ways"), enjoying being included at a strange family's dinner table at Thanksgiving, waiting to board a train which, it is to be hoped, is not already full of idle civilians, or delighting in the Chelsea cigarettes included in a K-ration. The man shown in bed enjoying the luxury of Pacific Sheets is a Pfc., not an officer, because he is alone. Yawning and stretching in an ad in *Life* in February, 1945, he thinks, " 'Hallelujah, what a day is coming! A day when a fellow can drop his gear in his tracks, climb into a real bed as soft as a marshmallow, and s-t-r-e-t-c-h every last muscle! A day when he can feel again the caress of sleek, soft, white Pacific Sheets against his tired body.' " But when women enter, the male models get promoted instantly to officer rank, and their looks improve, too. Thus the woman enjoying a Honeymoon in Mexico on behalf of DuBarry Beauty Preparations is attended by her young naval-officer husband in whites. A young woman fortunate enough to have found a lover who appreciates the benefits of an extremely smooth Barbasol Shave is doubly blessed, for he is also an officer (branch of service not revealed). One young woman appearing on behalf of a brand of woolen goods is being met at her front door at a snowy Christmastime by a young man in a sleigh bearing a Christmas tree. At first glance he seems to be wearing an enlisted soldier's rough overcoat, but the ad-man has saved the day by remembering to affix a gold bar to his shoulder. Another young woman, lonely, has been left behind as a result of Rough Hands, but in the background wiser women who have learned to use Campana Balm swarm past in crowds, each with her date: only two are servicemen, but one is a naval ensign, the other a commissioned Air Corps pilot. If an enlisted man must be depicted in close proximity to a desirable woman, as in one ad for Chesterfield cigarettes, the situation can be salvaged by displaying on his shoulder the insignia ("patch") not, surely, of the 3rd Armored Division but of the United States Army Air Corps. In fiction or film, the GI might be Jewish or Italian, Polish or Hispanic or "Colored," but never in advertising, a medium where only ideal imagery can be allowed to enter. In advertising, the Allied war is fought by white Anglo-Saxons, officers or aviators, with neat, short hair, clear eyes, gleaming teeth, and well-defined jawlines. That is the wartime "we," fighting against the beast-like yellow-skinned Japanese, the "sick" Germans, and the preposterous Italians. Naturally we won. As Admiral Halsey said in his victory message to his fleet when the Japanese surrendered, "The forces of righteousness and decency have triumphed."[42]

10

The Ideological Vacuum

For most of the troops, the war might just as well have been about good looks, so evanescent at times did its meaning and purpose seem. The puzzlement of the participants about what was going on contrasts notably with the clarity of purpose felt, at least in the early stages, by those who fought the Great War. For many, that war promised not merely the repression and punishment of Hunnish barbarism. It offered the prospect of a healthy adventure, starting with a body-building vacation at a holiday camp. Great outdoor fun—that's what the First World War seemed to promise at its outset, as well as the chance to dress up in neat officers' uniforms with Sam Browne belts, the costume of the attractive young in the early fiction of F. Scott Fitzgerald, Katherine Anne Porter, and Willa Cather. The British style of joyous anticipation was perhaps more dignified and literary than the American, but fully as intense. Rupert Brooke found cause for actual thanksgiving toward (in those days) an actual Deity who, in the generosity of His heart, had provided the war as an occasion for British youth to wake up and cleanse itself. Like the beneficent proprietor of a great moral laundry, God had intervened in time, plucking the young from filth and corruption and trivial flirtations and cleansing them by means of His Grace. Or, as Brooke put it in his famous sonnet "Peace,"

> Now, God be thanked who has matched us with His hour
> And caught our youth, and wakened us from sleeping;

With hand made sure, clear eye, and sharpened power,
To turn, as swimmers into cleanness leaping,
Glad from a world grown old and cold and weary,
Leave the sick hearts that honor could not move,
And half-men, with their dirty songs and dreary,
And all the little emptiness of love![1]

That way of looking at a war would almost persuade the giver of thanks to celebrate the Central Powers for violating Belgian neutrality, thus providing the means by which God might work his redemptive operations.

An emotion so innocent and bizarre, so confident of right and wrong and secure in its sense of divine intelligence and design, is not likely to surface more than once a century. Those who fought the Second World War didn't at all feel that it was good for them. For one thing, they had access to a lot of profoundly unbellicose literature not available to Brooke and his enthusiastic fellows. If the troops of the Second War had not read, they'd at least heard of the general point made by Remarque's *All Quiet on the Western Front* and Barbusse's *Under Fire,* as well as by the sardonic memoirs of Robert Graves and Siegfried Sassoon. Many were familiar with Hemingway's understanding of military experience as vividly unfair and dishonorable in *A Farewell to Arms,* as well as with Frederic Manning's exposure of army life as not just pointlessly hazardous but bureaucratic, boring, and chickenshitty in *Her Privates We.* The result of this awareness was, as Robert E. Sherwood said, that the Second World War was "the first war in American history [and of course even more so in British history] in which the general disillusionment preceded the firing of the first shot."[2] Or as Rupert Croft-Cooke recalls the outbreak of the war, "We were all conscientious objectors, and all in [the war]."[3] One of the actual COs, Edward Blishen, testifies that it was "the literature of disgust" from the Great War that persuaded him to opt out, and indeed, when it was all over, he concluded that "I think it was my father's war that I refused to fight."[4] The egregious contrast between the credulity and even the enthusiasm of 1914 with the disillusion of 1940 is the specific point of Herbert Read's poem "To a Conscript of 1940." For over twenty years Read had meditated, in memoirs and poems, on the meaning of the Great War to himself and others caught up in it. In this poem he posits the ghost of a soldier from the former war who addresses a "conscript"—the word seems carefully chosen—of this one. His message is one of disillusion bravely borne:

We went where you are going, into the rain and the mud;
We fought as you will fight
With death and darkness and despair;
We gave what you will give—our brains and our blood.

We think we gave in vain. The world was not renewed.
There was hope in the homestead and anger in the streets
But the old world was restored and we returned
To the dreary field and workshops, and the immemorial feud

Of rich and poor. Our victory was our defeat. . . .

Knowing that, the only wise course for the Second-War conscript is to
fight without any hope that his labor and suffering will result in good.
"My brother and my ghost," says the shade from the Great War,

> if you can go
> Knowing that there is no reward, no certain use
> In all your sacrifice, then honor is reprieved.

Indeed, the only appropriate awareness to bring to the new war is that

> To fight without hope is to fight with grace.[5]

Asked in 1940 what he feels about the war, E. M. Forster replies, "I
don't want to lose it. I don't expect Victory (with a big V!), and I can't
join in any build-a-new-world stuff. Once in a lifetime one can swallow
that, but not twice."[6] Virtually everyone agreed. As a motive for self-
immolation, patriotism was now obsolete, as a Canadian soldier perceived: "Who the hell dies for King and Country any more? That crap
went out in the first world war." What caused him to enlist was a consid-
erably less noble motive—revenge, for the death of a friend killed in
action.[7]

If for Americans, at least, the Great War could sometimes be imagined as a brief quasi-athletic lark, the Second War permitted no such
melioration by the spirit of adolescent optimism. In North Africa alone,
the 1st Infantry Division spent more time in mortal contact with the
enemy than all the time it spent—forming up, marching, drawing equipment, lining up at the mess hall, training, bitching—in all of the First
World War. And on December 7, 1941, the American navy lost in one
day more men killed—2,008, to be exact—than in all the days of the

earlier war. The Second World War, total and global as it was, killed worldwide more civilian men, women, and children than soldiers, sailors, and airmen. And compared even with the idiocies of Verdun, Gallipoli, or Tannenberg, it was indescribably cruel and insane. It was not until the Second World War had enacted all its madness that one could realize how near Victorian social and ethical norms the First World War really was. Unthinkable then would have been the Second War's unsurrendering Japanese, its suicides and *kamikazes*, its public hanging of innocent hostages, its calm, efficient gassing of Jews and Slavs and homosexuals, its unbelievable conclusion in atomic radiation. It was a savage, insensate affair, barely conceivable to the well-conducted imagination (the main reason there's so little good writing about it) and hardly approachable without some currently unfashionable theory of human mass insanity and inbuilt, inherited corruption. As novelists like Thomas Pynchon and Joseph Heller have understood well after the fact, the war was so serious it was ridiculous. Leonard Woolf notes that he and Virginia and their friends had determined to kill themselves if—*when* seemed a more accurate word at the time—the Germans arrived in England, and for this purpose they had provided themselves with poison. As Leonard Woolf correctly observes, "It is inconceivable that anyone in England in 1914 would have dreamt of committing suicide if the Kaiser's armies had invaded England."[8] Terrible as the Great War was, unthinkable then would have been such an eventuality as Magda Goebbels calmly poisoning her six beloved children before she and her husband killed themselves.

But if the Second War was that serious, it was never, like the First, imaginable as romantic. Even the air war had lost most of the chivalric magic attending it in 1914–18, and the use of the air as a medium and conduit for the German V-weapons quite thoroughly completed its deromanticizing. Forster wrote Christopher Isherwood in July, 1944, about the flying bombs: "I think they are going to be important psychologically." he said, "They will bitch the Romance of the Air—war's last beauty-parlor."[9]

Among those fighting there was an unromantic and demoralizing sense that it had all been gone through before. For all its danger, the Second War often came close to being boring, with a sigh, not a scream, its typical sound. If loquacity was one of the signs of the Great War—think of all those trench poets and memoirists—something close to silence was the byproduct of experience in the Second War. So demoralizing was this repetition of the Great War within a generation that no one felt it appropriate to say much, either to understand the war or to explain it. "When in 1939," says Peter Conrad, "the catastrophe occurred a second time, the imagination was more reluctant [than the first time] to be enticed into the fray. This was a war to which literature conscientiously objected."[10] Conrad goes on to note that writers like Isherwood, Aldous Huxley, and Virginia Woolf had little to say about the war, while Edmund Wilson, John Berryman, and Delmore Schwartz often acted as if the war were not taking place.

The Allied soldiery tended likewise to silence, or at least to a disenchanted brevity. Stephen Spender reports that early in September, 1939, a friend was traveling on a French train carrying British soldiers. They "sat all the way," he told Spender, "in absolute silence, no one saying a word."[11] One would have expected them to act somewhat like soldiers of the Great War, talking of the contemporary equivalent of *Chu Chin Chow* or the contemporary equivalent of brave little Belgium, or at least of all the chickenshit they had to bear. But they seemed to feel that the less said, the better. In a British hospital in Normandy in 1944, everyone was very badly off and men were dying all over the place. Yet, as a nurse observed, "There were no impassioned calls to God, no harking back to mother, only an infinitely sad 'Oh dear,' from colonels and corporals alike."[12] At one point Simon Boulderstone, Olivia Manning's young lieutenant in *The Danger Tree*, tries to write a letter to his parents informing them that his brother has been killed. He tries twice. He suspends the first letter when he finds that he doesn't know how to tell them decently that his brother's legs were blown off. He aborts the second when he finds he can't write the word *dead* about his brother. He then bursts into tears and sleeps. When he wakes, he studies both half-written letters and realizes "there was nothing to be said," as Manning writes. "He tore the pages into fragments and threw them to the desert wind."[13] A similar vacancy faced Robin Maugham, obliged to write the wife of his orderly, killed by the same shell that has wounded him. "Everything I could think of to say seemed so pitifully inadequate," he writes. "The conventional phrases seemed indecent."[14] Boulderstone's and Maugham's problem is ideologically the Allied problem: a German officer could write that these men had died for the Reich, or for the Führer, or to forward the struggle for *Lebensraum* and against Bolshevism. A Japanese officer could write that the dead soldier had glorified his family and his Emperor. But what could we say? That the man had died for the Four Freedoms or for the principle of World Government, to be realized after the war? In late

September, 1939, Spender found himself deeply puzzled by the big question, What are we fighting for? Typically, his sense of a positive effort becomes an acceptance of a negative, his *for* turns into an *against*, as he runs the problem through his mind: "What are we fighting for? Personally, I think that we ought to be fighting a kind of defensive rearguard action against the development of absolutely chaotic and brutal conditions." [15]

When the war was over, for most of the participants there was nothing to be said either. "When I came back," a Canadian soldier deposes, "I didn't realize how silent I had been through those four years, and I became silent, or I continued silent. It was funny." [16] When the war was over, men of letters became silent too. As Karl Shapiro says, speaking of John Ciardi and the rest of the young writers who'd actually been in the fighting and had plenty to testify about, "We all came out of the same army and joined the same generation of silence." [17] Kurt Vonnegut was of this group. When he returned from the war, he says, he wanted to tell everyone about the destruction of Dresden, which he had witnessed. He thought that would be easy, "since all I would have to do would be to report what I had seen." [18] But he found that it took him twenty-three years to overcome his urge to say nothing and to tell finally, in *Slaughterhouse-Five*, what had happened at Dresden in 1945 and the way it had affected his own life.

Less said the better, as John Pudney says in his poem "Missing," deploring the death of his friend "Smith," an unread book on a shelf.

> No roses at the end
> Of Smith, my friend.
>
> Words will not fill the post
> Of Smith, the ghost. [19]

No roses: as military-elegiac properties *roses* by this time have been thoroughly exhausted by their use in the Great War. Why repeat the roses again? Why repeat any of that stuff a second time? As Keith Douglas says in his poem "Desert Flowers," recalling the juxtaposition of a trench-flower and trench-death in Isaac Rosenberg's Great War poem "Break of Day in the Trenches,"

> Rosenberg I only repeat what you were saying.

While Pudney's minimalist little poem is implying that elegy is no longer possible, it is shrewdly at work demonstrating the opposite, if in eloquently attenuated form. It is like Gavin Ewart's "When a Beau Goes In," in which the point is made that

> Nobody says, "Poor lad,"

which is exactly what the poem says, but in sardonic mock-brisk lines. The irrelevance of traditional elegy, with all those accustomed words, is likewise the burden of the opening lines of Ewart's "For Whom the Bell Tolls":

> Aircrews have had it and the war goes on
> And I have had it if I die tomorrow,
> Not needing the marvellous conceits of Donne
> Or any word of fear or sound of sorrow.[20]

"The art of litotes"—that's one young officer's way of describing the British style of phlegmatic understatement.[21] It serves as well to suggest the mode of Second World War poetry. One inference might be that the more verbally confident poetry of the Great War emerged from a proud verbal culture, where language was trusted to convey and retain profound, permanent meaning, while the later world from which these laconic notations arise is one so doubtful of language that the responsible feel that only the fewest words, debased as they have been by advertising, publicity, politics, and the rhetoric of nationalism, should be hazarded. In his poem "Memorial to the Great Big Beautiful Self-Sacrificing Advertisers," Frederick Ebright, sick of self-serving ads like, say, the one proclaiming,

> Because Bomber Crews Must Have "Victory
> Vitamin C", maybe your *canned* Florida
> Grapefruit Juice IS OVER NAZI ROOF
> TOPS TONIGHT!

concludes with the line

> There is dignity in silence.[22]

Silence, or any related refusal to mourn, is so little associated with "poetry" that the phrase *war poetry* is likely less to evoke the emanations of the Second World War than those of the First. From this distance it's not hard to sense behind the Allied writing of the Second War what Susan Sontag will later designate, speaking of the plays of Pinter and Beckett, the films of Bergman, and the writings of Ponge and Robbe-Grillet, "The Aesthetics of Silence." "As the prestige of language falls," she says, "that of silence rises."[23] A similar suspicion of the taken-for-granted and the prolix is what Tom Wolfe seems to infer in the drawings Ronald Searle made while a prisoner of the Japanese in Malaysia. "His drawings of British soldiers dying of cholera," says Wolfe, "seemed all the more powerful for the sparseness of his technique. Some had been done with makeshift markers, such as burnt-out matches."[24] Second World War technology made it possible to be killed in virtual silence—at least so it appeared. When in a tank battle a distant tank was hit and entered by an armor-piercing projectile, the only sound heard by those connected in the same radio network was a light "click." A British tankman recalls:

> Suddenly, across the Squadron Leader's voice came a sharp ominous click. We'd heard it before. We couldn't see the tank but we knew what the click meant. Charlie took over the radio network. The others obeyed his orders calmly, resolutely, as if it were the most natural thing in the world for their comrade to depart suddenly like that—with a click as adieu.[25]

The war was simply "a bad job that had to be got through"[26]— Melvyn Bragg's designation is one that those close to the war would agree with. The war seemed so devoid of ideological content that little could be said about its positive purposes that made political or intellectual sense, especially after the Soviet Union joined the great crusade against what until then had been stigmatized as totalitarianism. After that embarrassment, less said the better indeed. Not that there wasn't quite a bit of trying to attach profound, noble meaning to events. In the middle of *The Last Enemy* (1942), Richard Hillary's account of early RAF fighting, Hillary has seen fit to insert a "philosophic dialogue" occupying many pages in which he and another pilot consider what the war's about. But the debate gets nowhere. Hillary's interrupting his exciting narrative to supply this inert passage suggests that some sort of explanation of the war is required and must be supplied, no matter how damaging aesthetically or intellectually. After this embarrassing *pro forma* ideological intrusion, the narrative resumes, re-installing the reader satisfyingly back into the middle of events, quite ready to forget and forgive the implausible intervention of the rationalizing intellect.[27]

The night before V-E Day the British poet Patric Dickinson wondered what it had all meant and came up with the lines,

> There are no words to be said . . .
> Tomorrow night a war will end.[28]

The war might be considered to have been about bringing to light the horrors of the German extermination camps and punishing the guilty. But if that turned out to be the purpose, what about the Katyn Massacre, where the Soviets murdered as much of the Polish officer corps as they could lay hands on, and the readiness with which "denazification" and "demilitarization" were scuttled when it was found that a revived Wehrmacht could prove useful in preventing one's former ally from advancing further west? Even regarded as a cleansing operation aimed at German wickedness, the war seemed to disappoint anyone avid for significant meaning. At the end in Europe, Martha Gellhorn was at Dachau.

> "The war is over," the doctor said. "Germany is defeated."
> We sat in that room, in that accursed cemetery prison, and no one had anything more to say.[29]

At the end the exhaustion of England was particularly awful, but even then few expected the end-of-the-war scene to promise much joy. On March 31, 1945, Waugh notes in his diary: "Everyone expects the end in a few weeks but without elation; all conditions expect worse from the peace than they have had in the war." And four days later he observes again: "No exhilaration anywhere at the end of the war."[30]

Although the Jews entertained a different view, to most American soldiers and sailors the United States, at least, was pursuing the war solely to defend itself from the monsters who had bombed Pearl Harbor without warning. For the troops the war was about avenging that event a thousand-fold. Writing a friend from Chanute Field, Illinois, in July, 1943, Randall Jarrell says: "99 of 100 people in the army haven't the faintest idea what the war's about. Their two strongest motives are (a) nationalism . . . and (b) race prejudice—they dislike Japanese in the same way, though not as much as, they dislike Negroes."[31] The feeling today that the war was in aid of the Jewish cause, the current resentment that more was not done to relieve Auschwitz and similar hell-holes, slights the Pacific, anti-Japanese dimension of the war, which was the official— and unofficial—reason America had gone to war in the first place. (Germany declared war on the United States in accord with its treaty with Japan; only then did the United States, which had been observing Nazi anti-Semitism for years without doing a great deal about it, declare that Germany was its enemy too.) It was difficult, if not impossible, for most Americans to see what the menace and perfidy and cruelty of the Japanese had to do with the ill-treatment of the Jews in Poland (both by Germany, and, incidentally, by the West's newest ally, the Soviet Union). For most Americans, the war was about revenge against the Japanese, and the reason the European part had to be finished first was so that maximum attention could be devoted to the real business, the absolute torment and destruction of the Japanese. The slogan was conspicuously *Remember Pearl Harbor.* No one ever shouted or sang *Remember Poland.* During the war Arthur Miller worked 14 hours a day in the Brooklyn Navy Yard and observed there, as he says, "the near absence among the men I worked with . . . of any comprehension of what Nazism meant—we were fighting Germany essentially because she had allied herself with the Japanese who had attacked us at Pearl Harbor." [32]

What were the troops to be told they were fighting for, as opposed to their clear understanding of what, in the Pacific at least, they were fighting against? The often-repeated Four Freedoms was one official answer, but even sentimentally set forth on the Norman Rockwell poster "Ours To Fight For," they didn't seem to grab the heart, let alone the mind. The American services made an attempt to fill the ideological vacuum with the series of seven training films titled *Why We Fight.* Made by Frank Capra and the U.S. Army Signal Corps from both friendly and enemy newsreel footage, these were perhaps more effective in stimulating a necessary hate than in providing satisfying answers to the question implied in the title. For example, the final film abjured argument or persuasion entirely in favor of murderous command: at the end it presented head-and-shoulder stills of some of the Nazi hierarchy and ordered, with a *March-of-Time* timbre, "If you ever see one of these men, KILL HIM!" Although perhaps obvious, it's worth observing that such films would not have been necessary to motivate the Japanese or German soldier. Even the dumbest understood what their war seemed to be about. But Ernie Pyle, the most important interpreter of the war to the American public, never did understand what it was about or even affect to. Pyle's biographer reports his saying at the time of American operations in North Africa, "Fellows like Bill Long and you, who have roots in Europe, can work up a real hate about this thing, but I can't. When you figure how many boys are going to get killed, what's the use of it anyway?" "An unmitigated misfortune" is what Pyle called the war, and from Sicily he wrote his wife: "The war gets so complicated and confused in my mind; on especially sad days it's almost impossible to believe that anything is worth such mass slaughter and misery; and the after-war outlook seems to me so gloomy and pathetic for everybody. . . ."[33]

And it was not just among soldiers and journalists that uncertainties about the war's meaning arose. Older men of letters joined younger in wonderment. At the end of the war Mark Van Doren, looking back over the poetry produced by the contemporary "war poets," such as they were, confessed, "I suspect any war poet now who says he knows what the current calamity means."[34] That no very precise ideological appeal would work on the wartime audience was a fact accurately sensed by ad-men, one of whom, assigned to sell a lot of "IRRADIATED CARNATION MILK. 'From Contented Cows' " contrived a full-color, full-page magazine display. It depicted a young soldier sitting on his bunk, a picture of his wife on the wall behind him. He is scratching his forehead in admiration and delight at the news contained in the letter he's holding. The copy reads:

IT'S A BOY AND HE'S THRIVING ON CARNATION.

Many a nervous buck private flops down on his cot—trying to take in such heart-jerking news! Could any news be better? New life . . . coming into a new world we're fighting to make ready!

Clearly, any attempt to define that new world would result only in bafflement, dispute, and a severe loss of confidence in Carnation products. Vagueness is all.

As the war went on and duty grew heavier, casualties more numerous, and Allied purposes more confused, there developed a sense that sheer pragmatic unverbalized action on behalf of the common cause would somehow substitute for formulations of purpose or meaning. Again, magazine advertising is the place to locate America's secret convictions. In 1943 appeared a full-color double-spread ad for Goodyear products (then, navy blimps, largely). On one side of the fold, a mother at her doorstep looks up with shattered features from a telegram just received. On the other side, this text:

> What can you say to those whose hearts bear the aching burden of this conflict? That their sons have died in a noble cause? That the nation mourns with them in their bereavement? That these men shall be avenged, that we shall see to it that they shall not have died in vain?

And then the startling answer, *No,* which in the First World War would have been thought intolerably cynical and brutal. "No," the text continues, "you can't say these things and have them really mean anything." And then the ad-man's equivalent of Pudney's

> The ocean lifted, stirred,
> Leaving no word,

and Ewart's

> . . . nobody says 'Poor lad':

"You can't say anything—you can only do." All you can do, concludes the text, is "bend a bit more grimly to whatever task is yours in these stern times." Which is to say that former ritual words of comfort won't work for this mother now, not just because the Great War and subsequent history have already exposed those words' lack of credibility but also because since then the general secularism has had another quarter-century in which to advance its gains. Between the wars, "belief" itself has eroded.

"The Marines didn't know what to believe in," Robert Sherrod reported from Tarawa, "except the Marine Corps."[35] That is, if you embraced the right attitude, you could persuade yourself that in the absence of any pressing ideological sanction, the war was about your military unit and your loyalty to it. At Anzio American private Jim Alcock "wondered a bit about what the guys with me thought they were fighting for, twenty-year-olds mostly from the Mid-West, never crossed the ocean before. . . . If we killed we could go on living. Whatever we were fighting for seemed irrelevant."[36] And to kill effectively and go on living, you had to believe in your comrades. "It took me darn near a whole war to figure what I was fighting for," reports one soldier. "It was the other guys. Your outfit, the guys in your company, but especially your platoon. . . .

When there might be 15 left out of 30 or more, you got an awful strong feeling about those 15 guys."[37]

And if loyalty to your unit might ever seem an insufficient reason to fight the war, there was always the fall-back reason, which close scrutiny might expose as equally irrational: namely, to get home. To get home you had to end the war. To end the war was the reason you fought it. The only reason. John Hersey asked the marines on Guadalcanal, "What are you fighting for?" "A piece of blueberry pie," they answered. "Scotch whisky." "Dames." "Books." "Music." "Movies." Hersey translated these answers into the real one: "To get the goddam thing over and get home."[38] Sometimes a soldier would respond to the question with the official answers, and then think again and speak more honestly. One disabled veteran says, "I knew what I was fighting for. . . . Fighting to keep slavery and hate away from my home." But then, perceiving that he hadn't done himself justice with that answer, he disclosed the real reason: "Fighting to end this war, so that I could go back to my family and start a normal life again."[39] Even more-or-less official explanations often arrived, finally, at this lame reason for sacrificing oneself. General Montgomery knew that his soldiers were in no way to be motivated by ideological appeals. Hence, preparing to attack at El Alamein in October, 1942, in his "Personal Message from the Army Commander," which was read to the troops, he stressed only the motif of getting back home. "The sooner we win this battle," he proclaimed, "the sooner we shall all get back home to our families."[40] And at approximately the same time, an anonymous poem in the quasi-official American *Infantry Journal* made the same point but about the Japanese rather than the Germans:

> To kill is our business and that's what we do.
> It's the main job of war for me and for you,
> And the more [Japs] we rub out, the sooner we're through
> To return where they wait for a soldier.[41]

The soldier would be likely to return home on a Greyhound bus, and in an ad in *Life* magazine the Greyhound Bus Company made the point that in its view the only thing the war could be said to be about was getting home. Two pictures are juxtaposed. One shows a fighter pilot happily walking away from his plane, holding up three fingers to signify the three Japanese Zeros he's just shot down. The second picture, a view of the future, depicts the same pilot waving as he arrives home—by means of a

Greyhound bus. *"Another zero nearer that HAPPIEST New Year!"* reads the copy:

> The fighter pilot who has just chalked up his third victory is three long steps nearer the front porch of his home—nearer the girl who's waiting— nearer the happiest New Year a war-tired world will ever know.

The reader is left in the usual ideological wonderment: should the soldier despise the enemy for his cruelty and totalitarianism, his bayoneting of civilians, gassing of Jews, and hanging of partisans, or simply as an impediment to returning home? In 1943 the Office of War Information issued a child's propaganda coloring book in English, French, and Spanish, titled *John's Book.* "John's father," the book explains to its infant addressee, "is a pilot in the United States Ferry Command and flies the big planes across the oceans":

> There are so many planes and so many ships John feels that soon they will win the war. Then John's father can stop fighting. He can come home and have fun with John. . . .

If at the end of the book there's a little canting about boys like John growing up to be "free men," the reader is left with the unmistakable impression that the purpose of the war is only to bring Daddy home to John. Although to an adult that point might at first seem grievously simplified to fit a child's understanding, the truth is that there was not much more than that to say even to a grown-up. As Jack Beeching of the Royal Navy put it, accurately, in his poem "1944—On the Invasion Coast,"

> Our tongueless khakied strangers
> Fight their way home.[42]

Now, fifty years later, there has been so much talk about "The Good War," the Justified War, the Necessary War, and the like, that the young and the innocent could get the impression that it was really not such a bad thing after all. It's thus necessary to observe that it was a war and nothing else, and thus stupid and sadistic, a war, as Cyril Connolly said, "of which we are all ashamed . . . a war . . . which lowers the standard of thinking and feeling . . . which is as obsolete as drawing and quartering . . ."; further, a war opposed to "every reasonable conception of what life is for, every ambition of the mind or delight of the senses."[43] Both civilians and soldiers were right to perceive in the war, as Dwight Macdonald has said, "the maximum of physical devastation accompanied by the minimum of human meaning."[44] It takes some honesty, even if that honesty arises from despair, to perceive that some events, being inhuman, have no human meaning. It thus seems natural for the Canadian bomber pilot J. Douglas Harvey, visiting rebuilt Berlin in the 1960s, to say: "I could not visualize the horrible deaths my bombs . . . had caused here. I had no feeling of guilt. I had no feeling of accomplishment."[45]

11

Accentuate the Positive

That was melodic advice from Bing Crosby (and the United States Government) in the early spring of 1945, when everyone's "morale" needed a special boost, the war having gone on months (or even years) longer than expected. By that time, almost everyone had had a relative killed or wounded or knew someone who had, and one would have to be pretty unobservant not to perceive by that time that the war had something very gruesome about it. In the absence of a credible positive ideology, motivation was always a problem. Consequently, raising and sustaining morale became all-important, and morale itself developed into one of the unique obsessions of the Allies in the Second World War.

It had never been unimportant in war, of course, and most military theorists had recognized for centuries the importance of what they sometimes called "the moral factor." Until the middle of the nineteenth century it was called *esprit de corps,* and why that term went out and why *morale* replaced it no one seems to have considered. Perhaps as secularism spread, the connotations of *esprit* began to seem objectionably proximate to things "spiritual." Perhaps some suggestion of moral justice or moral rectitude in one's "cause" was felt to be required, and *morale* supplied it. At any rate, by the time of the Second World War the term was *morale*, and that word, designating a mystique indispensable to Victory, echoed from all sides.

For those brought up in the neighborhood of the Great War, with its presumably clearer ethical purposes, a rather spare definition of *morale* had sufficed. The first edition of *Webster's Collegiate Dictionary*, published in 1936, defines the term this way: "Condition as affected by, or dependent upon, such mental or moral factors as zeal, spirit, hope, confidence, etc.; mental state, as of an army." But between the moment of that definition and 1951, when the revision titled *Webster's New Collegiate Dictionary* appeared, the Second World War had taken place, and now the definition of *morale* has swollen into a virtual treatise, even an *aria:*

> *Morale:* Prevailing mood and spirit, conducive to willing and dependable performance, steady self-control, and courageous, determined conduct despite danger and privations, based upon a conviction of being in the right and on the way to success and upon faith in the cause or program and in the leadership, usually connoting, esp. when qualified by the adjective *high*, a confident, aggressive, resolute, often buoyant, spirit of wholehearted co-operation in a common effort, often attended particularly by zeal, self-sacrifice, or indomitableness.

That's a definition sounding less like a lexicographer's than a rabid patriot's, and a patriot combining the characteristics of General Patton, George M. Cohan, a small sociologist, and Mrs. Miniver. Anyone feeling an urge to study seriously the intellectual damage wrought by the war could begin with an analysis of that definition, its rhetoric, its purpose, and its assumptions about its audience. In wartime, "high morale" became a substitute for all sorts of lost valuable things—the critical spirit, for example, or even, as John Knowles says, happiness itself, which "had disappeared along with rubber, silk, and many other staples, to be replaced by the wartime synthetic, high morale, for the duration."[1] In the Great War, the German home-front stomach had been the target of the former technique of mass coercion, blockade. In the Second World War, civilian morale was the target, and by the new technique, "strategic bombing."

On the Allied home front manufacturers of frivolous commodities like beer, chewing gum, and tobacco moved their products by arguing their indispensability to high morale. Tobacco especially. The whole matter of cigarettes in wartime deserves more attention than it can be given here. Let it suffice to note that anyone in the services who did not smoke cigarettes was looked on as a freak, and it was axiomatic that smoking, if a silly and costly and dirty pastime, was venial rather than fatal. A term like *addiction* was not heard, and one called a cigarette a *coffin-nail* with the deep-down knowledge that it was probably not all that harmful. Cigarettes were held to be absolutely indispensable to high morale and thus were issued freely, enclosed in field rations, passed out by visitors to the troops, awarded as prizes in sharpshooting matches. Part of the unique atmosphere of the war is provided by the constant scent of cigarette smoke, the automatic, ubiquitous actions of deep inhaling, borrowing and offering smokes, "field-stripping" cigarettes to dispose of the butts outdoors, and the cry, "Smoke if you've got 'em!" General Eisenhower, popular with the troops because in so many ways the typical Second World War American serviceman and thus sympathetic with their needs, smoked at least two packs of cigarettes daily, and when especially nervous, he went up to three or even four. As one advertiser put it,

MORALE IS A LOT OF *LITTLE* THINGS,

among them, beer, best consumed "with wholesome American food." Yes, "morale *is* a lot of little things like this. Little things that help lift the spirits, keep up the courage. Little things that are part and parcel of our American way of life." And again: "If your dealer doesn't have your favorite LIFE SAVERS flavor, please be patient. . . . It is because the shipment he would have received has gone to the Army and Navy."

One reason soldiers' and sailors' letters home are so little to be relied on by the historian of emotion and attitude is that they are composed largely to sustain the morale of the folks at home, to hint as little as possible at the real, worrisome circumstance of the writer. No one wrote: "Dear Mother, I am scared to death." Thus also the artificially cheerful servicemen's faces displayed in framed pictures in wartime living-rooms. From those pictures you'd get the impression that being in the war was really rather jolly, everyone's so smiling and jaunty. Sailors chose to be photographed with caps worn well back in a non-regulation manner, to enhance their air of boyish carelessness. Anyone in the army photographed wearing a "garrison cap"—the one with a visor and a disc-like flat crown—liked to remove the stiffening grommet—again, against regulations—and let the sides of the cap droop down, Air Corps fashion and thus romantic. In these service photographs "there seemed to be one pose

permissible," the cheerful "morale" pose.[2] As a result of the high value assigned to these morale photographs in frames, during the war advertisers learned that to depict anything within an easel frame was to imply its preciousness. Because framed photographs became, as Bevis Hillier notes, "all-important household icons," the easel frame moved into advertisements to enhance such goods as Yardley perfume, Jaguar cars, costly fountain pens, and items made of wool. "If it's in a frame, it deserves your attention"—both servicemen's relatives and ad-men would agree on that point.[3]

Those attentive to the maintenance of home-front morale became skilled at optimistic prose, one reason Robert Sherrod's grim *Tarawa* came as such a nasty surprise. Before his presence at that gruesome scene brought home the truth to him, Sherrod had taken a different line. A few months earlier, he had written about the fighting on Attu that destroyed the small Japanese garrison there. In a Luce magazine piece titled "Graves on Attu,"

Sherrod's object is clearly to soothe the home front by making sure that the truth does not leak through and threaten morale. The American dead on Attu, he writes, are wonderfully taken care of. "No nation handles its casualties as carefully as we do." For example, the contents of their pockets are carefully collected and placed in "a clean wool sock." To be sure, what might be called a mass grave—here, a "collective grave"—is scooped out with a bulldozer, but it is not really a communal pit, for at the bottom of this excavation "small one-foot-deep individual graves are dug by shovel" and "thus each man his his own grave. . . ." Those at home can be proud of the soldiers on Attu, for everyone has been "splendid." The chaplains have been especially splendid, braving fire just like the combat troops, laying aside doctrinal differences in burying the dead of each other's faiths. A fine example of Teamwork.[4] No wonder Sherrod, an honest man, finally rebelled and told the truth.

Sherrod's "collective grave" illustrates the indispensability to morale of euphemism, misnaming which is either disingenuous or cute. A panicky rout, at Kasserine Pass or in the Ardennes, is better not designated even a retreat: it is a *retrograde movement* or *disengagement*. A communiqué properly drafted can turn a disaster into a virtual victory, a Dunkirk into a triumph: "Our troops were successfully disengaged during the night," or "By magnificent co-operation among all arms, we succeeded in straightening the line." *Mopping up* after an attack suggests household cleansing, rather like *cleaning* an enemy *out* of some remaining positions, or quasi-domestically, *pockets* of resistance. (Impossible not to think of hot water and strong soap.) In a similar way, failure in flight school or officer candidate school is not really a disgrace and scandal: it is only *washing out,* suggestive of a hygienic household event and thus almost beneficial when you think of it the right way. *Battle fatigue* (United States) and *battle exhaustion* (United Kingdom) became ways of suggesting that a little rest-up would be enough to restore to useful duty a soldier more honestly designated *insane.* The morale of black work gangs, stevedores and pick-and-shovel crews, was a continuous problem for the Americans, who found it could be eased by honorific unit designations like Engineers or Quartermasters. But even before entering the army the troops had grown accustomed to euphemism, what with *Selective Service* for draft and *inductee* for conscript. When the Allies invaded France in 1944, they did no such thing: they *liberated* it (a usage suggested to Roosevelt by the newspaperman Douglas S. Freeman). One of Roosevelt's shrewdest euphemisms was the concept *Lend-Lease,* implying business-like, even profitable, transactions with Britain and the Soviet Union, with loans properly secured and interest promptly paid. Actually, Lend-Lease mostly meant outright gift: the British understood that they would never pay for the 30 billion dollars of tanks, planes, guns, and landing craft sent them. If they had been obliged to pay, the economic collapse of the British Empire might have occurred right during the war—an embarrassment for all hands—rather than waiting until it was over. Another American triumph of nomenclature was the term applied to the B-17 bomber, *Flying Fortress*, with its suggestion of a vaguely chivalric venue and a purpose largely defensive. These overtones could be reinforced by referring to the plane as *she*, a usage honored by *Life* magazine whenever possible. While the Germans chose to sustain morale by giving their tanks names suggesting ferocity, like *Tiger* and *Panther*, the Allies leaned toward high-mindedness, as in the name of the British tank *Crusader*.

The threat to British home-front morale by prolonged bombing required a whole collection of euphemisms. Not "Where did the bomb hit?" but "Where is the incident?" That term for a local disaster became so habitual that Tom Driberg, a skeptical and sophisticated person, still writes in 1977 of the effects of that ghastly experience known as "The Wednesday": "As I got near the incident I had to step over doors and window frames that had been hurled bodily into the road."[5] It was better for morale if the German V-1 flying bomb was designated, cutely, a "doodlebug," and when the more frightening V-2 rocket bomb came along, its booms and concussions at first were designated "gas main explosions." Half seriously and half skeptically, many were soon calling the rockets "flying gas mains." From General Montgomery's practice of designating a forthcoming battle a *party* to the RAF's calling a 4000-pound bomb a *cookie*, the British showed a marked talent for using subtle nomenclature to soothe fears. *Battledress* is an example. That term seems to redeem some of the horror of *battle* by associating it with the harmless charms of normal *dress*, as in "Do we dress for dinner?" or "Oh, what a lovely dress!" The British newspapers, adept as always at turning the serious trivial, devised many cute usages in aid of morale. One was the term *coventried* to describe any place as bomb-ruined as Coventry. This led untimately to such a headline as

HAMBURG HAS BEEN HAMBURGERED!

The CO Edward Blishen observed this example with horror, and interpreted it as an index of an undeniable "coarsening of responses. . . ."

On all sides, he says, "the tragic evolution of war was commented on in the language of a gang fight in a school playground." And prophetically he perceived that "such an orgy of brutal over-simplification [would] shape attitudes that would last a lifetime."[6]

Much accentuating of the positive—with attendant coarsening of responses—was the result of the Allies' adolescent "V for Victory" campaign. It is said to have been initially devised by the BBC, which got into the habit of associating the first notes of Beethoven's Fifth Symphony with the Morse signal for "V." Soon, the two became inseparable. "One of Beethoven's liveliest works," announced an ad for a British concert featuring the Fifth Symphony. "A grand piece, with victory emphasized throughout."[7] For years, nothing was apparently fit to appear without *Victory* attached to it. A vegetable garden was not a wartime garden but a *victory garden*. *Victory* taxicab companies sprang up everywhere. Film theaters were re-named *Victory*. The bad cigarettes issued British troops were called *Victory* cigarettes. Teenage girls friendly with soldiers became *Victory* girls.

Without *Victory*, advertising could hardly have survived: as a Pabst Beer ad commanded in August, 1942 (when, to be sure, the need was great), "Drink a Blue Ribbon Toast to Victory." Elizabeth Arden came out with a V-for-Victory (or "Victory Red") Lipstick, and in shop windows and on counters, any merchandise that could be arranged in Vs, like cakes of soap or canned goods, was. Ersatz or "utility" items justified their defectiveness with the Victory designation. In the United States, one cheap "he-man's utility coat," with fake fur collar, was depicted in an ad worn by a man with an air-raid warden's brassard. It was a "Victory Coat." In Occupied France, the victory knock (· · · ——) was said to be used by Allied escapees from German *Stalags* seeking sanctuary in French, Belgian, or Dutch houses, and the Morse signal was sent by flashlight, especially in the Vercors area of France, to Allied planes looking for the places to drop their loads of arms and supplies. Hardly anything visual was immune to the visitations of *Victory*. One standard three-cent U.S. postage stamp showed an eagle with hypertrophied wings extended abnormally high above it to form a V, with "Win the War" inscribed across its "waist." Publishers were not behindhand in joining the procession. In 1943 Random House was using a colophon combining their little-house trademark with a backdrop V, drawn as if made of wood.

Churchill's well-known V finger gesture was, in Britain at least, rich with ironic symbolism. He always made the gesture with the front of his hand to the audience, but by turning the hand with its back to the audience, especially with a brisk upward movement, you had the obscene gesture (equivalent to "the finger" in the USA) known among British schoolboys as "The Fig," betokening "Up yours!" Churchill, the perpetual schoolboy, was certainly aware that his gesture carried both positive and negative meanings, signaling to the British *Victory,* but to Hitler, *Guard Your Ass!* Members of the RAF were fond of making the V sign mock-innocently with the hand turned around. Once popularized, numerous variations could be worked on the official meaning of V. The Americans retreating in the Philippines in early 1942, critical of the native infantry swarming past toward the rear but giving the V sign as they passed and saying, "V for Victory, Joe," were met with the contemptuous response, "V for Vacate, Joe."[8] And soon the dispirited Americans were chalking Vs on the front of their helmets, which they said stood for *Victims.*[9]

The Allied V-for-Victory cliché became so popular as a morale raiser that the enemy had to adopt it, an easier task for the Italians, whose Vs displayed in public could be held to stand for *Vinceremos,* or We Will Win, than for the Germans, embarrassed by the fact that properly their V for Victory should be *S für Sieg.* No matter: just change *Sieg* to *Viktoria,* alluding to the "Germano-Latin" tradition, and an immense V made of light-colored panels could be run up on the Eiffel Tower above the words (this was before the Normandy invasion)

DEUTSCHLAND SIEGT AUF ALLEN FRONTEN.

The military has long known that the soldier's morale is sustained not just by plenty of badges and medals and by ample access to alcohol and, when possible, non-infectious sexual intercourse but by the irrational conviction on the part of each soldier that he has the honor of serving in the best squad in the best platoon in the best company in the best battalion in the best regiment, etc., in the army. Modify each of these units with *damned* or *goddamned* and you would come close to what an American soldier with high morale might be led to say. In Scottish units, a similar conviction would be expressed by the noisy whoop, "Wha's like us?" An equally useful irrational belief is the conviction that one is invincible and indestructible because one is so uniquely intelligent, agile, and skillful. Such self-delusion seldom survives a few bombing missions or a few weeks on the line. Then the terror and despair are the deeper as a result of cleaving to such happy delusions.

Another way for those in charge to raise service morale is by outright lies, as in the U.S. Navy's assuring its personnel that danger from sharks has been greatly exaggerated. Indeed, the Navy said, "Sharks are amazingly overrated, there being only three cases of shark bite in all Navy records."[10] Romantic fiction is another help, the kind Sherrod produced about tender loving care on Attu and the kind appearing in popular periodicals, both civilian and service, reporting *beaux gestes* and gaily heroic remarks. Morale depended deeply on these folk fictions. After the Battle of the Bulge, Louis Simpson found himself in a hospital in Paris, recovering from frozen feet. He learned nothing about the battle, he says, from his ward-mates. "We didn't want to discuss what we had seen. . . . But we read *Time* and *Yank* and *The Stars and Stripes* avidly, and what's more, we believed what we read. If Jimmy Cannon reported a 'doughboy' as saying, 'Well, they have us surrounded, the poor bastards!' perhaps the man *did* say it, and we liked to think we would have said it too."[11]

One reason the services were so concerned about morale, a reason that would never appear in *Time*, *Yank* or *The Stars and Stripes*, was the Allied desertion rate. At one point there were said to be around 12,000 armed deserters in Italy alone, 2000 of them British.[12] Of the 19,000 or so acknowledged deserters from the American army, only 9000 had been found by 1948, while at the same time some 20,000 in flight from British chickenshit and onerous duty remained unapprehended. As Pete Grafton reveals in his book *You, You, and You*, the British, having fought longer, came nearer than the Americans to exhaustion and despair. Grafton quotes a man from Glasgow: "If Churchill instead of his blood, sweat and tears thing had said 'Any man or woman in the forces who would like to give it all up and go home, can'—he wouldnae have got the microphone out of his mouth before he'd been trampled to death in the rush."[13]

Curiously, something like Victorian "tight-lacing" is a subtle sustainer of morale, at least in the ground forces. Tight leggings and boots, tight belts and equipment straps, make one feel especially able and confident, even perhaps, for a while, invincible. One of the paratroopers dropped into Normandy attests that the pressure of his pistol belt and web equipment and his tightly laced boots made him feel actually encased in armor.[14] Costuming is important in other ways as well. General Patton is an authority here, laying down the rule that "Generals . . . must always be very neat" and warning that "in cold weather, General Officers must be careful not to appear to dress more warmly than the men." Indeed, Patton on *Morale, How to Keep It High*, is worth attending to. Naturally he recommends frequent ostentatious visits to forward positions by officers of high rank, and he notes that "the more senior the officer who appears with a very small unit at the front, the better the effect on the troops. If some danger is involved in the visit, its value is enhanced." As Patton's words *appear* and *effect* suggest, he is a master of the difference between external theater and internal actuality. One of his most brilliant suggestions to high officers working on the morale of their troops is never to be seen *going to* the rear. In visiting the line, go up in a jeep for all to see, but coming back, fly.[15] One gauge of the morale in large units, a gauge familiar to all experienced generals, is the size of the sick-call. At the height of his successes in North Africa, General Montgomery was delighted that the morale of his troops was such that their sick rate was one out of 1000 per day.[16]

"Morale is Mightier than the Sword": that was the self-interested view of the publicity arm of the American Motion Picture Industry in the full-page ad it inserted in magazines in 1942. To win the war, it announced, "Our minds must be as keen as our swords, our hearts as strong as our tanks, our spirits as buoyant as our planes. For morale is a mighty force—as vital as the materials of war themselves."

> And just as it is the job of some industries to provide the implements that will keep 'em flying, keep 'em rolling, and keep 'em shooting, so it is the job of the Motion Picture Industry to *keep 'em smiling*.
>
> Yes, that is our war-time job. We cannot build combat planes or bombers . . . we cannot make tanks or guns or ships. But we *can* build morale. . . .

But for the real mystique of morale at its purest one would have to turn to the Germans, and to the Germans *in extremis*, in the black hours of 1944 and 1945. It was then that Hitler, caught up like everyone else in the publicity craze, had occasion often to designate cities hard pressed by the enemy *fortresses*. He imagined—or affected to imagine—that by calling a city a *fortress*, like *Fortress Karlsruhe*, and so designating it officially and publicly, you actually made it stronger. Sustained by his belief in the power of the will, persuaded that steady resolve is the equivalent of countless tanks and guns and planes, thoroughly agreeing with the American

Motion Picture Industry that "Morale is a mighty force—as vital as the materials of war themselves," Hitler saw to it that orders like the following, issued in August, 1944, streamed from his headquarters:

> The OKW [*Oberkommando Wehrmacht*] will henceforth often be no longer able to meet demands, however urgent and justifiable, for air, armor, and artillery support, even when enemy superiority is overwhelming. Any shortages of weapons, therefore, must be made good by strengthening the morale of the troops.[17]

To motivate those German soldiers you would remind them of their sacred oath to the Führer. To motivate Allied, and especially American, soldiers, you would persuade them that their actions would receive "credit" by means of the immense wartime publicity apparatus. A notable event in contemporary history occurred at the beginning of the war, when the Commandant of the United States Marine Corps, anxious that his arm of the service enjoy all the credit in his view due it, called on the J. Walter Thompson advertising agency in New York to supply an adviser. From this humble beginning grew the Second World War occupational specialty of Public Relations Officer. Swarms of these, emanating from ad agencies and newspaper and public-relations firms, attended the troops—in combat, not too closely—and provided for hometown consumption the necessary heroic-romantic narrative and imagery. Since the war could only doubtfully be understood as ideological, something else had to serve as a spring of action. The spring was found in publicity. Compared with all previous wars, the Second was uniquely the Publicity War, and by the 1960s service publicity had solidified into an institution. Visiting the United States then, Anthony Powell was told by one ex-marine that each month many men in the Corps chose to contribute a dollar or so to the USMC publicity fund.[18] And the army rapidly learned to ape the Marine Corps. The reader opening a *Pictorial Review*, published in 1944 at Fort Benning, Georgia, to indicate the sort of activities going on there, will find the first page of editorial matter devoted to photographs of ten officers—one lt.-colonel, three majors, two captains, and four first lieutenants. Are these officers commanders of troops? Or perhaps eminent instructors of the infantry cadets being trained for hazardous leadership at the Infantry School? Perhaps they are decorated heroes fresh from overseas action, brought home to inspire the officer candidates? No, they are Public Relations Officers, ten of them for Fort Benning alone, and their work is clearly considered a vital part of the operations there. The quasi-official army *Officer's Guide* (1942), outlining the qualifications and duties of staff officers, deals with the Chief of Staff, the Provost Marshal, and the Fire Marshal in a half-page each, but lavishes six and a half pages on the activities of the Public Relations Officer.

So fast was advertising developing between the two World Wars that by the time of the Second, there was prepared for it a well-organized profession skilled at disingenuous presentation and adept at imposing value on the neutral or the nugatory. It might be going too far to suggest that every public relations officer aspired to the condition of Dr. Josef Goebbels, but it should be noted that a person performing the functions of Dr. Goebbels would hardly be imaginable in any earlier war. To have a Goebbels you have to have an atmosphere where presentation replaces actuality—that is, you have to have something like what we now recognize as the media world, where things are conventionally asserted to be true which smart people know are false. Goebbels conceived that absolutely anything could be believed, so long as it was asserted officially with a straight face. For example, his propaganda magazine *Signal* reported in the early 1940s:

> When, after his work is completed, the Führer gives free rein to his thoughts and talks, these are the most beautiful hours for his closest collaborators. Drawing upon his limitless store of recollections, he tells the merriest anecdotes and the most delightful stories.[19]

As the current popularity of periodicals like the *National Enquirer, Star,* and *Globe* suggests, the Goebbels world, or something like it, is one of the most noticeable legacies from the Second World War to the present. And in wartime, outright lies were not necessary. Just a little shading, a little tinting, a little withholding of unpleasant facts would do, as practiced, for example, by St. Clair McKelway, publicist and apologist for General Curtis LeMay. Formerly an editor of the *New Yorker,* he easily brought to his wartime task the same optimism and instinct for euphemism and the habit of never mentioning certain actualities that he had been accustomed to employ on that magazine.

Since among Allied troops a non-ideological "Pride in Outfit" became an indispensable element of morale, this was one thing the publicity arm focused on. One way of generating this pride, it was thought, was to write songs for the troops and impose them from above, especially songs glorifying such hopelessly unromantic branches of the service as the infantry and the construction battalions, or Seabees. The fraudulent enthusiasm and bogus pride of these songs, like the infantry's "We Are the Kings of the Highway," suggest their generic similarity to the neo-Pindaric odes of the later seventeenth century, public poems in which everything can be said except what is natural or true. By congratulatory songs or other means, every unit had to have its due, whether, strictly speaking, earned or not. Receiving sufficient flattery, it would perform its tasks, even if boring or loathsome, moderately well. But unflattered, its morale would sink, and it would grow melancholy and depressed, and finally unruly and even mutinous. The principle worked the same on the home front. To keep the morale of war-workers from drooping, the E (for Excellence) flag was awarded with notable lack of discrimination to shipyards and similar industrial installations. When workers at food-processing plants (makers of Spam and the like) began to feel slighted, an A flag (for Award) was devised to keep them satisfied. A total of 231 was conferred before the war ended.[20]

Thus both on the line and behind it, *credit* became a crucial concept, for the soldiers suggesting that ultimate value is assigned by the distant, credulous home-town audience for whom one performs by means of letterpress rather than by one's nearby equals who know what the real criteria are. That all-important home-town audience the troops never forgot. After landing in Normandy with the American 1st Infantry Division and after the trauma of seeing men from his platoon blown up or mangled and after losing most of his anti-tank guns and all his personal belongings, Lt. Franklyn A. Johnson still retains a sufficiently strong publicity consciousness to wonder, in his diary, "What people are saying at home." As he goes to sleep that night, aware now that in addition to the other disasters of the day his best sergeant has been killed, he can't help thinking about the impression he and others are making on the media audience at home. "What are the folks back home thinking," he speculates, "now that the Great Invasion has begun?"[21] That they are awarding proper credit (almost like teachers or academic registrars) is the hope Lt. Johnson shares with everyone in the invasion.

It was the main concern of Ernie Pyle to confer credit upon the humble and the normally overlooked, and it was to be expected that, as General Omar Bradley once said, "My men always fought better when Ernie was around."[22] Pyle specialized in what his profession called "Joe Blow Stories"—charming or odd vignettes of home-town boys designed for home-town consumption. He helped raise morale in the navy as well, telling his readers from a midget aircraft carrier in the Pacific, "The smaller carriers have had very little credit and almost no glory, and I've always had a sort of yen for poor little ships that have been neglected."[23] Accompanying the marines about to land on Okinawa, Pyle spoke this morale-raising message over the ship's loudspeakers: "In writing about tomorrow and the days that will follow, I'll try to give the folks at home an honest picture of what happens—so that they can understand enough to give you the credit you deserve."[24] And the truth was that most servicemen would rather have had their names appear in one of Pyle's dispatches than a medal, unless the award of the medal was very widely publicized. There is a complicated mixture of satire and sensibility in a cartoon in *Yank* depicting one soldier crying while another explains to a buddy, "Ernie Pyle misspelled his name."[25] One American war artist attached to an infantry battalion in order to serve the cause of credit and publicity recalls being told by the battalion commander of Pyle's importance. "He doesn't write well and if you are looking for any penetration of ideas, his column is a dud." But "his immense popularity is because he writes about and writes to the great, anonymous American average. They . . . are thirsty for recognition and publicity."[26]

Indispensable as they were to keeping up the morale of the troops, the correspondents, at least in the European Theater, finally accrued immense power. It was they who tried to get General Patton sent home after the soldier-slapping incident in Sicily. They offered Eisenhower's Chief of Staff, General Walter Bedell Smith, a deal: if Eisenhower would relieve Patton, the correspondents would say nothing. It was only because Eisenhower, after deep consideration, decided to keep Patton for later use in Europe that the correspondents released the news of Patton's behavior.[27]

To read widely in the wartime correspondence exchanged by persons of high rank and important position is to find that about one-third of their attention is devoted to matters of publicity and "credit." Indeed, many behave as if their main duty is generating favorable publicity. Thus the head of RAF Bomber Command, Arthur Harris, writes his superior, Chief of Air Staff Charles Portal, on July 1, 1944:

> I think you should be aware of the full depth of feeling that is being aroused by the lack of adequate, or even reasonable credit to the Royal Air Force . . . for their efforts in the invasion. *I* have no personal

ambition that hasn't years ago been satisfied in full, but I for one cannot forbear a most emphatic protest against the grave injustice which is being done to my crews. . . . They have the right that their story be adequately told, and it's a military necessity that it should be.[28]

Notable there is the phrase *grave injustice,* a wrong which depends entirely on the amount and credibility of publicity vouchsafed. Notable also are the words *their story,* which carry the unwitting implication that the war is somehow about plausible public narrative rather than political, moral, humane, or even military issues. And Harris's insisting that it is a *military necessity* that the RAF "story" be told exposes the apparent unlikelihood that his crews will continue performing as ordered unless they get plenty of publicity out of it. A future historian might be forgiven who, looking back over some of the ways the publicity war documents itself, concludes that the war was largely about just that—publicity narrative, that is, heroic fiction. And to be sure, a powerful postwar drama like *Command Decision* (1947) seems credible and effective because its audience assumes as axiomatic the indispensability of the right publicity. It might be thought that this play (later, a film) is about the "strategic bombing" of Germany. But it is not. It is about the way the actuality of wartime events can be managed by public-relations releases, and it rings true. So does William Brinkley's best-seller of 1956, *Don't Go Near the Water,* even though it is comic rather than melodramatic. The book is a series of sketches in the *Mister Roberts* vein about a U.S. Navy unit in the Pacific. In organization and style it apes a combat outfit, but its real job is producing Joe Blow stories and developing publicity narratives glorifying various naval officers and operations. The comedy arises from the wide gap between the actual and the asserted, and the reader is expected to assume that public relations as an activity is inherently fraudulent and absurd. During wartime, that news could never have been uttered, and if uttered, it would never have been understood.

As General Patton seems to have realized, virtually everything—except, perhaps, a soldier-slapping incident—can be "fixed up" by augmenting or shifting the publicity emphasis so as to generate more "credit." At a press conference in Luxembourg in March, 1945, he stated, he recalls, "that three divisions of Marines in the Pacific were getting great credit by reporting their tremendous losses, while twelve or thirteen divisions in our [Third] Army are getting no credit because we did not have tremendous losses." And he concludes: "I asked the newspapers to fix it up." [29] The soldiers consigned to the China-Burma-India Theater had much to endure, but not the least of their complaints was the failure of their public-relations people to garner much credit for them. It seemed that the correspondents sending back Joe Blow stories were all in Europe, transmitting stuff like this, from the *Clarksburg* (West Virginia) *Exponent:*

> Four West Virginia boys played an active part in knocking down Germany's buzz bomb rockets. These soldiers attached to the 125th Anti-Aircraft Artillery Battalion are credited with helping their divisions in 700 direct hits on these bombs in the skies over England and Belgium. Their names:

And four names of youths from nearby West Virginia towns follow. [30] Anti-aircraft gunners like these needed frequent stroking by the publicity machine, with the result that fighter pilots claiming to have destroyed certain German planes were annoyed to be told that some of the damage "was being credited to the [anti-aircraft] guns 'because they must be encouraged.'" [31] The marines who took Saipan in June, 1944, were angry that the Normandy invasion had occurred nine days earlier, grabbing all the publicity. The upshot, says a marine, was that "the bloody victory on Saipan never received its just due from the American media." [32] Giving all branches of the service their just due was one purpose of the rhetoric of Eisenhower's "Communiqué No. 1" issued on the morning of the Normandy invasion and published all over the Allied world to be read by proud parents and wives: "Under the command of General Eisenhower," it read, "Allied *naval* forces, supported by strong *air* forces, began landing Allied *armies* this morning on the northern coast of France." [33] Thus, no one could feel that he had not received proper credit.

The publicity competition among the various services reflected in that communiqué resulted in each being celebrated in its own virtually official movie. The Marine Corps was first with *Wake Island* in 1942, which is said to have occasioned a great rush to USMC recruiting stations. It followed this up with more, the films *Guadalcanal Diary* and *Gung Ho* in 1943. The army retaliated quickly with *Bataan* (1943). Then it was the turn of the Air Corps (*Air Force*, 1943) and the navy (*Destination Tokyo*, 1943). Finally the merchant marine got its credit in *Lifeboat* (1944). But the army infantry divisions in the ETO had no movie made about them, although it was their sufferings that seemed to call for the most publicity and credit. For that, they had to depend upon the copy generated by their own public-relations officers. Once the German war was over and the troops began to be sent home, *The Stars and Stripes*, co-operating with the Information and Education Division of the army, produced a series of little 4- by 5-inch booklets for the troops to mail home, each devoted to the heroism and grandeur of a single division. For those who were there, all are funny, but the funniest is the one for the 106th Division, which is finally obliged to acknowledge that two regiments or large parts of them surrendered during the Bulge but still insists that the 106th won a famous victory by forcing the Germans to "expend" a lot of troops, matériel, and energy. Or, as the booklet puts it, "The losses and sacrifices of the 106th Infantry Division paid great dividends in eventual victory." Or, as the Dodo puts it in *Alice's Adventures in Wonderland*, "Everybody has won, and *all* must have prizes." And now, almost fifty years afterward, the quest for "credit" is still going on. Witness this letter to the *New York Times* of May 14, 1985:

> To the Editor:
> Drew Middleton's "All the Guys Who Won the War," like most of the accounts I've been reading, made no mention of the American merchant marine, who were the first in the war, with three vessels sunk before Pearl Harbor, and the last out (six ships sunk by mines as late as 1956). Moreover, next to the Marines, the merchant marine had the highest per capita losses.

All this morale-sustaining publicity works, of course, because it operates in a society which has not just developed advertising to a high pitch but trained an immense audience to believe it—and enjoy it. The bywords of the war like "I Shall Return," "The Four Freedoms," or "The Great Crusade" are hardly distinguishable from those which for years advertisers had accustomed their audience to believe conveyed significant meaning ("It Floats"; "Not a Cough in a Carload"; "It's Toasted"). Indeed, to get anywhere, a wartime political or military leader had to assume the role of a memorable phrase-maker in the tradition of advertising display copy: "France has lost a battle but she has not lost the war."—Charles De Gaulle. "We will fight on the beaches," etc.—W. S. Churchill. "A date which will live in infamy"—Franklin D. Roosevelt.

During the Great War names like Haig and Foch and Pershing were well known, but the publicity mechanisms that might trumpet the names and merits of lesser commanders had hardly been developed. By the time of the Second World War they were in vigorous condition, and army, corps, division, and even lesser-unit commanders could now be celebrated. Glorifying General Montgomery's leadership of the British Eighth Army was the task of his staff member Captain Geoffrey Keating, who is quoted as saying that because England had as yet no popular military hero, "he set out to make one and Montgomery was now 'it.' "[34] Montgomery assisted the process not just by his unfailing self-esteem but by his instinct for eccentric personal signs—the Australian bush hat, then the tanker's beret with not one but two insignia—and memorable gestures like passing out cigarettes to the troops despite his known disapproval of smoking. It was natural that the publicity thus accrued by Montgomery's Army should be resented by other British armies less well-favored. One soldier poet, W. G. Holloway, outraged by this "unfairness," registered his annoyance in a poem sardonically focusing on the sad death-without-publicity of a soldier who happened to be in the First Army rather than the Eighth:

> His blood flows just as steady,
> His sharp wound cut as deep,
> The sand soaked just as crimson,
> By booted, shattered feet.
>
> But Praise's voice is muted,
> Seek no record of his fame—
> The poor boy died at Medjez
> And not at Alamein.[35]

General Eisenhower thought Montgomery excessively avid for publicity, although he himself, on one visit to France during the Normandy battle, was met by fifty newsmen—cinema and still photographers as well as correspondents.[36] These would have been laid on by Eisenhower's media expert, U.S. Navy captain Harry Butcher, whose rank attested more to his usefulness in the publicity struggle than to any maritime expertise: actually, he once confessed he didn't know the difference between longitude and latitude. Before the war he had been a journalist, the editor of a magazine, and an executive of the Columbia Broadcasting System, and it was his "main job," says Stephen E. Ambrose, "to serve as a full-time, if unofficial [which means undesignated], public-relations officer."[37] Despite his occasional apparent lapses into Kansas naïveté, Eisenhower was a shrewd publicist, who at one time sent an urgent message to Washington requesting the immediate shipment to Europe of twelve more public-relations officers (captains and lieutenants) to "tell the story" of tactical air operations in his theater.[38] General Omar Bradley also seemed entirely homespun and guileless, but he equipped himself with a public-relations staff as able as any. When he appeared on the bridge of the cruiser *Augusta* on D-Day, photographers were commanded to stay away from him. A horrible boil had arisen on his nose, and he had covered it with a clownish bandage.[39] A bit later Bradley, together with Eisenhower, went ashore to look around. One of the photographers covering the event remembers, "You were told which was their good side and which was their bad side, and you only photographed them from their good side."[40]

But the pre-eminent publicity hounds were probably Generals Mark Clark, in Italy, and MacArthur, in the Pacific. Of Clark, David Hunt has said that "his reading of Clausewitz's famous dictum was that war was the pursuit of publicity by other means." His anxiety to get his troops speedily to Rome arose from his fear that if the city's liberation occurred after the invasion of France, the news from Italy would be relegated to the back pages. His main war aim, Hunt unkindly observes, was his need "to be photographed entering Rome in triumph."[41] And it would not be going too far to suggest that General MacArthur's reputation as a strategist who never failed was fabricated very largely by his own swollen publicity organization, whose communiqués issuing from his headquarters implied that the boss never made a mistake of either perception or decision. In 1942, Roosevelt, Stimson, and Marshall all recognized the degree of fraud in MacArthur but let him get away with his act because in those black days morale required an invincible hero in the Pacific as an earnest of eventual victory there.[42]

Perhaps the most energetic and far-reaching public-relations performance during the war was what must now be labeled The Great China Hoax, worked largely by the Luce magazines. This was the attempt to persuade the British and Americans that Chiang Kai-shek's China constituted a menace to the enemy as formidable as the U.S. and the U.S.S.R. and that its powerful belligerency should be fueled by constantly augmenting supplies of arms and cash. China was really one of the Great Powers, the argument went, and should be treated as such. For the United States especially, China posed a problem, considering the long American tradition of contempt for Orientals expressed even officially in the Oriental Exclusion Acts. But after Pearl Harbor, embracing the principle that My Enemy's Enemy Is My Friend, the United States threw its attitude into sudden reverse and decided that if the Japanese were still swine, the Chinese were now noble. Lin Yutang became a vendor of the highest wisdom, Mme. Chiang's loveliness and desirability were obvious to all, and the Bureau of Motion Pictures of the Office of War Information issued a "suggestion" to movie-makers: "Do not show Chinese in menial, servant positions."[43]

As Barbara Tuchman has perceived, the promotion of the Chiangs and their China to high honors was one of wartime's most successful feats of accentuating the positive:

> Journalists . . . richly nourished twice daily at Chinese government press conferences reported tales of heroism. . . . China was seen as fighting democracy's battle and personified by the steadfast Generalissimo and his marvelously attractive, American-educated, unafraid wife. In their image Americans saw China strong in will and united in purpose.

There was virtually no mention of Mao's constant chipping away at the Chiangs' institutions of greed, disorder, corruption, bribery, and extortion. "Once firmly fixed," Tuchman goes on,

> this impression was unaffected by . . . the fiasco of the [Chinese] Air Force, which, after trying vainly for weeks to hit the Japanese warships in the Whangpoo, by mistake loosed bombs that caused 2000 casualties including 900 dead among their own people and hit the U.S. liner *President Hoover*.[44]

Wendell Willkie's immensely popular book *One World*, published in 1943, helped to solidify the myth of a high-minded, powerful, united, "democratic," almost Christian, Western-world-loving China. *Nothing* is an uncompromising word, but when she invokes it here, Barbara Tuchman means it: "The American public, blanketed under the active propaganda of China's friends, partisans and church groups, knew nothing of actual conditions."[45] It was only in November, 1944, when General Joseph Stilwell was recalled and began to speak out, that the truth about China began to leak, occasioning, as Tuchman says, "the long-delayed washday for China's dirty linen."[46] Stilwell's job had been to try to persuade Chiang's troops to fight and his officers not to sell for their own profit the supplies entrusted to their units by the Americans. Stilwell felt sadly let down, and his initial pity for Chiang grew into vigorous contempt which he made little effort to conceal. Stilwell's men were as disgusted as he with the China hoax and achieved some small revenge by referring to Chiang Kai-shek as Chancre Jack. It is well to suspect fraud when encountering letters home from American troops serving with the Chinese and praising their valor and devotion to the cause. They are as little to be relied on as later soldiers' letters home celebrating the courage and determination of the armed forces of the Republic of Vietnam. One marine stationed in Peiping just after the war speaks for most of his buddies in his disdain for Chiang and his main American mouthpiece Henry Luce, who during the war had displayed Chiang's noble features on the cover of *Time* six times. "When I got out of the service," this marine says, "I switched to *Newsweek*. We hated Chiang Kai-shek. [His government] was all rich people . . . very corrupt. . . ."[47]

During wartime a few sensitive and decent people recoiled, although seldom publicly, from this plethora of show-business and fraud in aid of "morale." "It is the falseness of everything that drives me crazy now," said Anne Lindbergh as she scanned a newspaper, "the false hopefulness and the 'morale' of the lying headlines. . . ."[48] Some bright people never got over their resentment of their government. One such is Dollie Hahne, one of Studs Terkel's most energetic and self-respecting interviewees about "The Good War." "I was lied to," she says, "I was cheated. I was made a fool of":

> If they had said to me, Look, this has to be done and we'll go out and do the job . . . we'll all get our arms and legs blown off but it has to be done, I'd understand. If they didn't hand me all this shit with the uniforms and the girls in their pompadours dancing at the USO and all those songs—"There'll Be Bluebirds over the White Cliffs of Dover"— bullshit![49]

A fairly accurate characterization, that last, of the whole fictive world projected by wartime Public Relations. But it must be noted as well that this unreal war, even if the creation of ad-men, could hardly have been otherwise. The multitudinous military blunders obviously could not be mentioned, and other interesting things could not enter the scene considered real by the public because they were so deeply secret: the work on atomic fission, for example, or the Ultra project involving the breaking of the German military-operations code, or the decoding of Japanese naval signals, or the work of the civilian coast-watchers in the South Pacific. Because these fascinating actualities could not be mentioned until well after the war was won, what was projected to the contemporary audience almost had to be fictional, an image of pseudo-war and psuedo-human-behavior not too distant from the familiar world of magazine advertising and improving popular fiction.

The postwar power of "the media" to determine what shall be embraced as reality is in large part due to the success of the morale culture in wartime. It represents, indeed, its continuation. Today, nothing—neither church, university, library, gallery, philanthropy, foundation, or corporation—no matter how actually worthy and blameless, can thrive unless bolstered by a persuasive professional public-relations operation, supervised by the later avatars of the PR colonels and captains so indispensable to the maintenance of high morale and thus to the conduct of the Second World War.

12

High-mindedness

The China Hoax could probably not have been worked so successfully at any other time, for it required a unique context of public credulity and idealism. If elementary logic—the only kind wartime could accommodate—required the enemy to be totally evil, it required the Allies to be totally good—all of them. The opposition between this black and this white was clear and uncomplicated, untroubled by subtlety or nuance, let alone irony or skepticism. Paul Addison is right to note that "the war served a generation of Britons and Americans as a myth which enshrined their essential purity, a parable of good and evil."[1] In the absence of doubt, and with the positive enjoying constant accentuation, the view easily developed that Americans were by nature, by instinct really, morally wonderful. Observing some marines on Okinawa making pets of baby goats, Ernie Pyle comments: "Americans are the damnedest people! Why can't everybody be like them?"[2] It was easy to persuade oneself of one's goodness when, as one young marine officer wrote his parents, "The Big Guy is on our side."[3]

For the successful pursuit of uncomplicated High Purpose, a profound chasm had to be opened between good and evil, and those two terms were wonderfully available to make high-minded sense of the war, regardless of one's maturity. A woman adolescent at the time recalls her attitude, which was not far from the official one: "I really wanted to be a woman in uniform and support this terrible war and overcome evil with good. America represented nothing but good to me. Our boys were good."[4] And a grown-up looking back more than twenty years later accepts the same terms and (with the phrase *absolutely true*) without qualification: "If that fight was not holy," says Eric Severeid, "if it was not absolutely true that the contest was between good and evil, then no battle ever was such. . . ."[5] And the division between other dualisms had to be as total as that, without shading or complexity. One British pamphlet of 1940 indicated how simple the issues were and how little you needed any critical intelligence to sift the data and find your way:

> Readers and listeners must not forget that no confidence can ever be placed in statements coming from German sources. . . . British news can always be relied on. German news never. That is a distinction of vital importance.[6]

(Belief in this point was easier early in the war, before, say, one could gather from German sources only that it was the Soviet Union, not the Germans, which had butchered the four thousand Polish officers in the Katyn Forest.) That the world was divided rigorously between "slave" and "free" was axiomatic, and when in 1942 the OWI issued a set of "suggestions" for Hollywood film-makers, it declared, "This is total war. Everyone is either a friend or a foe."[7]

Belief in anything was easy, so long as the thing believed in seemed noble and supported the Allied cause. Analogous to the China Hoax and equally indicative of idealistic wartime credulity is what can be called the Brave Little Dutch Boy and Wonderful British People Hoax. This was

brilliantly engineered in the months before Pearl Harbor by a rabidly
pro-British interventionist working as an editor at the publishing firm of
Harcourt, Brace, the writer Stanley Preston Young. In January, 1941,
anxious for the United States to enter the war immediately and help Britain repel an invasion felt to be imminent, Young rapidly produced a little
book of 95 pages as if written by a twelve-year-old Dutch lad, "Dirk van
der Heide," and translated by "Mrs. Antoon Deventer." *My Sister and
I: The Diary of a Dutch Boy Refugee* was published by Harcourt, Brace
in an edition which finally sold 56,000 copies and occasioned the Tin Pan
Alley tear-jerking song "My Sister and I." Dirk's book delivers an "eye-
witness" account of the bombing of Rotterdam, resulting in the death of
his mother and his flight with his nine-year-old sister first to Britain and
finally to America. While appearing to be a sentimental celebration of
Dutch bravery, the book is really a shrewd attempt to depict the British,
presumably Hitler's next victims, as especially fine and noble—selfless,
sympathetic, faultless in every way. These exemplars of virtue are currently in serious danger, as even Dirk realizes: "I hope the Germans
don't come there the way they did in Holland." [8] High-mindedness and
selflessness are the sole British characteristics Dirk experiences. No one
in the whole United Kingdom is impatient, not to mention snotty, snob-
bish, inept, impatient, or in any way unadmirable. Dirk overhears no
anti-Semitic remarks nor does he observe any slackers, black-marketeers,
or envious grumblers against manifestations of class privilege.

What is notable is less Stanley Young's making his child spokesman
entirely uncritical than contemporary readers' and reviewers' embrace of
Dirk's goody-goody vision as a plausible registration of actuality. The
Christian Century found the book "an authentic document," and Dirk's
presumed naïve accuracy as a reporter of people's behavior was found by
a writer for *Books of the Month* to give the book special value for the
ultimate historiography of the war. Even if it was Pearl Harbor and not
My Sister and I that brought the United States in on Britain's side, Stanley Young could feel satisfied that at the time, in an atmosphere in which
anyone on the Allied side could easily be conceived of as without spot, no
one guessed that the book was a pious fraud. [9]

Given the wartime requirements of elevated morality, it was not hard
(for Americans, at least) to understand the war as virtually a religious
operation, as Isaiah Berlin noted while serving in the British Embassy.
Reporting back to the U.K. about Henry Wallace's "Free World Victory" speech in 1942, Berlin invoked the term *apocalyptic* and observed

that Wallace and his hearers imagined America's role almost in Old Testament terms, as if the Republic were "the chosen of the Lord." Berlin concluded that America has accepted a divine mission to save the world."[10] No wonder little skepticism greeted Eisenhower's stately pre-invasion message to the troops calling the forthcoming operation "the Great Crusade," and no wonder eyebrows did not rise at his later title, *Crusade in Europe* (1948). For him and for many of the troops (at that moment) and for the folks at home, the invasion was, as he said in his message, a high-minded affair. "This great and noble undertaking," he called it, and he urged God to bless it.[11]

And in those days perhaps He did. Then, the Higher Skepticism had not yet appeared, fueled by the assassinations of the Kennedys and Martin Luther King and the others and by the Vietnam war and by Watergate and by John Mitchell and Spiro Agnew and by Irangate, etc. In the 1940s, by contrast, one notes a very "period" association of high-mindedness with traditional piety. A British woman recalls watching some Allied troops heading in trucks for their invasion ships. "As they reached one corner [in Dorchester] a priest stood there all day long with a lad holding a cross while he made the sign of the cross as each vehicle went by and the men bowed their heads."[12] In the same way Roosevelt's public prayer on D-Day would seem unthinkable now, with its reminder to Almighty God that "our sons, pride of our nation," are undertaking "a struggle to preserve," among other things, "our religion." The virtue of those on the home front will be all-important in the coming battles:

> And for us at home—fathers, mothers, children, wives, sisters, and brothers of brave men overseas—whose thoughts and prayers are ever with them—help us, Almighty God, to rededicate ourselves in renewed faith in Thee in this hour of great sacrifice.

Let us join, his argument went on, in beseeching the Almighty to help us buy more and more war bonds: "Give us strength . . . to redouble the contributions we make in the physical and material support of our armed forces." With "faith in our united crusade," and if we are all virtuous enough, we will finally achieve "a peace that will let all of men live in freedom. . . ."[13]

If each member of the Allies was engaged on God's work, there arose from time to time uncertainty about one's entire moral worthiness for the task. Are we virtuous enough? That became the anxious question implied in many wartime attempts to understand what was going on. One had to be aware of an obligation not just to buy war bonds and stamps but to be consciously a virtuous person at all times. Eleanor Roosevelt is said to have carried in her purse, to be consulted when necessary, a prayer presented to her by Sir William Stephenson, the Canadian in charge of British intelligence operations in the United States:

> Dear Lord
> Lest I continue
> My complacent way
> Help me to remember
> Somewhere out there
> A man died for me today.
> —As long as there be war
> I then must
> Ask and answer
> Am I worth dying for?[14]

One way to help assure yourself of worthiness was to pitch in, to abandon disbelief, sarcasm, pessimism, or any sign of heterodoxy, and to play the game with sincerity and devotion. Performing your duty had immense consequences, as one advertisement rebuking the careless suggested: "What's it to you that a kid just got bumped off in the Solomons . . . because *you* couldn't be bothered with scrap collection."[15] Wartime was a moment when everyone felt obliged to instruct others in ethics. Thus the Pure Oil Company scolded malefactors in a full-page magazine ad:

AN OPEN LETTER TO TIRE THIEVES

Tire theft has risen to new heights.

This is not just petty larceny anymore.

It is a direct stab-in-the-back at American transportation which is hand-in-hand with vital American production.

. . . For want of a tire the car was lost; for want of a car the man was lost; for want of a man the job was lost; for want of the job the bomber was lost; for want of the bomber the battle was lost.

That, including the clichés, conveys a fairly accurate idea of the self-righteous popular tone in 1942, a tone to be expected in a world where it was the obligation of the Allies and of all virtuous people to teach lessons in correct thought and behavior to others. Thus Churchill speaking of the Japanese in 1942: "What kind of people do they think we are? Is it possible they do not realize that we shall never cease to persevere against them until they have been taught a lesson which they and the world will never forget?" [16] Was it possible to reprehend Axis evil without at the same time sounding the note of self-righteousness, even priggishness? Auden was one who encountered this embarrassment. In "Sept. 1, 1939," after condemning Nazi wickedness, he first demands that we all be morally better than we have been ("We must love one another, or die") and then ennobles those opposing Hitler (including, of course, himself) as "the Just," who "exchange their messages" across the wastes inhabited by those not so virtuous. He is asking his readers to believe that it is virtue rather than power that will defeat the Axis.

One notable repository of high-mindedness is *A Book of War Letters* (1943), edited by Harry E. Maule, which collects a number of unbelievably noble and happy letters sent home by servicemen. One young sailor is quoted as writing his wife on November 7, 1942 (a moment when, to be sure, lots of optimism and high purpose are required): "We will be greater and finer for all of this—and the inner justice of our deeds will one day be realized in peace, harmony and universal love." [17] Even the relative impurity of the Allied ethical cause once Joseph Stalin joined in seemed easily accommodated to the general high-mindedness. Another sailor reassures his father, "Remember, Pop, I've got the great Red Army on my side," and then finds no intellectual awkwardness in going on, "This is the fight for freedom. This is the chance to show that a free people will win." [18] In collecting these letters, Maule has been struck, he says, "by the essential *goodness* of the writers." There are no exceptions, or even nuances or slight qualifications. The letters indicate that "our cause is in good hands" as a result of these men's "bravery and determination." All of them, without exception, reveal "the consciousness of a noble cause." Without any doubt these letters "invariably show a clear grasp of what we are fighting for." [19]

In that way, totems of the totally good were required everywhere. Hector Bolitho quotes Churchill saying of the King and Queen, "They have the rare talent of being able to make a mass of people realize, in a flash, that they are good." Citing this, Bolitho goes on to wonder how important "goodness" is "in relation to the war," and he concludes that there emerges "one truth: . . . none of the rulers of the Axis powers is

a 'good' man, in the sense that Churchill spoke of the King and Queen."
Not even Mussolini? No, he has been guilty, says Bolitho, of "untidy
morals."[20]

It does not require great acuteness to perceive what this ethically pu-
rified atmosphere will mean for writing. It will mean, among other things,
that E. B. White will replace H. L. Mencken as one of America's most
attended-to observers and commentators. And in Britain it will mean the
apotheosis of the warm and plummy J. B. Priestley as the voice of society
in general. That is, the age will demand that analysis, criticism, evalua-
tion, and satire yield to celebration, charm, and niceness. Increasingly,
the tone that will be felt appropriate to wartime will be the folksy, coy,
over-simplified, self-satisfied sound mastered by E. B. White, as in this
sample of his quiet, secure Norman-Rockwellism. He has gone lobstering
with a friend and he has been thinking about the war at the same time:

> It struck me as we worked our way homeward up the rough bay with
> our catch of lobsters and a fresh breeze in our teeth that this was what
> the fight was all about. This was it. Either we would continue to have it
> or we wouldn't, this right to speak our own minds, haul our own traps,
> mind our own business, and wallow in the wide, wide sea.[21]

That alone would justify Russell Lynes's description of White as "a sort
of Eagle Scout of American letters":

> Mr. White has won all the merit badges, his heart is pure, he can tie
> and untie complicated knots, and he knows the names and habits of beast
> and fowl and sprout and loves them all.[22]

One of the most interesting events of the war was Mencken's turn
from lively satire and attack to such benign literary effusions as sentimental memoirs of boyhood and treatises on the American language and a
dictionary of quotations. This total change in Mencken's production might
be imputed to his difficulty, as a former celebrator of the Germanic in
general, of continuing that act with the Germans now cast as a particularly vicious enemy. But another explanation would be that in the context
of wartime moral canting, his former mode came to seem egregiously
cruel, and his audience turned elsewhere. Wartime also marked Sinclair
Lewis's turn from his wonderfully sardonic satires on American fatuity
to more conventional and harmless narratives. It is hard to imagine his

writing anything like *The Man Who Knew Coolidge* (1928) during the forties.

Virtually everyone who wrote anything evaluative—with the possible exception of Cyril Connolly and Edmund Wilson—succumbed in some measure to the appeal of the new self-congratulatory mode. Goodness became the all-but universal theme, just as for the Jacobeans rape and murder had been stylish and for the Victorians, child-abuse, industrial wickedness, and the consolations of Empire. Even E. M. Forster, normally a highly critical intelligence, capable of sending up with a vengeance such sacred items as the Queen's Dolls House, is to be found, in his broadcasts for the BBC, laying aside for the duration his critical as well as his ironic sense and, for example, celebrating Steinbeck's *The Moon Is Down:* "It is very moving and it contains a terribly practical lesson for us all." Descanting on Thornton Wilder's plays, Forster notes that "Mr. Wilder has two great qualities: sincerity and compassion." Considering Greek tragedy, he concludes that of "all the great tragic utterances," the one that "comes closest to my heart" is *Antigone.* Not *Oedipus the King,* notably, with its paradox and moral complexities and irony, but *Antigone,* with its entirely unironic moral message about resistance to unjust power. "The strength of Antigone" as a character is to Forster exemplary, available and useful to all. In a broadcast titled "Reading in Wartime," he notes without irony or any other critical coloration the current popularity of "books of war morality, which try to make us braver and more unselfish," and in a later BBC talk he dilates didactically on "The Unsung Virtue of Tolerance."[23]

An example of what might be learned from such "books of war morality" is provided by Jan Struther in a long free-verse poem "Wartime Journey," which appeared in the *Atlantic Monthly* in 1944. It is about a trip on a wartime train that keeps getting later and later and more uncomfortable with each delay. Aboard is a "cross-section"—mothers, wives, soldiers, train-crew—who all behave with remarkable decency and friendship. No one (like Dirk van der Heide's British civilians) gets impatient or angry. No one drinks too much, and the soldiers *(mirabile dictu)* drink only water. No one talks too loudly or blasphemes to be offensive. The general understanding of the sacredness of the common cause makes everyone polite and decent to each other. The view of humanity is pure Priestley-Saroyan. The proximity of others results, not as we should expect, in exasperation but in a magical release from the normal "self-forged barriers to the human heart," as we are shown by a vignette of a black soldier and an elderly white woman whose common exhaustion allows them to discard their social fears and to sleep with heads nodding together. All have learned goodness.[24]

In America, a place more devoted than elsewhere to unironic earnestness and sentimentality, the high-mindedness situation was especially severe, what with the Librarian of Congress, Archibald MacLeish, lecturing writers all the time like a commissar on their duties and responsibilities. The battle between wartime high-mindedness and sharp critical intelligence is enacted in the encounters between MacLeish and Edmund Wilson. As early as 1928 Wilson was tiring of MacLeish's "bathos" passing itself off as writing for grown-ups,[25] and ten years later, having had enough, he satirized *The Hamlet of A. MacLeish*, a pretentious verse monologue by MacLeish as Hamlet, with brief marginal prose summaries of the meaning, à la *The Rime of the Ancient Mariner*. Wilson's parody, *The Omelet of A. MacLeish*, ridiculed the poem's self-righteousness and self-concern, as well as its unpersuasive artistic means and its evident sacrifice of sharp original vision to middle-brow success. Wilson brilliantly parodied even the marginal glosses:

He puts plovers' eggs and truffles into his omelet.	Nimble at other men's arts how I picked up the trick of it. . . .
	And the Polacks and Dagoes and Hunkies undoubtedly dead:
He is obliged to reopen his omelet and put a little garlic in.	And behold these savage and sybarite-baiting strangers Had many among them like me well-mannered well-fed Bubbling over with schoolboy heroics. . . .
He is doomed to go on doctoring his omelet.	A clean and clever lad who is doing his best to get on. . . .[26]

But a more significant encounter between high-minded MacLeish and skeptical Wilson was occasioned by a speech MacLeish delivered in 1940 before the members of the American Association for Adult Education. Here MacLeish as the newly appointed Librarian of Congress conceived it his didactic duty to exhort American writers (in his mind apparently identical with "novelists") to abjure the critical and disillusioned view of war registered by Dos Passos and Hemingway, as well as Barbusse and Remarque. That view has stolen from the young their idealism and hence their main armor against fascism. The anti-war books of these authors, written as a result of the Great War, "have done more to disarm democracy in the face of fascism than any other single influence." These skeptical writers, says MacLeish, have satirized and thus devalued words and conceptions and slogans necessary for maintaining high morale in war.

Answering MacLeish's implicit argument on behalf of niceness, blindness, and blandness, Wilson invokes memory and asks, "Were there not . . . very good reasons why anyone who had served in the last war should have considered the Allied slogans an imposture?" But MacLeish's worst offense against honesty is his suggestion, writes Wilson, that these days "writers should censor themselves in the interests of—it is not clear what." (High-mindedness, it would appear.) According to MacLeish, before speaking out American writers should consider what effect their utterances might have in the battle between freedom and fascism. Nonsense, comments Wilson: is it really one's duty to persuade writers not to voice "their true opinions"?

> Mr. MacLeish is at pains to tell us that he does not want to burn any books or to regiment people's minds; but it is not very reassuring, at this moment of strain and excitement, to find the Librarian of Congress making a fuss about "dangerous" books. He has a good deal to say about liberty in the latter part of his speech, but he makes it perfectly plain that he believes that, as a matter of policy, certain kinds of dissentient writers should be discouraged from expressing their ideas.[27]

If MacLeish wanted to discourage the cynics and wits, what sort of writers did he want to encourage? Those with a wholesome message like Carl Sandburg, as he had suggested some years earlier in his essay "Mr. Sandburg and the Doctrinaires" (1936). Here he specifically rejects the Mencken view of the United States as home of "the great American boob." If the effect of Mencken's satire has been "to poison the belief of the people in themselves," Sandburg's achievement, says MacLeish, has been to restore their conviction that they are instinctively bright and able. Or as Sandburg has put it, *The People, Yes*.[28] During the war Sandburg fulfilled

MacLeish's faith in him by writing a column for the *Chicago Times* full of homely, folksy optimistic anecdotes and exhortations. Like a sub-literate E. B. White (one of Sandburg's overworked transitions is "Anyhow and ennyhoo"), in these columns Sandburg performed the rites of high-mindedness by celebrating the genius of Saroyan and admiring the poems in a volume *(America is Americans)* of one Hal Borlund. To Sandburg and his readers in 1942, it seemed important to ascertain whether Lincoln was religious. Sandburg is able to announce that he was, thus rescuing Lincoln for the side of decent Americanism. Like many others concerned that Americans might lack the goodness to overpower wickedness, Sandburg is liberal with moral instruction. In 1942 he counsels sincere self-examination as a device leading to self-improvement:

> It is not a bad exercise for a man to sit quiet once in a while and watch the workings of his mind and heart and notice how often he can find himself favoring five or six of the seven deadly sins, and especially the first of those sins, which is named pride.

He concludes this column with an account of a laudably modest tail-gunner who has told a press conference how he once dropped on the Japs seven bombs, on each written the name of one of his buddies killed at Pearl Harbor. His quiet goodness is so apparent that an officer present, Sandburg reports, said afterward, "Didn't you just feel that you wanted to reach out your arms and put them around him?" [29]

Some of Sandburg's poems of the period suggest the difficulties of registering precise ideas or emotion in the prevailing atmosphere of obligatory goodness. Vagueness is all but forced upon one (a good thing, really, considering the resistance of current events to precise ideological interpretation), and few terms extend a more powerful invitation to imprecision and even total non-meaning than *freedom* and *free*, buzz-words which appear everywhere and constitute the essential *leitmotif* of wartime high-mindedness. Sandburg's very titles, like "Is There an Easy Road to Freedom?" and "Freedom Is a Habit," are sufficient warning of flaccidity and crudity to come. MacLeish runs into the same difficulty. His poem "Brave New World," addressed to "Tom Jefferson," sets out to deplore the failure of the war to bring about real "freedom," but even MacLeish's repetition of that word eight times in fifteen four-line stanzas cannot invest it with literary meaning. (Any more than May Elizabeth Colman's invocation of ten *freedoms* in the 38 lines of her poem "For This Freedom Too."[30] The meaning of the word *freedom* was going to be a problem for the intelligent throughout the war. The difficulty was recognized as early as 1942 by a book *Freedom: Its Meaning,* in which Bertrand Russell, Albert Einstein, Thomas Mann, Henri Bergson, Harold Laski, and others tried their hands at definitions.) MacLeish issued "Brave New World" in 1948. He was slower to learn than Edna St. Vincent Millay, who, visited that year by Edmund Wilson, admitted that it had been a "mistake" to write bad wartime poems even to buck up morale.[31] She was thinking of the emissions in her book *Make Bright the Arrows* (1940) and the yards of banal, prolix dramatic dialogue in *The Murder of Lidice* (1942):

> Good people all, from our graves we call
> To you, so happy and free;
> Whether ye live in a village small
> Or in a city with buildings tall,
> Or the sandy lonesome beach of the sea,
> Or the woody hills, or the flat prairie:
> Hear us speak; oh, hear what we say;
> We are the people of Lidice![32]

But to single out as especially blameworthy MacLeish, Sandburg, and Millay is unfair, for many wrote even worse, persuaded that the war effort required the laying aside of all normal standards of art and intellect. I am thinking of Stephen Vincent Benét, Vachel Lindsay, Clemence Dane, Laurence Binyon, Robert Nathan, Wilfrid Gibson, John Gould Fletcher, Stuart Cloete, Oscar Williams, Robert Hillyer, Donald Ogden Stewart, and MacKinlay Kantor, names remembered today largely by the literary historian alone. Yet so demanding was the need for a morale-sustaining note of upbeat that despite this outpouring of patriotic drivel, the publisher of Louis Untermeyer's anthology *Modern American Poetry,* issued in the dark days of 1942, felt it appropriate to declare that "we are in the midst of another revival of poetry. . . . A fresh wave of creative energy is apparent." We are witnessing, in short, a "reawakening." (So much for the loss of Wake Island, Guam, Hong Kong, Singapore, and the Philippines.)

Only rarely was the wartime *freedom* closely inspected and debunked.

One nice attack on it was mounted by the Australian John Manifold, sounding in "A Satire on Liberty" like a sort of Marxist Byron:

> Freedom for all! For bankers in their slums
>   As for the pampered poor of Bethnal Green!
> Freedom from any distant threat there comes
>   To keep the racket tolerably clean!
> Freedom to make and keep gigantic sums
>   By cornering markets as a go-between!
> Freedom from any form of social plan
> For Beaverbrook's delight, the Little Man!
>
> Blest Little Man! Four Freedoms are your lot—
>   Freedom from thought which makes one Reason's slave;
> Freedom from change in your obedient trot
>   From house to office, cradle to the grave;
> Freedom from information so you'll not
>   Mind how your representatives behave;
> *Travail, Patrie, Famille*—for more facility
> Freedom from freedom and responsibility.[33]

And so on, for eighteen refreshingly un-high-minded stanzas. Manifold displays equal unwillingness to join the team and play the game in his sonnet "Ration Party," which locates the outrageous unreason of wartime relations between means and proclaimed ends:

> Across the mud the line drags on and on;
> Tread slithers, foothold fails, all ardors vanish,
> Rain falls; the barking N.C.O.'s admonish
> The universe more than the lagging man.
>
> Something like an infinity of men
> Plods up the slope; the file will never finish,
> For all their toil serves only to replenish
> Stores for tomorrow's labors to begin.
>
> Absurd to think that Liberty, the splendid
> Nude of our dreams, the intercessory saint
> For us to judgment, needs to be defended
>
> By sick fatigue-men brimming with complaint
> And misery, who bear till all is ended
> Every imaginable pattern of constraint.[34]

And both Dylan Thomas and Julian Maclaren-Ross were bright enough
to sense something funny in the elaborate investment of vague sentiment
in *free* and *freedom*, which sustained the current clichés about the Free
French, the Free Poles, the Free Dutch, and the like. Writing a film
script about the Home Guard (never produced), they amused themselves
by contemplating the introduction of a number of Free Japanese, whose
kimonos would astonish the inhabitants of a cosy English village.[35]

But most people thought the designation "The Free [collective nationality indication]" as little odd as the later cant phrases The Free World
or Freedom Fighters (for counter-revolutionaries). In the world of high-
mindedness, almost anything went so long as it sounded sincere and patriotic and seemed to minister to the spirit of group self-satisfaction.
Thornton Wilder's *The Skin of Our Teeth* (1942) is an early example,
Arthur Miller's *All My Sons* (1947) a late, of the sort of works the age
demanded. Of *All My Sons*, a critic noted, when it was revived in London in 1981, that it brought back "an age of innocence when we could
be moral with impunity."[36] "They were all my sons," concludes Joe Keller,
having discovered that the faulty airplane parts produced by his factory
have killed numerous fliers and that his own aviator son overseas, aware
of this, has decided out of shame and horror not to return from a mission.
In normal times, Joe would have felt terrible about this and would have
tried to make some sort of civilized amends. But this is wartime, when
the unmitigated high-minded seems called for, especially in the theater
and the "arts," and so he proceeds straightway upstairs and shoots himself. At the time, few thought this noble act of self-punishment, and
certainly not his son's, either morally excessive or artistically unbelievable. But if, as a theatergoer, after Joe Keller's expiation you needed
cheering up, you could get comfort and further simplifications at a musical like *Oklahoma!* (1943) or dance like Martha Graham's *Appalachian
Spring* (1944).

During the war Diana Trilling reviewed scores of novels for *The
Nation*. A great many of them dealt in a notably high-minded way with
a pressing ethical question of the period, the morality of certain careers.
Novel after novel, like Frederic Wakeman's *The Hucksters*, Helen Ha-
berman's *How About Tomorrow Morning?*, and Herman Wouk's *Aurora
Dawn*, explores the dishonor attaching to such "parasitical professions" as
advertising, the selling of cosmetics, commercial radio, low journalism,
making a living by working for Henry Luce, even selling. (Miller's
Death of a Salesman was the Broadway hit of 1949.) It was "the artist"—

in Ayn Rand, the architect—who became the hero resisting all invitations to low-mindedness and the corruption lurking in insincerity.[37]

All this focus on human goodness naturally led to imagining a Better World following the war. In one way, it couldn't help being a better world, for Hitlerism and the Japanese empire would be extirpated. But moral and political progress would result in more positive ends than that: international social justice, for example, as well as worldwide peace and harmony, and decency and goodness for all. Virtually everyone was persuaded, with George Herbert Clarke, that "something greater than the present stage of human worth and social justice is striving to be born." Evolution must be at work: "As a nobler world-order unfolds we shall see . . . a finer philosophy of life and purer modes of government." The doctrine of the survival of the fittest applies to conceptions as well as species, Clarke insists: "This war defines itself at last as a battle in the endless conflict between power to do evil and power to do good. . . ."[38] There were some warnings about simple-minded formulas for realizing the better postwar world, books like C. M. Joad's *The Adventures of a Young Soldier in Search of the Better World* (1944), which brought a Rasselas-like youth into contact with a number of glib proposers, all of whose plans are exposed as either fatuous or impossible. But if Joad warned against excessive optimism, H. G. Wells, in *Guide to the New World* (1941), came on as an unreconstructed believer in a World State, and in a world rational enough actually to desire such a thing. ("Wells," said Orwell, "is too sane to understand the modern world."[39]) To some, concentration on the new shape of "the postwar world" could be so intense as to be dangerous—indeed, mortal. Sandburg believed that Stephen Vincent Benét's death in 1943 was hastened by brooding too deeply on "the war, the American dream, human and international solidarity after the war, these shook his bones and writhed in his heart."[40] But the condition of things at the end of the war looked a lot like the scene at the beginning. Despite British exultation over the 1945 election, "The entry into the Promised Land," observes John Mortimer, "was indefinitely postponed and 'The Just City,' we were told with increasing irritation, would prove far too expensive to build."[41] There was ultimate disappointment everywhere, the result of too fond an indulgence in dreams of moral evolution and a necessary advance toward decency and justice. Of the United Nations in the 1980s Shirley Hazzard notes that "an entire generation has now grown up for whom the UN, as far as it is regarded at all, is an object of disbelief, ridicule, and boredom."[42]

What is missing from all the high-minded wartime moments is any awareness of the mind of the troops in the field. They were neither high- nor particularly low-minded. They were not -minded at all. One infantryman writes his mother on May 2, 1945, about the death of his friend Neal:

> I keep thinking of him . . . lying off the path looking as if he were asleep. I see him lying on his back, arms overhead with eyes and mouth open as if asking, "God, why?" . . . If you could only see us kids killed at eighteen, nineteen and twenty fighting in a country that means nothing to us, fighting because it means either kill or be killed not because you're making the world safe for democracy or destroying Nazism.[43]

And even when not struggling to save their lives instead of losing them, there were other military inhibitions on the expression of much high-mindedness by the servicemen, notably the constant chickenshit. "There are two wars here," concluded one British soldier—one against the designated enemy, the other, equally important psychologically, against the army. "I joined the army to fight fascism," says this man, "only to find the army full of fascists." Looking about in the barracks and the orderly room and the drill-field, "Anything I had been taught about the baddie and the Nazi and the fascists was plonk there in front of me, in this crowd of people who were supposed to be . . . informed and geared up to fight it."[44] And even though the brighter civilians perceived before the war was over that it would be prudent to stop talking about freedom versus something else, most people still believed in the war's high and simple moral purpose. Stalin and Tito? Better not dwelt upon too much. The bombing of civilians? Yes, but—. Gazing at the political condition of Mitteleuropa at the end of the war, those with good memories could hardly recall without irony and a degree of self-contempt the words of Chamberlain at the end of his broadcast of September 2, 1939: "It is evil things that we shall be fighting against—brute force, bad faith, injustice, oppression, and persecution. . . ."[45] And a few, a very few, noted with foreboding the general flight from complexity, irony, skepticism, and criticism. In 1942 Delmore Schwartz wrote in his notebook (but did not publish) his estimate of the cost of all this high-mindedness: "Our movies are bad, our plays, our books, our education, and winning the war without criticism will be the victory of Henry Luce."[46] If Luce and his crowd celebrated "Basic English" as a God-sent mechanism permitting all mankind to share the benefits of a simplified and literal-minded Anglo-American (but mostly American) understanding, there was at least Robert Frost around to designate Basic English "Basic Balls."[47] The proletarian James Jones, speaking in 1952, sensed the need for some antidote to the continuing postwar high-mindedness. Acknowledging his National Book Award, he paraphrased his editor Maxwell Perkins and said: "The only thing wrong with literature in our time is that it lacks . . . malice, envy, and hate. . . . This fear of rascality in our writers is unwittingly turning them into moralists."[48] Which is to say that the mood of wartime survived the war, at least until Vonnegut, Heller, and Pynchon succeeded in proposing an attractive alternative.

13

With One Voice

Because in wartime the various outlets of popular culture behaved almost entirely as if they were the creatures of their governments, it is hardly surprising to find that they spoke with one voice. Together with skepticism, irony, and doubt, an early casualty was a wide variety of views about current events. Radio, popular music, films, and magazines (whose essence reduced largely to their advertisements) conveyed the same sanguine message about the war as the singing commercial of the period delivered about housewifely chores:

> Rinso white! Rinso white!
> Happy little washday song.

In a way not easy to imagine in the present world of visual journalism, the war was mediated and authenticated by spoken language, whose conduit was the radio. For those at home the sound of the war was the sound of the radio. Actually, wartime was a special moment in the history of human sensibility, for in those pre-television days the imagination was obliged to fill in the missing visual dimension, and in those pre-tape days, there was in addition all the excitement of live transmission, when anything could happen. It might not be going too far to say that in those days the audience's "creative imagination" was, willy-nilly, honored as seldom before or after, by the very conventions of radio. Besides inviting listeners to imagine the appearance of speakers and scenes, broadcasting seemed to confer on utterance both intimacy and authority. Hence Roosevelt's choice of "Fireside Chats" as a format for enunciating the government line. Hence the satisfaction of Mussolini's government at having Ezra Pound calumniate the Jews not just in letterpress but slangily over the airwaves.

Henry Fairlie remembers:

> Radio sets were not then very powerful, and there was always static. Families had to sit near the set, with someone always fiddling with the knobs. It was like sitting round a hearth, with someone poking the fire; and to that hearth came the crackling voices of Winston Churchill, or George Burns and Gracie Allen, and of FDR. The fireside chats. . . . It was not FDR who was at his fireside . . . , it was we who were at our firesides.[1]

During the war the average listener spent four and a half hours a day attending to what came out of the speaker,[2] and when something especially significant was expected, one sat in front of the radio and looked at it intently. What issued from it was thoroughly censored, and it was puritan, chaste, and resolutely optimistic. Shortly after the United States entered the war the National Association of Broadcasters developed a code governing the conduct of its members, and one of its clauses prohibited programs "which might unduly affect the listener's peace of mind."[3]

It was not easy for the star radio reporters of the day to euphemize the bombing of London, the sinking of vessels in the Atlantic, or the defeat of Allied troops at Singapore, Hong Kong, and Bataan, or to avoid honest mention of bodies and body parts. But Edward R. Murrow, Richard Dimbleby, Eric Sevareid, and Richard C. Hottelet did their best, and these radio voices accrued immense authority and credibility. One American magazine cartoon depicted a torpedoed and sinking freighter with a lifeboat pulling away when an officer calls down from the door of the radio room, "Hold on a minute, men! I've got H. V. Kaltenborn on the radio. He's analyzing our predicament." For listeners to the BBC the big daily event was the nine o'clock news, with the speaker always identified ("Here is the news, and this is Bruce Belfrage reading it") to assure the audience that the station was still in British and not enemy hands. Everyone listened, even the highly sophisticated and skeptical. When in 1940 Virginia Woolf's biography of Roger Fry seemed to drop into a vacuum, entirely unnoticed by reviewers, she wrote in her diary, "Complete silence surrounds that book. It might have sailed into the blue and been lost. 'One of our books did not return,' as the B.B.C. puts it."[4] Most people believed what the radio news reported, but a few non-team-players and nay-sayers retained their critical faculties: "You would have a raid where the whole district would be shattered and everyone demoralized. Then on the news they'd tell you how many enemy planes had been shot down . . . , totally exaggerated. It has since been proved by officers of the ack-ack that some evenings they didn't shoot any down."[5]

After the BBC nine o'clock news on Sundays, a highly popular fixture was the ten-minute "postscript" talk by J. B. Priestley. As a man whose humane and sentimental identity as a lover of the British people had been established by his novel *The Good Companions* (1929), his was the perfect voice to enthuse over Dunkirk and to project sincere emotion over the "little boats" in action there. His performances were an undoubted sustainer of morale as he dilated week after week on the German fondness for destroying pastoral landscapes; the blessed Englishness of the Home Guard; various heartening things encountered during the week; our lads in the RAF—don't forget them after the war; how to relax and curb worry; Dickens's Sam Weller as an inspiration to us all; the need for more social justice (something to look for after the war); and the happiness of the many more important than the privileges of the few. As he went on, he dwelt increasingly on topics like these last and grew, in the view of Tories, dangerously socialistic, or, as he put it, "more aggressively democratic in feeling and tone," until finally he was taken off the air—by Churchill himself, he was persuaded.[6] Churchill's own distinguished radio oratory, while as highly valued in the United States as the later quasi-musical renderings of his own poems by Dylan Thomas, and of undoubted value in sustaining British morale, had a few severe critics at home. One radio speech in 1940 Hesketh Pearson found "very amateurish," suggesting the performance of "a gangster clergyman who has gone on the stage."[7] Evelyn Waugh was even less impressed. He summed up Churchill's achievement by finding him essentially "a 'Radio Personality' who outlived his prime." And he went on to testify: " 'Rallied the nation,' indeed! I was a serving soldier in 1940. How we despised his orations."[8] What many of the troops preferred was the serious music broadcast by the BBC. Participating in the reduction of Monte Cassino, Captain Peter Royle, R.A., attended to Schubert's *Unfinished Symphony* while the shells and bombs thundered away.[9] In the midst of the fighting in Normandy, Captain Douglas G. Aitken, of the Medical Corps, waited all day to hear Brahms's Fourth Symphony.[10]

Unless one had access to a short-wave receiver, the transmissions of the BBC were the only ones to be heard in Britain, and because it held so high an opinion of its dignity and the importance of its mission to educate and elevate, its standards were dramatically higher than those of American commercial radio. One heard on it extremely intelligent discourse: if the people conspicuous in American broadcasting included Norman Corwin, Alexander Woollcott, Archibald MacLeish, and Christopher Morley, from the BBC one heard such as George Orwell, Forster, T. S. Eliot, Cyril Connolly, and Louis MacNeice, as well as scholars and critics like Neville Coghill, Herbert Read, Bonamy Dobrée, Geoffrey Tillotson, and Edmund Blunden. The BBC Third Programme is sufficiently well known as a source of distinguished transmission, but it was on the mere Home Service, not at all aimed at highbrows, that Forster's regular program "Some Books" celebrated Harry Levin's *James Joyce* and Lionel Trilling's *Matthew Arnold*, Forster saying, "In the catastrophe that has befallen our civilization, we have all become callous as an alternative to insanity. . . . Arnold reminds us that it is possible to be sensitive as well as sane." A month before the invasion Forster was considering Wordsworth, and on D-Day itself he discussed Harold Laski's *Faith, Reason, and Civilization* and C. V. Wedgwood's biography of William the Silent.

Orwell, whose BBC title was Talks Producer, Indian Section, was in frequent communication with Eliot, asking him to broadcast on the plays of Marlowe and on Dryden's *The Indian Emperor*. The BBC "Books and People" series included talks on Bunyan and Cobbett, Yeats, Samuel Johnson, Crabbe, and Robert Frost. As stubborn as *Horizon* in implying that the war, no matter how total, should not be allowed to destroy intellectual and artistic amenities, in the darkest moments the BBC was calmly sending out unflappable talks on

Victorian Schooldays (July, 1941)

July in the Garden (July, 1941)

Two Aspects of Spanish Architecture (August, 1941)

The Greatest English Portrait Painter (Sir Joshua Reynolds) (August, 1941)

John Galsworthy: The Man and His Works (August, 1941)

The Tercentenary of Anthony Van Dyck (November, 1941).

The last was published in the *Listener* for December 11, 1941, together with a piece about the attack on Pearl Harbor. On September 17, 1942, while Russians and Germans were fighting hand-to-hand at Stalingrad and Japanese soldiers were being massacred on New Guinea and Guadalcanal, the Home Service brought listeners a talk on James Boswell by William Beattie. On July 29, 1940, with the Home Guard being organized as a defense against invasion and with Luftwaffe attacks on Dover offering a distinct warning that invasion was being prepared, M. H. Allen, the BBC Director of Features and Drama, wrote Eliot asking him to select a favorite passage of verse or prose to read over the air: "Just before the midnight news and after the dance music we offer our listeners the relief of four minutes' reading from the best prose or verse in English."[11]

But all transmission was not that elevated. In Britain as well as America there were, in addition to the dance music, book-and-idea features for middle-brows. On the BBC there was, weekly, "The Brains Trust," on which Julian Huxley, C. E. M. Joad, retired naval commander A. B. Campbell, and others came to grips with questions proposed by listeners, such as What is a Lady? Why is the *Mona Lisa* the most famous painting in the world? and How does a fly manage to "land" on the ceiling? In America the equivalent program was the weekly CBS "Invitation to Learning" (a title impossible to imagine seducing any substantial audience today). This presented people like Huntington Cairns, Allen Tate, and Mark Van Doren discussing one or the other of the Great Books.

But despite all this talk, popular music, as always, was the staple broadcast material, but now it was held to be invaluable for morale. Twice a day the BBC broadcast for the munitions workers "Music While You Work," consisting of one popular song after another—the instrumental music only, once it was found that otherwise workers were likely to stop to take down the words.[12] Given the Allied ideological vacuum, it would not be expected that a song like the highly popular Japanese one, addressed to a dead soldier, would be piped into the factories:

> Your mother weeps with joy;
> It's too great an honor for us,
> That you are worshipped as a god
> At the Yasukuni shrine.

Not that British and American governments didn't try encouraging a few lyrics equally wet, like "We're Gonna Hang Out the Washing on the Siegfried Line," "I Am a Canadian," and "There's a Star-Spangled Banner Waving Somewhere," not to mention, once the United States was thoroughly engaged against the Japanese, "The Japs Don't Have a Chinaman's Chance" and the "Remember Pearl Harbor March." The normally intelligent and skeptical Frank Loesser, known for his refreshingly cynical songs in *Guys and Dolls,* answered his country's call to supply material glorifying the infantry and came up with "The Ballad of Rodger Young," memorializing a (posthumous) winner of the Medal of Honor who had rushed a Japanese machine-gun nest:

> Oh, they've got no time for glory in the Infantry,
> Oh, they've got no use for praises loudly sung,
> But in every soldier's heart in all the Infantry,
> Shines the name, shines the name of Rodger Young.
>
> On the island of New Guinea in the Solomons,
> Stands a simple wooden cross alone to tell
> That beneath the silent coral of the Solomons
> Sleeps a man, sleeps a man remembered well.

This song proved too embarrassing for either the troops or the more intelligent home folks to take to their hearts. Loesser, sensing that some explanation of his behavior here was called for, commented later on this kind of song-writing: "You give [the folks at home] hope without facts; glory without blood. You give them a legend with the rough edges neatly trimmed." [13]

Rather, the songs that people actually listened to with delight and hummed and remembered were those not of triumph but of deprivation, largely sexual. Some points of view were explicitly female ("They're Either Too Young or Too Old") but most were male:

"I've Got a Girl in Kalamazoo"
"Don't Get Around Much Anymore"
"You'd Be So Nice To Come Home To."

Hopes for the fidelity of the loved one at home constituted another repeated theme:

"Don't Sit Under the Apple Tree with Anyone Else But Me"
"Paper Doll"
"Somebody Else Is Taking My Place."

Desperately wanting something currently unavailable generated numerous "dream" songs. If you couldn't have Linda, you could dream about her:

When I go to sleep
I never count sheep,
I count all the charms about Linda.
And lately it seems
In all of my dreams
I walk with my arms about Linda.

There were a lot more, including "Thanks for the Dream," "I Had the Craziest Dream," "A Soldier Dreams of You Tonight," "I Dream of You," "I'll Buy That Dream," "My Dreams Are Gettin' Better All the Time," and just plain "Dream":

Things never are as bad as they seem
So dream, dream, dream.

And of course "I'm Dreaming of a White Christmas," travestied by American troops in North Africa, tired of looking at veiled, dark-skinned women, as "I'm Dreaming of a White Mistress." Personal deprivation and hope for improvement were the themes that the troops, menaced by chickenshit and fear, responded to. They wept openly when Vera Lynn sang,

We'll meet again, don't know where, don't know when,
But I know we'll meet again some sunny day;
Keep smiling through, just like you always do,
Till the blue skies drive the dark clouds far away.

If there was one song that was the Allied song of the war, it was "Roll Out the Barrel." This was the war's equivalent morale-raiser to the Great War's "Pack Up Your Troubles in Your Old Kit Bag, and Smile, Smile, Smile." If the Great War soldiers and civilians sang, "What's the use of worrying? It never was worthwhile," twenty-five years later they shouted out, "We've got the blues on the run." The blues? Occasioned perhaps by being unable to forget, except with some liquor and raucous music, that the Germans aren't going to quit until you've personally killed what will amount to your quota, or that your son or brother or beau is in the bombers, or the infantry, or the tanks, with the *Royal Oak* at Scapa Flow or the carrier *Franklin* waiting for the *kamikazes* off Okinawa. "The Beer Barrel Polka" (the song's real name) in its secular hedonism was significantly the Second War's "Onward Christian Soldiers," and in its utter avoidance of anything like patriotism or ideology, it was the Second War's "Over There." One pious Briton who went to St. Paul's on VE-Day for the Thanksgiving Service was shocked, he reported in a letter to the *Times* (May 12, 1945), to find the Guards Band welcoming the congregation with "a spritely rendering of 'Roll Out the Barrel.' " But what else? By the end, says Alec Wilder, the historian of popular music, "It was no longer possible to sentimentalize any aspect of war. People knew too much."[14] (And he adds, encouragingly some will think, that the absence of the "war song" has been even more notable during the Korean and Vietnam wars.)

Very much a wartime fixture was the communal sing-along, and there was hardly a more popular item for belting out with one voice than "The Beer Barrel Polka." The bouncing ball on the movie screen indicated the words and the emphasis, a usage nicely caught in Noël Coward's film *In Which We Serve*, where the normally phlegmatic and genteel naval CPO on the destroyer *Torrin* is prompted by a sudden access of group spirit at the cinema to sing out lustily "Roll Out the Barrel!" In Britain probably the second most popular song for group singing was "Run, Rabbit, Run," which became a craze after meat rationing began in 1940, triggering the image of a rabbit scampering to escape augmented threats from hunters. But before long the rabbit of the song became identified, curiously, with Hitler: one postcard depicts a Hitler-faced rabbit being chased by a British bulldog. By loudly singing the song with others, you could suggest that you were actively doing something to win the war by urging something, at any rate, to run and advance. Because the "group" implied the preferable human image, numerous popular songs, especially in the United

States, went in for choral arrangements, making morale songs, like "Buckle Down, Winsocki" and "Coming In on a Wing and a Prayer," virtual recorded sing-alongs. Equally redolent of the group spirit are many other wartime musical arrangements, like Glenn Miller's pepped-up version of the "St. Louis Blues." It begins with many bars of a brisk military drumbeat which continues in the background, turning what was formerly a highly individualist blues ("*I* [not *We*] hate to see . . .") into a communal march scored for a group hardly smaller than a troop, battery, or company.

Group singing had its corollary in wartime communal dancing, as exemplified in the Conga line and the Boomps-a-Daisy craze, both long forgotten now in favor of the highly individual performances required by normal ballroom dancing and later, and more so, the individual showing-off of disco. The sort of community awareness verging on team-spirit characteristic of wartime is revealed by the all but universal knowledge of the same popular songs by all ages, classes, and genders. Not to have known them would have been not to play the game at all. In the American Eighth Air Force a great many aircrews named their bombers after current songs, certain that anyone seeing the title on a plane's nose would react with pleased recognition. Thus planes were named "Big Beautiful Doll," "Bom[b]boogie," "Cabin in the Sky," "Frenesi," "I'll Be Around," "In the Mood," "Jersey Bounce," "Margie," "Paper Doll," "Pistol-Packin' Mama," "Stardust," "Stormy Weather," and "Sunrise Serenade." A notable social cohesiveness is suggested there: today, no one would be expected to know all such allusions.

If the bumptious "Beer Barrel Polka" was the Allied song (the German one was the "sincere," self-pitying "Lili Marlene"), the Allied instrumental background music was "The Warsaw Concerto," a melodramatic piece of pseudo-Tschaikovsky written by the British film-music composer Richard Addinsell for *Dangerous Moonlight*, a movie released in September, 1941.[15] This depicted a heroic Polish pilot in the RAF who happened to be a brilliant pianist of the cinematic-Chopin type, and he nobly executed his chords and runs while the bombs were falling. Point? The Germans are enemies not just of the Allies but of Culture and Refinement. In aid of this premise, as well as in recognition of its melodic attractiveness, "The Warsaw Concerto" was played constantly.

A heroic Pole opposing bombs with pianism suggests folk-fantasy rather than real-life narrative, but it is entirely in the cinematic style of the period. Regardless of what it may have become later, in the 1940s the cinema delineated little but a fairy-tale world of uncomplex heroism and romantic love, sustained by toupees, fake bosoms, and happy endings. It was a medium whose conventions equipped it perfectly for the evasion of wartime actualities, and it adapted to its new requirements without in any way changing step. John Mortimer testifies, "I don't remember any of our films in which the characters complained about the war or tried to fiddle extra expenses on the fire-watching or had love affairs with the wives of soldiers posted to Burma or the Western Desert. . . ."[16] Despite appearances, there was really little difference between three popular films of 1940, *The Wizard of Oz*; Walt Disney's *Pinocchio*; and *The Fighting 69th*, which showed how clever and brave James Cagney and Pat O'Brien were in fighting the First World War. In the same year Chaplin's *The Great Dictator* seemed to keep alive the prewar hope that Hitler was really more absurd than sinister, a point suggested likewise in Noël Coward's song "Don't Let's Be Beastly to the Germans" or the song "Even Hitler Had a Mother," banned by the humorless Lord Chamberlain. A film like *Mrs. Miniver*, showing Greer Garson and Walter Pidgeon heroically suffering through the Blitz and Dunkirk, could be swallowed by all when it came out in 1942, but by early 1944, with the invasion forthcoming to remind everyone of the real price of the war, it went down less smoothly. In April, 1944, one Canadian flier got a 72-hour pass to London. He remembers: "There was something about . . . London that spring. Everybody knew the invasion was coming." Mindful of this, he spends a night with a girl he meets, and next morning they take a walk and decide to go to a film. *Mrs. Miniver* is still showing after two years. "What a phony," is now the Canadian's reaction, and it's shared by the rest of the audience. "You could hear the people muttering all around, making rude remarks about Greer Garson's clothes. Nobody dressed like that in Britain any more."[17]

By 1942 troops who knew something of the real war began to constitute a part of the cinema audience, and the grosser sorts of wartime whitewash sometimes flaked away a bit. In *In Which We Serve* there is shown an actual coward (later redeemed, to be sure) and in *Wake Island*, the first American film about U.S. troops in combat, there is a nasty quarrel between the Marine major and a civilian construction-crew boss. "Realism" began to be treasured. One of the British hits of 1943 was the official documentary *Desert Victory*. A young RAF pilot officer saw it in Alexandria, where it was so popular that it was showing in two theaters simultaneously. "I have never seen such a fine film," he told his diary. "No actors, no romance, no plot, just a true story taken entirely in action in the desert of desert rats. . . . I really felt very proud to be an English."[18] But as was revealed in 1981 in a BBC TV program about the Army Film Unit that made *Desert Victory*, it is not easy, even in making "documentaries," to overcome the cinema's natural instinct for "effects" and sentimental misrepresentation. In the 1981 BBC program, "a laconic cameraman . . . revealed that all those shots of grim-faced tommies marching through clouds of smoke and sand with bayonets fixed had been filmed at the infantry base depot." And the cameraman went on to interpret the motive cinematically. The film-makers, he pointed out, were trying to "fix up 'an ideal situation from a picture point of view, . . . trying to recreate war as we were all taught in history books.' "[19] That is, the action must be rendered in the received clichés: otherwise it will look inauthentic to the audience.

The American films *Bataan* and *Guadalcanal Diary* (1943) established the paradigm of the ideal infantry situation the audience was expected to credit. Infantry units are all melting-pots, with the "universal platoon"[20] comprising something like the following mixture:

> One leader who dies
> one inexperienced youth
> one comic
> one cynic (transformed before the end into
>   a true believer)
> one black or Hispanic, and
> one person each from
>> Brooklyn
>> Texas, and
>> the Middle West.[21]

Bataan showed the universal squad of this platoon in heroic defeat; *Guadalcanal Diary* showed it springing back. In this film there is so much choral music ("Sweet Genevieve," "Rock of Ages," "Chatanooga Choo-Choo," "Home on the Range") that it functions as a virtual musical, with other occasional elements of that genre as well: there is much New York City complacency and would-be attractive vulgarity, with William Bendix and Lloyd Nolan in charge. One and all are crazy about sports, and much is made of men's rigid and serious loyalties to various baseball teams. The jokes and raillery are unremitting, and all the characters are brave, many volunteering for hazardous duties. (A technical reason these films seem so "Hollywood" is that many, like *Bataan*, had to be shot entirely indoors, in sound studios, because the test-flying of planes by the Southern California aircraft industry made outdoor filming impossible.)

Since the infantry and marines had received their "credit" in these two films, other branches had to have theirs. Thus in 1943 *Sahara* (tanks in North Africa, with Humphrey Bogart); *Air Force* (air-gunner John Garfield on the loss of the Philippines: "We're gettin' kicked around all over the place by a lot of stinkin' Nips"); *Destination Tokyo* (adventures on a U.S. Navy submarine captained by Cary Grant); and finally, a tribute to the Merchant Marine, *Action in the North Atlantic*, with Bogart again. In 1944, two more big boosts for the Air Corps, *The Purple Heart*, about the ill treatment meted out by the Japanese to captured bomber crews, and *Thirty Seconds Over Tokyo*, which celebrated the Doolittle raid. By this time even a Hollywood film could go so far as to suggest that wounded men scream and cry and that men losing limbs experience severe shock, but as always there is a silver lining: at home salvation awaits, for their women will comfort them. In all these films, no matter how temporarily damaged the personnel, good triumphs, which means that the success story, Hollywood's dominant narrative model, was easily accommodated to the demands of wartime moral meaning. As the film historians Koppes and Black have emphasized, "Few pictures . . . dared breathe what everyone knew but found hard to voice aloud—that death was random and success only partly related to one's deserts."[22] Maybe the success-story cliché has been violated somewhat in recent films about the Vietnam war, but the Hollywood habit is hard to break, as *The Longest Day* (1972) indicates. Received by many as an authentic representation of D-Day, the film has been accurately called by Lawrence H. Suid "essentially a romance."[23] That no sort of originality should be expected in "war movies" is suggested by the example of *Dawn Patrol* (1938), dramatizing Basil Rathbone's torment sending his fliers out on mortal missions in the Great War. This establishes the invariable paradigm for the conventional strain-of-command films of the Second War like *Command Decision* (1948) and *Twelve O'Clock High* (1949), designed to argue that rank may have its privileges but that these provide no defense against anxiety and guilt.

The governmental device for assuring that the movies spoke with one optimistic and morale-sustaining voice was deadly simple. Because no film company could be expected to possess its own tanks, bombers, or war-

ships, the services' had to be used, and the services refused to co-operate
without approving the screenplay in advance, insisting on changes to make
sure that little remained but the bromides of wholesome behavior and
successful courageous action. As late as 1969 the U.S. Army's Public
Relations office refused to co-operate in the making of *The Bridge at Re-
magen* as long as one scene remained, depicting a GI removing binoculars
and a watch from a German cadaver.[24] "The military manages to improve
its image," says Suid, "in any film on which it assists."[25] No problem
was presented, of course, with films it made itself, instructional ones like
VD Hygiene and *How To Wash* or bellicose ones like the *Why We Fight*
series.

Their sort of easy bloodthirstiness was also to be met with in wartime
magazine advertising. Its cynicism and greed were nothing new. In an
American *Playbill* of 1918 the American Chicle Company touched the
hearts of readers with a drawing of a soldier suffering on a battlefield:
"Wounded, lying in No Man's Land—feverish from thirst—a stick of
gum to him might have been a matter of life and death." Therefore,

SEND A STICK IN EVERY LETTER TO YOUR SOLDIER BOY.

What distinguished that sort of relatively innocent Great War performance from its Second War counterparts is the absence of callousness,
the absence of sadistic delight in the pain and death of others—that delight being associated with the success, importance, and power of the
product being advertised. Its victory is virtually identical with Victory.
The contribution of canned Florida grapefruit juice to the mass murder
of civilians is a case in point. In *Life* for June 7, 1943, the manufacturers
of Texaco gasoline congratulated themselves on producing materials for
making " 'block-busting' bombs and shells" and illustrated their satisfaction with a painting of a stylized German military cemetery, each cross
topped by a swastika-emblazoned helmet, each crossbar tilted up in a
"Heil!" salute. The copy reads: "HEIL . . . ! They salute you, Fuehrer
. . . your dead warriors." Finding that sort of ghoulish, lip-smacking
approach in a Great War ad for anything would not be easy. Similarly,
at the same time the makers of the patent medicine Nujol were pleased
to associate themselves with the message "WORDS WON'T STOP THE
ENEMY—BULLETS WILL!," illustrating the point with a drawing of two
helmeted German soldiers running toward the reader. She will be able to
kill them, the copy indicates, by buying a 25-dollar war bond: that will

provide 104 .50-caliber bullets, of which only two or three will be enough to tear out the insides of these men. "The slippery messenger of death" is the way a torpedo being assembled by nice young people in an American automobile factory is described.[26] Canadian and British advertisers seemed as pleased as American to contemplate and brag about the agonies caused by their products. "DEATH RATTLE IN A NAZI TANK," says an ad of the Steel Company of Canada, which fairly slavers as it describes the way an armor-piercing projectile, white-hot, penetrates a German tank and rico-chets around inside, "spreading fire, death, and destruction."[27] And a British advertisement presented by a toothpaste manufacturer "as a public service" exhorts readers to salvage old rags (to be turned into naval charts and aviators' maps) with the display headline ENEMY SHIPS TORPEDOED WITH THE HELP OF OLD RAGS. The accompanying drawing depicts a violent torpedo explosion aboard what is clearly a merchant ship, and the reader is to enjoy the knowledge that his or her humble old rags can contribute to such a sudden, surprising, and eminently satisfying loss of life.[28]

In the Great War, Edmund Wilson noted as he looked at London at the end of this later war, some "humanitarian feeling survived and con-tinued to assert itself." But now, "No one pretends to give a damn any-more—unless they are one's close friends or relatives—whether people are killed or not." And there are long-range consequences:

> The long-continued concentration on killing people whom we rarely confront, the suppression of the natural bonds between ourselves and these unseen human creatures, is paid for by repercussions, the spitefulness and fear and stifled guilt, in our immediate personal relations.

And Wilson concludes: "Our whole world is poisoned now. . . ."[29]

But not all the magazine advertising would lead to a conclusion so sinister. Some would serve to expose merely the incorrigible fatuity of both advertisers and readers:

THE WINGS OF FREE MEN SWEEP OVER INDIA

No mysteries of India are more exciting than the modern miracle per-formed by Pan American Airways in collaboration with the Air Trans-port Command in transporting men and equipment to distant corners of the globe. Truly the spirit of freedom now moves forward on shining wings. And where these giant clippers touch ground, they leave something of America. Thus, at Pan American canteens famous Snider's Catsup is served.

Does it not stir your imagination when you see a bottle of Snider's Catsup on your table at home to realize that our boys—perhaps *your* boy—can enjoy this same treat thousands of miles away?[30]

And wartime magazine advertising also makes quite clear the profound social snobbery of the period which almost all public representation had to accommodate in order to succeed. Lucky the woman, nay, doubly lucky, whose perfect complexion has earned her an engagement to an officer.

Many magazine ads indicate considerable skill in projecting a subtext as well as the obvious message—like the beer ad with its phrase "a beverage of moderation" suggesting the subtext injunction, "Don't ruin our business and generate conditions that lead to flagrant criminality by imposing post-war prohibition as in 1919." There's a subtext ("Look how wonderful, how sympathetic and patriotic the New Haven Railroad is") in the most famous magazine ad of the war, since regarded as a Madison Avenue classic. "The Kid in Upper 4" was written by Nelson C. Metcalf, Jr., to justify the temporary want of amenity on New Haven trains. When you have to stand, or when you have to wait an unconscionable time for a seat in the dining car, you should *Remember the Kid in Upper 4*. He is a young soldier, shown lying in an upper berth, and he is blond, pretty, and contemplative. He is shipping out to the war, and the train is crowded with lads like him:

> Tonight, he knows, he is leaving behind a lot of little things— and big ones.
> The taste of hamburgers and pop . . . the feel of driving a roadster over a six-lane highway . . . a dog named Shucks, or Spot, or Barnacle Bill.
> The pretty girl who writes so often . . . that gray-haired man, so proud and awkward at the station . . . the mother who knit the socks he'll wear soon.
> Tonight he's thinking them over.
> There's a lump in his throat. And maybe—a tear fills his eye. *It doesn't matter, Kid.* Nobody will see . . . it's too dark.
>
> A couple of thousand miles away, where he's going, they don't know him very well.

But people all over the world are waiting, praying for him to
come.
And he will come, this kid in Upper 4.
With new hope, peace, and freedom for a tired, bleeding world.[31]

So acceptable were those sentiments that the same message could have
been conveyed without variation by radio, popular song, or film, to be
greeted by universal applause. As Eileen M. Sullivan has concluded,
"There was no room in this war-culture for individual opinions or personalities, no freedom of dissent or approval; the culture was homoge-
nous, shallow, and boring."[32] And the main tonality of the wartime advertising voice has resonated for years now as the voice of society at large,
with its "You've Got a Friend in Pennsylvania." and "Have a Nice Day."

Deprivation

For Americans emerging from the Depression assisted by their abundant accidental resources of oil, coal, iron, and other metals and their
impressive manufacturing capacity, the "shortages" and deprivations occasioned by the war were a distinct shock. And they were shocking not
just because of the accustomed milieu of easy excess but because the "fron-
tier" aura of "freedom" had governed for so long most Americans' imaginative and psychological relations with their peers. Visible possession and
conspicuous consumption had been the traditional signals of personal distinction and even satisfactoriness in America, and now to be told by the
government that one could not buy and exhibit a new car or wear new
shoes or silk stockings or have a new extension phone installed was a
heavy blow to the psyche.

The American citizen was first denied rubber. The Japanese seizure

of Southeast Asia meant no more raw rubber imports, and it was some
time before synthetic rubber could be devised as a substitute. The result:
purchase of tires was prohibited or severely restricted, and Americans of
all classes became adept at the jargon of re-capping, re-treading, "car-
casses," and the like. The supply of garden hoses, beach balls, overshoes,
rubber floormats, and hot-water bottles virtually dried up. (Although not
often mentioned in public, condoms remained in good supply during the
war.)

It was largely to save tires that gasoline was rationed from December
1, 1942, although the sinking of tankers by U-boats off the East Coast
was dramatically depleting petroleum supplies. Once gasoline-rationing
mechanisms were fully in place, the ordinary person, the possessor of an
"A" windshield sticker, could buy four gallons a week, later reduced to
three. That meant only about 60 miles of driving per week, but none of
those miles was to be wasted in "pleasure" driving. Those able to wangle
"B" or "C" stickers—people engaged in crucial deliveries or medical services or indispensable government work—got more gasoline, and there
was a lively black-market trade in those stickers. To save gasoline (but
also one imagines to oblige the home-front to suffer inconvenience, reminding them that "there is a war on"), a 35-miles-an-hour national speed
limit was imposed, and staying within this "Victory Speed" one learned
further gas-saving tricks, like coasting down hills and being careful about
letting the motor idle. Highways were soon almost deserted, grass growing up between pavement joints, and the "See America First" tourist
business suffered grievous damage. The resort industry was a frequent
complainer, especially since many of its hotels (most notably those in
Miami) became in addition dormitories for military and naval trainees.
The closing in January, 1945, of such appealing venues of frivolity as
horse- and dog-racing tracks may have been a further effort to save gasoline and tires, but was more likely ordered to remind stay-at-homes of
the sacrifices being undergone at the moment in the Battle of the Bulge
and the recapture of the Philippines.

But limits on driving came to matter less as cars themselves became
scarce. The manufacture of anything made of metal was soon forbidden
or drastically curtailed, which meant not only no new cars but no bicy-
cles, refrigerators, vacuum cleaners, stoves or household appliances in
general, typewriters, even alarm clocks. The consumer was not allowed
to forget that "tin" cans used the metal the troops needed for bayonets
and ammunition. Even the services found themselves metal-short before

the war was over. The brass buttons originally supplied on the army overcoat were soon being made of brown plastic, like the former brass NCO's whistle and the former metal flashlight. It may now seem hard to believe that at a women's basketball game at Northwestern University in 1944, play was stopped by the referee so that all ten players could search the floor for a bobby-pin fallen there. Copper was essential for rotating-bands on artillery shells as well as for military telephone and radio parts, and a fixture of the period not easily forgotten was the zinc penny, which looked distinctly hangdog and deprived.

Shoes were rationed from February, 1943, and everyone, not just proletarians, learned the advantages of half-soling. Men's clothing man-ufacturers were forbidden to supply cuffs on trousers or vests with suits, and artificial substitutes for silk were devised for the same reason that there was no natural rubber—Japanese conquests in Asia. The govern-ment promulgated this advice for citizens unable to replenish their ward-robes:

> Use it up, wear it out,
> Make it do, or do without.

Paper was in short supply, and Kleenex virtually disappeared, not to mention toilet paper. One man, ten years old at the time, remembers a signal event. "A neighbor woman, an otherwise normal, modest woman, came running down the street one day shouting at the top of her lungs, 'There's toilet paper at the A & P!' "[1] Newsprint and magazine stock grew coarser, and low-budget periodicals like *The New Republic* and *The Nation* soon looked as if printed on paper towels, and gray ones at that. Book paper often disclosed twigs, and those accustomed to prewar books feared that pages would soon yellow and brown and then flake away. Books apolo-gized for their straitened and nasty appearance and implied where the blame lay by carrying some version of this statement on the copyright page:

> This book has been published in full
> compliance with all War Production
> Board Conservation Orders.

All this was surely novel and not at all pleasant. But it was easier to bear than deprivations of food and drink and tobacco. Food rationing began a month after Pearl Harbor. First was sugar, and soon chewing gum, preserves, and candy became scarce, at least for civilians. One reason candy bars were hardly to be seen was that hundreds of thousands of troops in training, requiring instant energy to help them over the obstacle course, were buying them by the box of twenty-four at their PXs and consuming several a day. (One favorite: Clark bars.) Coffee went next, rationed from November, 1942. Soon butter, cheese, canned goods, and—worst of all—meat required coupons. Many Americans for the first time had rabbit for dinner, and macaroni and cheese became a staple dish. Oleomargarine was the favored butter substitute, and because the dairy lobby had prevented the oleo industry from selling its pure-white product tinted to resemble butter, a wartime home-front ritual was coloring the marge by mixing in the orange dye supplied until the stuff resembled the rarely seen "higher priced spread." By the end of the war virtually all foods were rationed except fruits and vegetables, and many people supplied these from their own gardens. It was always possible to beat the game by turning to the black market, but this required money and criminal cunning and often led to attacks of guilt stimulated by monitory advertising:

> Did you drown a sailor today because
> YOU bought a lamp chop without giving up the required coupons?

Most people played the game, and for them deprivation was the condition of wartime. One woman remembers:

> Rationing was awful, awful. I was always losing the ration books, and you just couldn't get anything good, even if you did have the ration coupons. I can remember thinking a can of corned beef was just marvelous. We ate a lot of Spam.[2]

Whisky, especially Scotch, was hard to find, and people learned to drink liquors like rum not requiring trans-Atlantic passage. Cigarettes grew scarce, most going in profusion to the troops, who bought them for almost nothing at the PX or received them free overseas. Unable to find their usual Chesterfields or Camels or Lucky Strikes, people endured horrible brands like Chelsea and Wings or learned to roll their own, plying little bags of Bull Durham or operating cigarette-rolling machines, likely to produce unsatisfactory objects—hypertrophied tubes thick as a finger or white sticks resembling toothpicks.

And even if they were generally well supplied with tobacco, the troops themselves frequently knew deprivation, their hunger occasioned sometimes by the rigors of combat, sometimes by the simplifications enjoined by institutional life. Starvation was endemic, for example, on Bataan well before the American surrender. "The first few days on Bataan," a soldier recalls, "we talked about booze and women. Later, it turned to food. Still later, not only did you talk about food, you dreamed about food, you fantasized about food. In February [1942], food became an obsession." The soldiers killed and ate lizards, snakes, cats, and dogs, and sometimes other things. Says one soldier: "Once I came back off the front line and on the trail ran across three guys with a pot on the stove. I lifted the pot lid to see what they had and I saw a little old bleached hand that looked exactly like a baby's. It was a monkey. 'Come on,' they said, 'stay for dinner.' I seen that little hand. 'No thanks, I'll see you later.' "[3]

But even in happier circumstances hunger gnawed at the troops, despite the official carbohydrates ladled out three times a day. Loneliness and frustration doubtless played a part, and any ex-serviceman can testify to almost constant pangs unsatisfied even by candy bars and similar PX supplements. The diaries of soldiers and sailors contain meticulous listings of the foods constituting the meals of the day. Like this: "Breakfast this morning: canned grapefruit juice, powdered eggs, oatmeal, biscuits, coffee. Lunch: Spam, fruit cocktail. Dinner: chipped beef on toast, apple, cookie." The motive, pathetic, to be sure, seems to be to set these items down to enjoy the food a second time by revisiting the literary record. Sometimes these entries would almost make you weep. The American sailor James J. Fahey notes in his diary in July, 1944: "We had Jello for chow at noon, this was the first time we had it in about a year." And eleven months later, another red-letter day: "This morning we had something for breakfast that we never had before. When they gave us fried eggs we almost passed out. This was the first time we ever had fried eggs while in the navy," he writes, and he's been in it for years.[4]

But accustomed as they became to their own national forms of deprivation, Americans discovered its deeper reaches when they began arriving in England in 1942 to train for the invasion. The official booklet of advice issued to U.S. forces reminded them that the British had been at war more than two years longer than they, and that deprivation had become for them a way of life.

So stop and think before you sound off about lukewarm beer or cold boiled potatoes, or the way English cigarettes taste. If British civilians look dowdy and badly dressed, it is not because they do not like good clothes or know how to wear them. All clothing is rationed. . . . Old clothes are "good form."[5]

They had to be, because in Britain a man was allowed to buy a new suit only every two years, a new shirt only every 20 months. Trousers came without cuffs, pleats, or zippers. All commodities scarce in the United States were even scarcer in the United Kingdom, and there were some shortages Americans never experienced, like blankets, bottles, drinking glasses, pots and pans and cutlery, soap, paper bags, bandages and drugs, bed sheets and towels, paper-clips, needles, thermos bottles, carpets, combs, and golf balls. If hairpins were unavailable, somehow pipe-cleaners were to be found, and women used them as hairpin substitutes. Of course petrol and heating oil were not to be had and coal was extremely scarce, so the roads were all but empty of civilian traffic and houses and buildings were even colder than usual. When Myra Hess played her noontime piano recitals at the National Gallery, the audience sat in overcoats and scarves and mittens. Babies' prams and nursing bottles and nipples almost disappeared, and so did children's toys. Paper became much more precious than in lumber-rich America. Newspapers dwindled to four pages, envelopes and greeting cards were hard to find, and theater programs shrank to little eight-page booklets four inches tall.

For the British almost all normal conveniences and even necessities became rarities: fountain pens, chamber pots, vegetable peelers, wedding rings (a "utility" wedding ring of nine carats was issued), cigarettes and matches, cosmetics, toothbrushes, and razor blades. If some standard items, like pencils, could now and then be found, they came without paint or varnish. Wood was so scarce that the manufacture of furniture was rigorously restricted, with "utility furniture"—22 standard items only—replacing previous stocks. The nightly blackout became even more tedious and dangerous once flashlights and batteries became unavailable. To this list of shortages could be added such a former convenience as window glass, now widely shattered and replaced with cardboard. The iron railings around parks disappeared, presumably to provide metal for weapons

*Myra Hess playing a noontime recital in the National Gallery,
London (Imperial War Museum)*

and matériel. Railway station signs were removed, like road signs, lest German invaders have too easy a time getting around. And to all these deprivations was added another: there was little "service," and shopping queues formed regularly. You could spend a whole day waiting in lines, acquiring the most common items.

Food especially, much harder to come by than in America. Almost half the food Britons required had to be brought in by ship, and the ships were programmatically sunk by submarines. Merchant seamen were drowned daily, the government proclaimed, because the British housewife was unwilling to make her family consume, say, soy beans instead of bacon. "FOOD IS A MUNITION OF WAR. DON'T WASTE IT," announced the Ministry of Food. Rigorous rationing began in January, 1940, and it did not end entirely until nine years after the war, in 1954. Virtually everything you liked to eat or drink was available only in minuscule quantities: meat, butter, cheese, eggs, sugar, sweets, apples, grapes, melons, fats, white bread (replaced by a gray "utility loaf"), tea, coffee, whisky, and pepper; and some things were so rare as to be virtually unobtainable and among some people not even known, like onions, oranges and lemons, and bananas. The only things usually available were fish (including whale meat), oatmeal, potatoes, carrots, parsnips, and turnips. Animal offal was occasionally offered by one's butcher, and older gentlemen sometimes laid their gout to so many livers and lights consumed during wartime.

This sorry scene was administered by one of the civilian heroes of the British war, Lord Woolton, head of the Ministry of Food. A peacetime social worker and former department store executive, Fredrick James Marquis, First Earl of Woolton, became widely respected for his fairness, resourcefulness, and cheerfulness in the face of terrible odds. His ministry was tireless in promulgating hints and devising substitutes, like carrot marmalade and the "soya link"—what you got instead of sausage. Or you could make a nice "Woolton Pie," consisting of potatoes, carrots, parsnips, and turnips, with perhaps a bit of fish stock for flavoring. Why not make a tasty soup by adding a bouillon cube to the water you've boiled the peapods in? (Thicken it with oatmeal if desired.) Have you tried mock-marzipan (made of beans, rice, marge, and almond flavoring)? How about a vegetable pie for dinner, with some parsnip wine? Carefully made, it can resemble champagne. If your tastes ran to the Scottish cuisine, you could make a mock haggis of a little bacon rind, some oatmeal, a leek, vegetable water, and bicarbonate of soda. Or if chicken or the usual game birds aren't available, try crow, cooked either fried or à la Lyonnaise. (A visitor to Mr. and Mrs. Dylan Thomas's wartime flat recalls being served "a particularly curious starling pie."[6]) No need to mourn too deeply the disappearance of coffee when you can survive on Victory Coffee, made of dried acorns ground up. Nothing to use for sandwich filling? Try mashed vegetables, especially mashed potatoes. "Potato Pete," a character in Lord Woolton's ads, gave cheerful advice:

> You get the *extra energy* you need in wartime from potatoes. They guard you against illness too. Don't just serve potatoes once a day, cook them often. . . . Give the family such tasty dishes as Floddies for supper or Potato Pancake for dinner.[7]

(Woolton's "Dr. Carrot" dispensed similar injunctions.) If you wanted to entertain American troops, you could offer them Mock Hamburger (two-thirds potato).

Woolton's people tried hard to feel, or affect, enthusiasm for the *ersatz* items they had to push, like powdered eggs, which were, they pointed out, the whole real egg with nothing added (certainly not plaster or wood pulp, as rumor said) and nothing removed but the water and the shell. Eileen Blair, George's Orwell's first wife, worked for the Ministry of Food's BBC program "The Kitchen Front" preparing recipes and writing slogans and copy to promote them. Bernard Crick points out that some of Oceania's "snappy slogans" in *1984* may derive from Eileen's wartime performances,[8] and certainly Orwell's emphasis in the novel on constant shortages refracts wartime actuality. Winston Smith's colleague Symes asks,

> "By the way, Smith old boy, I suppose you haven't got any razor blades you can let me have?"
>
> "Not one," said Winston. "I've been using the same blade for six weeks myself." (61)[9]

And Smith's description of the state of things distinctly recalls wartime Britain:

> There had been a famine of [razor blades] for months past. At any given moment there was some necessary article which the Party shops were unable to supply. Sometimes it was buttons, sometimes it was darning wool, sometimes it was shoelaces; at present it was razor blades. (49)

A bit later, Smith witnesses a fight between dozens of women at a shop selling a few rare saucepans. For a moment he thinks, rather hopefully, that the proles are rising at last. But no, it is just a conventional scarcity-and-rationing struggle familiar to any observer of early-forties Britain. Indeed, anyone curious about the feeling of deprivation in wartime Britain might simply turn to *1984* and watch Winston Smith pouring from an envelope Victory Coffee into boiling water and adding saccharine tablets; or wondering whether some tea is real or only ground-up blackberry leaves; or morosely drinking his Victory Gin; or realizing that some children do not know what a lemon is. In 1944 as in *1984*,

> always in your stomach and in your skin there was a sort of protest, a feeling that you had been cheated of something that you had a right to. . . . At any time that [Smith] could accurately remember, there had never been quite enough to eat, one had never had socks or underclothes

that were not full of holes, furniture had always been battered and rickety, rooms underheated, tube trains crowded, houses falling to pieces, bread dark-colored, tea a rarity, coffee filthy-tasting, cigarettes insufficient—nothing cheap and plentiful except synthetic gin.

That moment of awareness Smith experiences while sitting at a gravy-dribbled table in a crowded canteen with "bent spoons, dented trays, coarse white mugs . . . and a sour, composite smell of . . . bad coffee and metallic stew and dirty clothes" (60)—all remarkably suggestive of the wartime scene in one of the more than 2000 government cafeterias where you could get a meal for less than a shilling. To limit British consumption, it was essential for citizens to eat more of their meals in controlled environments, and early in the war these public cafeterias were established, for which the name "Communal Feeding Centres" was proposed. Upon which Churchill sent this classic comment to Lord Woolton:

> I hope the term "Communal Feeding Centres" is not going to be adopted. It is an odious expression, suggestive of Communism and the workhouse. I suggest you call them "British Restaurants." Everybody associates the word "restaurant" with a good meal, and they may as well have the name if they cannot get anything else.[10]

The so-called British Restaurants were of course deeply resented by the free-enterprise restaurant industry, whose establishments had further cause of complaint because they were forbidden to charge for a meal more than five shillings (a little over a dollar). But unless you had a lot of money, there seemed little to choose between private and public feeding, although most people agreed with Edward Blishen (and Churchill) about the curse of regimentation:

> It was always a bad day when you had to go to the British Restaurant. Maybe the little café round the corner served nothing much better in the way of food; but you felt Mrs. Bolton's variations on the theme of fish and chips were by some indefinable advantage of individuality and privacy an improvement on the anonymous offerings of the British Restaurant, [where eating] was awfully like being fed by the government—positively by the Minister of Food himself.[11]

Equally depressing was the daily struggle to get something decent to eat at home. A banana was so rare that even its discarded skin was exciting. One boy was brought a banana by his brother in the merchant navy. He ate it "sitting on the church wall and threw the banana skin down to watch people's faces. . . . Nobody had seen a banana."[12] A teenager who won a banana at an office raffle "took it home, where, after it had been inspected by the neighbors, 'it was cut up into pieces with a taste for each member of the family,' " after which the family amused itself by arranging the skin on the road outside to simulate a real banana and watching the "surprised looks" of passers-by.[13] It is said that a woman visiting the zoo watched with outrage a monkey addressing himself to a banana until she looked closer and perceived it was only a peeled potato cunningly clothed in a banana skin.[14] Occasionally a pear or a peach would surface in a shop, but it might cost as much as three shillings. Any kind of citrus fruit was seen less often. As a promotion for a theater near Trafalgar Square, a man announced through a public-address system that the two lemons he was displaying (they had just arrived in a convoy from Gibraltar) would be auctioned at the theater that evening.[15] At one point in 1944, an American soldier in Britain somehow achieved an orange. A little girl came walking past. "I hold the fruit out to the child," he recalls.

> "What is that?" says a squeaky soprano.
>
> "An orange for you to eat," is my reply. Her curiosity changes to wonder, and breathes with awe.
>
> "Oh, is *that* an orange? May I hold it? I won't drop it." When I again tell her that it is hers, she joyously runs home to show it to her mother.[16]

It was Axis control of the Mediterranean for so long that deprived Britons of bananas and citrus fruit, and it was the German occupation of Brittany, whose onion-sellers formerly visited England en masse every year, that made onions so rare a luxury that they became popular prizes at raffles and treasure hunts. By February, 1941, they had almost completely disappeared from the markets. One greengrocer displayed in the center of his shopwindow "one large onion, a pink ribbon tied round its middle, and, propped against it, a placard with the words 'Very rare.' "[17] Eggs were almost as rare, the powdered kind ("reconstituted" with water) being the only sort usually met with. When a whole egg was found, too often it proved rotten, especially those stamped CANADA (how old could these have been?). An ad for a boarding school in *Horizon* for March,

1942, specifies as an attraction not just "Moderate Fees" but "Eggs." In the absence of candy, children learned to relish Tums and cough drops, and the tenseness of the sweets situation in the winter of 1943 can be inferred from an ad for Mars bars in *Penguin New Writing*, No. 16. Inside the front cover is an illustration of a proud father passing to the members of his family a plate with slices of a Mars bar displayed attractively: "CUT THEM INTO SLICES," the reader is adjured,

> and let *all* the family enjoy them. Sweet rationing may have made "share and share alike" a good family motto . . . . By cutting these chunky candy-bars up into slices, every member of the family can enjoy a satisfying share of their delicious goodness.

And if children were forced to learn a quasi-adult discipline about hunger and disappointment, one effect of rationing was to bring out the schoolboy in grown men. "One morning," reports Anthony Powell, "I saw Prince Felix [of Luxembourg] (who wore the uniform of a brigadier) coming from the direction of Belgrave Square. He was carrying a large paper bag. 'I've just bought some buns, Major Powell. Come back to the Legation. We'll go up to my room and eat them.' "[18]

Being deprived of common conveniences and your favorite foods and drinks was bad enough, but some things were even worse—like being deprived of European and Middle Eastern travel for six years. No wonder one of the most popular of postwar books was Elizabeth David's *A Book of Mediterranean Food* (1950). Cyril Connolly almost died from longing for France ("Streets of Paris, pray for me; . . . summer rains on quays of Toulon, wash me away," he wrote in *The Unquiet Grave*[19]). But even this deprivation diminished when placed next to the ultimate one, not having close to you your son or husband, your sister or wife or father or mother or friend, and often not having even any news of them, for months and years—and in dark moments half-suspecting that you would never see them again. Clara Milburn, who lived near Coventry, was especially sensitive to wartime deprivations because even more than foodstuffs and 24-page newspapers and ample petrol she missed her son Alan John, captured near Dunkirk in 1940 and destined to spend five years in a German prison camp. If Mrs. Milburn can't have the things she hungers for she can at least fantasize about them in rhyme and meter as a small literary compensation. Her poem, for domestic consumption only, is titled

WHEN

How good 'twill be in days to come when peace is here again
To live in simple comfort free from worry, stress, and strain,
When breakfast is a cheery meal with coffee rich and rare,
And cream a-floating on the top and lashings still to spare.
From *Times* or *Telegraph* we're roused, "Please pass the marmalade,"
To hand a jar of jellied gold—real, genuine homemade!
When "butter" bends before it breaks in winter's icy grip,
When one may see without surprise the orange, and its pip.
When blackout curtains disappear and all may show a light,
When shop-assistants may be wrong—the customer be right.
When milkmen pour out milk in quarts, the butcher brings the joints,
And no one thinks of ration books, of coupons or of points.
When work has its allotted hours and there is time for play,
When no one needs to listen to the news but once a day;
When sugar's sweet and plentiful, and cakes are not a fluke,
When eggs are seldom mentioned, and Lord Woolton is a duke.
But oh, with hope and patience we are waiting for a day
When the tank is full of petrol and the dust sheet stowed away,
The engine's running smoothly and the M. G. free to roam,
When Oflag's gates have opened wide and Alan John is home.

When Alan John finally came home in May, 1945, Mrs. Milburn's grocer helped the family celebrate by letting her have some oranges.[20]

Compensation

Appearing in February, 1943, to the gratification of the sexually deprived troops and hungry civilians, was one of the prime American compensations for wartime deprivation, Walter Benton's free-verse sequence

This Is My Beloved. In its day this 43-page book was thought boldly erotic, and soldiers gave it to cautious girls in the hope that it might loosen them up. Like Kahlil Gibran's high-minded *The Prophet*, it was a dramatically popular wartime work, and it has remained in demand. The sort of high trash generally well below the dignity of literary criticism, by 1968 it had gone through thirty-six printings, and it still constitutes one of the trustworthy fixtures of the Alfred A. Knopf backlist, available in both standard and pocket editions.

Born in Austria of Russian parents, in 1943 Walter Benton was a 33-year-old lieutenant in the Signal Corps. The brief biographical notice at the end of *This Is My Beloved* observes the convention of American war-time authorship that a writer establishes his *bona fides* by having worked in a wide variety of manly and ostentatiously non-literary trades. "After working on a farm, in a steel mill, as a window washer, as a salesman, and at various other jobs, [Benton] entered Ohio University," later serving as a social worker in New York City. The war over, he returned to New York and wrote for magazines. He died in 1976.

Conflating the "Children of Adam" section of Whitman's *Leaves of Grass* with "The Song of Songs Which Is Solomon's" and then rendering the product in the medium of folk grammar ("You rise out of sleep like a growing thing rises out of the garden soil" [4]),[1] Benton proceeds to deliver his would-be erotic rhapsody on page after page of Knopf's elegant laid paper. But sometimes it is not easy to keep attention focused on the erotic element, so intense is the imagining of unrationed foodstuffs:

> O I drew love like honey-steeped wine from every mouth of you—and when we had loved our fill, we laughed, and we were very hungry. Then we ate fruit with cream and sugar, bacon—sausages and cakes with rich brown maple syrup . . . and drank strong, fragrant coffee. (20)

On another occasion, when his woman has been unable to meet him, the lover registers his disappointment by cataloguing the delicacies he has expectantly laid in:

> I had everything you love—shellfish and saltsticks . . . watercress, black olives. Wine (for the watch I pawned), real cream for our coffee. Smoked cheese, currants in port, preserved wild cherries. (37)

And if the troops could not always lay hands upon the liquors they remembered from peacetime, they could at least enjoy vicarious intoxication
and get an erotic lift at the same time from passages like this:

> What enslaving cocktail have I sucked from your full mouth . . . to
> leave me so totally yours! (42)

But if Americans were left hungry for food and sexual comforts by
wartime deprivation, in infinitely drearier Britain the need was more acute
for simulacra of prewar freedom, delight, warmth, abundance, and elegance. There, even less tolerable than in the U.S.A., was

> the bored banality, the seediness . . . waiting, forever waiting, mostly
> in queues, standing in over-crowded night trains that stop for hours in
> the middle of the black countryside, the frail consolations offered by the
> cinema . . . the seedy comforts dispensed by NAAFI and municipal
> restaurants, the heartless architecture of Nissen huts, the shabby, ugly,
> makeshift modes of war: headscarves, turbans, frayed overcoats, . . .
> cigarettes sold singly over the counters of pubs, . . . the dull dismal
> drudgery of the whole thing.[2]

Hence, in compensation, the welcome accorded the rich sauces of Churchill's oratory and the over-ripe poems of Edith Sitwell and Dylan Thomas,
the toothsome luxury of Osbert Sitwell's sinuous sentences, the elegance
of Cecil Beaton's wartime photographs: he could beautify even a street in
Calcutta and make of a hospital ward a lovely theatrical setting occupied
by supremely beautiful people. Hence the compensatory dandyism of Julian Maclaren-Ross's dress, which, as D. M. Davin notes,

> courted derision from the drunken and the spiv. At a time when clothing
> shortage forced most civilians into a drab uniformity, Julian ransacked
> Charing Cross Road for garments more striking—a huge teddybear over-
> coat, a liver-colored jacket perhaps and beige trousers. . . . His hair,
> too, was long in a way the army had made unfashionable, [and] his
> carnation buttonhole renewed each day from a barrow was a provoca-
> tion . . . ,[3]

not to mention his silver-headed walking stick, both flashy and supremely
irrelevant. And wartime deprivation is the cause, pre-eminently, of Cyril
Connolly's noble attempt to keep a rich and satisfying culture alive by

means of his monthly *Horizon,* one of the most civilized and civilizing of periodicals.

Connolly (born 1903) came from a good family and was polished at Eton and Balliol College, Oxford. In the late 1920s he was a literary journalist, writing largely for the *New Statesman,* where he earned a reputation as one of the best reviewers in London. In 1935 he published an attenuated novella, *The Rock Pool,* about a colony of British expatriates on the Riviera. It was his bid for notice as a "creative" writer, but Orwell was not alone in finding it conventional and tiresome, the sort of thing already better done by Aldous Huxley and Norman Douglas.[4] In his critical book *Enemies of Promise* (1938), written with intermittent brilliance, he lamented the paucity of contemporary literary masterpieces and considered some of the causes: the temptation or necessity of journalism (i.e., reviewing), the expenditure of energy on Left activism, and the contentment of writers with merely momentary fame. What he really seemed to be doing in this book, many thought, was explaining his own failure to produce a serious sustained work which would aim at a level above the stylish. At this point, stout, snub-nosed, and sartorially unsubtle, at the age of thirty-five he seemed doomed to remain a lifetime self-apologist, a producer of brief, perky critical essays instead of the major works presumably bottled up inside him. After all, he was called, by Kenneth Clark, "without doubt the most gifted man of his generation."[5]

It was wartime that conferred upon him the identity he had been seeking so long. The war allowed him to blossom as an "editor" and to become one of the most popular and sought-after cultural heavyweights in England. He had long been projecting a magazine. In April, 1934, he wrote in his journal: "Favorite daydream—edit a monthly magazine entirely subsidized by self. No advertisements, harmless title, deleterious contents."[6] And half-seriously he even proposed a title: *Meridian.* T. S. Eliot's decisions not to go on with the *Criterion* past January, 1939, left the field open, and several people besides Connolly were attracted by the image of themselves as cultural regulators, most notably the trio of Osbert Sitwell, Lord David Cecil, and Evelyn Waugh, who in the fall of 1939 proposed to start a magazine *("Duration")* like Connolly's, an idea they abandoned when the first number of *Horizon* appeared that December. For such a losing proposition as a cultural magazine an angel was required, and Connolly (and his assistant editor Stephen Spender) found one in "Peter" (actually Victor William) Watson, the heir of a margarine fortune and an aesthete and collector of modern painting. "A pansy of means," Waugh unkindly designated him.[7] Although Connolly constantly sought to reduce the deficit by enlarging the subscription list—it seldom rose above 5,000—Watson covered the loss, and for ten years *Horizon: A Review of Literature and Art* appeared monthly, comprising finally around 10,000 pages of exquisite poetry and prose and art reproductions, produced and read in the midst of the most discouraging and terrible destruction, not just of human bodies and buildings but of traditional stays against artistic and intellectual barbarism. The whole operation, which published some of the finest writing during the early years when Britain was widely assumed to be losing the war, constitutes one of the high moments in the long history of British eccentricity. As a cultural act, it was as stubborn as Churchill's political behavior.

Connolly's aims are set forth in a brochure advertising the magazine after its first year and soliciting more subscribers:

> Now we can say that *if . . . support continues and increases* we can carry on in 1941, improving upon our literary record, encouraging the young writers-at-arms who seem to find the need to write more irresistible as the War progresses, keeping them in touch with their French and American contemporaries—in short, continuing our policy of publishing the best critical and creative writing we can find in wartime England and maintaining the continuity of the present with the past.

And Connolly goes on to list *Horizon's* triumphs so far, under the heading "A Year of Achievement": Spender's "September Journal"; Orwell's "Boys' Weeklies"; Maclaren-Ross's notable story "A Bit of a Smash"; Brian Howard's memoir of his escape from France; Peter Quennell's "Byron in Venice"; political pieces by both liberals and conservatives—by Priestley, R. H. Crossman, and Peter Cromwell. The Forces have contributed impressively, Connolly notes, mentioning Alun Lewis and Goronwy Rhys. "But all-pervading though the War has become," Connolly observes, "it has never been allowed to dominate the essential literary values which *Horizon* upholds." Indeed, "during the months when London was severely bombed, when the offices of *Horizon* lay under dust and plaster, it was *D. H. Lawrence in Bandol*, by Rhys Davies, and *'The Temptation' by Hieronymus Bosch*, by Robert Melville, that were carried by hand (no other means of communication being available) to our printer."

The titles of those articles will suggest *Horizon's* focus and presumed readership. The magazine's assumptions about its audience merit a term like *noble*—it proceeded on assumptions hardly entertained by anyone since the days of Matthew Arnold's belief in the possibility of a high general culture. *Horizon* spoke to "general readers" of a humanistically educated kind, presumed to be equally interested in sensitive fiction and poetry; painting, architecture, and the history of styles; sophisticated travel; music; philosophy; and European political history. There was no talking-down whatever, and *Horizon* went so far—by printing an occasional essay in French—as to assume polylingual readers as interested in Continental aesthetic theory as in British. "Matthew Arnold Frenchified"—i.e., hedonized—would be a not too misleading indication of much of *Horizon*'s contents. Addressed with such steady intellectual respect, an audience fit though few, intensely loyal, was accumulated, and very many readers were servicemen sick of the stupidity and chickenshit who regarded their monthly *Horizon* as their only handhold on the civilized world. Many of these would agree with Captain J. R. Strick, who wrote in his diary just after the fall of Paris in 1940, "While style is still available one must live with style." Two years later, Strick is to be found reading *Horizon* on a transport bound for the Mediterranean and getting into trouble with his CO for reading to the troops Maclaren-Ross's "I Had to Go Sick," that memorable registration of the likelihood of service procedures to misfire. Strick's CO, he notes, "reproved me for undermining morale, a ridiculous attitude, I think."[8] Later, Strick's subscription copies arrived safely and regularly in Iraq.

Horizon probably meant most to such sensitive, unclubbable types as Ronald Blythe, who recalls how thin was the trickle of civilized discourse that sustained him in the midst of wartime deprivation:

> A few magazines and books—impossible now to convey their effect to anyone who did not read them at the time—provided the "civilization" with which to counter the pain, the general racket and the awful, though now much admired, bonhomie, through which we floundered.[9]

Actually, *Horizon* might convey the impression that the European war was being fought about literature and art history (e.g., "Some Notes on English Baroque," by Terence Heywood, in issue No. 11) rather than about Poland's territorial sovereignty or the right of the European Jews to survive. Spender reports that after the first few numbers of *Horizon*, "we received letters from pilots fighting in the Battle of Britain, often saying that they felt that so long as *Horizon* continued they had a cause to fight for." [10] But not everyone was enthusiastic. Those who thought "aesthetes" bogus and comic, like Waugh, heard in *Horizon* "an ugly accent—RAF pansy—which kept breaking in; not indeed from you," he wrote Connolly in 1953, "but from your artless colleagues." [11] And twice in his fiction Waugh frowned at—if he did not totally satirize—Connolly and his magazine, once in *Put Out More Flags* in the character of Ambrose Silk and his magazine *Ivory Tower*, and again in *Sword of Honor*, in the character of Everard Spruce, founder and editor of *Survival*. "The war had raised Spruce," says Waugh, "to unrivalled eminence," once his magazine, "devoted 'to the survival of values,' " got going. [12] Spruce is of course enthusiastic over the loathsome Ludovic's *Pensées*—a glance at Connolly's aperçus in *The Unquiet Grave*—and is quick to accept them for *Survival*.

On the night of Sunday, December 29, 1940, London experienced its worst air attack to date. Incendiaries ignited 1500 fires in the City and Westminster. Miles away, the journalist Hector Bolitho was watching from Knightsbridge with the actress Katina Paxinou: "I could hear her sobbing," he wrote, "as she clung to me." [13] Acres of docks, factories, offices, and warehouses were destroyed, including some of the warehouses near St. Paul's which held in publishers' storage five million books, now ashes. Another literary casualty was the fire-bombed roof of Samuel Johnson's house off the Strand, together with most of the garret where he had made his *Dictionary*.

Trying to get to work early the next week, an office worker would have climbed through streets piled with rubble and tried to avoid the shards of glass littered everywhere. He could peer into the still smoking craters in the street revealing obscene tangles of wires and cables normally decently concealed. Some fires would still be burning. Burnt-out vehicles would squat stupidly in the streets. Hot soot and charcoal would threaten clothing and skin. Wet hoses would still be spread around like giant spaghetti. This worker's office, when he finally got there, might be a pile of brick and mortar and blackened junk—furniture, telephones, typewriters, files, all destroyed. And he would begin to notice something else, the smell of the dead beginning to rise from deep underneath the rubble. But turning homeward, shocked and angry, if he had passed some newsagent whose premises were yet intact he would have seen in the rack the brown and beige cover of the latest *Horizon*, No. 13. For a shilling, he could have taken this home and used it to persuade himself that despite Sunday's happenings the world was not quite insane. Indeed, to persuade himself that mind and soul and the instinct for creation and beauty were alive and busy, as even a publisher's ad, facing the Contents page, suggests by asserting that Lewis Mumford's new book, *The Culture of Cities*, indicates "what beliefs and hopes will give the survivors the courage to resist to the death the present flood of barbarism, and to lay down the foundations of the future"—wonderfully rich ironic imagery in the light of Sunday's architectural havoc.

This particular issue opens with Connolly's more-or-less regular editorial feature, "Comment." Here he observes that those complaining that this new war has spawned no "War Poets" unreasonably expect new naive idealists like Rupert Brooke and Herbert Asquith instead of what this number of *Horizon* gives them, the tired, laconic, politely fed-up Alun Lewis of "All Day It Has Rained." "That we lack patriotic poetry at the moment is a healthy sign," says Connolly, "for if it were possible to offer any evidence that civilization has progressed in the last twenty years, it would be that which illustrated the decline of the aggressive instinct." And he goes on to derive some slight consolation from the destruction of historic architecture by the bombing, for at least it clears away the distraction of possessions and other irrelevancies to the life of art and thought. In this number the reader would also come upon such compensations for barbarity as Dylan Thomas's "Death and Entrances," an essay by G. W. Stonier on the differences between French and British literary life, the second of Peter Quennell's two essays on Byron in Venice, and reviews by Kathleen Raine of Auden's *Another Time* and by John Pope-Hennessey of Anthony Blunt's *Artistic Theory in Italy*. And a superb editorial touch: to provide an appropriate context for Alun Lewis's poem, with which this number opens, it closes with a review by Lewis of Edward Thomas's *The Trumpet and Other Poems*, a review which is virtually a prose gloss on "All Day It Has Rained." Lewis writes: "I have been garrisoned for six months in Edward Thomas's country and walked his walks. . . . I have read his poems often and often in tent and hut. . . . His poetry has the quality of bread, or tweed, or a ploughed field. . . ." And enclosed in this number is a single-sheet questionnaire ("Please let us have your views on *Horizon*") couched in the most "normal," unflapped and unflappable of terms, quite as if the magazine were not appearing regularly in the midst of unprecedented mass butchery and destruction:

How did you first *hear* of *Horizon?*

Would you like more or less: Poetry? _____
      Stories? _____ Book Reviews? _____

Would you please give us the following
particulars about yourself: Age? _____
      Sex? _____ Married or single? _____.

And on the back cover, there's a postal address form making it easy for
the reader to tie string around the magazine and "Send *Horizon* to a Man
in Uniform": no reason why he should be deprived of these 80 pages of
intelligence and sensibility just because he's forced to languish in some
stupid barracks somewhere.

One more illustration of the brave anomaly represented by *Horizon:*
on Wednesday, April 16, 1941, occurred the worst air raid on London
yet, memorable ever after as simply "the Wednesday" or sometimes "the
bad Wednesday night." Bolitho again: "We have been through London's
most terrible night." He was in the shelter underneath the Hotel Savoy
while 450 German bombers attacked for eight hours, killing 2000 civilians. "I think the most horrible thing was the sound of burning timber.
The crackling, malicious sound, like little devilish laughs. . . . Then
there seemed to be nurses and people bleeding. . . . Injured people in a
line, their faces cut, their hands cut, a few being carried, one with her
face slashed. . . ." Later, the Strand "looked amazed and broken in the
morning light. Buildings we had known for twenty years were no more
than cracked walls. . . . Little tongues of flame still licked the edge of
great advertisements. . . . Even the trees were wounded. There were
scars where the bark had been torn." [14] During that night Graham Greene,
an air-raid warden near the University of London, was engaged in clearing away the wounded and the dead. He was miraculously missed by the
bombs falling near him. Of one particularly close call, when a stick of
three bombs fell next to him, he remembered: "One really thought that
this was the end, but it wasn't exactly frightening—one had ceased to
believe in the possibility of surviving the night. Began an Act of Contrition." In Greene's area, the bodies under the rubble stank for days afterward. [15] But soon the ever trustworthy, imperturbable *Horizon* appeared,
this time offering an essay by Herbert Read on postwar culture; four
brief memoirs of the late Virginia Woolf, by Eliot, Rose Macaulay, Vita
Sackville-West, and William Plomer (Woolf had killed herself the month

before, motivated in part, Vera Brittain thought, by events like "the Wednesday," so typical of "the violent assaults which had caused . . . Woolf to escape from the disorderly barbarism of contemporary life");[16] an essay by A. J. A. Symons on "Wilde at Oxford"; an account by Sonia Brownell (one of Connolly's assistants on the magazine, later George Orwell's second wife) of a forthcoming show of paintings at Oxford; and a critical commentary by Arturo Barea reprehending Hemingway for numerous inaccuracies about the Spanish War in *For Whom the Bell Tolls*.

And thus it went. For the rest of the war and beyond, up to January, 1950, and a total of 120 numbers, readers of *Horizon* were regaled every four weeks with material of almost unbelievable excellence. If in his own editorials Connolly could sometimes be silly and sentimental and second-rate, especially soft-minded about the sort of cultural improvements to be expected from a future enlightened socialism, in his selection of others' writings he seldom slipped below a standard close to breath-taking. Maclaren-Ross recalls him at the Café Royal going over the galleys of an article on detective stories by W. Somerset Maugham, which Connolly had apparently commissioned. He passed over the sheets for Maclaren-Ross to read. Handing back Maugham's article with approval a bit later, he heard Connolly say, as he stuffed the proofs back into his bulging and untidy briefcase, "I've decided not to print it." "But it's by Maugham!," said Maclaren-Ross. Connolly: "I don't say this is a *bad* article. It's good enough to be accepted by *Horizon* but not quite good enough for me to publish."[17]

It was this brave, uncompromising attitude that sustained Connolly through the horrors and the darkness—and a paper shortage so severe as occasionally to reduce *Horizon* to sixty gray, crummy pages. It was Connolly's rare (and doubtless neurotic) commitment to distinction that determined *Horizon*'s superb contents, with essays by Benedetto Croce and Hermann Hesse and Bertrand Russell, Gide, Sartre, and Koestler, Aldous Huxley, Forster, and Orwell—it was in *Horizon* that many Orwell classics first appeared, including "Politics and the English Language." Connolly printed essays by Eliot ("The Man of Letters and the Future of Europe"), H. G. Wells, Greene, and Herbert Read, Nancy Cunard, Olivia Manning, and Nancy Mitford, who, in *Horizon* No. 35, permitted to surface her hunger for butter, eggs, cheese, and something good to drink in an essay on the Victorian autobiographer and travel writer Augustus Hare. "If a glance at his photograph reveals the face of a sulky badger," she wrote, "there is compensation lower down; the waistcoast, the watch chain are tightly stretched over dairy produce and fine wines—oh to have been Augustus Hare." Reprinting this essay in 1962, she adds a note to explain her interjection of 1942: "This essay was written in wartime."[18] Connolly gave space to Osbert Sitwell and A. J. Ayer and Sean O'Faolain and the aged Logan Pearsall Smith. Enid Starkie helped relieve wartime uniformity and deprivation by a series on French "Eccentrics of 1830," and although the *New Yorker* was unavailable in England because of severe restrictions on shipping space, Connolly got hold of one issue and extracted an essay by Edmund Wilson on Malraux and Silone. But the contents was not all literary and aesthetic. Major General J. F. C. Fuller wrote on military theory, and in the number for July, 1944, there was a sensitive anonymous "Mass-Observation" piece on emotions at home on D-Day: "It's a shame. I hate to think of it. All those fine young fellows being mown down. The pick of our boys, and there's more waiting in reserve. I can't help feeling depressed." Amidst the keening of air-raid sirens and the rumble of collapsing masonry, the most sensitive and intelligent writers Connolly could find (so distinguished that identification in contributors notes was almost never necessary) reassessed the achievements of Goethe and Schelling and Hölderlin, Benjamin Constant and Gerard de Nerval and Diderot and Rousseau and Flaubert, Balzac, Proust, Baudelaire, Rimbaud, Apollinaire, Anatole France and Henry Montherlant, Molière, Mallarmé, and Camus. There were considerations of Nietzsche, Kierkegaard, of Spengler and Jung and Karl Barth, of Yeats, Lorca, Seferis and Elytis, and of Donne, Boswell, Sterne, and Peacock. The merits were canvassed and displayed of Tolstoy, Turgenev, and Pasternak, Kipling, D. H. Lawrence, Joyce, Eliot, and Sir James G. Frazer and his *Golden Bough*. And there was a lot on Henry James, to Connolly an invaluable "symbol of a certain way of life, a way that is threatened not only by the totalitarian enemy but by the philistine friend. . . ."[19] Indeed, the quintessential *Horizon* article would be something like "Henry James's Year in France," recognizing the general hunger for such current rarities as subtlety and honor, on the one hand, and Continental travel (and cuisine) on the other. And that article did appear, written by Mervyn Jones-Evans, in *Horizon* No. 79.

Horizon's art consciousness was as intense as its sense of literature. Connolly published criticism of painting and sculpture and architecture by Matisse and Juan Gris and Giorgio de Chirico. Philip Hendy discoursed on Henry Moore, Robert Melville on Picasso, Kenneth Clark on Jack Yeats, Jankel Adler and Robin Ironside on Paul Klee, and Jean

Paulhan on Georges Braque. Ben Nicholson and John Piper and John Rothenstein wrote on contemporary practice and theory, and Ironside took a longer view with "The Art Criticism of Ruskin." All this was fleshed out with both monochrome and color reproductions of works by Monet and Picasso, Lipchitz and Arp and Gris and Duchamp, and even Grant Wood and the photographs of Cecil Beaton. In *Horizon* No. 40, for April, 1943, Connolly laments some of the magazine's younger contributors killed in combat and while doing so comes close to locating his magazine's bizarre focus on the highest art within a context of the most awful horror. He notes of Rollo Woolley, a promising writer of short fiction (e.g., "The Pupil," in No. 26), that his "death as a fighter pilot in Tunisia must now be presumed," an end especially unthinkable and ironic because, Connolly adds, "he was a charming, modest, dreamy young man, whom I last saw wandering round a picture gallery."

Likewise, Connolly's eye and ear missed few poets worth paying attention to. He printed Auden and MacNeice, Empson and Day Lewis, Roy Fuller, George Barker, and Vernon Watkins. Dylan Thomas's "Fern Hill" appeared first in *Horizon*, nor did Connolly fail to respond to a very different sort of excellence in practitioners like John Betjeman and Gavin Ewart. C. M. Bowra, *Horizon*'s Russian expert, translated poems by both Alexander Blok and Pasternak, but Connolly entertained a sufficiently high regard for his readers to allow the French of Louis Aragon and Paul Eluard to remain untranslated. Issue No. 50, in February, 1944, included "A Little Anthology of American Verse," a 17-page section put together by Oscar Williams, which included poems by Wallace Stevens and Marianne Moore, Allen Tate, and Karl Shapiro, Delmore Schwartz and E. E. Cummings, Muriel Rukeyser, Howard Nemerov, and Randall Jarrell. Later, in April, 1945, the war almost over, Connolly would suggest in little room its unspeakable cost by reprinting from the *Partisan Review* Jarrell's "Ball Turret Gunner." A similar instinct for the memorable is apparent in Connolly's choices among short stories: here his authors include V. S. Pritchett and Eudora Welty, Elizabeth Bowen and Robert Penn Warren, Henry Miller, Honor Tracy, Waugh, and Alberto Moravia.

Connolly's poets and fiction writers alone—Jarrell and Maclaren-Ross are good examples—would suggest his success in printing, as in 1950 he said he hoped he had, "what many years hence will be recognized as alive and original. . . ."[20] But he was just as alert to the merits of memoirs by Denton Welch and travel pieces by Graham Greene. A travel piece on New Zealand by Anna Kavan, in the form of a letter to "Dear John" answering his questions about living there after the war, set off a whole series focusing on the luscious fantasy of postwar travel and residence abroad titled "Where Shall John Go?," which considered the pros and cons of living in the U.S.A., Turkey, Syria, Persia, Egypt, Chile, and Argentina. But despite its sensitivity to the verbal and visual, *Horizon* might be thought somewhat tone-deaf, for it seldom dealt with music, although now and then the reader musically inclined was rewarded with essays like Pierre Jean Jouve's "The Present Greatness of Mozart," Gerland Abraham's "Shostakovich," or Béla Bartók's "Race Purity in Music." Film seemed an art not yet subtle enough for *Horizon*'s attention, although it did single out *Citizen Kane,* and with appropriate enthusiasm. Theater likewise it tended to leave to other magazines, even if once Peter Ustinov did write on the state of contemporary plays and Beyrl de Zoete on the choreography of Frederick Ashton.

Confronting the unlikelihood, if not the impossibility, of a phenomenon like *Horizon* appearing in the wartime U.S.A. is a way of recognizing the persistence in Britain of the impulses which led to the Aesthetic Movement of the 1890s. *Horizon* is one of that movement's late reverberations. Despite Connolly's "modern" abrupt idiom, the tone of Pater and Wilde is detectable in *Horizon*'s comment on having completed its fifth year: "Accused of 'aestheticism,' 'escapism,' 'ivory-towerism,' 'bourgeois formalism,' 'frivolity,' and 'preferring art to life,' *[Horizon]* pleads on all these counts 'guilty and proud of it.' " But as Connolly goes on in this self-evaluating "Comment," it becomes clear that *Horizon*'s "aestheticism" does not imply any abandonment of the powerful social, indeed satiric, obligations of criticism. Just the opposite. Wartime culture, Connolly points out, is appalling:

> Books are becoming as bad as they are ugly; newspapers continue to be as dull with four pages as they were once with forty; reviewing has sunk to polite blurb-quoting; nothing original is produced; journalists grow sloppier, vainer, more ignorantly omniscient than ever; the B.B.C. pumps religion and patriotism into all its programs; mediocrity triumphs. . . .[21]

But despite its admirable wartime fight against obviousness and banality, when peace came *Horizon* seemed to resemble increasingly just another Little Magazine, its compensations no longer so desperately needed. Exhausted after ten years of effort, Connolly closed it down in January,

1950, saying with a trace of bitterness, "A decade of our lives is quite enough to devote to a lost cause such as the pursuit and marketing of quality in contemporary writing."[22] It was ultimately the discouraging fact, the same in peacetime as in wartime, of the tiny-ness and finiteness of the intelligent humanistic audience that demoralized the Connolly who had once entertained such buoyant and joyous hopes for a postwar cultural redemption.

His faith in the existence of a civilized audience as well as his need for relief from the current deprivations permeate the little book of *pensées* he brought out late in 1944 and sold from the *Horizon* office, having coyly advertised it in the December *Horizon*: "We are able to offer our readers and the general public a beautifully printed limited edition of an original work by an English author entitled THE UNQUIET GRAVE, by Palinurus." Connolly then indicates what he thinks the book is conveying:

> *The Unquiet Grave* is a year's journey through the mind of a writer who is haunted by the turbulent Mediterranean figure of Palinurus, the drowned pilot [of Aeneas] whose uneasy ghost demands to be placated. Three movements indicate with deepening intensity the three blust'ring nights when he is adrift on the ocean, and the Epilogue examines the myth from both the historical and psychological aspects.

"Order in good time," readers are advised.

But all such high-powered insistence on the "mythic" theme of the little book doesn't disclose its unostensible subject, Connolly's acute and anguished sense of wartime deprivation, not just from food and drink and subtlety but from Continental and Mediterranean travel—and most of all from the company of his wife Jean Bakewell, now in the United States, his marriage having unravelled seriously—she would divorce him shortly after the war. "Cyril's lament," Waugh called *The Unquiet Grave*,[23] and there he has located Connolly's difficulty in objectifying his personal distress and rendering it in terms more universally gripping. The work seems to lack plot and point also because it is a collage put together without sufficient narrative design. *The Unquiet Grave* began as a journal and commonplace book Connolly kept during 1942 and 1943. After lots of tinkering, he had it set up in galleys, which he then scissored apart and arranged on the floor until the parts implied, in his view, a "quest myth"— an action of "initiation, a descent into hell, a purification and cure." Perhaps the total text can be said to do this, but a reader uninformed of Connolly's intentions is more likely to respond to the plaintive individual moments registering the familiar wartime dynamics of deprivation and desire. "*The Unquiet Grave* is inevitably a war book," Connolly noted in 1950. "As a Londoner [the author] was affected by the dirt and weariness, the gradual draining away under war conditions of light and color from the former capital of the world. . . ." The consciousness of deprivation included especially "the minds and culture of those across the channel who then seemed quite cut off from us, perhaps for ever. To evoke a French beach at that time was to be reminded that beaches did not exist for mines and pill-boxes and barbed wire but for us to bathe from. . . ." In short, "we must understand the author's obsession with pleasure at a time when nearly all pleasures were forbidden."[24]

And for Connolly, stranded in wartime London, pleasure means France and food and wine, or rather food, wine, and France, especially Paris and the Riviera and Périgord. The area bounded by Souillac in the north and Toulouse in the south Connolly embraces in what he calls "The Magic Circle," delimiting in the midst of wartime uniformity and anonymity that desideratum "A Charm Against the Group Man."[25] Connolly's text pathetically recalls the now-lost pleasures of the palate—truffles, "coffee being roasted," "smell of brioches from the bakeries"—and memories of happiness with Jane on the Riviera merge with memories of the cuisine: "At the local restaurant there would be one or two 'plats ǎ emporter,' to which I would add some wine, sausage, and Gruyère cheese. . . ."[26] And driving south down the Rhone Valley on Route Nationale 7 with access to unlimited petrol is made an emblem of the kind of civilized, unmilitary freedom the war has foreclosed, perhaps forever:

Peeling off the kilometres to the tune of "Blue Skies," sizzling down the long black liquid reaches of Nationale Sept, the plane trees going sha-sha-sha through the open window, the windscreen yellowing with crushed midges, she with the Michelin beside me, a handkerchief binding her hair.[27]

After much of this and a sober excursus on the worldwide neurosis which issues in wars, especially this one, Connolly brings his descant of deprivation to a close by designating La Napoule, on the Riviera, as the "real" terminus of Palinurus' journey, his *periplus*, not the place on the Gulf of Policastro specified by Vergil.

Looking back five years later, Connolly was aware how deeply his little book had been determined by its wartime context, and he was conscious now of a need to "explain" its excesses and apologize for its indulgences. In the same way, five years after the war Evelyn Waugh reported to Graham Greene that a re-reading of *Brideshead Revisited* had "appalled" him and that he proposed to rewrite it. The novel and its faults arose naturally, he acknowledged, as an act of compensation in a world of "spam, Nissen huts, black-out—but it won't do for peace-time."[28] When Waugh reissued the novel in 1960 with, as he explains in a preface, "many small additions and some substantial cuts," he recalled the wartime moment of composition—early 1944—as "a period of . . . privation, . . . the period of soya beans and Basic English." As a result, he notes,

> the book is infused with a kind of gluttony, for food and wine, for the splendors of the recent past, and for rhetorical and ornamental language, which now with a full stomach I find distasteful. I have modified the grosser passages. . . .[29]

One of these, registering Charles Ryder's initial reaction to Anthony Blanche, went: "I found myself enjoying him voraciously, like the fine piece of cookery he was."[30] In the revision Waugh perceives that now, in peacetime, the cookery simile will seem to go too far, and he cuts it. But enough of the original text remains to suggest the wartime environment, like Ryder's circumstantial, mouth-watering account of the dinner he orders for Rex Mottram in Paris:

> I remember the dinner well—soup of *oseille*, a sole quite simply cooked in a white wine sauce, a *caneton à la presse*, a lemon soufflé. At the last minute, fearing that the whole thing was too simple for Rex, I added *caviare aux blinis*. And for wine I let him give me a bottle of 1906 Montrachet, then at its prime, and with the duck, a Clos de Bèze of 1904.[31]

That fantasy of 1944 acquires poignancy when we hear Waugh a year earlier complaining of being served sheeps' hearts and a surfeit of "fish dinners and vegetable broth,"[32] and a bit later having to endure Randolph Churchill's cooking at their liaison post in Yugoslavia: "Randolph cooked dinner consisting of one enormous, raw potato each with a hard egg in the middle—uneatable."[33] (Twenty days later Waugh was reading the proofs of *Brideshead* for its serialization in the American luxury magazine *Town and Country*.) And once the war was over he found austerity closing in tighter than ever. "We have practically no meat," he wrote in his diary in October, 1945, "two meals a week—and live on eggs and macaroni, cheese . . . bread, and wine; very occasionally we get a rather nasty fish."[34]

There are additional ways in which *Brideshead Revisited* constitutes a compensatory fantasy of not-war. The framework of army crudity and dullness enclosing the text at beginning and end underlines the value of the contrasts within—the beauty and "charm" of Sebastian Flyte, the wit of Anthony Blanche, the eccentricity of Ryder's father. In place of the sadistic colonel, skilled in chickenshit, the nice Nanny Hawkins. Instead of the straight lines enjoined by the military—the posture of attention, the "dressing" of ranks, bunks, and tents, "the ultimate straight line of the bullet"[35]—the novel offers the inestimable relief of the baroque, with its benignly impertinent curves and surprises, and its joy in the counterfeit. The fountain at Brideshead effects Ryder's "conversion to the baroque," that antithesis in every way to the artifacts and tone of wartime:

> Sebastian set me to draw it. It was an ambitious subject for an amateur—an oval basin with an island of formal rocks at its center; on the rocks grew, in stone, formal tropical vegetation and wild English fern in its natural fronds; through them ran a dozen streams that counterfeited springs; and round them sported fantastic tropical animals, camels and camelopards and an ebullient lion all vomiting water. . . . This was my conversion to the baroque. Here . . . as I . . . sat, hour by hour, before the fountain, probing its shadows, tracing its lingering echoes, rejoicing in all its clustered feats of daring and invention, I felt a whole new system of nerves alive within me, as though the water that spurted and bubbled among its stones was indeed a life-giving spring.[36]

But that was years ago. Now, in wartime, the fountain is dry and dirty, a receptacle for the troops' cigarette butts and half-eaten sandwiches. And to Ryder's current residence "under canvas," what greater contrast than the former elegance of Brideshead, its decor exhibiting a plethora of "wreathed medallions," "Chippendale fret-work," and "gilt mirrors," and the life lived there such as to call for ample civilized allusion, to Quattrocento portraiture, Lear on the heath, the Duchess of Malfi, Ruskin and Pre-Raphaelitism, and Venetian architecture, whose visual recall merges with gustatory remembrance as we hear of "melon and *prosciutto* on the balcony in the cool of the morning" and "hot cheese sandwiches and champagne cocktails at the English [revised, 1960, to 'Harry's'] bar."[37] No wonder the first readers of *Brideshead Revisited* experienced so warm a feeling. As Harold Acton remembers, "By December 1944 it was a nostalgic luxury, if not a tonic, to read of an affluent epicurean society that had all but ceased to exist," to taste if only in imagination in colorful young people's Oxford rooms luncheons featuring plovers' eggs, lobster, and crab, all washed down, as Acton says, by "good vintages . . . available at reasonable cost."[38] And the excesses of *Brideshead Revisited* had the power to occasion excesses in its critics, like Rose Macaulay, who in *Horizon* while noting Waugh's overripeness betrayed her own wartime hunger for richness and complication. "There is . . . much subtly precise and intelligent writing [in the novel]," she observes, but then, instead of saying something like "But often it's too fancy," she says, "But it flowers too often into an orchidaceous luxury of bloom."[39]

But even more in need of redemption than Waugh's wartime circumstances were Osbert Sitwell's, for Waugh was only middle class. Sitwell was upper, and his peacetime environment had comprised not merely splendid and copious food and wine but ample theater and books, costly tailoring, dances and late suppers, ballets and concerts, parties and luncheons with society hostesses and their accumulations of chic writers and artists, afternoons at private art galleries, and holidays wandering among the baroque masterpieces in Italy. His was an elaborately full life organized on principles of pure anti-philistinism. Indeed, his family seat in Derbyshire, "Renishaw," was in a way a smaller Brideshead, straitened, to be sure (there was no electric light), but still with terraces and gardens and statues, endless corridors, fine furniture, pictures, and servants. In addition there was a "beach house" at Scarborough, and in London a town house and, in due course, a small house in Chelsea for Osbert and his brother and a flat for his sister, not to mention their father's mad hobby, the preposterous 100-room, thirteenth-century castle near Florence he had bought and restored. And there was a title, of a sort. Osbert's vigorously eccentric father, Sir George Sitwell, was the Fourth Baronet, and at his death Osbert became the Fifth.

"The war," says John Pearson, "cut [Osbert] off from almost everything he loved and valued—from society, from Italy, from art and travel, food and friendship."

> It had also left him, for the first time, with no distractions and a regular routine; so he began to recreate the rich, nostalgic dream-world of his past to set against the drab reality of Churchill's war.[40]

For this operation Osbert installed himself at Renishaw, where, writing the five successive volumes of his memoir, *Left Hand, Right Hand!*, from 1941 to 1949, he experienced the painful wartime dearth of clothing, cigarettes, and gasoline, as well as coal for heating and gas for cooking. And worse, he suffered powerfully from the abeyance of eccentricity, complication, variety, subtlety, irony, and sensitivity. Condemned to live in "this cruel and meaningless epoch" (vii),[41] he set out to redeem the time by means of diction, sentence structure, and wit. A fully complex use of language would be his weapon against wartime monosyllabism and primitive predication, which assumed for the duration the most stupid of audiences. "Complicated in surface and crowned with turrets and with pinnacles"—that's what he wanted his autobiography to be, "old-fashioned and extravagant" (xiii). His labyrinthine sentences and rococo usages would be his antidotes to such blunt, utilitarian injunctions as

Wage War on Waste,

or

Make Do and Mend,

or

Start a Rag Bag!

His sinuous ironies would be the counterweight to such cornball slogan-eering as "Waste the Food and Help the Hun," "A Clear Plate Means a Clear Conscience," and "Dr. Carrot Guards Your Health." His genuine wit would expose the false wit of utterances like "Steps You Can Take to Save Your Shoes."

Imaginative revisiting of a family past swarming with eccentrics is one of Sitwell's correctives to the obligatory uniformity of the wartime present. Among these refreshing oddities is his grandfather Lord Londesborough, one moment driven to a bizarre parsimony by a conviction of his imminent bankruptcy, the next throwing all his substance after "yachts, races, coaches, carriages, sport of every kind, especially shooting, speculation, and the stage . . ." (159). A great deal of his energy and money he poured into an extravagant musical comedy replete with costly tableaux and unprecedented scenic effects. *Babil and Bijou* ran for 160 performances in 1972 and seemed to one typical observer "the most scandalous waste of money on record" (165–66). But in his native Scarborough, Lord Londesborough was only one in an immense cast of human curiosities:

> There was, for example, Count de Burgh. A tradesman, retired and prosperous, who had bought a papal title, he always wore, over tightly laced stays, a frock coat, and to the rim of his top hat he had attached a row of curls, so that as he walked down the middle of the road . . . and doffed his hat to his acquaintance, in a gesture reminiscent of the court of old France, his hair swept off with it. . . . Then there was a lady who dressed, in the daytime, in a ball gown of blue chiffon sprinkled with silver stars, [and] a man who thought he was a cat and mewed. . . . (199)

"My ancestors," Sitwell writes, "have for generations been used to getting their own way" (93). Illustrative of this principle are his parents, Sir George and Lady Ida, he with his medieval obsessions and his constant nutty projects for "improving" his estate, she with her amazing stupidity and total inability to understand money, which once resulted in her dramatic victimization by a con-man and her imprisonment for three months. The world of these people was literally "colorful," and recalling it in wartime was a distinct relief from what Anthony Powell calls "the boundlessly unbecoming hue of khaki."[42] In Edwardian Scarborough were to be seen the jockey carts hired by the rich, their boy drivers wearing silk shirts striped "maroon and saffron, lemon and rusty pink, sapphire blue and water white," adding to the scene "an air that was almost gothic, giving it something of the checkered and slashed beauty of the Palio in Siena" (172). But even the poor formerly put on a show of color, delightful to remember as the war's olive drab and high-mindedness grow ever more menacing to the subversive values of wit and surprise. In the world now lost to the war,

> the gangs of miners returning from their work would tramp along the roads, wearing . . . scarlet tunics, the cast-off tunics of a happy army, then still dressed in musical-comedy uniforms, which the colliers bought

regularly; a costume which set off the blackness of their faces and their scarlet lips. (131)

The hallmark of Sitwell's style is a very un-wartime copiousness, implying both abundance and leisure. He seldom offers a single example when twenty-four will do as well. Thus, for example, the list of twenty-four of Sir George's topics for researches to be conducted and works to be written, a list containing such items as

> The Young Pretender's Court in Rome,
> The Origin of Surnames,
> Sweet Preserves in the Fourteenth Century,
> Wool-gathering in Medieval Times and Since,
> Introduction of the Peacock into Western Gardens,
> On the Colors of Flowers,

and Sir George's favorite topic,

> The History of the Fork.[43]

Long comic lists Osbert constructs as one of the few available antidotes to the prevailing poverty and utilitarianism. Verbal plethora becomes his form of rebellion. Of one of Sir George's many hypochondriacal illnesses, Osbert writes:

> Each of [the doctors] recommended at least one new cure, and more probably returned, after its failure, to prescribe a further experiment. The invalid tried them all, one after the other, in good faith and in swift rotation: continual fresh air . . . , no fresh air, to lay his head on hop pillows, to take exercise, to give up exercise, to stop smoking, to smoke special cigarettes, to live on meat, to touch no meat, to give up alcohol, to drink champagne and port, to walk, to run, to sing, to lie down for long periods without moving, never to keep still, to take up golf, to abandon it, "not to use his mind," and to "think of other things". . . .[44]

The striking popularity of Osbert's performance suggests that his copious sentences delighted hungry readers as well as the deprived author. As John Pearson notes, "A public jaded by the austerity of total war was ready for [Osbert's] endless sentences." Indeed, as if his words constituted a literal feast, "The verbally deprived could gorge themselves upon this convoluted prose, and relish the extravagance with which he recreated a suddenly familiar world which everyone had lost."[45] And while Osbert was doing this, his sister Edith was conducting her own poetic war against "utility" and drabness with her portentous imagery of ores and porphyry, diamonds, sapphires, emeralds, and rubies, amethysts, amber, myrrh, and viridian, and pre-eminently gold, all set in an archaic, non-utilitarian word-order ("Huge is the sun of amethysts and rubies"). Her poems are repositories of the "rich words," as Ronald Blythe observes, "which contrasted so vividly with the war's special poverty."[46] And Edith's onetime protégé Dylan Thomas, who, we are told, "regarded the war as a personal affront,"[47] developed his similar wartime line in abundance and extravagance. His surprising diction and strenuous lyricism are his counterweights to khaki, and the violent compassion of his poems is one of his responses to the obligatory wartime hate of the enemy that so depressed him. "Europe is hideously obvious and shameless," he wrote Vernon Watkins in the summer of 1940. "Am I to rejoice when a 100 men are killed in the air?"[48] And the stylistic lushness of Waugh and the Sitwells and Thomas was gratifying enough to deprived audiences to persist as a notable postwar style, from Christopher Fry's *A Phoenix Too Frequent* (1946) all the way to the late 1950s, with Lawrence Durrell's *Alexandria Quartet*.

Reading in Wartime

Until Sitwell's *Left Hand, Right Hand!* was available—1944 in the United States, 1945 in Britain—readers seeking literary relief from wartime had to utilize other reading matter. *Horizon*, of course, was a ready remedy, but intelligence, on the one hand, and peace and quiet, on the other, were to be found in the novels of Henry James and Anthony Trollope. It might not be going too far to suggest that the current vogue of both writers was solidified if not established by their popularity during the 1940s as counterweights to wartime utilitarianism and vulgarity of mind. Siegfried Sassoon favored James's middle-period works because they were " 'so all beautifully remote' from Hitlerism and its brutal behavior,"[1] and Trollope's novels were widely read because, in addition to their distance from the current violence and stupidity, they were handily available in the World's Classics pocket-sized editions, fit to be slipped into uniform pockets and gas-mask containers, like the equally popular unbellicose works of Dickens and Jane Austen. But Austen was valuable regardless of format. Ill with pneumonia in December, 1943, Churchill had *Pride and Prejudice* read to him by his daughter Sarah. It was his first encounter with this book, and he wrote later: "What calm lives they had, those people! No worries about the French Revolution, or the crashing struggle of the Napoleonic wars. Only manners controlling natural passion as far as they could, together with cultured explanations of any mischances."[2]

If D. H. Lawrence's reputation declined during the war (too angry? too close to the tone of the war itself?), E. M. Forster's rose, in part, doubtless, because of Lionel Trilling's thoughtful recommendation, in his critical study of 1943, of Forster's decidedly un-simple, ironic values, so useful in preserving sensitive and intelligent people from the war's more debilitating simplifications, especially from the consequences of the official and popular view that since the Axis is vile, the Allies must be morally wonderful. To Trilling, Forster is useful because he refuses "to play the old . . . game of antagonistic principles, . . . an attractive game because it gives us the sensation of thinking, and its first rule is that if one of two opposed principles is wrong, the other is necessarily right."[3] During the war Forster spoke on books frequently for the BBC, recommending "escape" reading sometimes—like A. J. A. Symons's *The Quest for Corvo*—but more often suggesting works bearing on the ethical complexities of the moment—*War and Peace, The Merchant of Venice,* Arnold Toynbee's *A Study of History,* T. S. Eliot's "Little Gidding." He assumed a bright and responsible reading public. "People are reading more, and reading good stuff," he declared in a broadcast in December, 1941. "It is as if the war has brought home to us all the seriousness of existence. We want to find out more about the universe while we can."[4] On the other hand, W. Somerset Maugham, broadcasting in the United States on the topic "Reading Under Bombing," came out for detective stories as the great distractor, but admitted that such immense nineteenth-century

novels as Ouida's and Charlotte Yonge's had their uses too.[5] Dull books
were what Anthony Powell wanted. At least during the Blitz, he used to
settle into bed with books whose monumental dullness offered some relief
from the prevailing noise, excitement, and terror. As he recalls, "War
[lent] attraction to the prosiest aspects of the past," and thus he read
"works like Toland's *History of the Druids* or Hearne's *Remarks and Recollections.* . . ." A comfort to re-visit so apparently stable a world "while
the blitz was reverberating through the night air."[6]

Nineteenth-century life at the universities, the quiet broken only by
learned demurrers over the port in the Senior Common Room, would
seem to lie at the farthest remove from life in wartime. Thus the popularity of books like Sir Charles Oman's *Memories of Victorian Oxford* and
G. B. Grundy's *55 Years at Oxford*. In fact, almost anything Victorian
would do, and both Thackeray and Willkie Collins enjoyed revivals. And
of course some books were popular because they managed to interpret the
contemporary scene in optimistic ways. The Great War had generated its
useful myth of the Angels of Mons—ghosts of British archers at Agin-
court who came back to assist a not very inspiring British retreat. Likewise, the Second World War had Paul Gallico's *The Snow Goose*, about
a beautiful, quasi-supernatural white bird flying above a small boat and,
as an omen of salvation, assisting the proceedings at Dunkirk. The *Times
Literary Supplement* found the story "beautiful and deeply moving," told
"with all the delicacy of touch and allegorical suggestion of a fairy tale,"[7]
and one dear, credulous reader, Vere Hodgson, allowed herself to entertain the idea that "perhaps it is founded on fact, like the Angels of Mons."[8]

Like Osbert Sitwell recovering his outlandish ancestors, some readers
went in search of past eccentric personalities as a way of opposing anonymity and uniformity, as well as offsetting the obedient, goody-goody
character the war had proposed as desirable. In "Reading in Wartime,"
Edwin Muir projected Samuel Johnson and Tolstoy's Ivan Ilyich as models
of the un-military and the un-subservient and the supremely human:

> Boswell's turbulent friend
> And his deafening verbal strife,
> Ivan Ilyich's death
> Tell me more about life,
> Both being personal,
> Than all the carnage can,
> Retrieve the shape of man,
> Lost and anonymous.

What is wanted now is

> the original face,
> The individual soul. . . .[9]

Joseph Wood Krutch's biography *Samuel Johnson*, published in 1944, was popular partly because it offered, and indeed, as a wartime book, over-stressed, just that original face and individual soul. An eccentric person-ality like Johnson could easily be imagined as an enemy of wartime cant and of the popular wartime character-type stigmatized by Connolly as the Group Man. One eloquent photograph of the period depicts Ernie Pyle's wife Jerry drawing sustenance from Krutch's *Samuel Johnson* in the Pyles' living room in Albuquerque while Ernie plays with the dog.[10] But some-times even the image of the brave, stable, tough-minded Johnson was of no use. After a ghastly tank battle in North Africa, Robin Maugham, in a state of shock among the burning tanks and cadavers, "felt horribly cold":

> I sat down in the small tent built out from the side of a 15 cwt. truck and began to read Boswell's *Johnson*, but it could not attract my interest from what had been before. While the bulky doctor tapped his way along the railings of eighteenth-century London I could hear the screamings of a man trapped to death.[11]

The hunger of the troops for something to read was even greater than for civilians, ample supply being less likely. And for those accustomed to artistic or intellectual life, isolation in remote spots without letterpress could be hell. Cecil Beaton, in China as an official photographer, at one point grew so starved for reading matter that he took down the pictures from *Sphere* someone had tacked to the walls of a billet in order to read what was on the back.[12] When books were available, soldiers relished in them the same images of peace and significant freedom as civilians, only more so. Although a CO, Edward Blishen lived a life regimented along military lines, except that he was treated with even more contempt than an enlisted soldier. His mitigation he found in Jane Austen: "All those choices of action! *That* was peace—to have ahead of one a hundred pos-sibilities of change."[13] Hiding from capture in Holland, the Germans all around, General Sir John Hackett was lucky enough to be brought by a Dutch friend a copy of *Vanity Fair* in English. His longing for subtle and ironic language finds its metaphor in the terms of literal hunger: "I felt a great longing for . . . a taste of elegant and lucid English prose." He found the novel "medicine for the condition in which I found myself, . . . restless . . . and uncertain, facing a future of which little could be predicted except that it was unlikely to be an easy one."[14]

Anyone hoping in some degree to measure cultural change between the two World Wars might consider the fate of *Pilgrim's Progress*, once a standard allusion invaluable to the menaced and the scared. In the Great War it seemed the common property of both highly educated, "literary" people and ordinary ones, and both called on it as a way of imposing some sense onto otherwise meaningless traumatic scenes and events. In the trenches of Flanders and Picardy from 1914 to 1918, there was a tradition of frequent instinctive reference to Christian and Appolyon, the Slough of Despond, the Valley of the Shadow of Death, the City of Destruction, and the Celestial City.[15] But by the time of the Second World War this cultural resource has grown obsolete: *Pilgrim's Progress* is almost never invoked, let alone read. A rare instance of its use in June, 1944, is recalled by Oliver Carpenter, a member of the 11th Battalion of the King's Royal Rifles, in Italy. At the end of a memorial service for the dead of the battalion, the "Epilogue" from *Pilgrim's Progress*—presumably the end of the narrative of Part I, on the transfiguration of the dead in the Celestial City—was read, followed by "The Last Post."[16] But aside from that (and the explanation may be that there was no Bible or Prayer Book handy), there's little evidence that *Pilgrim's Progress* was in anyone's mind or memory, suggesting not just the obvious attenuation of Christian belief and context between the wars but something perhaps more disturbing, the enfeeblement of traditional education involving the English classics. For example, compared with the popularity of their writings among troops of the Great War, Hardy and Housman seem much less read in the Second, a fact perhaps betokening the diminished capacity of Second War soldiers, accustomed to a secularized atmosphere, to enjoy that kind of irony—depending on a public Christian-optimistic setting—or their unwillingness to waste time exploding patriotic, nationalistic, sentimental, or religious respectabilities already thoroughly in tatters by 1939.

Indeed, it could not be said that the war occasioned any religious revival, at least among the troops, despite a generous provision of chaplains and chapels and free devotional materials. Chief among these was the pocket-sized, brown mock-leather New Testament issued to the Americans, with a letter from the nominally Episcopalian Commander-in-Chief Franklin D. Roosevelt on the flyleaf "commending the reading of the Bible to all who serve in the armed forces of the United States":

> Throughout the centuries men of many faiths and diverse origins have found in the Sacred Book words of wisdom, counsel and inspiration. It is a fountain of strength and now, as always, an aid in attaining the highest aspirations of the human soul.

In addition to the Biblical text, this 3- x 4½-inch volume contains the Ten Commandments (impossible to edit out "Thou shalt not kill") and a selection of "Psalms, Prayers, and Hymns," with "Hymns" including "America the Beautiful," "My Country, 'Tis of Thee," and "The Star-Spangled Banner." The psalms have been chosen with an acute eye to the needs of military morale, e.g., Number 91:

> I will say of the Lord, He is my refuge and my fortress. My God, in Him will I trust. . . .
> His truth shall be thy shield and buckler. . . .
> A thousand shall fall at thy side, and ten thousand at thy right hand; but it shall not come nigh thee.

(Writing his wife from Bataan in February, 1942, an American airman, beginning to understand that his death or capture is inevitable, consults his Testament and quotes at the end of his letter, "A thousand shall fall at thy side . . . but it shall not come nigh thee."[17]) But even an original "Prayer on Going into Battle" cannot endow the war with a purpose more positive than defense against "unprovoked aggression and unprovoked attack." Soldiers troubled by lewd fantasies are supplied with a "Prayer for a Pure Heart," and the back flyleaf advises readers to use specific passages to defend against anxieties and distress common in military service:

> If you are facing a crisis, read the 46th Psalm.
> When you are discouraged, think over Psalms 23 and 24.
> When you are lonely and fearful, read over Psalm 27.
> When you are very weary, seek St. Matthew 11:28–30.
> When everything seems to be going from bad to worse,
>   try 2 Timothy 3.
> If you have a fear of death, read St. John chapters 11,
>   17, and 20.

When Eugene Sledge, fighting on Peleliu, found his pocket New Testament getting sweat-stained, he took from a Japanese corpse one of the little rubber bags in which Japanese soldiers carried their family photos and personal papers and kept his Testament in that. The 23rd Psalm, ever popular with soldiers, was his support as he attacked under terrible fire, running across the airfield at Peleliu:

> I saw Marines stumble and pitch forward as they got hit. . . . The farther we went, the worse it got. . . . I gritted my teeth and braced myself in anticipation of being struck down at any moment. It seemed impossible that any of us could make it across.

But Sledge did, reciting over and over, "The Lord is my shepherd; I shall not want. Yea, though I walk through the valley of the shadow of death, I will fear no evil, for Thou art with me; Thy rod and Thy staff comfort me. . . ."[18]

The pocket New Testament could also be purchased in a version with a steel cover, for warding off flying metal and deflecting bayonet thrusts, and if you didn't have one of these, you could carry the issue Testament in your left breast pocket together with your small steel shaving mirror. The Testament in the breast pocket, whether fortified by steel or not, became one of the war's most common amulets, and to its mystical efficacy were imputed numerous miracles of salvation. And not merely during the war. When a B-24 bomber was hit during the Ploesti raid of August 1, 1943, and the crew was ordered to lighten ship by jettisoning everything, George Miller threw out all his personal possessions, including even his steel-jacketed Testament. These efforts failing, the crew bailed out over Hungary and Miller was captured. Thirty-four years later, Miller, now fifty-two years old and living in California, was near death following brain surgery when a package arrived. A Hungarian woman had found his Testament with his name and address written in it. Before it arrived, his wife said, George had been "morose and negative." But "when the book came back into his life," she said, "he became a happy, well-adjusted man."[19] The pocket Testaments were extremely popular among those captured by the Japanese after the fall of Bataan, but not for devotional reasons: their pages were the best size and weight for rolling cigarettes, "so these New Testaments," says one soldier, "were stole like crazy."[20]

The moment of the fall of Bataan in early 1942 was close to the nadir for the Allies, what with Pearl Harbor and the loss of Singapore and Hong Kong and the *Prince of Wales* and *Repulse*. During the first three months of 1942 not a single U-boat was sunk anywhere by any one of the Allies, and it appeared that the only sinkings of vessels were those accomplished by the Axis. In February, 1942, the *Normandie* burned and capsized at her pier in New York before she could be transformed into the much needed transport *Lafayette,* this while the German warships *Scharnhorst* and *Gneisenau* escaped destruction by an impudent dash up the English Channel. The news was so bad that in the United States the Wartime Guide of the National Association of Broadcasters forbade its member stations to use the transition "Now for some good news," and over Rome Radio Ezra Pound taunted Americans (troops included) by asserting, "You are at war for the duration of the Germans' pleasure. You are at war for the duration of Japan's pleasure."[21] An editorial in the *Infantry Journal* prepared soldiers for "a job of years," perhaps "decades."[22] "Never was the Allied cause in greater jeopardy than at this present moment," a member of the RAF wrote in his diary in that February,[23] and U.S. morale was so low by February 23, a day concluding, according to *Time* magazine, the worst week of the war, that Roosevelt was motivated to deliver an inspiring Fireside Chat invoking the spirit of Washington at Valley Forge when all looked black. Admitting that the Allies may, for a time, have to "yield ground," and that the government is confident that Americans are brave and mature enough "to hear the worst," he called for absolute national unity and resolution and quoted Thomas Paine's "These are the times that try men's souls."[24]

The year 1942 was thus the moment of the greatest need for uplifting reading matter, and in that year the troops were deluged with devotional works, many in olive-drab bindings and most in a size to fit the pocket. Typical is *Strength for Service to God and Country,* published in New York and Nashville and distributed by the Salvation Army. Chaplain Norman E. Nygaard assembled the contents of this little book from 365 Christian ministers' daily meditations with prayers, and one unacquainted with the date of publication could guess that it was a moment when many thought America might lose, or was in the process of losing, the war. Indeed, the rhetoric is not easily distinguishable from that required in Germany in early 1945:

These are the days when we are liable to become discouraged.

Discouraging things have happened, and perhaps more discouraging things are ahead.

Dark days are upon us.

We live in times that are disquieting and even terrifying.

This is a very difficult period in our lives.

And as the President himself would put it,

Worry and fear are the twin enemies that attack us,

and

To be able to take bad news without pessimism and reverses without losing our morale . . . is essential.

(At the same moment goods of a similar tendency were being provided civilians by Lloyd C. Douglas in the form of *The Robe*, his historical novel about the mystique of Christian fortitude in the first century. In less than 24 months it sold 1,450,000 copies and headed the best-seller list for eleven straight months, becoming "one of the great successes of publishing history," as Edmund Wilson designated it.[25]) American readers more secular and sophisticated could counteract the bad news in 1942 with *Past Imperfect*, a witty, fluffy autobiography by Ilka Chase, actress, author, and radio personality. Except for concluding with an obligatory three-page paean to "democracy," this is a thoroughly entertaining light read, and in selecting it, the Book-of-the-Month Club sensed that at the moment its members needed just this sort of antidote to darkness.

By 1943 things were beginning to look up. Some encouraging events were the surrender of the Germans at Stalingrad, the recovery of Guadalcanal by the Americans, the expulsion of the Afrika Corps from North Africa, the invasion of Sicily, the incineration of 50,000 German civilians in Hamburg, and the Allied landing at Salerno and the surrender of Italy. But the battle of the Atlantic was still going very badly for the Allies (convoys often arrived at their destinations with half their ships sunk), and devotional materials for the troops, while assuming a higher state of morale than the earliest models, now offer, like *A Book of Worship and Devotion for the Armed Forces* (Presbyterian Church of the U.S.A., 1943), prayers "For the Wounded," "For the Dying," "An Act of Contrition for a Dying Roman Catholic," "For Courage," and (now that hordes of wounded are beginning to constitute a special concern) "For Physicians, Nurses, and Hospitals."

To solace their men abroad, those at home could send parcels of comforts, and an apparent convention of the period was that mother sent food or socks, father books. Michael Adams, once a member of an RAF bomber crew, now a prisoner at Stalag III-E, after three months without reading matter joyously received from his father

> a wooden box, perhaps twenty-four inches long and fifteen across, which when it was opened in front of me . . . caused me to gasp in wonder and anticipation, . . . Here . . . was a whole library in itself.

His father had sent a complete Shakespeare on India paper, a Nonesuch Milton, 1000 pages of Browning, a collected Voltaire, and four Trollope novels—"ideal reading in a prison camp because Trollope, like the Dutch painters of the seventeenth century, paid such leisurely attention to detail, to the textures and nuances of everyday life." And from his father's thoughtful selection Adams derived consolations especially needed by prisoners of war: "From *Paradise Lost*, for instance, . . . came Milton's reminder that no external force can bind a man into submission against his will, since:

> The mind is its own place, and in itself
> Can make a Heav'n of Hell, a Hell of Heav'n."

Adams also found himself treasuring, in the text of *Richard II*, a "warning" against that common POW threat, self-pity, and he grew fond of a passage in Browning's "Bishop Blougram's Apology" suggesting that one make beautiful what one has rather than bemoan what one has not.[26] At the same time, on the other side of the world, a young American naval officer on a destroyer escort in the Pacific received a monthly package from his father. Before shipping out, this ensign had checked off in a catalogue of the Modern Library the titles he wanted to read (95 cents each, in those days), and every month his father sent him four books. By this means he first read *Crime and Punishment*, *The Possessed*, and *The*

Brothers Karamazov, as well as *Remembrance of Things Past.*[27] And even if you had no father to send you the volumes of the Modern Library, you could still get them easily by mail—if you subscribed to *The Infantry Journal,* that monthly trade-magazine of the ground forces, which in a section offering "Books, Manuals, Binders," listed over 100 Modern Library titles procurable by subscribers, in addition to such useful professional items as Dollard's *Fear in Battle,* Applegate's *Kill or Get Killed* and *What to Do Aboard the Transport,* as well as Walker's *The Physiology of Sex.*

By offering Modern Library books, even this non-humanistic journal seemed to be recognizing that the war provided some unique circumstances for genuine "liberal education," the accumulation of literary experience without ulterior or utilitarian motive. You might achieve promotion to staff sergeant or lieutenant commander by assiduous study of field manuals, Navy Regulations, *The Infantry Journal, The Bluejacket's Manual,* or *The Officer's Guide,* and you might persuade yourself to vote Labour in 1945 by reading the Beveridge Report, but neither result would be likely from hurling yourself into Marlowe and Ben Jonson and Beaumont and Fletcher, or Madame de Sévigné or Flaubert, Melville or Darwin or Alfred North Whitehead, Blake, Coleridge, Burns, Byron, Logan Pearsall Smith, A. A. Milne, Lewis Carroll, Saki, or Ronald Firbank, not to mention Rilke, Joyce, and T. S. Eliot. Yet all these were consumed devotedly by the few while the more visible many were deep in their comic books and westerns and thrillers. Recalling the grinding boredom of his almost two years as a soldier on a remote Alaskan outpost, Irving Howe remembers reading for once in a truly liberal way:

> In later years, driven by ambition or trying to fill gaps in my knowledge, I would read in a quick, grasping way, vulgar with purpose, but here I could read for the unalloyed pleasure of knowledge. I read about the Maoris and Matthew Arnold's critical thought, the Bolshevik Revolution and the decline of Rome. In nearly two years in Alaska I must have read 150 solid books, more and better ones than any time before or since.[28]

A similar valuable experience was Louis Auchincloss's when he was stranded as a naval officer performing absurd work in the Panama Canal Zone. Here he too learned to read without an impure purpose:

> I did not have a grade to make, a review to write, a person to talk to, or even an opinion to formulate. I was alone with Henry James, and this

was the time that I learned to love the late style, the last novels and the memoirs, and to take in what E. M. Forster has so rightly described as "the unique aesthetic experience" of *The Ambassadors* and *The Golden Bowl*.[29]

From 1943 on, an American serviceman so minded could get his Henry James free—at least *Daisy Miller and Other Stories*, one of the 1,322 titles comprising the 22,000,000 copies of the Armed Services Editions. These were the brainchild of a group of publishers organized as the Council on Books in Wartime. The idea was to issue special paperbound editions of books for servicemen overseas only, to be distributed free with the proviso that none must be allowed to enter the civilian market—the whole issue was to be pulped at the end of the war. At the height of the operation forty titles were to be issued per month in a curious side-stapled horizontal format, 4 by 5½ inches, sized to fit the upper left-hand pocket of the army shirt. Although they received only one-half cent per copy royalty, the publishers were glad to co-operate in this mass enterprise because they assumed it would generate a large postwar audience for their product among the hitherto unreached.

The titles were selected by a publishers' committee which included one member each from the army and navy. There was some censorship: Isabel Dubois, chief librarian for the navy, blackballed James T. Farrell's *Studs Lonigan*—too exciting erotically. And there were some conspicuous absentees in the list of titles, books of a pacifistic tendency which the selection committee considered possible threats to morale. Thus the troops were not vouchsafed acquaintance with such First World War masterpieces of disillusion as Robert Graves's *Good-bye to All That*, Remarque's *All Quiet on the Western Front*, Barbusse's *Under Fire*, Sassoon's *Memoirs of George Sherston*, Richard Aldington's *Death of a Hero*, Cummings's *The Enormous Room*, Hemingway's *A Farewell to Arms*, John Dos Passos's *Three Soldiers*, or even Edmund Blunden's quiet and gentle *Undertones of War*. And certainly not Dalton Trumbo's jolting account of the consciousness of a Great War multiple amputee, *Johnny Got His Gun*. About three-quarters of the list consisted of contemporary ephemeral fiction—not trash, really, just forgettable, and now forgotten, books, like Philip Wylie's *Salt Water Daffy*, Mildred Walker's *The Quarry*, William Colt MacDonald's *Master of the Mesa*, and Max Brand's *The Border Kid*. But more artistically and intellectually ambitious soldiers could find plenty of good stuff among the chaff: Henry Adams, Whitman, Melville, Twain, Dickens, Charlotte Brontë, *Tristram Shandy* (abridged), Browning, Conrad, Emerson, Faulkner, Frost, Homer (*Odyssey* only: *Iliad* too bloody and ironic?), Isherwood, Aldous Huxley, and Mann *(Selected Short Stories)*, as well as Herrick, Tennyson, Wordsworth, and Keats (but curiously, no Shakespeare). An allusion to Charles A. Beard's *The Republic* (1943) found its way into Pound's *Pisan Cantos* because a copy of the Armed Services Edition of Beard's book found its way into Pound's cage at the Disciplinary Training Center in 1945. Assuming correctly that the troops could use some cheering up, the committee provided lots of "humor": the first Armed Services Edition, produced in September, 1943, was *The Education of H*Y*M*A*N K*A*P*L*A*N*, by Leonard Q. Ross (Leo Rosten), copies of which—in morocco slip-cases—were presented to Roosevelt, General Marshall, and Admiral King. And soon there were reprints of H. Allen Smith, Dorothy Parker, Robert Benchley, Ring Lardner, James Thurber, and Ludwig Bemelmans. And there were two popular anthologies of poems, Louis Untermeyer's *Great Poems from Chaucer to Whitman* and *The Fireside Book of Verse: Favorite Poems of Romance and Adventure.*

At the front, a carton of these paperbacks would arrive with the ammunition and the rations, and men would devise some system of presumably fair access. Of course officers were likely to pick over the titles first. Trading after reading was the common practice, and in times of shortage expedients were devised, like soldiers' "tearing out portions of the books . . . in order to pass them on to others quickly." One typical platoon of combat engineers possessed a cache of eight or ten beat-up Armed Services Editions, guarded by their lieutenant, "who refused to let any man have a book unless he would agree to read it aloud to the fellows in his shack or tent."[30] One Armed Services Edition was issued to each soldier boarding a ship for the Normandy invasion, and while waiting for the awful moment the troops read and swapped.[31] It seems probable that this wartime experience of twelve million people with pocket-sized paperbacks helped propel the notable postwar mass-market paperback revolution in publishing.

That revolution began timidly before the war, when in June, 1939, Pocket Books brought out ten titles, to be had for a quarter each in drug stores and at news stands. Avon Books came along in 1941, and its ad writers began to realize the full wartime potential: "Because the new Avon Books are easy to open, light to hold, thrilling to read and compact to carry or store in clothing or bags, they are ideal gifts to the boys in the Armed Forces."[32] Popular Library joined the rush in 1942, Dell in 1943,

Bantam in 1945, and finally New American Library in 1949. Portable, cheap, easily mailed and easily left behind when vacating barracks or ships and moving on, these small paperbacks were indeed splendid things to send the troops. Starting with a sale of several hundred thousand, Pocket Books alone sold more than ten million in 1941, twenty million in 1942, and almost forty million in 1943.[33] In April, 1945, a *Stars and Stripes* survey found that among soldiers in Europe the most popular titles were *The Pocket Book Dictionary* (help in writing letters); *The Pocket Book of Cartoons, The Pocket Book of Boners,* and (the best selling paperback of the war) *See Here, Private Hargrove* (levity); Erle Stanley Gardner's *The Case of the Curious Bride* (mystery, with a whiff of sex); Zola's *Nana* (French: promise of considerable sex); and *The Pocket Book of Verse.*[34]

This last, edited by Professor of English Morris E. Speare, appeared first in June, 1940, and proved surprisingly popular: it had to be reprinted nine times before Pearl Harbor. Although the services were probably unable to influence the selection, the book posed no danger to morale, for it contained no poems whatever from 1914–18 exposing war as stupid slaughter, neglecting the ironies of Wilfred Owen and Siegfried Sassoon in favor of Rupert Brooke's satisfaction that

> there's some corner of a foreign field
> That is for ever England.[35]

Some soldier left behind a copy of *The Pocket Book of Verse* in the latrine at the Pisan detention center, with the result that Pound's *Pisan Cantos* are enriched by allusions to its canonical poems. The book proved equally sustaining to one soldier whom basic training had reduced to extreme loneliness and self-contempt. Prayer failing, he was delighted when a fellow trainee, one David Susskind, showed him his copy of *The Pocket Book of Verse.* "Picking it up idly," says Private Ross Parmenter, "I opened it at Michael Drayton's

> Since there's no help, come let us kiss and part. . . .

"I heard in those lines the voice of a living man and was moved. . . . I knew I would find in the volume the companionship I was not getting in the barracks and that the poetry would help to compensate for the beauty that was lacking in my life. I bought the anthology as soon as I could."[36] Parmenter memorized a great many of the poems. So did an infantryman who, forty years later, remembered the way the poems he'd memorized helped him keep sane as he slogged into Germany: "Then I knew them all: 'I could not love thee, dear, so much, loved I not honor more,' 'It was roses, roses all the way,' 'How do I love thee? Let me count the ways,' 'If this be error and upon me proved,' and a silly thing that always stuck with me, 'And down the long and silent street / The dawn with silver-sandalled feet / Crept like a frightened girl. . .'."[37]

Both the reduced-size Armed Services Editions and Pocket Books saved paper and shipping space and pleased soldiers who had enough to carry already. Similar weight- and paper-saving expedients were the "pony" editions of stateside magazines supplied free to troops overseas. There was no pony edition of *Life*, because its large photographs could not be shrunk without contravening the whole point of the magazine, but the pages of *Time* and *The New Yorker* could be reduced in number and size by eliminating some text and all advertising, and those magazines were shipped overseas in small sizes—6 by 8¾ inches. In its Overseas Edition, the *Infantry Journal* shrank even further, to 5½ by 7½ inches, a size readily carried (if one couldn't stand being parted from it) in a field-jacket pocket. If pockets were full, you could stash several pony editions in your helmet-liner, keeping them dry and ready to be whipped out whenever time or the tactical situation allowed.

British troops had no Pocket Books, but they had something even better—Penguins. Better at least for the thoughtful, for Penguins (and their siblings, Pelicans) offered not just fiction, from the lightest fluff to *A Farewell to Arms* and Forster's *Howards End*, but political controversy, archaeology, economic geography, biography, English classics, H. G. Wells's *A Short History of the World*, Shakespeare and Shaw, and such subversive items as Norman Douglas's *South Wind*, Samuel Butler's *Erewhon*, and Hašek's *The Good Soldier Schweik*. Books for grown-ups, the Penguins were, the tone of the list intelligent, critical, and leftish. Some observers thought the 1945 Labour Party victory greatly forwarded (especially among the troops) by the politics of the Penguin list, and one commentator observed that the Penguin enterprise could be called "the publishing arm of the Beveridge Report."[38]

The Penguin publisher Allen Lane first got the idea of a series of cheap paperbacks in 1935, when he brought out ten titles and merchandised them through Woolworth's. By 1941 there were 87 titles, by 1945, seven hundred. The first Penguins sold for only sixpence—the price of ten cigarettes. The popularity of Penguins among British servicemen was

A view of some Penguin Pockets (Imperial War Museum)

in part due to their size—they slipped into a compartment in the service gas-mask haversack "as if it had been tailored for the purpose," and when the British army battledress was devised, the troops found that the outer pocket above the left knee, intended for an entrenching-tool in combat and used sometimes for carrying a field dressing, "conformed exactly to the shape of a Penguin."[39] "The Penguin pocket," it was sometimes called, and a *Horizon* was sometimes found in it as well. During the war Penguins seemed available everywhere. If your family didn't mail you a few every month you could buy them at NAAFIs, or at the bookshops in Cairo. Or you could subscribe to Penguin's Forces Book Club and choose what you wanted mailed you from each month's selections. Penguins were so well known as a fixture of British wartime life that when, in November, 1942, a deception plan was needed to persuade the enemy that Anglo-American forces were going to land not in North Africa but in France, it was put about that a recent shortage of Penguin titles—a shortage apparently well known to the Germans—was the result of the print-order being postponed in favor of a million French-English phrase books for the troops.[40]

Also sized for the Penguin pocket was John Lehmann's miscellany, *Penguin New Writing*, which began in November, 1940, and for ten years continued as a competitor to *Horizon*, bringing soldiers and civilians, at first monthly, later quarterly, such reading as Orwell's "Shooting an Elephant"; stories by V. S. Pritchett, Dylan Thomas, Graham Greene, Sartre, Silone, Maclaren-Ross, Henry Green, and Denton Welch; poems by Auden, MacNeice, Day Lewis, and Alun Lewis; critical essays by Spender, Walter Allen, and Henry Reed; Isherwood's Berlin memoirs; a one-act play by Brecht; and intelligent, sensitive testimony and reportage about the war. *Penguin New Writing* sometimes sold as many as 100,000 copies per issue, very many of them read by military subscribers and beneficiaries of the injunction on the back page of a typical number: "FOR THE FORCES. Leave this book at a Post Office when you have read it, so that men and women in the services may enjoy it too." Compared with *Horizon*, which could seem precious, remote, and merely aesthetic, *Penguin New Writing* appeared "committed"—to the reality of the active life, to the necessity of politics in all its vulgarity, and to the redemption of postwar life by new imperatives of fairness and decency. Alan Ross, a sailor during the war, declares that now, when he picks up a faded issue of the old *Penguin New Writing*, he is

> transported, with quickening pulse, to those five or six years of my life, first at Oxford, then at sea, when I discovered that writing was not simply entertainment or a course to be studied, but at its best something that sustained one's existence and conditioned one's view of it.

By means of the writings published by John Lehmann, says Ross, "I came to see what was happening in a new and vivid way." With its frequent focus on proletarian life, *Penguin New Writing* "put literary values at the service of human, rather than narrowly doctrinaire ones."[41] "Shooting an Elephant" would illustrate what Ross seems to be getting at.

An anthology, appearing regularly and sized for the pocket—that describes *Penguin New Writing*, and as an anthology it was typical of its moment. Wartime was notably the age of anthologies. One ready explanation is that people manning the production lines or drilling on the parade grounds didn't have time for prolonged periods of reading and gravitated thus toward short pieces and "selections." But the popularity of such sustained experiences as reading *War and Peace* and Proust and Trollope and Austen suggests that a special wartime busyness is not the only reason anthologies were in demand. There are other, and perhaps more plausible, reasons. For one thing, there were still plenty of credible and authoritative anthology-makers, popular mass-merchandising book-men and men of letters like Clifton Fadiman, Alexander Woollcott, William Rose Benét, Henry Seidel Canby, and Bennett Cerf, a breed almost entirely departed from the current world of "visuals." Their *imprimatur*—delivered as often by radio as by print—carried weight. During the war, when *The Saturday Review of Literature* dared to be so titled and was flourishing, readers tended to credit these well-known popular critics with taste and authority, and to receive with gratitude what they selected and recommended. An even more important reason for the large number of anthologies during wartime was the desire in both anthologist and reader to survey "the heritage" as a way of seeking an answer to the pressing question, What are we fighting for? The war forced everyone back onto traditional cultural possessions and responses and forced people to consider which things were valuable enough to be preserved and enjoyed over and over again. If the enemy insisted on the principle *Ein Volk, Ein Reich*, the principle of variety honored by the anthologies was a way of taking an anti-totalitarian, anti-uniformitarian stance, a way of honoring the pluralism and exuberance of the "democratic" Allied cause.

Thus in 1941 Clifton Fadiman's *Reading I've Liked* (906 pages, selections from 36 authors) and E. B. and Katharine White's *A Subtreasury of American Humor* (814 pages, over 100 authors). In 1942, Whit Burnett's *This Is My Best* (1,180 pages of writings chosen by their authors, 93 of them); Hemingway's *Men at War* (1,072 pages of war narratives by over 80 authors); Storm Jameson's *London Calling*, presenting the verse, prose, and drama of 31 British writers invited by Jameson to submit pieces of special interest to American readers, the profits going to the U.S.O.; and Allen Tate and John Peale Bishop's *American Harvest: Twenty Years of Creative Writing in the United States* (544 pages of canonical works by Hemingway, Sherwood Anderson, Robert Penn Warren, Conrad Aiken, T. S. Eliot, Marianne Moore, Frost, Stevens, R. P. Blackmur, Hart Crane, and William Carlos Williams). "For the first time in the history of this country," Tate and Bishop announce, "it is possible to

produce an anthology in which the editors can feel confidence that it represents what is, properly speaking, a literature," and a literature in its
variety analogous to the variety of the peoples constituting the Allies.
"The energy that has gone into the contents of this anthology," Tate and
Bishop declare, "has derived some substance from the sidewalks of New
York; its origin is to be sought in the New England Village, the Ohio
factory town, the Wisconsin farm, the Southern plantation, the dry plains
of New Mexico."[42]

In 1943 there was not just *The Infantry Journal Reader,* offering selections of "professional" interest. There was Klaus Mann and Hermann
Kesten's *The Best of Modern European Literature,* designed to represent a
better Europe than the one currently dominated by Hitler. In 1943 there
was also W. Somerset Maugham's *Great Modern Reading,* a collection
aimed specifically at Americans and intending to lure them into a love of
letters by a reversed chronology, starting with the most recent and presumably most accessible modern works (Welty, Saroyan, Auden, Spender)
and moving back through Fitzgerald and Hemingway, D. H. Lawrence
and Sassoon, finally to Housman, Yeats, Hardy, and the ultimate challenge of Henry James ("The Beast in the Jungle"). Maugham's Introduction reflects the obligatory democratic, "One World" tone of the period: "I have made this anthology," he says, "for the plain people of
America, for the woman who goes into the store to buy a spool of cotton
or a cake of soap, for the man who goes in to buy a pound of nails or a
pot of paint. . . . I believe in people and I believe in their taste."[43]

In 1944, there was Benjamin A. Botkin's *A Treasury of American
Folklore,* which ministered to the wartime obsession with the national
identity and value, as well as Lawrence Spivak and Charles Angoff's *The
American Mercury Reader,* containing a number of pungent pieces, but
not so pungent as to menace morale, by such as Mencken, Sinclair Lewis,
Ben Hecht, and Sherwood Anderson. Finally, in 1945, as if after all this
there was a need for a contemplative summing-up and a quiet consideration of what it all might be thought to have meant, there was *The Practical Cogitator, or Thinker's Anthology,* compiled by Charles P. Curtis,
Jr., and Ferris Greenslet, a collection of high-minded paragraphs and
brief essays conveying, the editors promise, "nothing cynical."[44]

"Books Are Weapons in the War of Ideas": so read the ribbon in the
beak of the angry eagle, book in claws, chosen by The Council on Books
in Wartime to embellish copyright pages of American wartime books.
These wartime anthologies were conceived as distinct contributions to the

war effort, and it is unthinkable that any materials of a pacifistic, subversive, or even very skeptical tendency would find an entrance. A reader of them over forty years afterward will be astonished to find what admirable people Americans are, how generous, tolerant, imaginative, and charming, how resolute in pursuing Victory, how selfless in sacrifice and noble in courage. As well as how literate and tasteful in their reading. It is as if the whole country were the invention of E. B. White.

Just as civilians had anthologies tailored for them, so did the troops. In the Great War British soldiers could peruse in the trenches Robert Bridges's pocket-sized anthology *The Spirit of Man*, as well as such ubiquitous handy poetry collections as Palgrave's *Golden Treasury* and *The Oxford Book of English Verse*. In the Second World War British troops could carry in haversack or Penguin pocket an ingenious little 4- by 6½-inch anthology of prose and verse edited in 1939 by Herbert Read and designed specifically for troop use, not just substantively, in the selection, but physically, in the binding. The cloth covers of this little book— brown, for camouflage—join and overlap to form a slip-case with a snap closure, protecting the over 600 India-paper pages from damage. *The Knapsack* it is called, *A Pocket-book of Prose and Verse*. Read opens his Preface with what some might think a disconcerting if undeniably courageous implication—that since there seems to be a world war every quarter-century it's best to learn to deal with its exigencies efficiently and phlegmatically:

> During the last war, as a soldier on active service, I was very conscious of the need of a book which I could carry about with me as part of my kit, and which would suit the various moods and circumstances of my unsettled existence. . . . Because one book at a time is the most that the average soldier can conveniently accommodate . . . an anthology of some kind is . . . indicated.[45]

The previous war's *Spirit of Man*, he points out, now seems too elevated, too morally serious, and too abstract in its "idealism" (i.e., Platonism) to do the present job. He has wanted to create something more earthy, representing more honestly the "extreme contrasts" met with in actual life. Hence his inclusion of both Plato and "She Was Poor But She Was Honest," Spinoza and "The Dong with the Luminous Nose." Any soldier reading *The Knapsack* could feel flattered by Read's assumptions about him, for the selections posit a highly intelligent reader with an acute aesthetic sense, brave enough to confront the truth about war and about himself. In addition to accounts of battle from the *Iliad* and *Beowulf* and *The Song of Roland*, the book includes plenty of uneuphemized and therefore depressing military narrative from the Great War, implying all the gross uncertainties and blunders inevitable in battle. Read includes many poems of "masculine interest," not excepting Swift, and the selections from philosophers are largely stoical, emphasizing the value of intellectual courage. Near the end, Read has included three sets of noble "last words," those of St. Louis to his son, Raleigh to his wife, and Nicola Sacco to his son. And the book concludes with three prayers of a humanistic, un-mystical kind. The last selection is the prayer of the dying Socrates begging the great god Pan to strengthen his instinct for moral beauty. *The Knapsack*, implying the usefulness of a marriage between beauty and wisdom, struck T. S. Eliot as providing good matter for a BBC program, which would suggest among other things "the point that good English has a vital connection with the highest national achievement."[46] (A concept not excluding winning the war.)

The main portable anthology designed for American soldiers was a significantly different matter, as different as the U.S.A. from the U.K., as different as the character of its editor, the sentimental newspaperman and publicity "personality" Alexander Woollcott, from that of the scholar, philosopher of art, poet, and combat veteran of the Great War, Herbert Read. If the selections in *The Knapsack* tended to stress wisdom and virtue, those in Woollcott's anthology were designed to provide "entertaining reading," as asserted in a Viking Press advertising brochure for *As You Were: A Portable Library of American Prose and Poetry Assembled for Members of the Armed Forces and the Merchant Marine:*

> Mothers, wives, and sweethearts are seeking the perfect book to send their boys—and girls—in uniform. Here it is—more than 200,000 of the most readable words in the language, deftly fitted into a volume little larger than a deck of cards!

The purpose of *As You Were* is

> recreation—in every sense of the word. It offers humor in abundance . . . as well as melodrama, suspense, and romance.

In a fey Foreword whimsically arguing by anecdote that books are good things, Woollcott thanks friends who have helped him make his selections, and by naming such as Thornton Wilder, E. B. White, and Carl Sandburg, he signals that in the book will be found much high-mindedness and charm. Thus one encounters Williston Fish's "A Last Will," John Howard Payne's "Home, Sweet Home," and lots of James Whitcomb Riley, Vachel Lindsay, Edna St. Vincent Millay, and Sandburg. The final section, "American Fact," includes documents delivering uniquely American themes—The Declaration of Independence, Lincoln's Second Inaugural Address, a Thanksgiving Day Proclamation by Governor Wilbur Cross of Connecticut, the words of Emma Lazarus from the Statue of Liberty, and the inscription on the tomb of the Unknown Soldier. Sentimental nostalgia is the dominant tone, as the punning title implies, and there is hardly a nay-sayer in the whole 655 pages, with the exception of E. E. Cummings, represented by "my sweet old etcetera," and Ring Lardner, with "Some Like Them Cold." More typical are the poems "Scum of the Earth," by Robert Haven Schauffler, a complacent, undiscriminating paean to American immigration, and "American Laughter," by Kenneth Allen Robinson, an apotheosis of "democratic" humor, offensive to Bostonians, perhaps, but highly valued out where the buffalo roam and the corn grows tall. The first printing of *As You Were* was of 30,000 copies, and if your loved ones didn't send you a copy (price, $2.50), you could get yours at the serviceman's price of $1.00 from the subscribers' service of *The Infantry Journal* and such. The small size of the book (4¼ by 6½ inches), enjoined in part by the paper shortage, became standard for the subsequent volumes of the Viking Portable Library, those marvelous one-volume collections of the 1940s and 1950s: Hemingway, Faulkner, Fitzgerald, Melville, Hawthorne—and, of all things, Woollcott. James Jones, who collected them, designated them "my influences."[47]

Although neither Read's nor Woollcott's anthology for soldiers was in any way official, they can't help suggesting two quite distinct national ways of bringing interpretation to bear on the war. The two ways are not quite as simple as the way of experience and the way of innocence, but that would begin to suggest the difference. It would be impossible to infer anything like a tragic view of life from *As You Were*, impossible to gather a hint that good will, a sense of humor, and warm patriotism would not be found sufficient for dealing with a soldier's forthcoming experiences.

But all this might convey a highly erroneous image of the troops' reading. The terrible fact is that the comic-book was the book of the war, "the favorite reading of the armed forces," as Stanley Kauffmann testifies. In wartime Kauffmann worked for a publisher of comic-books, one of which featured the hero Major Mighty. "There was a Major Mighty Club, with membership cards and secret code." About half the 100,000 members were servicemen. "I saw many a letter," says Kauffmann,

> from a serviceman overseas confiding his troubles to the Major because there was no one around he could really talk to. I saw more than one letter from a serviceman overseas applying for membership and asking Major Mighty to rush the membership card so that the soldier or sailor could have it before he went into combat.[48]

And meanwhile, what were the Germans reading? Clearly, under the strict censorship and the general National Socialist enthusiasm, they enjoyed little of the variety offered even by Allied writing. For entertainment and escape, they leaned toward the pseudo-American westerns of Karl May, or the romantic peasant novels of Josefa Berens-Totenohl, or the melo-dramatic anti-Semitic narratives of Tüdel Weller, or Walter Dach's stories glorifying Nazi labor. In all these, earnestness was the tone, as it certainly was in the other kind of writing popular during wartime in Germany, ideological works useful in defining and strengthening the national spirit. *Mein Kampf,* of course, and the "philosophical"-sociological works of Alfred Rosenberg, Hans Frank, and Ludwig Klauss, as well as the frequent essays by Goebbels in the *Völkischer Beobachter* and the treatises and articles on "racial science," National Socialist law, and the proper relations (totalitarian) between the Party, on the one hand, and the churches and universities, on the other, produced by Bert Roth, Hanns Anderlahn, Hermann Paull, Hanns Löhr, and Hans Globke.

As the war began to turn bad with Stalingrad, the defeat in North Africa, and the invasion of Italy; and then very bad with the bombing of German cities and the invasion of France; and then insupportably bad with the rapid advance of the Allies in the west and the Russians in the east, the German hierarchy turned repeatedly to the consolations available in the career of Frederick the Great and the presumed parallel it offered with the present situation. Just as the fortunes of Frederick, at a low ebb in the Seven Years' War, had been miraculously rescued by the unexpected death in 1762 of the Russian Czarina Elizabeth, so Hitler, Goebbels, and Doenitz hoped that some similar miracle would save Germany. The unexpected death of Roosevelt in April, 1945, seemed the very miracle required, and for a few hours there was joy at Hitler's headquarters. The main work triggering this hope was Carlyle's *History of Frederick the Great*, as well as Frederick's letters and the records of his conversations, which the Nazis studied enthusiastically, and not merely in hope of the miracle. Frederick's military career demonstrated, they thought, the value of "will"—spirit, morale, and sheer belief in victory, despite evidence of its unlikelihood. This devotion to Carlyle's version of things might seem to imply some small respect for literature, but more indicative of the German wartime conception of letters would be Hitler and Speer's elaborate plans for the ultimate reconstruction of Berlin, which made no provision for a library. The new main avenue was to be furnished with cinemas, opera houses, concert halls, buildings for congresses and conferences, hotels, restaurants and indoor swimming pools, but was quite innocent of bookshops.

Fresh Idiom

Disappointment threatens anyone searching in published wartime writing for a use of language that could be called literary—that is, pointed, illuminating, witty, ironic, clever, or interesting. What one finds, rather, is the gush, waffle, and cliché occasioned by high-mindedness, the impulse to sound portentous, and the slumbering of the critical spirit. Here is James Truslow Adams commenting on his essay "The American Dream," which he has selected to represent him in Whit Burnett's *This Is My Best:*

> Our type of civilization, the American way of life, the American dream are all at stake. I cannot go into details of prophecy here, and the

entire world will be different when the war is over. Life will be altered
in countless ways, but I believe that the cause of free men will prevail,
and that the American dream is so deeply rooted in the American heart
that it, too, will survive, translated into perhaps a greater reality than
ever. It can be lost only by us Americans ourselves, and I do not believe
we want to forget it or cease striving to make it real.[1]

It would not be easy to contrive a parody-prose at once as pretentious and
incompetent as that, and yet during wartime such utterances passed for
profound and ennobling.

For relief one turns to a different wartime tradition, the precise,
skeptical, demotic mode of the troops—and an idiom different from and
well above the habitual witless obscenities employed for rhythm and emphasis when abuse or disgust are being expressed. Impatient of dullness,
high purpose, and official euphemisms, the troops delighted in automatic
obscene abuse, but they also delighted in defaming the sometimes insufficiently rugged officers of the Medical Administrative Corps in scurri-
lous verses suggesting sprung rhythm:

> MACs,   MACs,
> Ball-bearing WACs.

One pleasant irony is that while servicemen's language often exhibited
such literary qualities as originality and energy, "literature" languished
in respectability, caution, and prudery. It was almost as if the cause of
literary "modernism," temporarily abandoned by "authors" and "artists,"
had descended to the troops. It was they during the war who behaved as
if continuing the modernist impulse toward subversion and Making New.

Their main technique of subversion was, of course, obscenity. It was
nowhere but in the Army of the United States, says Norman Mailer, that
he learned the joy of surprising and comical sudden obscene interjection.
Coming out with "shit" before an earnest audience priming itself for a
protest march on the Pentagon, Mailer recognizes that for soldiers of all
sorts, the humor that guards individual dignity and sanity must take the
form of obscenity. Thus, "Mailer never felt more like an American than
when he was naturally obscene—all the gifts of the American language
came out in the happy play of obscenity upon concept. . . ." And only
those in possession of the extremes of the social spectrum of language
could grasp and convey moral reality: "What was magnificent about the

word *shit*," Mailer says, "is that it enabled you to use the word *noble*." In sum, the important thing for an observer and registrar of actuality in this most bizarre and most canting of violent, vicious centuries is to say goodbye "to the literary corset of good taste."[2]

But popular, demotic traditions offered further opportunities than resourceful foul-mouthing for attaining something like literary and artistic effects, for having the experience of literature without the literature. What relation is there, one might ask, between the man writing *Four Quartets* and the woman writing "Still Falls the Rain," on the one hand, and, on the other, the soldier who has never heard of either but to whom "poetry" extends an appeal so deep he can't even talk about it? Witness his devotion to, say, "In Apple-Blossom Time" or "I'll Be Seeing You." In singing those two typical wartime songs, or identifying himself with the voice that sings, the soldier experiences an essential artistic action unattempted by either Eliot or Sitwell in their two works: namely, throwing himself into a voice and a character not his own—female, in these songs. While the troops were singing these, back home Cleanth Brooks and other New Critics were insisting that the most interesting poetry often involves this sort of dramatic situation, often achieves "irony" by revealing some imaginative distance between the maker of the poem and the voice that speaks in it. The troops were by no means critics, but in their way they were celebrating this poetic principle forgotten for the moment by most of their literary betters, for whom stark literal statement or sentimental platitude seemed to suffice.

Thus while official authors were descanting about Freedom and the American Way and the Postwar World, soldiers were busy at creative and often ironic language work, the Americans devising, for example, the concept of the *Dear John letter*, more often referred to simply as a *Dear John* (or, in the Pacific theater, a *Green Banana*, i.e., a cause of pain). This was the feared letter from home beginning harmlessly but exploding finally with the news that the beloved female writer has (of course, experienced soldiers would say) taken up with someone more accessible. Thus you could hear, "Don't bother him now. He just got a Dear John." And if that reveals talents for a literary use of language, how about the very term *G. I.*, now such a cliché that it's easy to forget what an original advance it was on the First World War's *doughboy*. G. I. was one of the very few euphemisms the troops permitted themselves. In the E. T. O. one heard observations like "I don't mind seeing dead Krauts, but I can't stand seeing a dead G. I.," where it's doubtful that the remark could be made at all if the speaker were forced to confront the emotion of the literal and say "a dead American soldier."

Diarrhea, common among combat soldiers and for centuries one of the inconveniences, seldom mentioned, of the trade, has generated a large body of comic reference, like the "Tennessee Trots" and "Virginia Quickstep" of the American Civil War. Infantry units on one's flanks which "retreat" without notice, thus, can be said to have a bad case of the runs. The United States Army Medical Corps term for a diarrheaic attack was, fortunately, "gastro-intestinal upset," which abbreviated eloquently to G. I., so that a GI could speak of experiencing the G. I.s, creating thus a rhetorical moment which should be of interest to semioticians and critics. Given the tire shortage, a *retread* is a rich term for an elderly NCO or officer unexpectedly called back into service, and it would be hard to think of a more effective way of conveying all that is implied by a stomach wound than to say *gut-shot*. On the other hand, the sort of wound known in the British Great War as a *blighty*—one just severe enough to send one home, but without amputation or disfigurement—is now called a *Hollywood wound*.

The U.S. Marines made from their motto a greeting capable of what later critics will laud as multisemiousness. Depending on tone and facial expression, "Semper Fi, Mac" can convey both such hostile messages as

> Fuck you, buddy, I'm all right,
> Tough shit: deal with your own problems, *or*
> Hell no!,

and friendly greetings like

> Hello, buddy, glad to see you, *and*
> Hang in there: help is coming.

The American military way with prepositions creates a whole special idiom, resolutely anti-Latinate and anti-pretentious, by which you can *put in for* the Air Medal or *put yourself in for* the Bronze Star, or (by a superior) *be put in for* (rather than the high-falutin' *recommended for*) the Silver Star. In the same way, you can be *up for* something: He's *up for* sergeant or *up for* the Medal of Honor. The Air Corps had its own brilliant usages, like *creepback,* a term recognizing the fear that causes bomber crews to drop their loads on the near edge of the target rather than in the more hazardous center. Successive instances of *creepback* will result in bombs falling ten miles short of the target, while everyone goes home convinced that a great and heroic job has been done. These practitioners of *creepback* become known as *fringe merchants*. And since the long thin strips of metal foil thrown from bombers to confuse enemy radar had early been given the random code-name *window*, throwing them out—now from a literal window, of course—became known as *windowing:* "The waist gunner began windowing the moment we got across the Channel."

Here, it may not be going too far to invoke R. P. Blackmur's definition of "fresh idiom," a characteristic of memorable poetry. Fresh idiom involves, he says, "language so twisted and posed . . . that it not only expresses the matter in hand but adds to the stock of available reality."[3] That is what *windowing* does, and such an achievement seems to belong not at all to the world of Sandburg or MacLeish or James Truslow Adams. The same can be said of thousands of other usages, like the term sailors of the Royal Navy (never called that, but rather "The Andrew") use to refer to themselves. *Sailors* would be uninteresting, but to call themselves *matelots* (rhymes with *matzos*) when none is French is to give reality a distinct twist: surprise now enters discourse and things perk up. As when a British sailor refers to soldiers as *pongos* and airmen as *erks*, not to mention designating testicles *goolies*—a notable advance on the customary and excessively literal *balls*. The principle of popular military idiom is the oblique approach: never use the expected civilian or "sincere" word or phrase but send it up with a surprising substitute. For "What's the news?" say, "What's the *griff?*" For toilet paper, say *Army Form Blank*, or *bumf*, short for *bum-fodder* and thus a one-syllable satire on the cant of horse-age military supply. One way to put newcomers "in the picture" is to give them *the gen*, the necessary information, a term most likely deriving from the conventional heading, "For the General Information of All Ranks." *Gen* comes in two varieties: there is *pukka gen*, or trustworthy information, and *duff gen*, its opposite. A retailer of either is a *gen merchant*, who can be, on the one hand, an intelligence officer or, on the other, the person on the adjacent commode in the latrine. *Gen* the intelligence officer may not want to pass on is *secret gen*. *Poop* is the American equivalent. In general, American usage seems to go in for more pessimistic and sardonic effects than British. American company officers entering combat were required to show yellow or white bars on the front of their helmets to indicate their rank. These were referred to as *aiming stakes*, and they were usually soon obscured by netting or by mud. And as a technique, folk-metonymy offers many pleasures. No need to say *a shower of shit*. Say simply, *a shower:* "You should have heard the brigadier chew out the battalion commanders. An absolute shower." Or: "How was the Colonel's reception?" "A shower."

But it was members of the youngest British service, the RAF, who developed perhaps the most original idiom, one often suggesting the nursery: being drunk was *screechers*, money was *ackers*, mosquitos were *mozzys* and mosquito-nets *mozzy-nets*, an aircraft engine was a *donk*, a recruit a *sprog*, and anyone in his barracks cot was *in the wanker*, i.e., the *wanking pit*. London was *The Big Smoke*, Berlin *The Big City*. Being called to the CO's office to be reprimanded was *being shit on from a great height*. Originally a term for any impressive or particularly destructive mission, a *prang* was said to be a *wizard prang* if especially memorable. Or *wizard* could be used, as in the nursery, for anything wonderful: "How was your date?" "Wizard!" But *prang* ultimately came to denote a crash, and thus one heard, "Any prang you walk away from is a good prang." Having your plane shot down was *getting the chop*, and certain girl friends, whose successive men seemed always to get chopped, were feared as *chop girls*. An easy way to be chopped over the Continent was to get *coned*—caught simultaneously by multiple searchlight beams. Then, if you were lucky you could escape with the assistance of your *brolly*, known to adults as a parachute.

To suggest the "poetic quality" of many of these usages is not as loose as it might seem, for many wartime phrases became popular because they exploited that sure-fire charm, rhyme. Or assonance. Perhaps the real "poetry of the war" is to be found not so much in genteel printed materials as in the evanescent assonances of the service rhymers who coined the term *crotch rot* for certain fungus ailments and *ruptured duck* for the American discharge button. Not to mention such obvious rhymings as the charge-of-quarters' morning wakey-wakey call, "Okay, men. Drop your cocks and grab your socks!," or *chow hound* or *shit list* or *walkie-talkie* or the favorite term for those unhappy in the army, *nervous in the service*. Rhyme can both familiarize and demean, as in *repple-depple* for an overseas replacement depot. The popularity of *This is it!* to mark dangerous or significant moments, like the arrival of a landing craft on an enemy beach or hooking up for a mass parachute drop, may stem in part from the pleasures of the short-*i* echo, like the short-*o* echo in the British POWs' term for their camp shows involving female impersonators, *sods' operas*. The same principle operates in *stupor juice*, any liquor like rum or Schnapps or Calvados used to raise morale or make attacks easier, and in such well-known popular formulations as *fuck-up, grabass, chickenshit, ass bandit* (Royal Navy for an aggressive homosexual), *beating one's meat* (brought over from civilian life), and pre-eminently *Sad Sack*, where a further appeal is doubtless the alliteration.

Comic as the results may be, much service rhyme is fueled by anger: "I've been screwed, blewed, and tattooed" and "They can just jam it and cram it—and ram it—up their ass!" And much represents powerful condescension and contempt, as in such hospital usages as *pecker checker, prick smith,* and *penis machinist* for the medical officer obliged to scrutinize genitals for sign of gonorrhea. The place their unfortunate owners are sent for treatment is the *clap shack*. A hapless medical orderly is demeaned by rhyme into a *bedpan commando*, a phrase leaning in the direction of *chairborne*, describing troops (officers, largely) working in offices rather than descending in parachutes or landing in gliders. And no student of contemptuous rhyming demotics should overlook *Dugout Doug*, the troops' name for General MacArthur.

The Beast of the East, the title of an American anti-Japanese film of 1942, became a favorite epithet for any especially cruel Japanese guard in an American POW camp, and little folk-poems registered the hopes of Americans in the Pacific that the war would end sometime:

> Home alive in '45,

and

> Out of the sticks in '46,

and

> Hell to heaven in '47,

and finally

> Golden Gate in '48.

When the thoroughly exhausted American infantry neared Rome in spring, 1944, their hope that their torments might just possibly find significant recompense took rhyming form like a charm. "On to Rome," they said to each other, "then home." And of course the official government slogan manufacturers, many drawn from advertising, made their contributions:

> Nimitz Has No Limits.
> Loose Lips Sink Ships.
> We're in it! Let's win it!

Victory gardeners were urged to "Grow More in '44," while laggard female enlistees were advised, "Hurry Them Back! Join the WAC!" One should buy war bonds to *Back the Attack,* but some official poemlets were artistically more subtle than that, like *Buy a Share in America* and *Loose Talk Costs Lives,* where because of the spelling, the assonance is not instantly obvious, unlike the situation in, say, *Zip Your Lip.*

The hope entertained by both Allies and Axis that they were conducting the war with maximum efficiency and thoroughly up-to-date methods was nourished by the widespread employment of acronyms and abbreviations, and indeed their current popularity (HMO, IRA, CEO) is one of the legacies of the war, a survival of the wartime—as well as the New Deal—urge toward utility over former notions of traditional linguistic beauty and grace. The most satisfying wartime abbreviations were those that made words that were fun to say, like ETOUSA (European Theater of Operations, United States Army), CINCPAC (Commander-in-Chief, Pacific), SHAEF (Supreme Headquarters, Allied Expeditionary Force), and SEAC (Southeast Asian Command), as opposed to monstrosities like COMAMPHIBFORSOPAC—Commander, Amphibious Force, South Pacific. Some acronyms were virtually identical with code-names, like PLUTO (Pipe Line Under the Ocean), laid on the floor of the Channel to convey fuel to the Normandy invasion. The Germans had great success with GESTAPO *(Geheim Staats Polizei)* for Secret State Police, FLAK *(Flieger-Abwehr Kanone)* for anti-aircraft gun, SS *(Schutzstaffel)* for Protection Service, and of course NAZI, for *National-sozialistische Deutsche Arbeiter Partei,* for National Socialist German Workers Party.

Special wartime verbal entertainment was to be had in this context of abbreviations. Just as wags in the Great War rendered the British decoration DSO as "Dick shot off," in this war they took LDV (Local Defense Volunteers, the original term for the Home Guard) to stand for Look, Duck, and Vanish, and they imputed the award of the OBE to Other Bastards' Efforts. In the British army a standard term for an officers' indoor map or sand-table exercise was TEWT, Tactical Exercise

Without Troops. Those preparing for action in Burma and similar places assembled for what became known as JEWTS, or Jungle Exercises Without Trees. Some abbreviations entered the language as perfectly sober new words, like RADAR (Radio Direction and Ranging), while others became delightful or funny fresh idiom, like HUFFDUFF, for High Frequency Direction Finding. As usual, American troops seemed especially fertile with insult and cynicism, calling women marines BAMS (Broad-assed Marines) and devising SNAFU, with its offspring TARFU (Things Are Really Fucked Up), FUBAR (Fucked Up Beyond All Recognition), and the perhaps less satisfying FUBB (Fucked Up Beyond Belief). In the United States Navy, a popular retort (at least in imagination) to a superior mistakenly giving an order to a casual or detached sailor was FUBID—Fuck You, Buddy, I'm Detached—or FUBIS, Fuck You, Buddy, I'm on Shipping. The pomposity implied by official acronyms could be undercut by providing unexpected meanings, the way Anglophobic Americans turned SEAC into Save England's Asiatic Colonies, or the way British troops engaged in the immediate postwar operation in Southeast Asia designated RAPWI (Rehabilitation of Allied Prisoners of War and Internees) took the letters to deliver the injunction, Rape All Pretty Women in Indonesia. Indeed, every military or naval word or name, not just acronyms, invited travesty and ridicule: men stationed at Fort Eustis, Virginia, came up with Even Uncle Sam Thinks It Sucks. But levity was certainly not the motive among Hitler's entourage who invented for their Führer the acronym GRÖFAZ (*Grösster Feldherr aller Zeiten*, Greatest Military Commander of All Time). Pointing in quite a different direction are the coy affectionate acronyms beloved by the troops of all wars for writing on the flaps of envelopes containing letters home— SWAK (Sealed with a Kiss), SWALK (Sealed with a Loving Kiss), FLAK (Fond Love and Kisses), and ITALY, favored apparently by those with some doubts about fidelity at home: I Trust and Love You. With all this acronyming, blunders were bound to occur, and because of insufficient attentiveness or research, some official acronyms had to be hastily withdrawn, like AMGOT (American Military Government of Occupied Territory), which proved obscene in Turkish. It took the American government six months, from July, 1941, until December, to notice that its Bureau of Economic Defense made an inappropriate acronym and to replace it with Bureau of Economic Warfare. And although well-intentioned, the acronym for the Central Registry of War Criminals and Security Suspects (CROWCASS) perhaps was too risible to catch on. In subsequent wars the acronym and abbreviation habit, so gratifying to the technological in-group spirit, has grown until it seems almost unmanageable. Its domination of the "intellectual" dimension of the Vietnam War can be measured in Michael Lee Lanning's *Vietnam, 1969–1970: A Company Commander's Journal* (1988), where the abbreviations cascade forth, sometimes badly impeding discrimination and understanding (perhaps the point). Thus "VR in area of LOH this afternoon" (25), as well as BMB (Brigade Main Base), BDA (Bomb Damage Assessment), FB (Fire Base), AO (Area of Operations), OPCON (Operational Control), BH (Battalion Headquarters), UCMJ (Universal Code of Military Justice), and RIF (?), and such well-known "terms" as ARVN, VC, MIA, and KIA, whose functions can be regarded as, variously, satiric, serious, and euphemistic.

But the most successful acronym (perhaps "of all time") was *Jeep*, made from GP (General Purpose), the vehicle's official designation. Other names for this item failed to catch on, perhaps because they ignored the wartime principle that the best name for a thing derives from its initials (*Seabees* for Construction Battalions is a classic). General Patton tried to popularize "Peep," but it didn't go. Neither did "jitterbug" or such obvious "morale" coinages as "blitzbuggy" and "iron pony," which had not even assonance to recommend them. And *Jeep* was already familiar as the name of a cute non-human character in E. C. Segar's comic strip "Thimble Theater," which starred Popeye and constituted not-to-be-missed reading for the troops. One could indicate a significant distance between German and Allied understandings of the war by contemplating differences in tone between the two terms for their infantry's hand-carried anti-tank weapon. The Germans solemnly designated theirs *Panzerfaust*, or tank-fist. The Americans called theirs the *bazooka*, after the item it resembled in its clumsy tubularness, the absurd, home-made tuba-like bass trombone played by the harmless Ozarks entertainer Bob Burns.

As well known among the troops as Popeye (and Bob Burns) were three wartime characters. One is tempted to call them *literary* characters. They are Kilroy; Chad; and Spokeshave, the Shithouse Poet. If during the Vietnam War the favorite graffito was FTA—Fuck the Army, in the Second World War it was undoubtedly the more imaginative and stylish KILROY WAS HERE. This was best inscribed in the most unbelievable or inaccessible places as a testimony to Kilroy's bravery and enterprise—on a sign in not-yet-conquered enemy territory, for example, or on a virgin invasion beach. But it could be scrawled to advantage anywhere it was likely to occasion amusement or wonder. Sergeant Francis J. Kilroy, of the U.S. Air Corps, claimed to be the namesake and originator, but some believed, on the contrary, it was one James J. Kilroy, an inspector in a Massachusetts shipyard, said to have OK'd work by chalking "Kilroy was here" on parts of ships under construction—a flagrantly unlikely story, considering how much easier it would be to write JK, or K, or OK, or to make a check mark. No, there was no real Kilroy, and that is essential to the myth. Like Sad Sack reversed, Kilroy is a character fulfilling everyone's army fantasies of success, indeed, victory, without effort or strain or fear. He is ubiquitous and agile, cleverly overcoming all limitations of time and space. Though in the army, he retains identity and individuality: he is a name, and he has no serial number. And he is immortal, impervious to shot and shell, terror and humiliation. For those who have been in the wartime services, the ultimate lifetime joke would be for the first Americans or Soviets landing on Mars to be greeted with the sign KILROY WAS HERE.

Chad, who figures in the favorite graffito of British forces, conveys a different message. He is the universal comic military complainer, always depicted bald with his large nose peering over a fence or wall and saying, "Wot, no ———?", the blank filled with anything desirable and, because of the army, unavailable. Thus: Wot, no

Women?
Sausages?
Chips?
Beer?
Whisky?
Leave?
Cigarettes?
Hot Water?
Sweets?
Peace in Our Time? etc.

Late in the war, in some drawings of Chad his head disappears entirely behind the fence, leaving only his hands visible. Now he says, "Fuck! I'm slipping." Spokeshave, on the other hand, is never depicted. He is the new, fugitive Shakespeare appropriate to the modern scene who signs

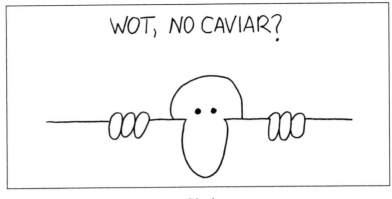

Chad

his writings appearing on British latrine walls, like this work recalled by
Maclaren-Ross:

> When apples are ripe
> And ready for plucking
> Girls of sixteen are ready for
> NOT WHAT YOU THINK THEY'RE READY FOR,
> YOU FILTHY-MINDED FUCKERS.[4]

Spokeshave is identifiably a British creation: impossible to imagine
U.S. graffiti signed with a sent-up name with literary resonance. The
British troops' comic songs are different from the American also. They
tend to use fucking less as an image, lubricious or otherwise, than as an
entirely de-sexed conventional adjective. From the American repertory,
for example, we have "The Great Fucking Wheel," which goes in part
as follows:

> Round and round went the great fucking wheel,
> In and out went the great prick of steel,
> Balls of brass all loaded with cream
> And the whole mechanism was driven by steam.

That is all very well, but what about the masterful deployment of the
word *fucking* as an abundant throwaway modifer, a modifer refusing to
be literal even when modifying *dames*, in this classic song about Halkirk,
a town in Scotland hated by the troops:

This fucking town's a fucking cuss
No fucking trams, no fucking bus.
Nobody cares for fucking us
In fucking Halkirk.

No fucking sport, no fucking games,
No fucking fun. The fucking dames
Won't even give their fucking names
In fucking Halkirk.

And so on for ten stanzas, with the *f*-word making 57 appearances. Another song exhibiting equal anonymous talent is this one, titled "The Twats in the Ops Room" (that is, the imbeciles [cf. cunts] in the RAF Operations Room), sung to the tune of "John Brown's Body":

We had been flying all day long at one hundred fucking feet,
The weather fucking awful, fucking rain and fucking sleet;
The compass it was swinging fucking south and fucking north,
But we made a fucking landfall in the Firth of fucking Forth.

(Chorus) Ain't the Air Force fucking awful?
Ain't the Air Force fucking awful?
Ain't the Air Force fucking awful?
We made a fucking landing in the Firth
of fucking Forth.

We joined the fucking Air Force 'cos we thought it fucking
right,
We don't care if we fucking fly or if we fucking fight,
But what we do object to are those fucking Ops Room twats,
Who sit there sewing stripes on at the rate of fucking knots.

Less well known than such sentimental selections as "I've Got Sixpence" and "Tavern in the Town" and "Bell-Bottom Trousers" but treasured by the troops were songs which could never be sung, and hardly understood, by civilians. Like the song from the North African desert delivered in the voice of a rear-echelon soldier, who asks,

"Why don't we grease all our nipples today,
So we can run faster when we run away?"[5]

Bitterness is the general tone of these songs, together with disdain for civilian ignorance and pomposity. The religious views of many of the troops are to be inferred from

> I am Jesus's little lamb,
> Yes, by Jesus Christ I am.

One collector of service songs goes so far as to suggest that "a conspiracy of silence" has kept most people unaware of the songs of wartime, for few want to know "the intensity of the bitterness that comes through the humor—directed, above all, towards the folks back home."[6] And of course towards the service itself, as retaliation for the chickenshit. As one airman remembers, the coarseness of service songs helped release

> the pent-up hostility each airman harbored against an official service that had stationed him in some ghastly hole, halfway round the world. . . . Why did we sing? Helpless to control our lives, we turned to song to express the insanities of the moment.[7]

In a world without electronic entertainment, drunken group singing was a staple of evening parties. Samuel Hynes, once a U.S. Marine Corps flier, remembers such parties near an air station in California attended by pilots who'd not yet been overseas. Girl friends and even some wives would be present:

> Everyone drank a lot, and there was a good deal of stumbling affection, but not sex. What there was mostly was singing. . . . The songs we sang were the ones that had been brought back from the war, a separate repertoire of songs suitable for Marines to sing while drunk. . . . None had ever been written down, I'm sure, and many had been remade to fit new circumstances. They were a genuine oral tradition, like folk ballads. Most of them were about sex or death, though a few were devoted to despising senior officers and the military life. All were comic, or were intended to be.

The pilot who led the singing, Hynes recalls, was "a sort of mnemonic curator of the collection" of dirty songs, and

> with a glass swinging in his hand in time to the music, and a happy grin on his face, he would finish one song and begin another, all night, inex-

haustibly. "There were *cats* on the roof," he would begin, and we'd be singing

> And cats on the tiles,
> Cats with the shits
> And cats with the piles,
> Cats with their a-a-ass ho-o-o-les
> Wreathed in smiles,
> As they revelled in the joys of fornication.

(The retard in the fourth line was best rendered by one pilot "with a high pure voice like a choirboy's"—his "church-in-the-wildwood tenor," he called it.) Later, in the South Pacific, Hynes met a flier who had both a beautiful voice and the capacity to make a slow song

sound like a hymn or a choral work for a hundred voices; it didn't matter how dirty it was, it came out like the songs we had all sung in Sunday school. "I love to see Mary make water," he would sing, with tender yearning in his voice,

> She can pee such a beautiful stree-ee-ee-eam.
> She can pee for a mile and a quarter *(long pause)*
> And you can't see her ass for the steam.

One song Hynes heard later from a Marine aviator begins as an easy parody of "Casey Jones," but turning to the matter of each soldier's $10,000 Government Service Life Insurance policy, arrives finally at the sort of satire sadly missing from most of the real poetry of the war:

> He was found in the wreck with his hand on the throttle,
> And his airspeed reading forty knots.
> They searched all day for the poor pilot's body,
> But all they could find were spots,
> Hundreds and hundreds of spots.

(In *spots*, a good example of Blackmur's "fresh idiom.")

> *(Chorus)* Ten thousand dollars going home to the folks.
> Ten thousand dollars going home to the folks.
> Oh won't they be delighted!
> Oh won't they be excited!
> Think of all the things they can buy![8]

Some, it is true, were singing "Lili Marlene," and some were singing "Scatterbrain" and "Mairzy Doats" and "Paper Doll," but others, sensing that peacetime attitudes would not do for wartime and requiring a way to object to the war without openly doing so, were singing (to the tune of "She Was Poor But She Was Honest"),

> Life is full of disappointments,
> Dull and empty as a tomb,
> Father's got a strictured penis,
> Mother has a fallen womb.
>
> Uncle Ted has been deported
> For a homosexual crime.
> Sister Sue has just aborted
> For the forty-second time.
>
> Now the fun has really started,
> Now we're really up the spout:
> Auntie Jane has gone and farted,
> Blown her asshole inside out.
>
> The maid has chronic constipation.
> Never laughs, and seldom smiles;
> Hates her dismal occupation:
> Crushing ice for Grandpa's piles.

Meanwhile, up above, as it were, and in no danger from shell fragments, public wartime rhetoric pursued its customary course, leaping from cliché to bromide to would-be bright phrases like "for the duration" and "books-krieg" (for a charity book sale) and "Operation ————" for any organized thing at all, the more trivial and harmless the better. In the midst of this most dehumanizing of wars, both the Allies and the Axis tried to create a warm human illusion by naming things—deadly, most of them—after the human being associated with them. In the absence of personality, things had to have "personality." In the First World War the rifle used by American forces was called a Springfield, after the arsenal in the Massachusetts city where it was made. In the Second World War, the American rifle was humanized to the Garand, after its inventor, John C. Garand. That was the hope, at least: but the troops, declining to play, called it simply the M-1. In the same way there was the Higgins landing craft, the Churchill tank, and the Kaiser freighters, while Germany had its

Organization [Fritz] Todt and later its Speer Construction Staff. And the U.S. Marines came up with units named Carlson's and Edson's and Roosevelt's Raiders.

If such usages were mild forms of what the troops' fresh idiom was protesting, more severe forms were to be met with on public celebratory occasions. On July 21, 1945, Churchill dedicated a soldiers' club in Berlin to be used by the remnants and replacements of the 7th Armored Division, the Desert Rats. In his speech, he raised his voice and said to the listening troops, "May the fathers long tell the children about this tale! May your glory ever shine! May your laurels never fade! May the memory of this glorious pilgrimage of war never die!"[9] If (despite the exclamation marks) that exemplifies stale idiom, as well as illustrating a notable aborted hope and failed prophecy, other official utterances equally illustrate what happens when fresh idiom is not to be found. Disaster is especially likely when a speaker unaccustomed to the hazards of such an operation essays telling metaphors. Are Yanks more likely to disgrace themselves here than the British? One might think so encountering MacArthur's thirsty ear: "I listen vainly," he tells the West Point cadets in his farewell speech to them, "I listen vainly, but with thirsty ear, for the witching melody of faint bugles blowing reveille. . . ."[10] The troops may have talked and sung dirty, but they never uttered anything as offensive as that.

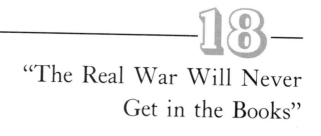

"The Real War Will Never Get in the Books"

What was it about the war that moved the troops to constant verbal subversion and contempt? It was not just the danger and fear, the boredom and uncertainty and loneliness and deprivation. It was rather the conviction that optimistic publicity and euphemism had rendered their experience so falsely that it would never be readily communicable. They knew that in its representation to the laity what was happening to them was systematically sanitized and Norman Rockwellized, not to mention Disneyfied. They knew that despite the advertising and publicity, where it counted their arms and equipment were worse then the Germans'. They knew that their automatic rifles (World War One vintage) were slower and clumsier, and they knew that the Germans had a much better light machine gun. They knew that despite official assertions to the contrary, the Germans had real smokeless powder for their small arms and that they did not. They knew that their own tanks, both American and British, were ridiculously under-armed and under-armored, so that they were inevitably destroyed in an open encounter with an equal number of German Panzers. They knew that the anti-tank mines supplied them became unstable in sub-freezing weather, and that truckloads of them blew up in the winter of 1944–45. And they knew that the greatest single weapon of the war, the atomic bomb excepted, was the German 88-mm flat-trajectory gun, which brought down thousands of bombers and tens of thousands of soldiers. The Allies had nothing as good, despite one of them designating itself The World's Greatest Industrial Power. The troops' disillusion and their ironic response, in song and satire and sullen contempt, came from knowing that the home front then (and very likely historiography later) could be aware of none of these things.

The Great War brought forth the stark, depressing *Journey's End;* the Second, as John Ellis notes, the tuneful *South Pacific.*[1] The real war was tragic and ironic, beyond the power of any literary or philosophic analysis to suggest, but in unbombed America especially, the meaning of the war seemed inaccessible. As experience, thus, the suffering was wasted. The same tricks of publicity and advertising might have succeeded in sweetening the actualities of Vietnam if television and a vigorous uncensored moral journalism hadn't been brought to bear. America has not yet understood what the Second World War was like and has thus been unable to use such understanding to re-interpret and re-define the national reality and to arrive at something like public maturity.

In the popular and genteel iconography of war during the bourgeois age, all the way from eighteen- and nineteenth-century history paintings to twentieth-century photographs, the bodies of the dead, if inert, are intact. Bloody, sometimes, and sprawled in awkward positions, but except for the absence of life, plausible and acceptable simulacra of the people they once were. But there is a contrary and much more "realistic" convention represented in, say, the Bayeux Tapestry, where the ornamental border displays numerous severed heads and limbs. That convention is honored likewise in Renaissance awareness of what happens to the body in battle. In Shakespeare's *Henry V*, the soldier Michael Williams assumes the traditional understanding when he observes,

> But if the cause be not good, the King himself hath a heavy reckoning to make when all those legs and arms and heads, chopp'd off in a battle, shall join together at the latter day and cry all "We died at such a place"— some swearing, some crying for a surgeon, some upon their wives left poor behind them, some upon the debts they owe, some upon their children rawly left. (IV, i)

And Goya's eighty etchings known as "The Disasters of War," depicting events during the Peninsular War, feature plentiful dismembered and beheaded cadavers. One of the best known of Goya's images is that of a naked body, its right arm severed, impaled on a tree.

But these examples date from well before the twentieth-century age of publicity and euphemism. The peruser—*reader* would be the wrong word— of the picture collection *Life Goes to War* (1977), a volume so popular and widely distributed as to constitute virtually a definitive and official anthology of Second World War photographs, will find even in its starkest images no depiction of bodies dismembered. There are three separated heads shown, but all, significantly, are Asian—one the head of a Chinese soldier hacked off by the Japanese at Nanking; one a Japanese soldier's badly burnt head (complete with helmet) mounted as a trophy on an American (light) tank at Guadalcanal; and one a former Japanese head, now a skull sent home as a souvenir to a girlfriend by her navy beau in the Pacific. No American dismemberings are registered, even in the photographs of Tarawa and Iwo Jima. American bodies (decently clothed) are occasionally in evidence, but they are notably intact. The same is true of other popular collections of photographs, like *Collier's Photographic History of World War II* (1946), Ronald Heiferman's *World War II* (1973), A.J.P. Taylor's *History of World War II* (1974), and Charles Herridge's *Pictorial History of World War II* (1975). In these, no matter how severely wounded, Allied troops are never shown suffering what was termed, in the Vietnam War, traumatic amputation: everyone has all his limbs, his hands and feet and digits, not to mention expressions of courage and cheer. And recalling Shakespeare and Goya, it would be a mistake to assume that dismembering was more common when warfare was largely a matter of cutting weapons, like swords and sabers. Their results are nothing compared with the work of bombs, machine guns, pieces of shell, and high explosives in general. The difference between the two traditions of representation is not a difference in military technique. It is a difference in sensibility, especially in the ability of a pap-fed mass public to face unpleasant facts. To this date, the appearance of the site of a major airplane accident is unknown to almost everyone. One may hear of *fragments*, but one is not shown them in images deemed suitable for public viewing.

What annoyed the troops and augmented their sardonic, contemptuous attitude toward those who viewed them from afar was in large part this public innocence about the bizarre damage suffered by the human body in modern war. The troops could not contemplate without anger the lack of public knowledge of the Graves Registration form used by the U.S. Army Quartermaster Corps with its space for indicating "Members Missing." You would expect front-line soldiers to be struck and hurt by bullets and shell fragments, but such is the popular insulation from the facts that you would not expect them to be hurt, sometimes killed, by being struck by parts of their friends' bodies violently detached. If you asked a wounded soldier or marine what hit him, you'd hardly be ready for the answer, "My buddy's head," or his sergeant's heel or his hand, or a Japanese leg, complete with shoe and puttees, or the West Point ring on his captain's severed hand. What drove the troops to fury was the complacent, unimaginative innocence of their home fronts and rear echelons about such experiences as the following, repeated in essence tens of thousands of times. Captain Peter Royle, a British artillery forward observer, was moving up a hill in a night attack in North Africa. "I was following about twenty paces behind," he says,

> when there was a blinding flash a few yards in front of me. I had no idea what it was and fell flat on my face. I found out soon enough: a number of infantry were carrying mines strapped to the small of their backs, and either a rifle or machine gun bullet had struck one, which had exploded, blowing the man into three pieces—two legs and head and chest. His inside was strewn on the hillside and I crawled into it in the darkness.[2]

In war, as in air accidents, "insides" are much more visible than it is normally well to imagine. To soldiers they are deplorably familiar. Dropping in his parachute over Arnhem, General Sir John Hackett saw "an inert mass . . . swinging down in a parachute harness beside me, a man from whose body the entrails hung, swaying in a reciprocal rhythm. As the body moved one way the entrails swung the other."[3] Sometimes damage to the body was well beyond endurance, for those perceiving as well as those damaged. Once in the Normandy battles a British major accompanied a stretcher party searching for a wounded man earlier parties had missed. "Sure enough," he says,

> we found a poor little chap with both legs blown off above the knees, moaning softly and, I remember, he was saying, "Oh dear! Oh dear!" The stretcher-bearer shook his head and, I thought, looked pointedly at my revolver.[4]

And there's an indication of what can be found on the ground after an air crash in one soldier's memories of a morning after an artillery exchange in North Africa. Neil McCallum and his friend "S." come upon the body of a man who had been lying on his back when a shell, landing at his feet, eviscerated him:

> "Good God," said S., shocked, "here's one of his fingers." S. stubbed with his toe on the ground some feet from the corpse. There is more horror in a severed digit than in a man dying: it savors of mutilation. "Christ," went on S. in a very low voice, "look, it's not his finger."[5]

In the face of such horror, the distinction between friend and enemy vanishes, and the violent dismemberment of any human being becomes equally traumatic. After the disastrous Canadian raid at Dieppe, one German soldier observed: "The dead on the beach—I've never seen such obscenities before":

> There were pieces of human beings littering the beach. There were headless bodies, there were legs, there were arms.

There were even shoes, "with feet in them."[6] The soldiers on one side know what the soldiers on the other side understand about dismemberment and evisceration, even if that knowledge is hardly shared by the

civilians behind them. Hence the practice among German U-boats of
carrying plenty of animal intestines to shoot to the surface to deceive those
imagining that their depth charges have done the job. Some U-boats, it
was said, carried (in cold storage) severed legs and arms to add verisi-
militude. But among the thousands of published photographs of sailors
and submariners being rescued after torpedoings and sinkings, no evidence of severed limbs, intestines, or floating parts.

If American stay-at-homes could be all but entirely sanitized from
awareness of the looks and smells of the real war, the British, at least
those living in bombed areas, could not. But even then, as one Briton
noted in 1941, "We shall never know half of the history . . . of these
times." What has prompted this observation was this incident: "The other
night not half a mile from me a middle-aged woman [in the civilian
defense] went out with an ambulance. In a smashed house she saw something she thought was a mop. It was no mop but a man's head."[7] So
unwilling is the imagination to dwell on genuine—as opposed to fictional
or theatrical—horrors, that indeed "We shall never know half of the
history . . . of these times." At home under the bombs on "The
Wednesday," Frances Faviell is suddenly aware of the whole house coming down on top of her, and she worries about "Anne," who has been in
bed on the top floor:

"With great difficulty I raised my head and shook it free of heavy, choking, dusty stuff. An arm had fallen round my neck—a warm, living
arm, and for one moment I thought that Richard had entered in the
darkness and was holding me, but when very, very cautiously I raised
my hand to it, I found that it was a woman's bare arm with two rings on
the third finger and it stopped short in a sticky mess."[8]

You can't take much of that sort of thing without going mad, as
General Hackett understood when he saw that the wild destruction of
enemy human beings had in it less of satisfaction than distress. Injured
and on the German side of the line at Arnhem, he is being taken to the
German medical installation. Along the road he sees "half a body, just
naked buttocks and the legs joined on and no more of it than that." To
those who might have canted that the Only Good German is a Dead
German, Hackett has a message: "There was no comfort here. It was like

being in a strange and terrible nightmare from which you longed to wake and could not."[9]

In the Great War, Wilfred Owen was driven very near to madness by having to remain for some time next to the scattered body pieces of one of his friends. He had numerous counterparts in the Second War. At the botched assault on Tarawa and Betio Atoll, one coxswain at the helm of a landing vessel went quite mad, perhaps at the shock of steering through all the severed heads and limbs near the shore. One Marine battalion commander, badly wounded, climbed above the rising tide onto a pile of American bodies. Next afternoon he was found there, mad.[10] But madness did not require the spectacle of bodies just like yours messily torn apart. Fear continued over long periods would do the job, as on the Royal and merchant navy vessels on the Murmansk run, where "Grown men went steadily and fixedly insane before each others' eyes."[11] Madness was likewise familiar in submarines, especially during depth-bomb attacks. One U.S. submariner reports that during the first months of the Pacific war, such an attack sent three men "stark raving mad": they had to be handcuffed and tied to their bunks.[12] Starvation and thirst among prisoners of the Japanese, as well as among downed fliers adrift on rafts, drove many insane, and in addition to drinking their urine they tried to relieve their thirst by biting their comrades' jugular veins and sucking the blood. In one way, of course, the whole war was mad and every participant insane from the start, but in a strictly literal sense the result of the years of the bombing of Berlin and its final destruction by the Russian army was, for much of the population, widespread madness. Just after the surrender some 50,000 orphans could be found living in holes like animals, "some of them one-eyed or one-legged veterans of seven or so, many so deranged by the bombing and the Russian attack that they screamed at the sight of any uniform, even a Salvation Army one."[13]

Although in the Great War madness among the troops was most conveniently imputed to the effects of concussion ("shell shock"), in the Second it was more frankly attributed to fear, and in contrast to the expectations of heroic behavior which set the tone of the earlier war, now it was recognized that the fact of fear had to be squarely faced. The result was a whole new literature of fear, implying that terror openly confessed argues no moral disgrace, although failure to control its visible symptoms is reprehensible. The official wartime attitude toward the subject was often expressed by quoting Marshal Ney: "The one who says he never knew

fear is a compound liar." As the U.S. *Officer's Guide* goes on to instruct
its anxious tyros,

> Physical courage is little more than the ability to control the physical fear
> which all normal men have, and cowardice does not consist in being
> afraid but in giving away to fear. What, then, keeps the soldier from
> giving away to fear? The answer is simply—his desire to retain the good
> opinion of his friends and associates . . . his pride smothers his fear.[14]

The whole trick for the officer is to seem what you would be, and the
formula for dealing with fear is ultimately rhetorical and theatrical: regardless of your actual feelings, you must simulate a carriage which will
affect your audience as fearless, in the hope that you will be imitated, or
at least not be the occasion of spreading panic. Advice proffered to enlisted men admitted as frankly that fear was a normal "problem" and
suggested ways of controlling it. Some of these are indicated in a 1943
publication of the U.S. National Research Council, *Psychology for the
Fighting Man*. Even if it is undeniable that in combat everyone will be
"scared, terrified," there are some antidotes: keeping extra busy with tasks
involving details, and engaging in roll-calls and countings-off, to empha-
size the proximity of buddies, both as support and as audience.[15] And
there is a "staff" solution to the fear problem which has been popular
among military theorists at least since the Civil War: when under shelling
and mortar fire and scared stiff, the infantry should alleviate the problem
by moving—never back but forward. This will enable trained personnel
to take care of the wounded and will bring you close enough to the enemy
to make him stop the shelling. That it will also bring you close enough
to put you within rifle and machine-gun and hand-grenade range is what
the theorists know but don't mention. The troops know it, which is why
they like to move *back*. This upper- or remote-echelon hope that fear can
be turned, by argument and reasoning, into something with the appearance of courage illustrates the overlap between the implausible persuasions
of advertising and those of modern military motivators. There was a lot
of language devoted to such rationalizing of the irrational. A little booklet
issued to infantry replacements joining the Fifth Army in Italy contains
tips to ease the entry of innocents into combat: Don't believe all the horror stories circulating in the outfit you're joining. Don't carry too much
stuff. Don't excrete in your foxhole—if you can't get out, put some dirt
on a shovel, go on that, and throw the load out. Keep your rifle clean

and ready. Don't, for fear of their flying off accidentally, tape down the handles of your grenades—it takes too long to get the tape off. Learn to dig in fast when shelling starts. Watch the ground for evidence of mines and bobby traps. On the move, keep contact, and don't bunch up. And use common sense in your fight against fear:

> Don't be too scared. Everybody is afraid, but you can learn to control your fear. And, as non-coms point out, "you have a good chance of getting through if you don't lose your head. Being too scared is harmful to you." Remember that a lot of noise you hear is ours, and not dangerous. It may surprise you that on the whole, many more are pulled out for sickness or accident than become battle casualties.[16]

(After that bit of persuasion, the presence of first-aid sections on "If You Get Hit" and "If a Buddy Gets Hit" may seem a bit awkward.)

This open, practical confrontation of a subject usually unmentioned has its counterpart in the higher reaches of the wartime literature of fear. The theme of Alan Rook's poem "Dunkirk Pier," enunciated in the opening stanza, is one hardly utterable during earlier wars:

> Deeply across the waves of our darkness fear
> like the silent octopus feeling, groping, clear
> as a star's reflection, nervous and cold as a bird,
> tells us that pain, tells us that death is near.[17]

In "Fear of Death," a piece of testimony appearing in *Penguin New Writing* in spring, 1943, the British naval rating F. J. Salfeld confronts without evasion and analyzes carefully the terror of being below decks and passing up shells and powder while under fire. If he manages to survive the shock and even has the satisfaction of passing the test and not letting his fear show, not all are so lucky. In the mess quarters after the battle,

> grimy men clustered around the tables smoking, talking of the action and of friends who were wounded or dead, and of how they had died. At the end of the table a youngster sat crying openly like the child he had so recently been. He had seen his "winger," his best friend, decapitated. Grief and shock joined in the tears that drew two pink lines down his grease-stained cheeks.[18]

William Collins's "Ode to Fear," published in 1746 when your average citizen had his wars fought by others whom he never met, is a remote allegorical and allusive performance lamenting the want of powerful emotion in contemporary poetry. C. Day Lewis's "Ode to Fear" of 1943 is not literary but literal, frank, down-to-earth, appropriately disgusting:

> Now Fear has come again
> To live with us
> In poisoned intimacy like pus. . . .

And fear is exhibited very accurately in its physical and psychological symptoms:

> The bones, the stalwart spine,
> The legs like bastions,
> The nerves, the heart's natural combustions,
> The head that hives our active thoughts—all pine,
> Are quenched or paralyzed
> When Fear puts unexpected questions
> And makes the heroic body freeze like a beast surprised.[19]

The new frankness with which fear will be acknowledged in this modernist, secular, psychologically self-conscious wartime Auden registers in "September 1, 1939," where the speaker, "uncertain and afraid," observes the "waves of . . . fear" washing over the face of the earth. And the new frankness becomes the virtual subject and center of *The Age of Anxiety*, written from 1944 to 1946.

Civilian bombing enjoined a new frankness on many Britons. "Perfect fear casteth out love" was Connolly's travesty of I John 4:18, as if thoroughly acquainted with the experience of elbowing his dearest aside at the shelter entrance. "WHY WORRY?" asked an ad in *Penguin New Writing* for April-June, 1943:

> Worry uses an immense amount of vital force. . . . People who worry can't sleep. They lose their appetite. . . . If the men and women who worry could be shown how to overcome the troubles and difficulties that cause worry, they soon would cease wasting their very life-blood in worrying.

The answer: Pelmanism, a mail-order course

fully described in a little book entitled *The Science of Success.*

And then a significant addendum: "Half Fees for all serving members of His Majesty's Forces." (This at the moment when Leslie Howard was killed when his plane from Lisbon was shot down. In a month Sicily would be invaded and the American paratroops killed in the Great Palermo eff-up, brought down by the fire of the United States Navy. In the same month the permanent steel gallows would be erected outside the kitchen building at Auschwitz I. Ample occasions for worry, some might think, and worry beyond the power of Pelmanism to alleviate.)

If the anonymous questionnaire, that indispensable mechanism of the social sciences, had been widely used during the Great War, more perhaps could be known or safely conjectured about the actualities of terror on the Western Front. Questionnaires were employed during the Second War, and American soldiers were asked about the precise physical signs of their fear. The soldiers testified that they were well acquainted with such impediments to stability as (in order of occurrence)

> Violent pounding of the heart,
> Sinking feeling in the stomach,
> Shaking or trembling all over,
> Feeling sick at the stomach,
> Cold sweat,
> Feeling weak or faint.

Over one-quarter of the soldiers in one division admitted that they'd been so scared they vomited, and almost a quarter said that at terrifying moments they'd lost control of their bowels. Ten percent had urinated in their pants. As John Ellis observes of these data,

> Stereotypes of "manliness" and "guts" can readily accommodate the fact that a man's stomach or heart might betray his nervousness, but they make less allowance for his shitting his pants or wetting himself.

And furthermore: "If over one-fifth of the men in one division . . . admitted that they had fouled themselves, it is a fair assumption that many more actually did so."[20] One of the common fears, indeed, is the very fear of wetting oneself and betraying one's fear for all to see by the most childish symptom. The fear of this fear augments as the rank rises:

for a colonel to piss his pants under shellfire is much worse than for a PFC. Landing at Peleliu, U. S. Marine E. B. Sledge confesses, "I felt nauseated and feared that my bladder would surely empty itself and reveal me to be the coward I was."[21] If perfect fear casteth out love, perfect shame can cast out even agony. During the Normandy invasion, a group of American soldiers came upon a paratroop sergeant caught by his chute in a tree. He had broken his leg, and shit and pissed himself as well. He was so ashamed that he begged the soldiers not to come near him, despite his need to be cut down and taken care of. "We just cut off his pants," reports one of the soldiers who found him, "and gently washed him all over, so he wouldn't be humiliated at his next stop."[22] Men more experienced than that paratrooper had learned to be comfortable with the new frankness. A soldier new to combat heard his sergeant utter an obscenity when their unit was hit by German 88 fire:

> I asked him if he was hit and he sort of smiled and said no, he had just pissed his pants. He always pissed them, he said, when things started and then he was okay. He wasn't making any apologies either, and then I realized something wasn't quite right with me. . . . There was something warm down there and it seemed to be running down my leg. . . .
>
> I told the sarge. I said, "Sarge, I've pissed too," or something like that and he grinned and said, "Welcome to the war."[23]

Other public signs of fear are almost equally common, if even more "comic." One's mouth grows dry and black, and a strange squeaking or quacking comes out, joined sometimes with a stammer. Very hard for a field-grade officer to keep his dignity when that happens.

For the ground troops, artillery and mortar fire were the most terrifying, partly because their noises was so deafening and unignorable, partly because the damage they caused the body—sometimes total disappearance or atomization into tiny red bits (cf. "spots")—was worse than most damage by bullets. To be killed by bullets seemed to Sledge "so clean and surgical. But shells would not only tear and rip the body, they tortured one's mind almost beyond the brink of sanity."[24] "Emasculating" was the effect Vernon Scannell imputed to the special fear caused by shelling, "the pure physical terror that savages you when loud and violent death is screaming down from the sky and pounding the earth around you, smashing and pulping everything in the search for you."[25] An occasional reaction to the terror of shelling like this was audible "confession." One

American infantryman cringing under artillery fire in the Ardennes suddenly blurted out to his buddies, "In London I fucked prostitutes and then robbed them of their money." The shelling over, the soldier never mentioned this utterance again, nor did his friends, everyone understanding its stimulus and its meaning.[26]

But for the infantry there was something to be feared almost as much as shelling: the German *Schü* mine, scattered freely just under the surface of the ground, which blew your foot entirely off when you stepped on one. For years after the war, ex-soldiers seized up when confronted by patches of grass and felt safe only when walking on asphalt or concrete. Fear among the troops was probably greatest in the staging areas just before D-Day: that was the largest assembly of Allied troops yet unblooded and combat-virgin. "Don't think they weren't afraid," says one American woman who worked with the Red Cross. "Just before they went across to France, belts and ties were removed from some of these young man. They were very, very young."[27] It is to be suspected that early in the war the commanders of the RAF knew as well as anyone how silly it was to send bombers over Germany not with bombs but with pamphlets from *"Englische Arbeiter an ihre deutschen Brüder,"* that they were aware how little good that sort of approach was going to do. But perhaps the idea was not to drop pamphlets specifically but to drop something, so that aircrews would get accustomed to their fear of night-formation flying over hostile territory. Frightened fliers had to be got to fly through flak and searchlights: pamphlets would do for a reason.

For those who fought, the war had other features unknown to those who looked on or got the war mediated through journalism. One such feature was the rate at which it destroyed human beings—friendly as well as enemy. Training for infantry fighting, few American soldiers were tough-minded enough to accept the full, awful implications of the term *replacement* in the designation of their Replacement Training Centers. (The proposed euphemism *reinforcement* never caught on.) What was going to happen to the soldiers they were being trained to replace? Why should so many "replacements"—hundreds of thousands of them, actually—be required? The answers came soon enough in the European theater, in Italy, France, and finally in Germany. In six weeks of fighting in Normandy, the 90th Infantry Division had to replace 150 per cent of its officers and over 100 per cent of its men. If a division was engaged for more than three months, the probability was that every one of its second lieutenants, all 132 of them, would be killed or wounded.[28] For those

*Infantry replacements being prepared at a Replacement Training
Center, Spring, 1943. (The author is second from left in the
top row.) (U.S. Army Signal Corps)*

being prepared as replacements at Officer Candidate Schools, it was not
healthy, mentally, to dwell on the oddity of the schools' turning out
hundreds of new junior officers weekly after the army had reached its full
wartime strength. Only experience would make the need clear. In Normandy, when the 120th Infantry relieved the 82nd Airborne,

> the green, unblooded newcomers gazed in shock and awe at the para-
> troopers they were to succeed. We asked them, "Where are your offi-
> cers?," and they answered, "All dead." We asked, "Who's in charge,
> then?," and some sergeant said, "I am."[29]

The British were equally unprepared for this rate of destruction. The
commanding officer of the King's Own Scottish Borderers, his unit arriving finally in Hamburg in 1945 after fighting all the way from Nor-

mandy, found an average of five original men remaining (out of around 200) in each rifle company. "I was appalled," he said. "I had no idea it was going to be like that."[30]

And it was not just wounds and death that depopulated the rifle companies. In the South Pacific it was malaria, dengue and blackwater fever, and dysentery; in Europe, dysentery, pneumonia, and trenchfoot. What disease did to the troops in the Pacific has never been widely known. The ingestion of atabrine, the wartime substitute for quinine as a malaria preventive, has caused ears to ring for a lifetime, and decades afterward, thousands still undergo their regular malaria attacks, freezing and burning and shaking all over. In Burma, British and American troops suffered so regularly from dysentery that they cut large holes in the seat of their trousers to simplify things.[31] But worse was the mental attrition upon combat troops, who learned by experience the inevitability of their ultimate mental breakdown, ranging from the milder forms of treatable psychoneurosis to outright violent insanity.

In war it is not just the weak soldiers, or the sensitive ones, or the highly imaginative or cowardly ones, who will break down. Inevitably, all will break down if in combat long enough. "Long enough" is now defined by physicians and psychiatrists as between 200 and 240 days. As medical observers have reported, "There is no such thing as 'getting used to combat'. . . . Each moment of combat imposes a strain so great that men will break down in direct relation to the intensity and duration of their experience." Thus—and this is unequivocal: "Psychiatric casualties are as inevitable as gunshot and shrapnel wounds in warfare."[32] Given this ultimate collapse into blubbery tears of the strongest and most experienced soldiers surviving in every outfit, the whole front line would dissolve except for two things: at any given moment, not all men have yet reached the stage of collapse; and there is a constant flow of replacements for those who have. Because "combat is torture, and it will reduce you, sooner or later, to a quivering wreck," to spare themselves the awful moment of psychological breakdown, with its appearance of cowardice, soldiers wanted to be wounded: except for death, a severe wound was the only way out that did not imply letting the side down. For every front-line soldier in the Second World War there was the "slowly dawning and dreadful realization that there was no way out, that . . . it was only a matter of time before they got killed or maimed or broke down completely." As one British officer put it, "You go in, you come out, you go in again and you keep doing it until they break you or you are dead."[33]

This "slowly dawning and dreadful realization" usually occurs as a result of two stages of rationalization and one of accurate perception:

1. It *can't* happen to me. I am too clever / agile / well-trained / good-looking / beloved / tightly laced, etc. This persuasion gradually erodes to

2. It *can* happen to me, and I'd better be more careful. I can avoid the danger by watching more prudently the way I take cover / dig in / expose my position by firing my weapon / keep extra alert at all times, etc. This conviction attenuates in turn to the perception that death and injury are matters more of luck than skill, making inevitable the third stage of awareness:

3. It *is going to* happen to me, and only my not being there is going to prevent it.

Because of the words *unconditional surrender*, it became clear in this war that no sort of lucky armistice or surprise political negotiation was going to give the long-term front-line man his pardon. "It soon became apparent," says John Ellis, "that every yard of ground would have to be torn from the enemy and only killing as many men as possible would enable one to do this. Combat was reduced to its absolute essentials, kill or be killed." [34] It was this that made the "Western Front" war unique this time: it could end only when the line (or the Soviet line) arrived in Berlin. In the Second World War the American military learned something very "modern"—modern because dramatically "psychological," utilitarian, unchivalric, and un-heroic: it learned that men will inevitably go mad in battle and that no appeal to patriotism, manliness, or loyalty to the group will ultimately matter. Thus in later wars things were arranged differently. In Vietnam, it was understood that a man fulfilled his combat obligation and purchased his reprieve if he served a fixed term, 365 days, and not days in combat either but days in the theater of war. The infantry was now treated somewhat like the Air Corps in the Second War: performance of a stated number of missions guaranteed escape.

If most civilians didn't know about these things, most soldiers didn't either, since only a relatively small number did any fighting which brought them into mortal contact with the enemy. For the rest, engaged in supply, transportation, and administrative functions, the war constituted a period of undesired and uncomfortable foreign travel under unaccustomed physical and social conditions, like enforced obedience, bad food, and absence of baths. Thus, as William Manchester has said, "All who wore uniforms are called veterans, but more than 90 percent of them are as uninformed about the killing zones as those on the home front."[35] In 1943 the Army of the United States grew by two million men, but only about 365,000 of those went to combat units, and an even smaller number ended in the rifle companies. The bizarre size and weight of the administrative tail dragged across Europe by the American forces is implied by statistics: between 1941 and 1945, the number of troops whose job was fighting increased by only 100,000.[36] If by the end there were 11 million men in the American army, only 2 million were in the 90 combat divisions, and of those, fewer than 700,000 were in the infantry. Regardless of the persisting fiction, those men know by experience the truth enunciated by John Ellis that

> World War II was not a war of movement, except on the rare occasions when the enemy was in retreat; it was a bloody slogging match in which mobility was only occasionally of real significance. Indeed, . . . the internal combustion engine was not a major consideration in the ground war.[37]

The relative few who actually fought know that the war was not a matter of rational calculation. They know madness when they see it. They can draw the right conclusions from the fact that in order to invade the Continent the Allies killed 12,000 innocent French and Belgian civilians who happened to live in the wrong part of town, that is, too near the railway tracks. The few who fought are able to respond appropriately— that is, without surprise—to such data as this: that in the Netherlands alone, more than 7000 planes tore into the ground or the water, afflicted by bullets, flak, exhaustion of fuel or crew, "pilot error," discouragement, or suicidal intent. In an article about archaeological excavation in Dutch fields and drained marshes, Les Daly has emphasized the multitudinousness, the mad repetitiveness of these 7000 crashes, reminding readers that "the total fighter and bomber combat force of the U. S. Air Force today amounts to about 3400 airplanes." Or, "to put it another way, the crash of 7000 aircraft would mean that every square mile of the entire state of New Jersey would have shaken to the impact of a downed plane."[38] Similarly, no one who fought will be surprised to hear that in planning air support for D-Day and concerned that fog might be a problem, the American Air Corps generals Spaatz, Doolittle, and Kepner "privately agreed in advance to send their air fleets out regardless of the weather even if they were all lost."[39] And in Papua, New Guinea, where today plane wrecks (from the Fifth Air Force) are strewn all over the forests, bad weather and mountainous terrain, together with incompetent piloting, caused more crashes than any Japanese opposition.[40] In the same way, the few who fought have little trouble understanding other outcroppings of the irrational element, in events like Hiroshima and Nagasaki, or for that matter the bombing of Hamburg or Darmstadt or Tokyo or Dresden. Recently a survivor of the bombing of Dresden has ventured to ask, "Was there any sense to this mass annihilation, military or otherwise?" Why, he asks, didn't some "humane bomber crews" choose to drop their bombs "off target?"[41] Overlooking the palpable oxymoron *humane bomber crews*, any experienced soldier would ask in turn, Why would they do that? To do that would delay the ending of the war and extend their own period of mortal risk. Not to mention, given the inaccuracy of bombing, how the bombardiers could even have directed their bombs to a safe place. Had they tried, they might, given the likelihood of ironic military blunders, really have hit Dresden worse. The problem is that this questioner has somehow been led to expect "sense," not to mention decency, in a war actually characterized by insensate savagery. This questioner seems innocent of such standard wartime materials as the British *Handbook of Irregular Warfare* (1942): "Never give the enemy a chance; the days when we could practice the rules of sportsmanship are over. . . . Every soldier must be a potential gangster. . . . Remember you are out to kill." At the same time the *Infantry Journal* was instructing its readers in the technique of dealing with enemy sentries: kick them very hard in the balls; hammer their heads in (tip off the helmet first); stab them with ladies' hat-pins; strangle them with piano wire. And those who imagine the Allies motivated by an infinitely higher morality than the Axis are probably unaware that in 1943 the Allied Chiefs of Staff seriously considered invading neutral Spain as an easier way of getting onto the Continent than an elaborate crossing of the Channel.[42] The destruction of Dresden *et al.* was as little rational as the German shooting of hostages to "punish" an area, or the Jewish conviction that if you were submissive you might come through, or the American belief that an effective way into Germany was to plunge through the Hürtgen Forest, or the British and Canadian belief, years earlier, that a great raid on Dieppe would be worthwhile. Revenge is not a rational motive, but it was the main motive in the American destruction of the Japanese empire. A compiler of *An Oral History of the War Years in America* observes,

> I distrust people who speak of the [atom] bombings today as an atrocity they strongly opposed in 1945. . . . . I don't believe them. At that time virtually everyone was delighted that we dropped the bombs, not only because they shortened the war and saved thousands of American lives but also [quite irrationally, notice] because the "Japs" deserved it for the terrible things they had done to our boys at Pearl Harbor, Bataan, Guadalcanal, and all the way through the Pacific.[43]

Those who fought know this, just as they know that it is as likely for the man next to you to be shot through the eye, ear, testicles, or brain as (the way the cinema does it) through the shoulder. A shell is as likely to blow his whole face off as to lodge a fragment in some mentionable and unvital tissue. Those who fought saw the bodies of thousands of self-destroyed Japanese men, women, and infants drifting off Saipan—sheer madness, but not essentially different from what Eisenhower describes in *Crusade in Europe*, where, not intending to make our flesh creep or descend to nasty details, he can't help reporting honestly on the carnage in the Falaise Pocket: "It was literally possible to walk for hundreds of yards at a time, stepping on nothing but dead and decaying flesh"[44]—formerly German soldiers who could have lived by surrendering but who chose, madly, not to.

How is it that these data are commonplaces only to the small number who had some direct experience of them? One reason is the normal human talent for looking on the bright side, for not receiving information likely to cause distress or occasion a major overhaul of normal ethical, political, or psychological assumptions. But the more important reason is that the large wartime audience never knew these things. The letterpress correspondents, radio broadcasters, and film people who perceived these horrors kept quiet about them on behalf of the War Effort. As John Steinbeck finally confessed in 1977, "We were all part of the war effort. We went along with it, and not only that, we abetted it. . . . I don't mean that the correspondents were liars. . . . It is in the things not mentioned that the untruth lies." By not mentioning a lot of things, a correspondent could give the audience at home the impression that there were no cowards in the service, no thieves and rapists and looters, no cruel or stupid commanders. It is true, Steinbeck is aware, that most military operations are examples of "organized insanity," but the morale of the home front must not be jeopardized by an eye-witness saying so. And even if a correspondent had wanted to deliver the noisome truth, patriotism would join censorship in stopping his mouth. As Steinbeck notes, "The foolish reporter who broke the rules would not be printed at home, and in addition would be put out of the theater by the command. . . ."[45]

The way censorship operated to keep the real war from being known is suggested by Herbert Merillat, during the war a bright and sensitive public-relations officer attached to the Marine Corps on Guadalcanal. In addition to generating Joe Blow stories, his job was that of censor: he was empowered to pass stories consonant with "the war effort" and to kill all others. Of a day in November, 1942, he writes:

> A recently arrived sergeant-reporter came around this afternoon, very excited, very earnest. Having gone through one naval shelling and two bombings he has decided that war is hell, and that he should write something stark. He showed me a long piece on the terror of men during bombings and shellings, the pain of the wounded, the disease and unpleasantness of this place. It was a gloomy and distorted piece; you would get the idea that every marine on the island is a terror-stricken, beaten man. I tried to tell him the picture was badly skewed.[46]

That's how the people at home were kept in innocence of malaria, dysentery, terror, bad attitude, and "psychoneurosis." Very occasionally there might be an actual encounter between home-front sentimentality and front-line vileness, as in an episode recalled by Charles MacDonald, a rifle company commander in Europe. One glib reporter got far enough forward to encounter some infantrymen on the line, to whom he put cheerful questions like, "What would you like best from the States about now?" At first he got nothing but sullen looks and silence. But finally one soldier spoke:

> "I've got something to say. Tell them it's too damned serious over here to be talking about hot dogs and baked beans and things we're missing. Tell them . . . they're [sic] men getting killed and wounded every minute, and they're miserable and they're suffering. Tell them it's a matter more serious than they'll ever be able to understand"—

at which point "there was a choking sob in his voice," MacDonald remembers. Then the soldier got out the rest of his inarticulate, impatient message: " 'Tell 'em it's rough as hell. Tell 'em it's rough. Tell 'em it's rough, serious business. That's all. That's all.' "[47]

Ernie Pyle, well known as the infantry's friend and advocate, was an accredited correspondent, which meant that he too had to obey the rules, that is, reveal only about one-third of the actuality and just like the other journalists fuel all the misconceptions—that officers were admired, if not beloved; that soldiers, if frightened, were dutiful; and that everyone on the Allied side was sort of nice. (Although representing the North American Newspaper Alliance, Pyle's copy makes him not easily distinguishable from a writer for *The New Yorker*.) One of Pyle's best-known pieces is his description of the return to his company in Italy of the body of Captain Henry T. Waskow, "of Belton, Texas." Such ostentatious geographical precision only calls attention to the genteel vagueness with which Pyle is content to depict the captain's wound and body. Brought down from a mountain by muleback, Captain Waskow's body is laid out on the ground at night and respectfully visited by officers and men of the company. The closest Pyle comes to accurate registration is reporting that one man, who sat by the body for some time, holding the captain's hand and looking into his face, finally "reached over and gently straightened the points of the captains' shirt collar, and then he sort of arranged the tattered edges of the uniform around the wound. . . ."[48] While delivering an account satisfying on its own terms, this leaves untouched what normally would be thought journalistically indispensable questions, and certainly questions bound to occur to readers hoping to derive from the Infantry's Friend an accurate image of the infantry's experience. Questions like these:

1. What killed Captain Waskow? Bullet, shell fragments, a mine, or what?

2. Where was his wound? How large was it? You imply that it was in the traditional noble place, the chest. Was it? Was it a little hole, or was it a great red missing place? Was it perhaps in the crotch, or in the testicles, or in the belly? Were his entrails extruded, or in any way visible?

3. How much blood was there? Was the captain's uniform bloody? Did the faithful soldier wash off his hands after toying with those

"tattered edges"? Were the captain's eyes open? Did his face look happy? Surprised? Satisfied? Angry?

But even Pyle's copy, resembling as it does the emissions issuing directly from the Office of War Information, is frankness itself compared with what German correspondents were allowed to send. They were a part of the military, not just civilians accredited to it, and like all other German troops they had taken the oath to the Führer. Their job was strictly propaganda, and throughout the war they obeyed the invariable rule that German servicemen were never, never to be shown dead in photographs, moving or still, and that if ever mentioned their bodies were to be treated with verbal soft-focus.[49] Certainly, as far as the German home front knew, soldiers' bodies were not dismembered, decapitated, eviscerated, or flattened out by tank treads until they looked like plywood. Even more than the testimonies sent back by such as Steinbeck and Pyle, the narratives presented to the German people were nothing but fairy stories of total heroism, stamina, good-will, and cheerfulness. This meant that for almost six years a large slice of actuality—perhaps one-quarter to one-half of it—was declared off-limits, and the sanitized and euphemized remainder was presented as the whole. That is, each side was offered not just false data, but worse, false assumptions about human nature and behavior, assumptions whose effect was to define either a world without a complicated principle of evil or one where all evil was easily displaced onto one simplified recipient, Jews on the Axis side, Nazis and Japs, on the Allied. The postwar result for the Allies, at least, is suggested by one returning soldier, wounded three times in Normandy and Holland, who disembarked with his buddies to find on the quay nice, smiling Red Cross or Salvation Army girls. "They give us a little bag and it has a couple of chocolate bars in it and a comic book. . . . We had gone overseas not much more than children but we were coming back, sure, let's face it, as killers. And they were still treating us as children. Candy and comic books."[50]

Considering that they were running it, it is surprising how little some officials on each side knew about the real war and its conditions. Some didn't care to know, like Adolf Hitler, who refused to visit Hamburg after its terrible fire storm in the summer of 1943. Some thought they knew about the real war, like Josef Goebbels, who did once visit the Eastern Front. But there he "assimilated reality to his own fantasies," as Neil Acherson has noted, and took away only evidence establishing that the troops were "brave fellows" and that his own morale-building speeches were "rapturously received." His knowledge of ground warfare remained largely literary: the course of the Punic Wars and the campaigns of Frederick the Great had persuaded him (or so he said) that in war "spirit" counts for more than luck or quantity of deployable men and munitions.[51] In addition to a calculating ignorance, a notable but not unique emotional coldness in the face of misery helped insulate him from the human implications of unpleasant facts. In September, 1943, airily and without any emotion or comment, even a conventional "I was sorry to see" or "It is painful to say," he tots up the casualty figures for two years on the Eastern Front alone: "Our total losses in the East . . . from June 22, 1941, to August 31, 1943, were 548,480 dead, of whom 18,512 were officers; 1,998,991 wounded, of whom 51,670 were officers; 354,957 missing, of whom 11,597 were officers; total 2,902,438, of whom 81,779 were officers."[52] If it was callousness that protected Goebbels from the human implications of these numbers, it was King George VI's rank and totemic identity that protected him from a lot of instructive unpleasantness. According to his official biographer, what the King saw on his numerous visits to bombed areas fueled only his instinct for high-mindedness. He concluded that among the bombed and maimed he was witnessing "a fellowship of self-sacrifice and 'good-neighborliness,' a comradeship of adversity in which men and women gave of their noblest to one another, a brotherhood of man in which the artificial barriers of caste and class were broken down. . . ."[53] The King never saw perfect fear operating as Connolly saw it, and it is unlikely that anyone told him, while the Normandy invasion was taking place, that "almost every police station and detention camp in Britain was jam-packed full. In Glasgow alone . . . deserters were sitting twelve to a cell."[54] It is hard to believe that the King was aware of all the bitter anti-Jewish graffiti his subjects were scrawling up in public places.[55] Nor is it recorded that he took in news of the thievery, looting, and robbing of the dead widely visible in the raided areas. Thirty-four people were killed in the cellar ballroom of the Café de Paris on March 8, 1941, when a bomb penetrated the ceiling and exploded on the bandstand, wiping out the band and many of the dancers. Nicholas Monsarrat recalls the scene a few moments later:

> The first thing which the rescue squads and the firemen saw, as their torches poked through the gloom and the smoke and the bloody pit which had lately been the most chic cellar in London, was a frieze of other

shadowy men, night-creatures who had scuttled within as soon as the echoes ceased, crouching over any dead or wounded woman, any *soignée* corpse they could find, and ripping off its necklace, or earrings, or brooch: rifling its handbag, scooping up its loose change.[56]

That vignette suggests the difficulty of piercing the barrier of romantic optimism about human nature implicit in the Allied victory and the resounding Allied extirpation of flagrant evil. If it is a jolt to realize that blitzed London generated a whole class of skillful corpse robbers, it is because, within the moral assumptions of the Allied side, that fact would be inexplicable. One could say of the real war what Barbara Foley has said of the Holocaust—not that it's "unknowable," but "that its full dimensions are inaccessible to the ideological frameworks that we have inherited from the liberal era."[57]

Finding the official, sanitized, "King George" war unbelievable, not at all in accord with actual human nature, where might one turn in search of the real heavy-duty war? After scrutinizing closely the facts of the American Civil War, after seeing and listening to hundreds of the wounded, Walt Whitman declared: "The real war will never get in the books." Nor will the Second World War, and "books" includes this one. But the actualities of the war are more clearly knowable from some books than from others. The real war is unlikely to be found in novels, for example, for they must exhibit, if not plot, at least pace, and their characters tend to assume the cliché forms demanded by Hollywood, even the new Hollywood, and even if the novels are as honorable as Harry Brown's *A Walk in the Sun* and Mailer's *The Naked and the Dead*. Not to mention what is perhaps the best of them, James Jones's *The Thin Red Line*. Sensing that action and emotion during the war were too big and too messy and too varied for confinement in one 300-page volume of fiction, the British tended to refract the war in trilogies, and some are brilliant: Waugh's *Sword of Honor* (1965), of course, collecting his three novels about Guy Crouchback's disillusioning war written from 1952 to 1961; Olivia Manning's *Balkan Trilogy* (1960-65); Anthony Powell's volumes VI, VII, and VIII of *A Dance to the Music of Time* (1964-68); and again Manning's *Levant Trilogy* (1977-80). The American way, on the other hand, seems less to conceive a trilogy than to produce three novels of different sorts and then, finding them on one's hands, to argue that they constitute a trilogy, as James Jones does. Despite undoubted success as engaging narrative, few novels of the war have succeeded in making a motive, almost a character, of a predominant wartime emotion, boredom, or persuading readers that the horrors have not been melodramatized. One turns, thus, from novels to "non-fiction," especially memoirs, and especially memoirs written by participants not conscious of serving any very elevated artistic ambition. The best are those devoid of significant dialogue, almost always a sign of *ex post facto* novelistic visitation. Because forbidden in all theaters of war lest their capture reveal secrets, clandestine diaries, seen and censored by no authority, offer one of the most promising accesses to actuality. The prohibition of diaries often meant increased devotion and care on the part of the writer. In Cairo in April, 1943, RAF Pilot Officer D. A. Simmonds addressed his diary thus:

> I understand that the writing of diaries is definitely forbidden in the services, and you must therefore consider yourself a very lucky diary to have so much time and energy expended on you when you're not entitled to be in existence at all.

And a month later: "You are becoming quite a big lad now, my diary; slowly but surely your pages swell."[58]

One diary in which much of the real war can be found is James J. Fahey's *Pacific War Diary* (1963). Fahey, a seaman first class on the light cruiser U.S.S. *Montpelier*, was an extraordinarily patient, decent person devoid of literary sophistication, and the authenticity of his experience can be inferred from his constant obsession with hunger and food, subjects as interesting as combat:

> For breakfast we had some hash and 1 bun, for dinner baloney sandwich, and for supper we had coffee, baloney sandwich, 1 cookie and a candy bar. This morning our ship shot down its lucky #13 Jap plane and one probable.[59]

Almost as trustworthy as such daily entries unrevised later are accounts of events written soon after by intelligent participants, like Keith Douglas (*Alamein to Zem Zem*, 1946), John Guest (*Broken Images*, 1949), and Neil McCallum (*Journey with a Pistol*, 1959). Those are British, and they are typically literary British performances, educated, allusive, artistically sensitive, a reminder of the British expectation that highly accomplished and even stylish young men will often be found serving in the

infantry and the tanks. There they will be in a position to create the sort
of war memoirs virtually non-existent among Americans, the sort which
generate a subtle, historically conscious irony by juxtaposing traditional
intellectual or artistic images of transcendence against an unflinching, fully
mature registration of wartime barbarism.

The best American memoirs are different, conveying their terrible
news less by allusion and suggestion and ironic learned comment than by
an uncomplicated delivery of the facts, conveyed in a style whose literary
unpretentiousness seems to argue absolute credibility. No American would
write of his transformation from civilian into soldier the way John Guest
does: "I am undergoing a land-change into something coarse and strange."[60]
American attempts to avoid the plain frequently backfire, occasioning embarrassing outbreaks of Fine Writing. Speaking of the arrival, finally, of
American planes on Guadalcanal, one U. S. marine has written:

> All Guadalcanal was alive with hope and vibrant with the scent of vic-
> tory. . . . The enemy was running! The siege was broken! And all through
> the day, like a mighty Te Deum rising to Heaven, came the beat of the
> airplane motors. Oh, how sweet the air I breathed that day! How fresh
> and clean and sprightly the life that leapt in my veins.[61]

By contrast, the American procedure at its best, unashamed of sim-
plicity, is visible in Eugene B. Sledge's memoir of a boy's experience
with "the old breed," the United States Marines. His *With the Old Breed
at Peleliu and Okinawa* (1981) is one of the finest memoirs to emerge
from any war, and no Briton could have written it. Born in Mobile,
Alabama, in 1923, Sledge enlisted in December, 1942. After his mirac-
ulous survival in the war, he threw himself into the study of nematology
and ultimately became a professor of biology at the University of Mon-
tevallo, Alabama. The main theme of *With the Old Breed* is, as Sledge
indicates, "the vast difference" between what has been published about
these two Marine Corps battles, which depicts them as more or less sane
activities, and his own experience "on the front line" (xiii).[62] One reason
Sledge's account is instantly credible is the detail with which he registers
his presence at the cutting edge, but another is his tone—unpretentious,
unsophisticated, modest, and decent. Despite all the horrors he recounts,
he is proud to be a marine. He is uncritical and certainly uncynical about
Bob Hope's contribution to the entertainment of the forces, and on the
topics of medals and awards he is totally unironic—he takes them seri-

ously, believing that those who have been given them deserve them. He doesn't like to say *shit,* and he prays, out loud. He comes through as such a nice person, so little inclined to think ill of others, that forty years after the war he still can't figure out why loose and wayward straps on haversacks and the like should be called, by disapproving sergeants and officers, *Irish pennants:* "Why Irish I never knew" (218). Clearly he is not a man to misrepresent experience for the momentary pleasure of a little show-business.

If innocent when he joined the Marines, Sledge was not at all stupid, and he knew that what he was getting into was going to be "tough": in training the emphasis on the Ka-Bar knife and kicking the Japs effectively in the balls made that clear. But the remaining scales fell from his eyes when he saw men simply hosed down by machine-gun fire on the beach at Peleliu: "I felt sickened to the depths of my soul. I asked God, 'Why, why, why?' I turned my face away and wished that I were imagining it all. I had tasted the bitterest essence of war, the sight of helpless comrades being slaughtered, and it filled me with disgust" (60). Before the battle for Peleliu is over, with casualties worse even than at Tarawa, Sledge perceived what all combat troops finally perceive: "We were expendable. It was difficult to accept. We come from a nation and a culture that values life and the individual. To find oneself in a situation where your life seems of little value is the ultimate in loneliness. It is a humbling experience" (100). He knew now that horror and fear were his destiny, unless a severe wound or death or (most unlikely) a Japanese surrender should reprieve him. And his understanding of the world he was in was filled out by watching marines levering out Japanese gold teeth with their Ka-Bar knives, sometimes from living mouths (120). The Japanese "defense" encapsulated the ideas and forms and techniques of "waste" and "madness." The Japanese knew they could neither repel the marines nor be reinforced. Knowing this, they simply killed, without hope and without meaning.

Peleliu finally secured, Sledge's ruined unit is reconstituted for the landing on southern Okinawa. It was there that he saw "the most repulsive thing I ever saw an American do in the war"—he saw a young Marine officer select a Japanese corpse, stand over it, and urinate into its mouth (199). If much of this would be incomprehensible to a home front nourished on athletic and heroic models of "combat," it wasn't understandable even to marines a few hundred yards back. Speaking of the "incredible cruelty" commonplace when "decent men were reduced to a brutish existence in their fight for survival amid the violent death, terror, tension, fatigue, and filth that was the infantryman's war," Sledge notes that "our code of conduct toward the enemy differed drastically from that prevailing back at division CP." Unequivocal is Sledge's assertion: "We lived in an environment totally incomprehensible"—not just to civilians at a great distance but "to men behind the lines . . ." (120-21).

But for Sledge the worst of all was a week-long stay in rain-soaked foxholes on a muddy ridge facing the Japanese, a site strewn with decomposing corpses turning various colors, nauseating with the stench of death, "an environment so degrading I believed we had been flung into hell's own cesspool" (253). Because there were no latrines and because there was no moving in daylight, the men relieved themselves in their holes and flung the excrement out into the already foul mud. It was a latter-day Verdun, the Marine occupation of that ridge, where the artillery shellings uncovered scores of half-buried Marine and Japanese bodies, making the position "a stinking compost pile":

> If a Marine slipped and slid down the back slope of the muddy ridge, he was apt to reach the bottom vomiting. I saw more than one man lose his footing and slip and slide all the way to the bottom only to stand up horror-stricken as he watched in disbelief while fat maggots tumbled out of his muddy dungaree pockets, cartridge belt, legging lacings, and the like. . . .
>
> We didn't talk about such things. They were too horrible and obscene even for hardened veterans. . . . It is too preposterous to think that men could actually live and fight for days and nights on end under such terrible conditions and not be driven insane. . . . To me the war was insanity. (260)

And from the other side of the world the young British officer Neil McCallum issues a similar implicit warning against the self-delusive attempt to confer high moral meaning on these grievous struggles for survival. Far from rationalizing their actions as elements of a crusade, McCallum and his men, he says, "have ceased largely to think or believe at all":

> Annihilation of the spirit. The game does not appear to be worth the candle. What is seen through the explosions is that this, no less than any other war, is not a moral war. Greek against Greek, against Persian, Roman against the world, cowboys against Indians, Catholics against

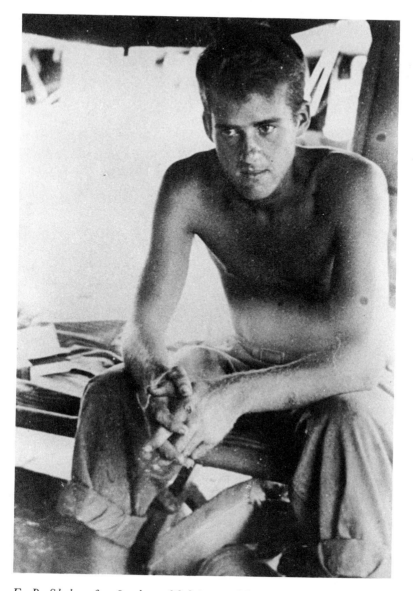

E. B. Sledge after 82 days of fighting on Okinawa. "There I sat trying to figure out how I was still in one piece, and depressed by the losses we suffered." (In Sledge's company alone, casualties of 153%.) "A tentmate had an ancient box camera and snapped this unposed photo." On Sledge's hands and forearm: sores from the filth. "I had entered the campaign weighing about 145 pounds, and weighed about 120 lbs. at the end. All the men lost 20–25 pounds." (E. B. Sledge)

Protestants, black men against white—this is merely the current phase of an historical story. It is war, and to believe it is anything but a lot of people killing each other is to pretend it is something else, and to misread man's instinct to commit murder.[63]

In some wartime verses titled "War Poet," the British soldier Donald Bain tried to answer critics and patriots arguing that the poets were failing to register the meaning of the war, choosing instead to notate mere incoherent details and leaving untouched and uninterpreted the great design of the whole. Defending contemporary poets and writers, Bain said:

> We in our haste can only see the small components of the scene;
> We cannot tell what incidents will focus on the final screen.
> A barrage of disruptive sound, a petal on a sleeping face,
> Both must be noted, both must have their place.
> It may be that our later selves or else our unborn sons
> Will search for meaning in the dust of long deserted guns.
> We only watch, and indicate, and make our scribbled pencil
>   notes.
> We do not wish to moralize, only to ease our dusty throats.[64]

But what time seems to have shown our later selves is that perhaps there was less coherent meaning in the events of wartime than we had hoped. Deprived of a satisfying final focus by both the enormousness of the war and the unmanageable copiousness of its verbal and visual residue, all the revisitor of this imagery can do, turning now this way, now that, is to indicate a few components of the scene. And despite the preponderance of vileness, not all are vile.

One wartime moment not at all vile occurred in June 5, 1944, when Dwight Eisenhower, alone with himself, for the moment disjunct from his publicity apparatus, changed the passive voice to active in the penciled statement he wrote out to have ready when the invasion was repulsed, his troops torn apart for nothing, his planes ripped and smashed to no end, his warships sunk, his reputation blasted:

> Our landings in the Cherbourg-Havre area have failed to gain a satisfactory foothold and I have withdrawn the troops.

Originally he wrote *the troops have been withdrawn*, as if by some distant, anonymous agency instead of by an identifiable man making all-but impossible decisions. Having ventured this bold revision, and secure now in his painful acceptance of full personal accountability, he is able to proceed unevasively with *My decision:*

> My decision to attack at this time and place was based on the best information available.

Then, after the conventional "credit," distributed equally to "the troops, the air, and the navy," Eisenhower's noble acceptance of total personal responsibility:

> If any blame or fault attaches to this attempt, it is mine alone.[65]

As Mailer says, you use the word *shit* so you can use the word *noble,* and you refuse to ignore the stupidity and barbarism and ignobility and poltroonery and filth of the real war so that *it is mine alone* can flash out, a bright signal in a dark time.

Notes

(IWM = materials in the Imperial War Museum, London)

1. From Light to Heavy Duty

1. Betty Ann Webster, letter to *Atlantic*, October, 1984, pp. 9–10.

2. *The United States Army in World War II* (Washington, 1955), II: 361 ff.

3. Michael Davie, ed., *The Diaries of Evelyn Waugh* (London, 1976), 448–49.

4. H. L. Sykes, memoir, IWM.

5. Geoffrey Perrett, *Days of Sadness, Years of Triumph: The American People, 1939–1945* (Baltimore, 1973), 82.

6. John Verney, *Going to the Wars* (London, 1955), passim.

7. Eric Newby, *A Traveller's Life* (New York, 1982), 44.

8. Quoted by Studs Terkel, *"The Good War": An Oral History of World War Two* (New York, 1984), 562.

9. Robert Wernick, *Blitzkrieg* (New York, 1976), 21.

10. Miss H. A. Harrison, diary, IWM.

11. Herbert Christian Merillat, *Guadalcanal Remembered* (New York, 1982), 168.

12. 9th ed. (Harrisburg, 1942), 179.

13. Capt. J. R. Strick, memoir, IWM.

14. The photograph is available in Michael Bloch, *The Duke of Windsor's War: From Europe to the Bahamas* (New York, 1983).

15. Stephen E. Ambrose, *Eisenhower: Soldier, General of the Army, President-Elect, 1890–1952* (New York, 1983), 149.

16. *The Pacific War* (New York, 1981), 416.

17. *Posters of World War I and World War II in the George C. Marshall Research Collection* (Charlottesville, 1979).

18. Peter Young, *The World Almanac Book of World War II* (New York, 1981), 362.

19. *Days of Sadness*, 67.

20. *Caviare at the Funeral* (New York, 1980), 28.

21. Quoted by Terkel, *"The Good War,"* 13.

22. Barry Broadfoot, ed., *Six War Years, 1939–1945: Memories of Canadians at Home and Abroad* (Toronto, 1974), 289.

23. *Fighter: The True Story of the Battle of Britain* (New York, 1977 [1979]), 290–91.

24. *The Civil War* (New York, 1971), 185.

25. Derek E. Johnson, *East Anglia at War, 1939–1945* (Norwich, 1978), 93–94.

26. Antoinette May, *Witness to War: A Biography of Marguerite Higgins* (New York, 1983 [1985]), 80–81.

27. Rafael Steinberg, *Island Fighting* (New York, 1978), 118.

28. (New York, 1944), 147–49.

2. Precision Bombing Will Win the War

1. Lee Kennett, *For the Duration: The United States Goes to War: Pearl Harbor–1942* (New York, 1985), 169.

2. Randall Jarrell, *The Complete Poems* (New York, 1969), 145.

3. John Grigg, *1943: The Victory That Never Was* (London, 1980), 142.

4. Michael Balfour, *Propaganda in War, 1939–1945* (London, 1979), 378.

5. *All England Listened: The Wartime Broadcasts of J. B. Priestley* (New York, 1967), xxii.

6. Nigel Hamilton, *Master of the Battlefield: Monty's War Years, 1942–1944* (New York, 1984), 287.

7. Gavin Lyall, *The War in the Air, 1939–1945* (London, 1968), 99.

8. "Mercury on a Fork," *Listener*, Feb. 18, 1971, p. 208.

9. (London, 1954), 23.

10. Terkel, *"The Good War,"* 209.

11. Vere Hodgson, *Few Eggs and No Oranges* (London, 1976), 54.

12. John W. Wheeler-Bennett, *King George VI: His Life and Reign* (London, 1958), 468.

13. *Few Eggs and No Oranges*, 63–64.

14. *Testament of Experience* (New York, 1957), 336–37.

15. *Overlord: D-Day and the Battle for Normandy* (New York, 1984), 253.

16. Omar N. Bradley and Clay Blair, *A General's Life* (New York, 1983), 280.

17. *Ibid.*, 249.

18. *Brave Men* (New York, 1944), 439.

19. Albert Speer, *Inside the Third Reich*, trans. Richard and Clara Winston (New York, 1970), 229.

3. Someone Had Blundered

1. Louis Simpson, *Collected Poems* (New York, 1965), 3–4.
2. Quoted by Robert E. Conot, *Justice at Nuremberg* (New York, 1983), 488.
3. J. Douglas Harvey, *Boys, Bombs, and Brussels Sprouts* (Halifax, 1983), 185.
4. *Extracts from Army Training Memorandum No. 46.*
5. Hastings, *Overlord*, 71.
6. *The Straw Giant: Triumph and Failure, America's Armed Forces* (New York, 1986), 60.
7. Conot, *Justice at Nuremberg*, 418–19.
8. Broadfoot, *Six War Years*, 240.
9. J. E. Johnson, *Wing Leader* (London, 1956), 208.
10. Hastings, *Overlord*, 90.
11. *The Second Front* (New York, 1978), 175.
12. *Ibid.*, 197.
13. Quoted by Peter Grafton, *You, You, and You* (London, 1981), 27–28.
14. *The Invasion Before Normandy: The Secret Battle of Slapton Sands* (New York, 1985), 133.
15. *The Second Front*, 71.
16. Page references to Davie, ed., *Diaries*.
17. Page references to Maclaren-Ross's *Memoirs of the Forties* (New York, 1984).
18. (New York, 1969), 87.
19. *The Poems of Lincoln Kirstein* (New York, 1987), 179.
20. *Ibid.*, 196.
21. Letter from Humphrey Spender, Jan. 24, 1982.
22. *The Collected Ewart, 1933–1980* (London, 1980), 308–10.

4. Rumors of War

1. Richard R. Lingeman, *Don't You Know There's a War On?: The American Home Front, 1941–1945* (New York, 1970), 212, 301.
2. Eric Morris, *Salerno: A Military Fiasco* (New York, 1983), 89.
3. *Ibid.*, 139.
4. *Few Eggs and No Oranges*, 263.
5. Anthony Hopkins, ed., *Songs from the Front and Rear* (Edmonton, 1979), 85.
6. Lee Kennett, *G. I.: The American Soldier in World War II* (New York, 1987), 132.
7. (Annapolis, 1944), 88.
8. *Kiss Me Goodnight, Sergeant Major: The Songs and Ballads of World War II* (London, 1973 [1975]), 140.

9. *Ibid.*, 145.

10. Franklyn A. Johnson, *One More Hill* (New York, 1949 [1983]), 36.

11. *Propaganda in War*, 180.

12. Diary, IWM.

13. John Lehmann, *Thrown to the Woolfs* (New York, 1979), 90.

14. Vernon Scannell, *Argument of Kings* (London, 1987), 121.

15. Neil McCallum, *Journey with a Pistol* (London, 1959), 24.

16. Henry Berry, *Semper Fi, Mac* (New York, 1982), 332.

17. Donald Knox, *Death March: The Survivors of Bataan* (New York, 1981), 260–61.

18. Edward Blishen, *A Cackhanded War* (London, 1972), 155.

19. *From the Ruins of the Reich: Germany, 1945–1949* (New York, 1985), 147–48.

20. *II Henry IV*, III, i, 97–98.

21. *War as I Knew It* (New York, 1947), 266–67.

22. *Ibid.*, 335, 203.

23. Bradley and Blair, *A General's Life*, 172.

24. *The Levant Trilogy* (New York, 1979), 118.

25. Charles B. MacDonald, *Company Commander* (New York, 1947), 246.

26. Michael Monihan, *People at War, 1939–1945* (London, 1974), 180.

27. *Levant Trilogy*, 266. For Maskelyne's North African performance see David Fisher, *The War Magician* (New York, 1983).

28. Knox, *Death March*, 36, 55, 86.

29. *Propaganda in War*, 98.

30. *Undercover Girl* (New York, 1947), 2.

31. *Ibid.*, 14.

32. *Ibid.*, 178.

33. *Ibid.*, 88–89.

34. Annette Tapert, ed., *Lines of Battle: Letters from American Servicemen, 1941–1945* (New York, 1987), xix.

35. Johnson, *One More Hill*, 128.

36. *Boy in the Blitz* (London, 1972), 131.

37. *Propaganda in War*, 192.

38. *Convoy* (New York, 1978), 202.

39. Robert Rhodes James, ed., *Chips: The Diaries of Sir Henry Channon* (Harmondsworth, 1970), 288–89.

40. Mike Henry, *Air Gunner* (London, 1964), 50.

41. "Stephen's Diary," Lord Deramore papers, IWM.

42. Norman Longmate, *How We Lived Then* (London, 1971), 132.

43. *Memoirs of the Forties*, 103.

44. Knox, *Death March*, 431.

45. IWM.

46. Quoted by Lyall, *The War in the Air*, 100.

47. Memoir, IWM.

48. IWM.

49. *Once There Was a War* (New York, 1958 [1977]), 21–23.

5. School of the Soldier

1. Frank F. Mathias, *G. I. Jive: An Army Bandsman in World War II* (Lexington, Ky., 1982), 30.

2. *The Face of War* (New York, 1959), 71, 94.

3. Page 428.

4. Broadfoot, *Six War Years*, 105.

5. *Ibid.*, 120.

6. Conversation with Wolfgang Iser, Heidelberg, 1957.

7. Charles Whiting, *Siegfried: The Nazis' Last Stand* (New York, 1982), 228.

8. *A Margin of Hope* (New York, 1982), 88.

9. *Jill* (London, 1946 [1976]), 10.

10. *With the Old Breed: At Peleliu and Okinawa* (Novato, Calif., 1981), 19.

11. *The Licentious Soldiery* (London, 1971), 25.

12. *Ibid.*, 37–38.

13. Hamilton, *Master of the Battlefield*, 576.

14. Henry, *Air Gunner*, 110.

15. *Alamein to Zem Zem* (New York, 1966), 15.

16. George Orwell, *A Collection of Essays* (New York, 1954), 25.

17. Lt. Peter Royle, Memoir, IWM.

18. *A Writer's Capital* (Minneapolis, 1974), 107.

19. Davie, *Diaries*, 646.

20. *The Military Orchid* (London, 1948 [1981]), 47, 80.

21. *The Tiger and the Rose* (London, 1971), 88.

22. James Lansdale Hodson, *Before Daybreak* (London, 1941), 101.

23. *Ibid.*, 66.

24. Croft-Cooke, *The Licentious Soldiery*, 33.

25. *Faces in My Time* (New York, 1980), 116.

26. Newby, *A Traveller's Life*, 125.

27. *Children of the Sun* (New York, 1976), 311–12.

28. *Mrs. Miniver* (New York, 1940), 260–61.

29. Page 478.

30. (New York, 1980), 23.

31. Graduation Program, The Infantry School, Ft. Benning, Ga., April 18, 1944.

32. Mary Jarrell, ed., *Randall Jarrell's Letters* (New York, 1985), 96–97.

33. James J. Fahey, *Pacific War Diary, 1942–1945* (New York, 1963), 79–80.

34. *A Separate Peace* (New York, 1960), 113.

35. *Collected Poems of Siegfried Sassoon* (New York, 1949), 72.

36. *Poems*, 149.

37. *The Complete Poems*, 401.

38. *Ibid.*, 145.

39. *Ibid.*, 143.

40. *Ibid.*, 397–98.

41. *Collected Poems, 1930–1960* (New York, 1960), 90.

42. Letter to Tania Stern, May, 1945, quoted in Stephen Spender, ed., *W. H. Auden: A Tribute* (New York, 1975), 126.

43. *Ibid.*, 131.

44. Edward Mendelson, ed., *W. H. Auden, Collected Poems* (New York, 1976), 259–62.

45. Don M. Wolfe, ed., *The Purple Testament* (Garden City, N.Y., 1947), xxvi.

6. Unread Books on a Shelf

1. *With the Old Breed*, 267.

2. *Testament of Experience*, 215.

3. Robert Lowell, ed., *Randall Jarrell, 1914–1965* (New York, 1967), 44.

4. *The Complete Poems*, 174.

5. P. J. Kavanagh, ed., *Collected Poems of Ivor Gurney* (Oxford, 1982), 102.

6. *Collected Poems* (New York, 1938), #204.

7. Quoted by Julian Green, *Diary, 1928–1957*, trans. Anne Green (New York, 1964), 182.

8. *Caviare at the Funeral*, 23–24.

9. *Infantry Journal*, Jan., 1945, p. 56.

10. Richard de Yarburgh-Bateson, IWM.

11. Ed., *Components of the Scene: Stories, Poems, and Essays of the Second World War* (Harmondsworth, 1966), 13.

12. *The Licentious Soldiery*, 21.

13. Oscar Williams, ed., *The War Poets: An Anthology of the War Poetry of the 20th Century* (New York, 1945), 214.

14. See Mauricio Mazón, *The Zoot-Suit Riots* (Austin, Tex., 1984).

15. *Last Chapter* (New York, 1946), 115–16.

16. (New York, 1942 [1970]), 21–22.

17. *Ibid.*, 267–68.

18. Broadfoot, *Six War Years*, 213–14.

19. *The Face of War*, 112.

20. *Complete Poems*, 198.

21. Brian Gardner, ed., *The Terrible Rain: The War Poets, 1939–1945* (London, 1966), 90–91.

22. *The Journey Not the Arrival Matters* (London, 1969), 9–11.

23. Richard Baron et al., *Raid! The Untold Story of Patton's Secret Mission* (New York, 1981), 86.

24. *Inside the Third Reich*, 237.

25. Blishen, *A Cackhanded War*, 146.

26. Angela Wright, "An Unlikely Romantic: William Scott in the 40s," *London Magazine*, July, 1981, p. 33.

27. Elaine Steinbeck and Robert Wallstein, eds., *Steinbeck: A Life in Letters* (New York, 1975), 264.

28. Hodson, *Before Daybreak*, 33.

29. Oliver Carpenter, IWM.

30. IWM.

31. Diary, IWM.

32. Page 119.

7. Chickenshit, An Anatomy

1. Gardner, *The Terrible Rain*, 70–72.

2. MacDonald, *Company Commander*, 99.

3. William Mulvihill, *Fire Mission* (New York, 1957), 13.

4. *Air with Armed Men* (London, 1972), 101.

5. Donald Pfarrer, *Neverlight* (New York, 1982), 206.

6. Desmond Flower and James Reeves, eds., *The Taste of Courage: The War, 1939–1945* (New York, 1960), 490.

7. (New York, 1946), 39.

8. "Britain and America," *Times Literary Supplement*, May 17, 1985, p. 544.

9. Kennett, *For the Duration*, 90.

10. Page references to *Heart of Oak* (New York, 1984 [1986]).

11. *Contemporary Authors*, vols. 73–76, p. 322.

12. *Memoirs of the Forties*, 228.

13. *Ibid.*, 265–66.

14. Page references to *My Enemy's Enemy* (New York, 1963).

15. *Times Literary Supplement*, Oct. 24, 1980, p. 1190.

16. Middlebrook, *Convoy*, 3.

17. *Ibid.*, 298.

18. Herbert Mitgang, *Dangerous Dossiers* (New York, 1988), 256.

19. *The Right Stuff* (New York, 1979. [1980]), 119.

20. Berry, *Semper Fi, Mac*, 192.

21. Knox, *Death March*, 406.

22. Harvey, *Boys, Bombs, and Brussels Sprouts*, 104.

23. Jones, *Heart of Oak*, 221.

24. *A Cackhanded War*, 120, 185–86.

25. *Extracts from Army Training Memorandum No. 41* (Oct. 7, 1941).

26. Linda Van Devanter, *Home Before Morning* (New York, 1984), 236.

27. Merillat, *Guadalcanal Remembered*, 154.

28. Lee G. Miller, *The Story of Ernie Pyle* (New York, 1950), 343.

29. Hopkins, *Songs from the Front and Rear*, 11.

8. Drinking Far Too Much, Copulating Too Little

1. McCallum, *Journal with a Pistol*, 133.

2. Broadfoot, *Six War Years*, 309.

3. *Ibid.*, 285.

4. Edward Mendelson, ed., *The English Auden* (New York, 1977), 245; Gellhorn, *The Face of War*, 107.

5. Victor Selwyn et al., eds., *Return to Oasis: War Poems and Recollections from the Middle East, 1940–1946* (London, 1980), 190.

6. *Life*, April 21, 1941, p. 80.

7. Page references to Strome Galloway, *With the Irish Against Rommel* (Langley, British Columbia, 1984).

8. J. Q. Hughes, IWM.

9. D. A. Simmonds, Diary, IWM.

10. *Come to Dust* (London, 1945), 10.

11. D. A. Simmonds, IWM.

12. Henry, *Air Gunner*, 98.

13. *Boys, Bombs, and Brussels Sprouts*, 144.

14. Quoted by John Ellis, *The Sharp End of War* (London, 1980), 289.

15. *Ibid.*, 292.

16. Quoted by Terkel, *"The Good War,"* 257.

17. *Ibid.*, 23–24.

18. Miller, *The Story of Ernie Pyle*, 341.

19. D. A. Simmonds, IWM.

20. Kenneth Young, ed., *The Diaries of Sir Robert Bruce Lockhart* (London, 1973–80; 2 vols.), II: 130.

21. *Ibid.*, 333–34.

22. M. J. Brown, Diary, IWM.

23. *WWII* (New York, 1975), 130.

24. *Preventive Medicine in World War II* (Washington, 1955), III: 247, 263–68.

25. Mathias, *G. I. Jive*, 146.

26. John R. Elting et al., eds., *A Dictionary of Soldier Talk* (New York, 1984), 218.

27. Page 20.

28. Lowry, *Casualty*, 74.

29. Donald Vining, ed., *American Diaries of World War II* (New York, 1982), 261.

30. *Ibid.*, 43.

31. Mark Jonathan Harris, Franklin Mitchell, and Steven Schechter, *The Homefront: America During World War II* (New York, 1984), 58.

32. Archie Satterfield, *The Home Front: An Oral History of the War Years in America, 1941–1945* (New York, 1981), 57.

33. *Ibid.*, 181.

34. Berry, *Semper Fi, Mac*, 202.

35. Page 71.

36. Page, *Kiss Me Goodnight*, 149.

37. Harvey, *Boys, Bombs, and Brussels Sprouts*, 29.

38. Broadfoot, *Six War Years*, 186.

39. *Poems of Lincoln Kirstein*, 224.

40. Knox, *Death March*, 419.

41. Newby, *A Traveller's Life*, 131–32.

42. Broadfoot, *Six War Years*, 70, 179.

43. *Boys, Bombs, and Brussels Sprouts*, 15.

44. *The Hand-Reared Boy* (London, 1970), 48.

45. Page references to *A Soldier Erect, or Further Adventures of the Hand-Reared Boy* (London, 1971).

46. *A Rude Awakening* (New York, 1978 [1980]), 254.

9. Type-Casting

1. *A Soldier Erect*, 202.

2. (New York, 1948 [1979]), 134.

3. Dwight Macdonald, *Memoirs of a Revolutionist: Essays in Political Criticism* (New York, 1957), 93.

4. *Into the Valley* (New York, 1943), 20, 56.

5. *Collected Poems: 1937–1962* (New York, 1962), 121.

6. Samuel Cosman Papers, U. S. Marine Corps Historical Center, Washington, D. C.

7. *Pacific War Diary*, 231.

8. Peter Donnelly, ed., *Mrs. Milburn's Diaries: An Englishwoman's Day-to-Day Reflections, 1939–1945* (London, 1979 [1980]), 248.

9. *Why Singapore Fell* (Bombay, 1945), 58.

10. John W. Dower, *War Without Mercy: Race and Power in the Pacific War* (New York, 1986), 36.

11. Knox, *Death March*, 364.

12. *With the Old Breed*, 142, 148.

13. John Costello, *The Pacific War* (New York, 1981), 616.

14. Longmate, *How We Lived Then*, 404.

15. No. 51, between pp. 248–49.

16. *I Was a Stranger* (London, 1977 [1979]), 74–75.

17. Fred Taylor, ed., *The Goebbels Diaries, 1939–1941* (New York, 1983), 148.

18. (1980), 5, 148.

19. Donnelly, *Mrs. Milburn's Diaries*, 216.

20. *Ibid.*, 185.

21. Napier Crookenden, *The Battle of the Bulge* (New York, 1980), 124.

22. Arthur Marshall, "Odd Man In," *New Statesman*, Nov. 21, 1980, p. 15.

23. John Strawson, *Hitler's Battles for Europe* (New York, 1971), 113.

24. Louis Lochner, ed., *The Goebbels Diaries, 1942–1943* (Garden City, N.Y., 1948), 317.

25. Johnson, *One More Hill*, 157.

26. *Overlord*, 24.

27. *The Past Is Myself* (London, 1970), 148.

28. M. J. Brown, Diary, IWM.

29. Anthony Deane-Drummond, *Return Ticket* (London, 1953 [1967]), 82.

30. Oliver Carpenter, Diary, IWM.

31. *Testament of Experience*, 258.

32. C. C. Rand, *The Ordinary Fellow* (Magazine of the 1st Bn., London Irish Rifles), I, #5, 54–55.

33. *And No Birds Sang* (Boston, 1979), 143.

34. James MacGregor Burns, *Roosevelt: The Soldier of Freedom* (New York, 1970), 214.

35. *A Cackhanded War*, 119.

36. Memoir, IWM.

37. (New York, 1929), 260.

38. Longmate, *How We Lived Then*, 422.

39. McCallum, *Journey with a Pistol*, 145.

40. Gillian Freeman, *The Undergrowth of Literature* (London, 1967), facing p. 86.

41. Diary, IWM.

42. E. B. Potter, *Bull Halsey* (Annapolis, Md., 1985), 348.

10. The Ideological Vacuum

1. Geoffrey Keynes, ed., *The Poetical Works of Rupert Brooke* (London, 1946 [1970]), 19.

2. *Roosevelt and Hopkins: An Intimate History* (New York, 1948), 438.

3. *The Licentious Soldiery*, 66.

4. *A Cackhanded War*, 13, 228.

5. *Collected Poems* (London, 1966), 152–53.

6. Mary Lago and P. N. Furbank, eds., *Selected Letters of E. M. Forster* (Cambridge, Mass., 1984; 2 vols.), II: 170.

7. Broadfoot, *Six War Years*, 19.

8. *The Journey Not the Arrival Matters*, 15.

9. P. N. Furbank, *E. M. Forster: A Life* (New York, 1978; 2 vols.), II: 254.

10. "Tones of Fear," *New Statesman*, July 28, 1978.

11. *Horizon*, Feb. 1940, p. 116.

12. Brenda McBryde, *A Nurse's War* (London, 1979), 86–87.

13. Pages 204–5.

14. *Nomad* (London, 1947), 16.

15. Lee Bartlett, ed., *Letters to Christopher: Stephen Spender's Letters to Christopher Isherwood, 1929–1939* (Santa Barbara, Calif., 1980), 190.

16. Broadfoot, *Six War Years*, 398.

17. *The Bourgeois Poet* (New York, 1964), 112.

18. *Slaughterhouse-Five*, 2.

19. *For Johnny: Poems of World War Two* (London, 1976), 21.

20. *The Collected Ewart*, 75.

21. McCallum, *Journey with a Pistol*, 40.

22. Williams, ed., *The War Poets*, 126–27.

23. *A Susan Sontag Reader* (New York, 1982), 195.

24. Review of Ronald Searle, *The Situation Is Hopeless*, in *New York Times Book Review*, March 8, 1981.

25. William Woodruff, *Vessel of Sadness* (London and Amsterdam, 1978), 94.

26. *Speak for England* (New York, 1977), 268.

27. (New York, 1942 [1983]), 86–96.

28. Gardner, *The Terrible Rain*, 183.

29. *The Face of War*, 242.

30. Davie, *Diaries*, 623, 624.

31. *Randall Jarrell's Letters*, 103.

32. "The Face in the Mirror: Anti-Semitism Then and Now," *New York Times Book Review*, October 14, 1984, p. 3.

33. Miller, *The Story of Ernie Pyle*, 219, 277.

34. Williams, ed., *The War Poets*, 17.

35. *Tarawa: The Story of a Battle* (New York, 1944), 35.

36. Quoted by Raleigh Trevelyan, *Rome '44* (London, 1981), 169.

37. Broadfoot, *Six War Years*, 208–9.

38. *Into the Valley* (New York, 1943), 74–75.

39. Wolfe, *Purple Testament*, 89.

40. *The Memoirs of Field-Marshal Montgomery* (Cleveland and New York, 1958), 116.

41. Joseph I. Greene, ed., *The Infantry Journal Reader* (New York, 1943), 274.

42. Williams, ed., *The War Poets*, 88.

43. "Writers and Society, 1940–1943," in Peter Quennell, ed., *Selected Essays of Cyril Connolly* (New York, 1984), 130–31.

44. *Memoirs of a Revolutionist*, 96.

45. *Boys, Bombs, and Brussels Sprouts*, 210.

11. Accentuate the Positive

1. *A Separate Peace*, 183.

2. Mary Lee Settle, *All the Brave Promises* (New York, 1966 [1980]), 127.

3. *The Style of the Century, 1900–1980* (New York, 1983), 119.

4. Gordon Carroll, ed., *History in the Writing* (New York, 1945), 191–93.

5. *Ruling Passions* (London, 1977), 158.

6. *A Cackhanded War*, 123.

7. *This England* (Baltimore, 1969), 59.

8. Knox, *Death March*, 46.

9. Costello, *The Pacific War*, 200.

10. Quoted by Michael Anglo, *Service Newspapers of the Second World War* (London, 1977), 130.

11. *Air with Armed Men*, 118.

12. Davie, ed., *Diaries of Evelyn Waugh*, 616, 597.

13. Pages 157–58.

14. Hastings, *Overlord*, 73.

15. *War as I Knew It*, 336, 169.

16. Hamilton, *Master of the Battlefield*, 133.

17. Matthew Cooper, *The German Army, 1933–1945* (New York, 1978), 487.

18. *The Strangers All Are Gone* (New York, 1982), 102.

19. S. L. Mayer, ed., *Signal: Years of Triumph, 1940–42* Englewood Cliffs, N.J., 1978), n. p.

20. A. Marjorie Taylor, *The Language of World War II* (New York, 1948), 11.

21. *One More Hill*, 138, 145.

22. Quoted by Miller, *The Story of Ernie Pyle*, 227.

23. *Last Chapter* (New York, 1946), 57.

24. Miller, *The Story of Ernie Pyle*, 414.

25. Oct. 6, 1944.

26. George Biddle, *Artist at War* (New York, 1944), 178.

27. Ambrose, *Eisenhower*, 251.

28. Wilbur H. Morrison, *Fortress Without a Roof: The Allied Bombing of the Third Reich* (New York, 1982), 258.

29. *War as I Knew It*, 248.

30. Aug. 15, 1945.

31. Deighton, *Fighter*, 285.

32. Berry, *Semper Fi, Mac*, 10.

33. *San Francisco Chronicle*, June 6, 1944, p. 1.

34. Hamilton, *Master of the Battlefield*, 339.

35. "1st Army Soldier," in Victor Selwyn et al., eds., *From Oasis into Italy* (London, 1983), 84–85.

36. Hamilton, *Master of the Battlefield*, 709–10.

37. *Eisenhower*, 175.

38. Matthew Bruccoli, ed., *In Time of War:* [James Gould Cozzens's] *Air Force Diaries and Pentagon Memos, 1943–45* (Columbia, S.C., 1984), 116.

39. Hastings, *Overlord*, 92.

40. Terkel, *"The Good War,"* 384.

41. "After Husky," *Times Literary Supplement*, June 8, 1984, p. 634.

42. Roland H. Spector, *Eagle Against the Sun: The American War with Japan* (New York, 1985), 118.

43. Lingeman, *Don't You Know There's a War On?*, 187.

44. *Stilwell and the American Experience in China, 1911–1945* (New York, 1971), 170.

45. *Ibid.*, 322.

46. *Ibid.*, 506.

47. Terkel, *"The Good War,"* 177.

48. *War Within and Without* (New York, 1980), 173.

49. *"The Good War,"* 121.

12. High-mindedness

1. *New Statesman*, March 14, 1978, p. 405.

2. *Last Chapter*, 107.

3. Henry E. Maule, ed., *A Book of War Letters* (New York, 1943), 29.

4. Terkel, *"The Good War,"* 559.

5. Introduction to *All England Listened: The Wartime Broadcasts of J. B. Priestley* (New York, 1967), ix.

6. *Hitler's Words and Hitler's Deeds* (n.p., n. d.), 30.

7. Koppes and Black, *Hollywood Goes to War*, 68.

8. Dirk van der Heide, *My Sister and I: The Diary of a Dutch Boy Refugee* (New York, 1941), 74.

9. I have interpreted *My Sister and I* more fully in "Writing in Wartime: The Uses of Innocence" in *Thank God for the Atom Bomb and Other Essays* (New York, 1988), 53–81.

10. H. G. Nicholas, ed., *Washington Despatches, 1941–1945: Weekly Political Reports from the British Embassy* (Chicago, 1981), 46.

11. David Eisenhower, *Eisenhower: At War, 1943–1945* (New York, 1986), 256–57.

12. Longmate, *The Home Front*, 193.

13. Rosenman, *The Public Papers . . . of Roosevelt*, 152–53.

14. William Stephenson, *A Man Called Intrepid* (New York, 1976), 111–12.

15. Richard Polenberg, *One Nation Divisible* (New York, 1980), 49.

16. Charles Eade, ed., *The War Speeches of . . . Winston S. Churchill* (London, 1952; 3 vols.), II: 150.

17. (New York, 1943), 287.

18. Pages 274–75.

19. Pages xi, xiii.

20. *A Penguin in the Eyrie* (London, 1955), 66–67.

21. *One Man's Meat* (New York, 1944), 82.

22. "The Divided Life of Stuart Little's Father," *New York Times Book Review*, Feb. 26, 1984, p. 9.

23. Forster's broadcast scripts are preserved in the BBC Written Archives, Reading.

24. Feb., 1944, pp. 82–84.

25. Elena Wilson, ed., *Edmund Wilson, Letters on Literature and Politics, 1912–1972* (New York, 1977), 307.

26. Dwight Macdonald, ed., *Parodies* (New York, 1960), 224–26.

27. "Archibald MacLeish and the Word," *Classics and Commercials* (New York, 1950), 3–9.

28. Archibald MacLeish, *A Time to Speak* (Boston, 1941), 36–41.

29. Carl Sandburg, *Home Front Memo* (New York, 1943), 230, 231.

30. In *Voices of Victory: Representative Poetry of Canada in War-time* (Toronto, 1941), 50–51.

31. Leon Edel, ed., *Edmund Wilson: The Forties* (New York, 1983), 290.

32. *The Murder of Lidice* (New York, 1942), 30.

33. John Manifold, *Selected Verse* (New York, 1946), 49.

34. *Ibid.*, 72.

35. Maclaren-Ross, *Memoirs of the Forties*, 130–31.

36. John Elsom, "Uprooted," *Listener*, Nov. 5, 1981, p. 552.

37. Diana Trilling, *Reviewing the Forties* (New York, 1978), v–xiv.

38. Introduction, *The New Treasury of War Poetry* (Boston, 1943), xxxii.

39. Sonia Orwell and Ian Angus, eds., *The Collected Essays, Journalism and Letters of George Orwell* (New York, 1968; 4 vols.), II: 145.

40. *Home Front Memo*, 258.

41. *Clinging to the Wreckage* (New York, 1982), 90.

42. "The Betrayal of the Charter," *Times Literary Supplement*, Sept. 17, 1982, p. 988.

43. Tapert, *Lines of Battle*, 261.

44. Grafton, *You, You, and You*, 43, 44.

45. Flower and Reeves, *The Taste of Courage*, 4.

46. Elizabeth Pollet, ed., *Portrait of Delmore* (New York, 1986), 75.

47. William R. Evans, ed., *Robert Frost and Sidney Cox: Forty Years of Friendship* (Hanover, N.H., and London, 1981), 248.

48. George Garrett, *James Jones* (New York, 1984), 102.

13. With One Voice

1. "The Voice of Hope," *New Republic*, Jan. 27, 1982, p. 16.
2. Lingeman, *Don't You Know There's a War On?*, 224.
3. *Ibid.*, 225.
4. Leonard Woolf, ed., *A Writer's Diary* (New York, 1954), 327.
5. Grafton, *You, You, and You*, 26.
6. *All England Listened*, xviii-xx.
7. *Hesketh Pearson by Himself* (New York, 1965), 282.
8. Amory, ed., *Letters of Evelyn Waugh*, 630.
9. IWM.
10. IWM.
11. BBC Written Archives, Reading.
12. Longmate, *How We Lived Then*, 422.
13. Lingeman, *Don't You Know There's a War On?*, 212.
14. *American Popular Song* (New York, 1972), 502.
15. Longmate, *The Home Front*, 159.
16. *Clinging to the Wreckage*, 63.
17. Broadfoot, *Six War Years*, 147.
18. D. A. Simmonds, IWM.
19. William Boyd, "Symbolism and the Ripper," *New Statesman*, May 29, 1981, p. 24.
20. Koppes and Black, *Hollywood Goes to War*, 259.
21. Jeanine Basinger, *The World War II Combat Film* (New York, 1986), 65, 74.
22. *Hollywood Goes to War*, 89, 308.
23. *Guts and Glory: Great American War Movies* (Reading, Mass., 1978), 143.
24. *Ibid.*, 241.
25. *Ibid.*, 136.
26. Eileen M. Sullivan, "Refraction and Fantasy: A Study of Magazine Advertising During World War II," Senior Thesis, University of Pennsylvania, May, 1986, p. 12.
27. Mary Jane Lennon, *On the Homefront* (Erin, Ontario, 1981), 48.
28. Minns, *Bombers and Mash*, 142.
29. *Europe Without Baedeker* (New York, 1947 [rev. 1966]), 34–36.
30. *Life*, Dec. 7, 1942, p. 82.
31. *The Style of the Century*, 114.
32. "Refraction and Fantasy," 47.

14. Deprivation

1. Satterfield, *The Home Front*, 219.
2. Roy Hoopes, *Americans Remember the Home Front* (New York, 1977), 220.

3. Knox, *Death March*, 84.

4. *Pacific War Diary*, 199, 334.

5. Norman Longmate, *The G.I.'s: The Americans in Britain, 1942–1945* (New York, 1975), 23.

6. Constantine Fitzgibbon, *The Life of Dylan Thomas* (Boston, 1965), 256.

7. Minns, *Bombers and Mash*, 101.

8. *George Orwell: A Life* (New York, 1981), 434.

9. Page references to *1984* (New York, 1949).

10. Winston Churchill, *The Grand Alliance* (Boston, 1950), 747.

11. *A Cackhanded War*, 184.

12. Melvyn Bragg, *Speak for England* (New York, 1977), 268.

13. Longmate, *How We Lived Then*, 146.

14. Minns, *Bombers and Mash*, 98.

15. Hodgson, *Few Eggs and No Oranges*, 302.

16. Johnson, *One More Hill*, 174.

17. Margaret Crompton, Diary, IWM.

18. *Faces in My Time*, 167.

19. (New York, 1945 [1957]), 65.

20. Donnelly, ed., *Mrs. Milburn's Diaries*, 5, 372–73.

15. Compensation

1. Page references to *This Is My Beloved* (New York, 1943 [1954]).

2. Richard Cobb, "Survivors of the Home Front," *Times Literary Supplement*, Oct. 2–8, 1987, p. 1073.

3. *Closing Times* (London, 1975), 8.

4. S. Orwell and Angus, eds., *Collected Letters . . . ,* I: 226.

5. David Pryce-Jones, *Cyril Connolly: Journal and Memoir* (New York, 1984), 57.

6. *Ibid.*, 244.

7. Amory, ed., *Letters*, 137.

8. IWM.

9. *From the Headlands* (New York, 1983), 77.

10. Stephen Spender, *World Within World* (London, 1951), 292.

11. Amory, ed., *Letters*, 414.

12. *Sword of Honor* (Boston, 1961), 571.

13. *War in the Strand* (London, 1942), 54.

14. *Ibid.*, 77–81.

15. *Ways of Escape* (New York, 1980), 115.

16. *Testament of Experience*, 282.

17. Maclaren-Ross, *Memoirs of the Forties*, 78.

18. Nancy Mitford, *The Water Beetle* (New York, 1962 [1986]), 34.

19. *Horizon*, May, 1943, p. 295.

20. *Ibid.*, Jan., 1950, p. 361.

21. *Ibid.*, Dec., 1944, p. 367.

22. *Ibid.*, Nov., 1949, p. 285.

23. Davie, *Diaries*, 609.

24. *The Unquiet Grave: A Word Cycle, by Palinurus* (rev. ed., London, 1951), xi-xii.

25. *The Unquiet Grave* (New York, 1945), 29.

26. *Ibid.*, 117.

27. *Ibid.*, 87.

28. Amory, ed., *Letters*, 322.

29. *Brideshead Revisited* (New York, 1962), 7.

30. *Ibid.*, 33.

31. *Ibid.*, 171–71.

32. Davie, *Diaries*, 531.

33. *Ibid.*, 588.

34. *Ibid.*, 637.

35. McCallum, *Journey with a Pistol*, 13.

36. *Brideshead Revisited* (1945), 81–82.

37. *Ibid.*, 101.

38. "Golden Youth Doomed," *Dial*, Jan. 1982, pp. 46–47.

39. *Horizon*, Dec., 1946, p. 372.

40. *The Sitwells: A Family's Biography* (New York, 1978), 349–50.

41. Page references to *Left Hand, Right Hand!* (Boston, 1944), vol. I.

42. *The Military Philosophers* (London, 1968), 34.

43. *The Scarlet Tree* (London, 1946 [1977]), 56.

44. *Ibid.*, 77.

45. *The Sitwells*, 381–82.

46. *Components of the Scene*, 19.

47. Fitzgibbon, *Life of Dylan Thomas*, 232.

48. Vernon Watkins, ed., *Dylan Thomas, Letters to Vernon Watkins* (New York, 1957), 100.

16. Reading in Wartime

1. Rupert Hart-Davis, ed., *Siegfried Sassoon: Letters to Max Beerbohm, and a Few Answers* (London, 1986), 84.

2. Quoted by John Grigg, *1943: The Victory That Never Was* (London, 1980), 192.

3. Lionel Trilling, *E. M. Forster* (New York, 1943), 9.

4. "Some Books: A Backward Glance over 1941," BBC Written Archives.

5. John Whitehead, ed., *A Traveller in Romance: Uncollected Writings (1901–1964) of W. Somerset Maugham* (New York, 1984), 175–76.

6. *Faces in My Time*, 147.

7. Feb. 7, 1942, p. 65.

8. *Few Eggs and No Oranges*, 240–41.

9. *Collected Poems*, 148–49.

10. Lee G. Miller, ed., *An Ernie Pyle Album* (New York, 1946), 117.

11. *Come to Dust*, 78–79.

12. Hugo Vickers, *Cecil Beaton: A Biography* (New York, 1975), 284.

13. *A Cackhanded War*, pp. 140–41.

14. *I Was a Stranger* (London, 1977 [1979]), 126–27.

15. I have dealt with this in *The Great War and Modern Memory* (New York, 1975), 137–44.

16. IWM.

17. Tapert, *Lines of Battle*, 20.

18. *With the Old Breed*, 79.

19. Wilbur H. Morrison, *Fortress Without a Roof: The Allied Bombing of the Third Reich* (New York, 1982), 133.

20. Knox, *Death March*, 340.

21. Charles Norman, *The Case of Ezra Pound* (New York, 1948), 38.

22. Greene, *The Infantry Journal Reader*, 542.

23. R. S. Raymond, IWM.

24. Rosenman, *Public Papers*, 1942 vol., pp. 105–16.

25. *Classics and Commercials*, 204.

26. Michael Adams, *The Untravelled World* (London, 1984), 92–93.

27. Letter from Edwin S. Fussell, Jan. 24, 1984.

28. *A Margin of Hope*, 95.

29. *A Writer's Capital* (Minneapolis, 1974), 93.

30. *History of the Council on Books in Wartime, 1942–1946* (New York, 1946), 81.

31. John Y. Cole, ed., *Books in Action: The Armed Services Editions* (Washigton, 1984), 9.

32. Geoffrey O'Brien, *Hardboiled America: The Lurid Years of Paperbacks* (New York, 1981), 37.

33. Perrett, *Days of Sadness, Years of Triumph*, 382.

34. Ellis, *The Sharp End of War*, 300.

35. *Poetical Works*, 23.

36. Ross Parmenter, *School of the Soldier* (New York, 1980), 42.

37. Letter from Ted Dow, June 27, 1985.

38. J. E. Morpurgo, *Allen Lane, King Penguin* (London, 1979), 366.

39. *Ibid.*, 157.

40. Charles Cruickshank, *Deception in World War II* (Oxford, 1979), 39.

41. *Times Literary Supplement*, June 16, 1978, p. 667.

42. Allen Tate and John Peale Bishop, eds., *American Harvest: Twenty Years of Creative Writing in the United States* (New York, 1942), 11.

43. Whitehead, *A Traveller in Romance*, 89.

44. Charles P. Curtis, Jr., and Ferris Greenslet, eds., *The Practical Cogitator* (Boston, 1945), v.

45. Herbert Read, ed., *The Knapsack: A Pocket-book of Prose and Verse* (London, 1939), v.

46. Letter to Christopher Salmon, Nov. 15, 1940, BBC Written Archives.
47. Garrett, *James Jones*, 91.
48. Stanley Kauffmann, *Albums of Early Life* (New York, 1980), 111–12.

17. Fresh Idiom

1. *This Is My Best* (New York, 1942), 190.
2. Norman Mailer, *The Armies of the Night* (New York, 1968), 61.
3. Edward T. Cone, Joseph Frank, and Edmund Keeley, eds., *The Legacy of R. P. Blackmur* (New York, 1987), 247.
4. *Memoirs of the Forties*, 81–82.
5. These songs are to be found in Martin Page, *Kiss Me Goodnight, Sergeant Major* and Anthony Hopkins, *Songs of the Front and Rear*.
6. Page, *Kiss Me Goodnight*, 11.
7. Harvey, *Boys, Bombs, and Brussels Sprouts*, 148.
8. Samuel Hynes, *Flights of Passage: Reflections of a World War II Aviator* (New York and Annapolis, 1988), 127–30; 169; 195.
9. George Forty, *Desert Rats at War: North Africa, Europe* (London, 1980), 329.
10. Douglas MacArthur, *Reminiscences* (New York, 1964), 426.

18. "The Real War Will Never Get in the Books"

1. *The Sharp End of War*, 53.
2. Memoir, IWM.
3. *I Was a Stranger*, p. 47.
4. Ellis, *The Sharp End of War*, 115.
5. *Journey with a Pistol*, 104.
6. William Whitehead and Terence Macartney-Filgate, eds., *Dieppe 1942: Echoes of Disaster* (Toronto, 1979), 144.
7. Hodson, *Before Daybreak*, 61.
8. Longmate, *The Home Front*, 106–7.
9. *I Was a Stranger*, 24.
10. William Manchester, *Goodbye Darkness: A Memoir of the Pacific War* (New York, 1980), 228–29.
11. Jones, *Heart of Oak*, 164.
12. Maule, *A Book of War Letters*, 269.
13. Botting, *From the Ruins of the Reich*, 130.
14. Page 497.
15. Quoted by Greene, *The Infantry Journal Reader*, 266–72.
16. *Combat Tips for Fifth Army Infantry Replacements* (Italy, 1945), 43.
17. M. J. Tambimuttu, ed., *Poetry in Wartime* (London, 1942), 146.
18. *Penguin New Writing*, No. 17 (April–June, 1943), 46.

19. C. Day Lewis, *Word Over All* (London, 1943), 34.

20. Ellis, *The Sharp End of War*, 103.

21. *With the Old Breed*, 56.

22. Elliott Johnson, quoted by Terkel, *"The Good War,"* 258.

23. Broadfoot, *Six War Years*, 234.

24. *With the Old Breed*, 74.

25. *The Tiger and the Rose*, 94.

26. Stevan Dedijer, "Heracleitos, Me, and a Damned Place Called Bastogne," copy of MS memoir in my collection, p. 3.

27. Frieda Wolff, quoted by Terkel, *"The Good War,"* 294.

28. Spector, *Eagle Against the Sun*, 383.

29. Hastings, *Overlord*, 156.

30. *Ibid.*, 12.

31. Tuchman, *Stilwell*, 449.

32. Ellis, *The Sharp End of War*, 251–54.

33. *Ibid.*, 239.

34. *Ibid.*, 317.

35. "The Bloodiest Battle of All," *New York Times Magazine*, June 18, 1987, p. 74.

36. Ellis, *The Sharp End of War*, 296.

37. *Ibid.*, 74.

38. *Smithsonian*, April, 1986, p. 107.

39. Morrison, *Fortress Without a Roof*, 231.

40. See Susan Sheehan, *A Missing Plane* (New York, 1986).

41. Dieter Georgi, "The Bombing of Dresden," *Harvard Magazine*, March-April, 1985, pp. 56–64.

42. Cruickshank, *Deception*, 140.

43. Satterfield, *The Home Front*, 7.

44. Page 279.

45. *Once There Was a War*, viii–xii.

46. *Guadalcanal Remembered*, 240–41.

47. *Company Commander*, 49–50.

48. *Brave Men*, 156.

49. Phillip Knightley, *The First Casualty: From the Crimea to Vietnam, The War Correspondent as Hero, Propagandist, and Myth Maker* (New York, 1975), 226.

50. Broadfoot, *Six War Years*, 392.

51. "Pooter in The Twilight of the Gods," *New Statesman*, May 5, 1978, 603.

52. Lochner, ed., *The Goebbels Diaries, 1942–1943*, p. 460.

53. Wheeler-Bennett, *King George VI*, 479.

54. Grafton, *You, You, and You*, 130.

55. Margaret Crompton, Diary, IWM.

56. *Breaking In, Breaking Out* (New York, 1971), 288.

57. "Fact, Fiction, Fascism: Testimony and Mimesis in Holocaust Narratives," *Comparative Literature* XXXIV (Fall, 1982), 333.

58. IWM.

59. Page 262.

60. *Broken Images*, 5.

61. Robert Leckie, *Helmet for My Pillow* (New York, 1957 [1979]). 111.

62. Page references to *With the Old Breed*.

63. *Journey with a Pistol*, 106–7.

64. Gardner, *The Terrible Rain*, 159.

65. Douglas Botting et al., *The Second Front* (New York, 1978), 88.

Index

PAUL FUSSELL

was born in Pasadena, California, and educated at Pomona College. In the Second World War he was a twenty-year-old Army lieutenant, the leader of a rifle platoon in the 103rd Infantry Division in France. He was severely wounded in the spring of 1945. After the war he earned a Ph.D. at Harvard and has since pursued a career as a literary scholar and critic, writing and editing many books on eighteenth-century British literature, poetic technique, Samuel Johnson, and travel writing, together with two volumes of essays in social and cultural criticism. His book *The Great War and Modern Memory* won the National Book Award for Arts and Letters in 1976 as well as the National Book Critics Circle Award for Criticism and the Ralph Waldo Emerson Award of Phi Beta Kappa. He has held fellowships from the Guggenheim Foundation, the National Endowment for the Humanities, and the Rockefeller Foundation and taught at Connecticut College, the University of Heidelberg, and Rutgers. Currently he holds the Donald T. Regan Chair of English Literature at the University of Pennsylvania and lives in Philadelphia.